THE SILE

Stephen Dorril is editor of *Lobster*, the most authoritative journal in Britain about the security services. Widely respected in the media and read by members of the intelligence community, *Lobster* was at the forefront of exposing the MI5 plots against Harold Wilson and the Colin Wallace affair. His previous books include *Honeytrap* (with Anthony Summers), the definitive book on the Profumo Affair, and *Smear!: Wilson and the Secret State* (with Robin Ramsay).

Also by Stephen Dorril

Honeytrap: The Secret Worlds of Stephen Ward
(*with Anthony Summers*)
Smear!: Wilson and the Secret State
(*with Robin Ramsay*)

STEPHEN DORRIL

THE SILENT CONSPIRACY

Inside the Intelligence Services in the 1990s

Mandarin

A Mandarin Paperback
THE SILENT CONSPIRACY

First published in Great Britain 1993
by William Heinemann Ltd
This edition published 1994
by Mandarin Paperbacks
an imprint of Reed Consumer Books Ltd
Michelin House, 81 Fulham Road, London SW3 6RB
and Auckland, Melbourne, Singapore and Toronto

A CIP catalogue record for this title
is available at the British Library
ISBN 0 7493 1094 4

Printed and bound in Great Britain by
BPC Paperbacks Ltd

Contents

Preface

Nothing is so secret that it needs to be kept secret.

'Ned' in John le Carré's *The Secret Pilgrim*

In early November 1991, a magazine ran an article which noted that the process for selecting a new chief for the Secret Intelligence Service (henceforth to be called by its more popular title, MI6) to replace the incumbent, Sir Colin McColl, was about to be put into play. A few days later, a journalist on a London newspaper telephoned this author for suggestions on who might be on the short list. I suggested that it would probably go to McColl's deputy. I did not know his name but joked that perhaps, following the appointment of Stella Rimington as director-general of the Security Service (MI5), it was time a woman headed the service. Did I know of any likely candidates? Off the cuff, I speculated on Margaret Ramsay.

I thought no more about it until I was informed that, much to my surprise and amusement, the newspaper had run a diary item indicating that Ms Ramsay was a favourite to become the next chief. Then the rumour mills began to grind away. Every major UK newspaper, and a number in the United States, ran a piece on the next chief of MI6, with each new article taking the story further forward. 'Meta' Ramsay had been identified as an MI6 officer by the *Leveller* magazine in February 1976. She had attended Glasgow University and had been elected president of the Scottish Union of Students, a good source of MI6 recruits. After graduating with an MA degree, in 1962 she landed a post as associate secretary of the International Student Conference, at Leiden, Holland, a student anti-communist body which was prominent during the Cold War. Between 1965 and 1967 she was secretary for the Fund for International Student Co-operation, later identified as a recipient of CIA funds. The Diplomat List of the Foreign Office showed that in 1969 Ramsay was made a second secretary and later served in Stockholm and Helsinki, before promotion to counsellor in 1987. The latter appointment was an indication that she was a senior figure inside MI6, possibly a division head looking after a particular region. These basic facts were already known, but every new story brought forth extra biographical details.

Meta's colleagues at university included a number of today's leading Scottish-born politicians. The press were told by an ex-MI6 colleague that the unmarried Ms Ramsay 'became one of MI6's most effective divisional heads'. An 'active' member of the Labour Party, she had attended Labour Party conferences where party officials had been 'unaware' of her intelligence connections. According to the *Intelligence Newsletter*, she had been head of the MI6 team liaising with the CIA during Desert Storm and had 'slept in the office' during the Gulf War. Other profiles later asserted that she had counter-terrorism experience and, while in Scandinavia, had been responsible for collecting intelligence on the IRA, in particular the arms shipments by the *Eksund* which was captured by French coastguards. In Northern Ireland, she had, apparently, worked closely with fellow Scot Craig Smellie, MI6 chief of station in the province between 1973 and 1975. However, former MI6 staff at the Northern Ireland office do not recall her serving in the province.

Even though Ms Ramsay had officially retired from the service in July 1991 on her fifty-fifth birthday, a former colleague told the *Sunday Express* that this would not rule her out of the job. In the event, Sir Colin McColl, who was due to retire as chief in September 1992, was asked by Prime Minister John Major to stay on for another two years to oversee changes inside MI6. That was not quite the end of the

Ramsay story because, in August 1992, the *Daily Telegraph* revealed that she had been appointed foreign policy adviser to Labour Party leader John Smith, a friend since university days. While she was not to be 'C', the new appointment did raise a few eyebrows.[1]

The Ramsay saga illustrates the difficulties encountered when writing on the British intelligence services. Researching the security service – the collective term for MI5, the Government Communications Headquarters (GCHQ) and MI6 – is somewhat akin to psychoanalysis, which Freud said, was analogous to an iceberg: only a small part is visible while three-quarters remains hidden. (This book does not deal in depth with GCHQ since the subject is covered in great detail in Hugh Lanning's and Richard Norton-Taylor's *A Conflict of Loyalties: GCHQ 1984–1991.*)

Despite Britain's draconian Official Secrets Act and lack of a Freedom of Information Act, there is, as this book will illustrate, a surprising amount of material in the public domain. These surface manifestations – the odd snippets which appear in the media – have, of course, to be sifted carefully for the story behind the story, while the words of an officer who provides anonymous information cannot always be trusted. Misinformation and disinformation are rife, which is inevitable, given that lying is second nature in any secret environment. The last few years, though, have been unqiue. We have seen a torrent of leaks from inside the security services and from senior officers from such diverse agencies as HM Customs and Excise and the Special Branch. Fortunately, during the eighties, officers such as Cathy Massiter, Michael Bettaney and others provided solid information about the internal affairs of the security services. This has proved to be both reliable and an excellent body of material against which to test the more dubious accounts and leaks.

The purpose of this book is to open up the debate which, hitherto, has taken place behind closed doors in Whitehall. Since the end of the Cold War there has been a continuous review of the role of intelligence services, but only a select band of anonymous officials are party to what has been resolved. Although ministers may proclaim their public desire to 'demystify the process of Whitehall decision-making', in truth they hide behind veils of secrecy when it comes to matters concerning the security services. The government, senior civil servants of the permanent government and members of the secret state do all they can to stifle debate.

Nowhere was this more in evidence than during the *Spycatcher* court case in Australia, in November 1978, when the Cabinet Secretary, Sir Robert Armstrong, was asked what harm publishing the book might do, since most of the information contained in it was already known to the KGB. He answered that 'the mere fact of publication in this country will undoubtedly promote discussion of, and articles about, the topics here, and thus lead to a heightened sensitivity and awareness of the methodology, philosophy, and organization of the services'. This, said Armstrong, was to be avoided at all costs.[2]

I hope this book will play a small role in heightening awareness about the activities of the security services. It is only right that, in a democracy, organisations which cost the taxpayer over £1000 million per annum should be subject to some form of scrutiny. In Britain, it is only when a scandal is brewing, such as the Matrix Churchill affair, that a little light is thrown on the activities of the security services. The taxpayer and, to a large extent, the media are excluded from asking simple questions about effectiveness, oversight, value for money, and even what it is that the security services actually do. In effect there is a silent conspiracy to conceal.

In researching this book, I owe a particular debt to Richard Norton-Taylor, who, since 1976, has reported on Whitehall, including security matters, for the *Guardian*. Unfortunately, investigative reporting is regarded with little affection in the print medium and Richard, as far as I am aware, is the only journalist in the media whose brief includes the activities of the security services. Similarly, many thanks must go to Richard Donkin of the *Financial Times*, the only newspaper with a proper investigative unit, for his work on banks and their intelligence ties.

Thanks are due to Nick Davies for his generous help with information and for the pioneering series of articles in the *Guardian* and the *Observer* during the mid-eighties which mapped out the, until then, largely uncharted territory of the work of MI5; likewise to David Leigh and Paul Lashmar (*Observer*), Barrie Penrose (*Sunday Times*) and Duncan Campbell (*New Statesman*) for their work during that decade. None of this work would have been possible, of course, without those members of the security services who had the courage to speak out or at least whisper during a period when, despite talk of 'sweeping away the cobwebs', the government has attempted to shut everything down.

I would also like to acknowledge the work of David Leppard on Lockerbie, John Ware and Geoffrey Seed on Northern Ireland, Mark Urban on the SAS in Northern Ireland, John Pilger on Cambodia, Dr Paul Rogers on international arms, Kenneth R. Timmerman on the Middle East and weapons of mass destruction, Kevin Cahill on the international computer trade, Mark Hollingsworth, David Rose and Patrick Fitzgerald on the work of the Security Service, Peter Taylor and David Murphy on Stalker, Nick Kochan and Bob Whittington on BCCI, Andrew Scott and Iain Mcleary on William McRae, and others who, in one way or another, contributed to this book. Essential reading were the encyclopedic *Statewatch* (PO Box 1516, London N16 OEW) and *Intelligence Newsletter* (10 rue du Sentier, 75002 Paris). Many thanks to Tony Bunyan and Olivier Schmidt for keeping the issues coming. *Lobster* is now available from 135 School Street, Netherthong, Holmfirth, HD7 2YB.

Tom Weldon and Sarah Hannigan, at Heinemann, deserve

credit for initiating the idea for this book and for their patience as the number of chapters doubled. My gratitude goes to literary agent Andrew Lownie, for making this project possible and providing constructive criticisms. Special thanks are owed to my former colleague on *Lobster*, Robin Ramsay, who read the bulk of the manuscript and supplied an endless stream of material from his own files. My wife, Stephanie, has been unstinting in her help and support.

This book is dedicated to the 'British Telecom engineer' who turned up and 'repaired' the unreported and non-existent fault on my telephone. May he find a more worthwhile occupation.

Stephen Dorril, January 1993

1

MI5: The Thatcher Years

We were brought up to feel we did terrible things so ordinary punters could sleep safely at night.

David Cornwell (John le Carré),
former MI5 and MI6 officer

By 1979, when Margaret Thatcher was elected Prime Minister and became nominal head of the security services, minor changes had already taken place within MI5. These had followed allegations from former Prime Minister Harold Wilson, which MI5 director-general Michael Hanley and MI6 chief Maurice Oldfield confirmed, that a right-wing section of MI5 had been actively engaged in undermining Wilson and his government. As a consequence, in 1976 there had occurred something of a 'review', during which the then Prime Minister, James Callaghan, met with Hanley and discussed, among other things, 'the nature of the procedures for positive vetting . . . management and recruitment . . . [and] whether grounds existed for continued suspicion in the Security Service'. Following the review MI5 was encouraged to recruit more officers from the working class and from red-brick universities in the hope of preventing anti-Labour factions forming. Junior Home Office minister Dr Shirley Summerskill then informed the House of Commons that 'arrangements' [for accountability to ministers] had been 'reviewed and further improved' and that she was 'authorised to assure the house that on the basis of these arrangements' Home Secretary Merlyn Rees and Prime Minister James Callaghan 'are confident that the service concerned [MI5] is carrying out its duties within the limits laid down in the directive to the Director-General issued in September 1952 and which remains in force'.[1]

Similar statements became commonplace in the next decade and reflected a startlingly complacent and naïve view of the security services. Labour Cabinet minister Tony Benn was repeatedly assured by his colleagues that 'it's all under Ministerial control'. Before the revelations of Peter Wright and Colin Wallace turned Merlyn Rees's view of the intelligence world upside down, he was able to claim: 'I am in complete charge of the security services, twenty-four hours a day, and nothing is done without my approval.' He was backed by Foreign Secretary David Owen: 'I took complete control of security, just like Merlyn.' These macho stances had little to do with reality, and the professionals in the Home and Foreign Offices knew it. During 1978 it was rumoured that Hanley was to 'quit in a sensational shake-up of the Intelligence apparatus. The Whitehall mandarins, who believe that . . . MI5 should be placed under tight ministerial control, have yet to give up the battle to place "amateurs" in charge of [MI5].'[2]

Although friends of Spycatcher Peter Wright regarded John Jones as a 'disappointing deputy', the experienced intelligence officer had been expected to replace Hanley. Jones was the first director-general of MI5 to come from a working-class background. His father had been a colliery repair man below ground in the Welsh mining village of Maerdy in the Rhondda. Jones won a scholarship to Christ's College, Cambridge, and after serving in Germany, later with the Sudan government and then in Malaya, joined MI5 in 1955 as a junior operative in E Division, traditionally responsible for internal security in the colonies. He later served overseas as a security liaison officer in Hong Kong. In the fifties, he met his wife, Daphne Redman, who worked inside MI5 headquarters as a typist, transcribing telephone tapping recordings. She later became the secretary to Arthur Martin in K Branch, which operated from Gower Street on counter-espionage. The shy, unassuming but well-liked Welshman rose through the ranks – director of A Branch and head of Registry – before joining F Branch, which monitors internal subversion. His success in F Branch during the period of the miners' strike in 1972 was rewarded with a CMG and he eventually became Branch director. At the end of 1976 he was made deputy director-general under Hanley, after studying the use of computers in intelligence work at GCHQ, Cheltenham. This gave Jones an advantage, as many of the senior officers seemed reluctant to promote technical advances within the service. The rather Civil-Service-minded Hanley retired in 1979, telling his friends that he was frustrated about the problems of computerisation of the service's vast records system.[3]

Callaghan had insisted on an outsider being brought into the service as the new director-general. To the fury of the old guard in MI5, the Prime Minister appointed an ex-Foreign Office man, Sir Howard Smith, who had worked with Callaghan in Northern Ireland. Morale among the senior ranks appeared to slump. Like most bureaucracies, and particularly those which are introverted and secretive, the service resents an outsider as head and generally makes his time as uncomfortable as possible. In 1965, when Harold Wilson had tried to impose another 'honest copper' on MI5 – the Chief Constable of Lancashire, Sir Eric St Johnston – the service did all it could to oppose the appointment. Officers falsely claimed that the last outsider appointed, the former gang-busting Chief Constable of Sheffield, Sir Percy Sillitoe, had almost 'wrecked MI5 by introducing police methods and attitudes'. Bitter resentment of Sillitoe from senior officers had been evident from the start. Rivals for the post were known to ridicule him by peppering their conversation with Latin epigrams. After one such episode Sillitoe returned home in a rage telling his wife, Dollie, 'I sometimes think I'm working in a madhouse. Now I know what MI stands for – it's the Muttonhead Institute.' The main reason for the resentment was that an outsider 'set back everybody's promotion prospects for several years'. When Howard Smith took up his post, Barry Russell-Jones, the head of S Branch, which dealt with computerisation, wrote to Peter Wright that 'It is not a happy ship.'[4]

Although she had no knowledge or experience of the security services, unlike previous prime ministers Mrs Thatcher had ensured that she was briefed about the intelligence world before she entered 10 Downing Street. Initially, she received 'intelligence briefings from a free-lance group' which Chapman Pincher confirmed 'was associated with' the right-wing think-tank on subversion, the Institute for the Study of Conflict, which numbered among its directors the right-wing cold warrior Brian Crozier and Robert Moss, a Thatcher speech writer. James Callaghan later allowed her official briefings from MI6 chief Maurice Oldfield. A similar arrangement appears to have continued with Oldfield's successor, Dickie Franks, who along with Crozier was involved with an influential European–American network of conservative politicians and intelligence operatives known as the Pinay Circle. Added to this, Thatcher's closest adviser, until his assassination shortly before her electoral triumph in 1979, was Airey Neave, who, like a number of MPs in the Tory Party, was extremely experienced in the shadowy world of security and intelligence. What characterised all these advisers was their loyalty to MI5's traditional rival, MI6. It is therefore likely that Mrs Thatcher's personal views were highly coloured by this partisan advice. Neave had gone as far as to suggest that, once in power, the Conservative government would need to purge the traitors in security.[5]

Mrs Thatcher's first scrape with the security services came shortly after her election, when Anthony Blunt was publicly identified in early November 1979 as a traitor. Jones drafted a memorandum to the Cabinet Office suggesting that a full statement on the immunity deal given to Blunt would inhibit MI5's use of the same tactic in any future dealings with traitors. Jones took the standard security line that any disclosure would be damaging to the service. Mrs Thatcher overruled him, believing that as the scandal had taken place under different administrations she could afford to make a clean break with the past on the matter. Two years later, Mrs Thatcher was forced to respond in the House of Commons to allegations that a former head of MI5, Sir Roger Hollis, had been a Soviet mole. The misleading statement, in which she suggested that all breaches of security could be explained by 'reference to Philby or Blunt', was dismissed by the mole-hunters as a 'masterly piece of Whitehall deception'.[6]

When Howard Smith retired in 1981, fifty-eight-year-old Jones finally took over the reins. Although he was given the obligatory knighthood (KCB) in 1983, he was not regarded as a great success. Some officers found him difficult to deal with and he was seen as a rather remote figure. Although senior government figures thought he was 'totally on top of his job' and were said to have 'the greatest respect for him', colleagues regarded him as 'a figure-head really. It was the deputy Director-General [Cecil Shipp] who was more in control.' It was said that Mrs Thatcher got on well with Jones but she was not pleased that when, in April 1982, the child-molester Geoffrey Prime was arrested for spying at GCHQ it was the local CID which uncovered his activities and not MI5. As a result, Jones was forced to accept new guidelines which conceded a degree of political independence. No longer was the Security Service the sole arbiter of what Downing Street needed to know. In future all potential breaches of security were to be reported to Number 10, to protect the Prime Minister from any political attack. Such acquiescence was not viewed favourably by older officers. Internally, MI5 appears to have been split between Jones' supporters, who came primarily from F Branch, and an opposition made up of the old guard of K Branch, who regarded their work as more important, and the younger officers, who had difficulty accepting the political role which the service, with its increased concentration on subversion, was expected to undertake.[7]

Over the previous ten years, F Branch had gradually become the service's senior branch, its investigation of subversion overtaking in importance K Branch's traditional role in monitoring Soviet bloc espionage operations. Events had conspired against K Branch; in September 1971, hard-line Foreign Secretary Alec Douglas-Home had authorised the mass expulsion of 105 Soviet diplomats who were alleged to have been KGB officers. According to KGB defector Oleg Gordievsky, who was deputy rezident in the mid-eighties, 'The London residency never recovered from the expulsions.' He added that the new KGB Resident from 1972 to 1978, Yakov Lukasevics, 'made little progress in rebuilding KGB operations in Britain'. Even when they did manage to mount operations, Gordievsky disclosed, 'contrary to popular myths generated by media "revelations" about Soviet moles . . . the KGB found it more difficult to collect high-grade intelligence in London than in almost any other Western capital'. Senior civil servants dealing with the intelligence community were therefore aware that K Branch claims about KGB penetration of British political life and the threat to security from Soviet bloc operations were generally exaggerated. Increasingly, security officials viewed the subversive threat as coming from a new direction.[8]

In *Spycatcher*, Peter Wright recalls the meeting in 1972 when director-general Michael Hanley told the assembled senior staff of A and F Branch that the Prime Minister and the Home Office wanted to see more resources poured into monitoring what was known as the 'far and wide left'. The Home Office had repeatedly complained that they were being kept in the dark about important areas and that when they were given the required information 'the quality of intelligence was not there'. By the early seventies senior civil servants had become extremely nervous about the rise of terrorism, particularly by largely unknown Middle East groups, and the ability of the IRA to inflict damage on mainland Britain. The activities of England's only home-grown terrorist organisation, the Angry Brigade, had taken them completely by surprise and the Home Office were angry that MI5 had not given them any warning. 'We had to press and press to get them to take a real interest.' Civil servants were extremely angry to discover that MI5, whose primary purpose was the Defence of the Realm, had failed in its task of protecting members of the ruling élite.[9]

The climax of this internal bureaucratic conflict came with the miners' strike of 1972. On 8 February 1972, the Cabinet Emergencies Committee decided to declare a state of emergency, and two days later came the Saltley depot incident, when National Union of Miners 'flying pickets' under the direction of the then largely unknown Arthur Scargill prevented the movement of coke from a depot in Birmingham – 'an event that has haunted contingency planners ever since'. Brendon Sewill, special adviser to the Chancellor, commented of this period

> At this time many of those in positions of influence looked into the abyss and saw only a few days away the possibility of the country being plunged into a state of chaos not so very far removed from that which might prevail after a minor nuclear attack. If that sounds melodramatic I need only say that – with the prospect of the breakdown of power supplies, food supplies, sewage, communications, effective government and law and order – it was the analogy that was being used at the time. This is the power that exists to hold the country to ransom: it was fear of that abyss which had an important effect on subsequent policy.[10]

In response to these events, Prime Minister Edward Heath set up a review of the government's Emergency Organisation which had remained unreformed since the 1940s. The review was headed by Lord Jellicoe (Lord Privy Seal) and John Hunt (Cabinet Office Deputy Secretary). The Cabinet Office assumed responsibility for civil emergency planning in the aftermath of the 1972 crisis, setting up the Civil Contingencies Unit (CCU). Parallel to this, the national 'war plan' was reconstituted with greater emphasis on meeting an 'internal enemy' – i.e. the left and the unions. The CCU has a close relationship with the Security Service. During important strikes, MI5's F2 section worked closely with the CCU –

supplying ministers with detailed information based on telephone tapping and agents-in-place, on the motivations and political allegiances of the strike leaders, internal divisions and prospects of industrial action.

The convention of political information not being provided to a new administration meant that this major change of policy was not communicated to the following Labour government. Merlyn Rees later admitted in the House of Commons that he had not been informed when he became Home Secretary, and that there had been 'great concern in the Home Office about what was going on in MI5'.[11]

At the review meeting in 1972, Michael Hanley handed over to 'a young and ambitious' F2 officer, David Ransom, 'who outlined the activities and structure of a host of left-wing splinter groups, like the Workers' Revolutionary Party (WRP) and the Socialist Workers' Party (SWP)'. Hanley and the F Branch officers argued for an increase in the use of telephone tappings and the interception of mail. There would have to be a massive increase in technical resources. Wright says that 'John Jones was a forceful advocate' of the new policy. 'I was not alone', Wright reveals, 'among the old-guard, anti-Soviet officers in being disturbed by these new developments. We could see all that we had worked to achieve frittered away chasing these minor left-wing groupings.' He and other K Branch officers did not take the threat from the New Left seriously. 'The SWP and WRP, despite their frightening names, were about as dangerous as a pond of ducks.'[12]

Both the tiny Workers' Revolutionary Party and the Socialist Workers' Party, handled by MI5's F7 section, were heavily infiltrated. Circumstantial evidence suggests that MI5 was active in the raid on the WRP's 'Red House' in the mid-seventies and in promoting the split of the party in 1985–6. Libyan financial support of the WRP made the organisation a prime target for the Security Service. The resultant disintegration of the WRP led to the creation of up to nine even smaller groups. Labour MP Ken Livingstone claimed at a meeting in

March 1990 that MI5 had used one of their agents, who was 'a high-ranking member of the leadership', to foment the split. In a letter to David Hyland, leader of one of the groups, he stated that 'copies of some Special Branch reports on [WRP] meetings had been made available'.[13] He commented to a leader of another fragment that 'democratic centralist organisations [Trotskyist groups] are particularly vulnerable to internal disruption by MI5/Special Branch because of their traditional expulsions and their secretive style of operations'.

The expansion of F Branch also had, according to Wright, an effect on the role of an intelligence officer. 'The move into the computer generation signalled the relegation of the role of the individual officer. From now on we were going to be data processors, scanning tens of thousands of names at the press of a button.' Wright thought that the 'fun had gone'. He also believed that the move into domestic subversion raised problems of accountability and ethics. 'It was easy to believe that we had the public's consent when we broke into a Soviet diplomat's house. But the wholesale surveillance of a large proportion of the population raised more than a question mark. "Big Brother" loomed.'[14]

After the 1972 miners' strike, a group of industrial managers with suitable political views and experience were recruited into F Branch. Most were hard-liners from K Branch with many years of combating the KGB behind them. With a limited experience of the outside world and the changes occurring in the social arena – the perceptible shift among the public to a more liberal attitude to civil liberties – they were not well suited to 'judging one's fellow citizens'. Roy Jenkins was Home Secretary in the mid-seventies when the expansion of F Branch activities was at its height. Jenkins, who considered security matters 'grubby', was not informed about the new orientation within the service. He later told the House of Commons that MI5 'should be pulled out of its political surveillance role'. He had become convinced that 'an organisation of people who lived in the fevered world of espionage and counter-espionage is entirely unfitted to judge between what is subversion and what is legitimate dissent'.[15]

An indication of this lack of judgement was given to an editor of a Sunday newspaper who, in the early eighties, was invited to a large Home Counties house to address the assembled MI5 staff on how to improve their 'public image'. He was shaken to hear the agency's head, Sir John Jones, talking about the danger posed by the trade unions and of the 'threat within'. Sir John was not talking in isolation; he had the complete support of the Prime Minister, who had recently referred to the miners as the 'enemy within'. Although there may have been deep divisions at times about MI5's management style, when it came to the question of 'subversion' the permanent government, in the shape of the Cabinet Office, the Home Office and the small group of politicians who had dealings with MI5, were in agreement with the secret state (made up of the security services and other intelligence offshoots) as to what constituted a threat to the state.[16]

It is worth quoting at length a remarkable passage from a May 1982 White Paper which came on the heels of a Security Commission report on security procedures. Mrs Thatcher revealed its contents to the House of Commons.

> The internal threat has altered considerably . . . It has become more varied and viewed as a whole has grown more serious . . . The threat offered by the Communist Party of Great Britain (CPGB) has probably diminished as a result of the fall in numbers of its members and the disillusionment of many of them with Soviet policy since 1968 in invading Czechoslovakia and, more recently, Afghanistan. The fall in CPGB membership, however, has been accompanied by the proliferation of new subversive groups of the extreme Left and the extreme Right (mainly the former) whose aim is to overthrow democratic parliamentary government in this country by violent or other unconstitutional means, not shrinking in the most extreme groups from terrorism to achieve their aims. Membership of individual groups is small

> but, for the most part, active and conspiratorial. They might well seek to make public information injurious to the interests of this country, not at the behest or for the benefit of any foreign power, but simply to harm this country itself, whether by causing a rift between it and its allies or otherwise, and by these means to weaken its defences against the overthrow of democratic government by force.[17]

This passage illustrates how far to the right policy on 'subversion' was allowed to drift in the Thatcher years. Senior officials admitted that 'the momentum in that direction has perceptibly increased since 1979'. The Commission report clearly referred to what the Security Service termed the 'far and wide left', which encompassed groups such as the WRP and SWP. However, none of these groups supported terrorism. In a letter to a Labour MP, Home Secretary William Whitelaw stated that 'The preservation of public order may require information to be kept on individuals who are active in a political movement, not because of the views they hold, but because the activities of the group could be such as to encourage public disorder.' The subversion net was being substantially widened and legitimate political activism was now seen as supporting violence and terrorism. Whitelaw's successor, Leon Brittan, stated subversives included those 'who, for tactical reasons or other reasons choose to keep (either in the long or the short term) within the letter of the law in what they do'. The next Home Secretary, Douglas Hurd, told the Commons that subversives were not only 'those who breach the criminal law'. This went beyond Lord Denning's broad definition of 'subversion' in his report on the Profumo affair in 1963, in which he described a 'subversive' as someone who 'would contemplate the overthrow of government by unlawful means'. Hurd went on to claim: 'We must be able to know the plans and intentions of those who abuse the freedom that we provide under the law to infiltrate our institutions and structures.' There were no longer any clear-cut definitions and a grey area opened up.[18]

Just how big was this grey area, was disclosed in April 1985, in a written answer to the House of Commons on new vetting procedures by Mrs Thatcher. Referring to her own belief of what constituted subversion she spoke of an individual who 'is a Member . . . of a subversive group, acknowledged to be such by the Minister, whose aims are to undermine or overthrow parliamentary democracy by political, industrial or violent means . . . is, or has recently been, sympathetic to or associated with members or sympathisers of such organisations or groups, in such a way as to raise reasonable doubts about his reliability . . . is susceptible to pressure from such organisations or groups.' The Cabinet Office realised that this was a sensitive statement and released it only three hours before the parliamentary Easter recess, which meant that MPs were not allowed the opportunity of questioning or debating such a controversial change of policy. According to Richard Norton-Taylor, one Whitehall view on Mrs Thatcher's statement was that the government wanted to 'legitimise' activities which MI5 engaged in by retrospectively signalling that 'subversive' activity covered more people and groups than the public assumed.[19]

Thatcher's written answer was, in effect, MI5's secret definition of subversion; a definition which went far beyond the charter and directives that governed its operations. Subversives were no longer solely those who sought to undermine parliamentary democracy by unlawful means, but those who may have had the most fleeting acquaintance with particular groups or individuals. This was guilt by association and a throw-back to McCarthyism. In 1983, when MI5 wanted to open a file on the future chair of the Campaign for Nuclear Disarmament (CND), Joan Ruddock, 'It was recognised that she had no subversive affiliation.' She did not, therefore, fit the official criteria for opening a file. According to former MI5 officer Cathy Massiter, whose desk dealt with CND, the problem was solved when, by chance, Mrs Ruddock was interviewed by a Soviet journalist, who was a KGB officer. 'Joan Ruddock didn't know that, but it provided the grounds for recording her as a "contact of a hostile intelligence service", which was ridiculous.' Another prominent CND member, Cathy Ashton, a former executive officer, had a file opened because she was 'a communist sympathiser'. The sole basis for the tag was that she shared a house with a member of the Communist Party. Although absurd, the criteria fitted Mrs Thatcher's definition of a subversive.[20]

While admitting that the change had been 'very, very significant' and that 'civil liberties do go by the board', a senior security official refused to 'apologise for it because it's the only way that we can possibly meet the threat'. He regretted that it was no longer possible to take people's 'loyalty for granted . . . within the organs of Government you now have to be looking at almost everybody whereas before you looked at one per cent. But although I regret it, it is necessary.' Even hard-liners such as Peter Wright thought that this was nonsense. The threat from the Soviet bloc intelligence agencies had diminished, and the targeting of groups like CND and the charity for the homeless, Shelter, made MI5 look 'more and more like a Gestapo'.[21]

2

Bettaney and Massiter

> Other British agencies have got into the spying business – house breaking, forgery and bribery – what they have not realised is that these things are not merely useless, they can be dangerous . . . they want to run spying as a branch of politics using factions and rampant careerism, deceit and manipulation. Well, you can achieve results at first but there is a price to be paid. Once you put results before loyalty you leave your agents without any centre and then you will open your gates to three short steps . . . from disillusion . . . to disaffection . . . to defection.
>
> Mansfield Cummings, chief of MI6, 1917

The career of sixty-one-year-old Sir John Jones came to an ignominious end with the Bettaney affair. On 16 September 1983, Michael Bettaney, a middle-ranking officer in the élite K Branch, which dealt with Soviet counter-espionage, was arrested by Special Branch Detective Superintendent Peter Westcott. Bettaney quickly admitted that in the spring of 1983 he had attempted to offer himself to the KGB as an agent-in-place. His first 'sweetener' was delivered in April and contained background details of the expulsion of three Soviet officials from Britain. This was followed two months later by an approach to the resident KGB officer in the London embassy, Arkadi Gouk.

Deputy to Anne Orr-Ewing (wife of Hamish Orr-Ewing, the chairman of Rank Xerox), the section head of K4 (responsible for monitoring Soviet diplomats, trade delegations, merchant shipping and Aeroflot employees), Bettaney had tried to hand over MI5's 'crown jewels'. These included the service's assessment of the KGB's order of battle in London, the background to the expulsion of a number of Soviet diplomats, incorporating information from a KGB defector, and information Bettaney had been given while working in counter-espionage about British agents and contacts in Eastern Europe and the Soviet Union. MI5's first captured traitor since the Second World War had deliberately set out to neutralise the Security Service's operations against the KGB.[1]

On 16 April 1984, Bettaney was convicted of ten offences under the old Official Secrets Act and sentenced at the Old Bailey to a total of twenty-three years' imprisonment. The length of sentence and the fact that Bettaney was the first MI5 officer to appear in the dock devastated many inside the service. Although Sir John Jones may have wished the Security Service to deal with its own traitor 'in-house', when Mrs Thatcher saw the director-general at Downing Street she had been uncompromising in her demand that there would be no back-door deals. There was to be no replay of the immunity deal given to Blunt. MI5 was going to have to wash this particular piece of dirty linen in public. This contrasted sharply with her refusal to set up public inquiries into the security services' history of dirty tricks and scandals.

Disturbed at yet another security scandal, Whitehall moved into action calling for fundamental reforms. In March 1984, three Security Commission members – Sir Michael Palliser, former head of the diplomatic service, Air Chief Marshal Sir Alastair Steedman, and Lord Allen of Abbeydale – under the chairmanship of Lord Bridge, were told by Mrs Thatcher to look beyond the Bettaney case to any fundamental weaknesses in MI5's management and vetting procedures. While no Commission member had direct experience of the security services, Allen had been Permanent Under-Secretary at the Home Office from 1966 to 1972 with responsibilities for supervising MI5. It had been a fraught period when, according to one commentator, Allen and the Home Office 'had never succeeded in dominating the stubborn Director-General of MI5'.

He had also been 'alarmed about the service's cavalier use of immunities and poor calibre of MI5 management'.[2]

One former member of the Commission, which had been set up in 1965 to look at lapses of security and lessons to be drawn, said, 'People are never overjoyed about being investigated in this way. But in my experience no member of the Commission would ever agree to a whitewash. We always had and could get full access to everyone and all the documents we needed.' That was hardly credible given past experience, however, for there was a bitter debate between the Home Office and MI5 about whether the investigators should be allowed total access to all documents or should be offered only partial revealing of the material. It revolved around what became known as 'the ring of confidence'. Eventually the Cabinet Office opted for total access, as it was felt that only a comprehensive investigation would be likely to prevent further scandal. Even though the focus of the inquiry was narrow, it was the first detailed investigation of MI5 – a service which had successfully evaded past efforts by outside bodies to examine its activities. The last major report had been Lord Denning's 1963 report on the Profumo affair. As with the Bettaney inquiry, the rather innocent Master of the Rolls later said that he had 'complete access to their files, memoranda, correspondence'. The truth was, as a senior MI5 officer admitted, 'Denning had the wool pulled over his eyes'. Director-general Sir Roger Hollis destroyed a number of key documents as the judge started his inquiry and the service went so far as to organise a fake operation for Denning to view; he was suitably impressed. In private, Peter Wright admitted that 'what they do is, they cook the files for an inquiry'.[3]

Within the service, the Commission was treated with derision and regarded as a 'stable door operation'. When Commission members did make the occasional visit to MI5 headquarters in Curzon Street, Mayfair, officers received advance warning and cleared their desks of sensitive files.

Material was deliberately withheld, and some details of Bettaney's uncovering and the circumstances of his arrest included disinformation given to the Commission to protect the still secret MI6 agent, KGB officer Oleg Gordievsky. The service is intolerant of outsiders and was naturally on the defensive. Those officers who expected 'heads to roll', which the *Daily Express* concluded was inevitable, were likely to hinder any real inquiry.[4]

However, not only did the Commission hear evidence from those officers directly involved with the specifics of Bettaney's case, it also spread its net wider, being particularly impressed by the quality of evidence coming from the younger and more junior officers – who often expressed criticism about the management set-up and style. According to one former officer, morale inside the service was very low. 'Some of the best young people are unhappy and are leaving.' There was unease in sections of F Branch dealing with controversial 'targets' such as surveillance of the Left. Bettaney himself had criticised senior MI5 officials, including Sir John Jones, for encouraging the Security Service to expand its monitoring of the activities of domestic groups including CND, trade unions and, increasingly, the investigation of leaks to journalists. New desks had been opened in the seventies to investigate subversion in the media and even lawyers became targets of surveillance. Officers dealing in these areas expressed their disquiet at the way official rules on targeting were circumvented and insisted that they needed more opportunity to discuss strategy. There was a view, which even former senior officers admitted, that MI5 was being increasingly politicised in common with the Civil Service.[5]

Security and confidentiality were of paramount importance to Mrs Thatcher and she was ferocious in her reaction to leaks. Although James Callaghan had authorised several leak inquiries, he did not invoke the services of MI5 with the ease or frequency of Mrs Thatcher. In 1971, just before he retired as director-general, Sir Martin Furnival-Jones told the Franks

Committee on Reform of the Official Secrets Act that MI5 had no specific responsibility for what are known as 'leak investigation procedures'. He said that 'if there is a leakage of information from [a] Department the Minister has responsibility, and he cannot push it off on to me.' The Security Service only became interested in leak inquiries 'where an hostile intelligence service is involved'. However, ministers did push on to MI5 inquiries which clearly broke its own charter. Conservative MP Jonathan Aitken later said in Parliament that 'such journalistic inquiries could be stretched into the area of national security only by the most vivid leaps and arabesques of febrile imagination'. Even the consistent supporter of the security services Rupert Allason (spy-writer 'Nigel West') was 'appalled' to discover that one inquiry into the leak of a document from the Department of Health and Social Security was headed by a Cabinet official, whom he knew to be 'a long-standing member of the Security Service'. Dennis Payne, who had been Director and Co-ordinator of Intelligence in Northern Ireland in the mid-seventies, had retired from the service shortly before being selected by the Prime Minister to investigate leaks from the Cabinet Office during the 1983 general election.[6]

In the first five years of Mrs Thatcher's administration she ordered MI5 to undertake ten leak inquiries. Only one concerned a possible threat to national security; the rest centred on leaks of documents on family and industrial policy, privatisation, welfare, and the Civil Service. A Department of Employment official was sacked for leaking a conversation between the Master of the Rolls and a civil servant to the magazine *Time Out*, but the results of all the other inquiries were officially classed as 'inconclusive'. Mrs Thatcher's obsession with secrecy became counter-productive. As Sissela Bok noted in her book on secrets: 'Leaking has a symbiotic relationship with secrecy. Without secrecy there would be no need to leak information.'[7]

Although Bettaney had given a full confession to Special

Branch, he decided to plead not guilty at his trial. This was a political action on the part of Bettaney, who hoped to force into the public arena a debate on the way that, as he saw it, an increasingly politicised MI5 was now operating. That wish was undermined by the official disruption of a trial which increasingly took on the hallmarks of an Eastern European style show-trial. Crucial documents were judged to be inadmissible, key witnesses were not allowed to be cross-examined and the majority of the trial was conducted *in camera*, added to which the jury was vetted by MI5. At one stage Bettaney considered refusing to recognise the court.

In another move which characterised the Thatcher period's open politicisation of the work of the security services, in August 1980 Attorney-General Sir Michael Havers drew up guidelines for use in vetting jurors in major trials, which might include national security matters. He referred to 'political beliefs . . . so biased as to go beyond normally reflecting the broad spectrum of views and interests in the community'. However, this would also include trials such as that of the senior civil servant Clive Ponting, which although involving leaks of government documents did not constitute a breach of national security.

The man responsible for vetting the Ponting and Bettaney juries was Sir Graham Lake, head of C3, which is responsible for vetting the staff of government departments. An Old Etonian 'Senior Technical Adviser at the MoD', Lake joined MI5 in 1959 and spent a period in New Delhi and was attached to MI6 before his posting to C Branch. The process involves 'record checks to establish whether a juror is a member of, or sympathiser with, any subversive party or organisation'. According to Michael Bettaney, the 'subversive' category extends to members of the Labour Party who were thought to be associated with Militant Tendency and other 'extremist' elements within the party. 'These checks are supplemented by "in-depth" discreet inquiries by the Special Branch amongst a person's colleagues, workmates, neighbours and friends with the aim of compiling a dossier on the person's political and social activities, his standing in the community, and so forth. In this area, a man or woman's involvement in the Peace Movement or in "industrial militancy" might be seen in the eyes of the authorities as sufficient to debar him or her from jury service.'[8]

The Security Commission chose to ignore Bettaney's genuine complaints about the activities of MI5. Instead, it focused on his alleged personal shortcomings, even when these stemmed from his increasing disenchantment with the service. Motives for his behaviour, where they could not be placed firmly within his personal make-up, were to be avoided. From prison, Bettaney later wrote to researchers that the Committee had diverted attention away from political questions in order to present a 'false idea of what was going on inside the service'. Despite its 'aura of judicial high-mindedness and detachment', the Committee report was, Bettaney wrote, 'a continuation of the strategy of disinformation and slander'.

Bettaney was a working-class conservative whose patriotism led him to the Security Service. He had attended state schools and had been recommended for recruitment while completing an English degree at Pembroke College, Oxford. He had undergone the normal routine of two preliminary interviews, followed by two personnel branch interviews and the positive vetting procedure which demanded no less than eight referees. His last hurdle had been the final appointments board chaired by Michael Hanley, Ronald Symonds and two MI5 directors. Bettaney supposedly represented the new breed of career intelligence officer who would supplant the hard-liners, the KGB obsessed and right-wingers who had contributed to MI5's poor reputation. As Tory MP Jonathan Aitken put it in a savage attack on MI5 in the House of Commons: 'The retired military and police personnel who are so present in the service are not the stuff of which deep thinkers are made.'[9]

The closed, isolated and rather stifling atmosphere of the Security Service provided cover for Bettaney's lonely, insecure persona; the inevitable cloak of secrecy acquired by officers helped to mask social and personal problems. Colleagues tolerated Bettaney's sometimes eccentric behaviour, expressed in drunken boorish bouts when he would openly declare he was working for the Soviets. His induction into security work had been disastrous both personally and as an example of the service's general incompetence. Young and inexperienced, this Catholic officer was thrown into the dirty world of Irish terrorism. In Northern Ireland, he was injured in a car-bomb attack and witnessed, while hiding in a cupboard, the horrifying spectacle of one of his informants being shot through the knee-caps by his terrorist colleagues. These traumatic experiences were soon followed by the death of two of his remaining relatives and a close personal friend. While he supported the continuing monitoring and surveillance of terrorism as a legitimate concern of MI5, he began to question Britain's role in Ireland.

The personnel section and the vetting system failed to monitor Bettaney's personal turmoil and his growing disillusionment with his work. Even during his last year in service, when the instability of his behaviour was such that two independent inquiries were being conducted into it, each was unaware of the other's existence. In October 1982, he was convicted for being drunk and disorderly and, the very next week, for fare dodging on the railways. He had missed one positive vetting scheduled in 1980 and by the time of his third, in January 1984, he was drinking heavily – a bottle of spirits a day – and was being treated for alcohol dependency by MI5's in-house doctor. There is, however, an ethos within MI5 which accepts heavy drinking – one reason why Bettaney escaped attention. The Pig and Eye, MI5's bar on the sixth floor of Curzon Street, was set up to discourage officers from talking shop outside the office in pubs. The intelligence world probably produces as many people with alcohol problems as journalism and medicine. Peter Wright revealed that psychiatric problems were quite common inside the service. 'Many senior officers in MI5 had counselling of one form or another during their careers to assist them in carrying the burdens of secrecy.' Despite his heavy drinking, Bettaney was promoted into K Branch, which dealt with counter-espionage. By the early eighties he had turned towards a dogmatic form of Marxism, with the same fervour he had once expressed in his Catholicism. Bettaney had become deeply concerned by the surveillance of his fellow citizens and the increasingly political way in which information was being used by MI5. He later wrote that he found these 'activities repugnant to my conscience'. By the spring of 1983 his political views, which 'had been steadily maturing since the days of my service in Northern Ireland', had 'crystallised'.[10]

A former colleague in K Branch, Miranda Ingram, wrote shortly after Bettaney's sentencing that the aura of glamour – largely a myth, she said – and secrecy surrounding intelligence work combined to make MI5 a very élite club. There was still a sharp class distinction in the service. 'Some expect membership as a birthright. To those of the new broader intake, who were not born to expect easy superiority, membership is a privilege. To both types, belonging to MI5 offers a private thrill . . . the danger is that officers are tempted to enjoy the secrecy surrounding their work . . . this hinders independent thinking and critical self-questioning. To retain, against all this, their sense of perspective and ability to question demands a strong character and an independence not encouraged by the service.' The decision by the Labour government in 1976 to encourage more working-class recruitment had not overcome class barriers. Like other working-class recruits, Bettaney still felt 'uncomfortable'. Although he appeared to ape his public school colleagues with his noted politeness, faultless manners and smart appearance, these masked a deep cynicism. 'He despised them, which was unusual for such an affable man.' This feeling was shared by others in the middle ranks of MI5, who resented their superiors who seemed trapped in the traditions of the service.[11]

Secrecy encourages closed minds and, according to Ingram, the tone was still right wing. 'There is an absence of open political debate inside the service. In this atmosphere it is not only the socially inferior who can feel uncomfortable. Those who dissent from the overall tone are also faced with a problem.' This was seen particularly in the area of subversion dealt with by F Branch. 'Working here means monitoring one's fellow citizens.' There was, Ingram found, 'a lack of flexible debate about the interpretation of "subversion" . . . [and] an officer who dissents from the official line does not feel encouraged to voice his concern.' In such an atmosphere someone like Bettaney 'keeps quiet'. 'This is where the situation becomes dangerous. What might begin as a moderate dissent will be silently nurtured and will fester until it grows into a much more serious dissent. Because it is not drawn out into open debate, it may eventually seek a clandestine outlet . . . The Bettaney case is an extreme manifestation of how dangerous this situation can become.'[12]

The disenchanted Bettaney had come to the conclusion that he should use his position inside MI5 to stop what he saw as the deteriorating international situation, in which the West was drifting into war against the Soviet Union. He claimed that the Thatcher government, 'by its slavish adherence to the aggressive and maverick policy of the Reagan administration, has contributed to an alarming heightening of tension to a point where the danger of war and the threat of nuclear extinction, surely the gravest crime against humanity, is closer than it has ever been'. He added that the 'cult of force' had been aided by the CIA and MI6, 'some of whose sections are permeated by an atmosphere of lurid anti-Soviet hysteria'. This had led to the use of 'subversive actions and other more sinister and immoral methods' against the Soviet Union. While working in K Branch, where he came into regular contact with MI6 officers, Bettaney was privy to the identity of a number of British agents who were working behind the Iron Curtain. Fortunately for the British, he did not have time to reveal the names to the Soviet embassy and was arrested before he made his planned trip to Vienna to meet up with KGB contacts. While Bettaney's view, made in a statement given to the media following his conviction, could easily be dismissed by the tabloids as the ravings of a disturbed individual, it was not without substance.[13]

The irony was that the man who had betrayed Bettaney to the British authorities, KGB defector Oleg Gordievsky, provided his MI6 case officers with evidence which did much to back up the dissident MI5 officer's claims. Gordievsky later told his debriefers about the KGB's ultra-secret Operation Ryan. President Reagan's simplistic view of the Soviet Union as the 'Evil Empire', an apocalyptic vision derived from his biblical readings of the Book of Revelation, together with the massive build-up of the United States' strategic nuclear forces and the announcement of the Star Wars programme, led the already paranoid and conspiracy-minded Soviet leadership to conclude that the West was considering a nuclear first strike. On the orders of the Kremlin, Ryan became a worldwide intelligence operation to discover evidence of planning for a third world war. From 1982 onwards, Ryan, which stood for 'Nuclear Missile Attack', was given top priority by the KGB residencies in NATO countries. In London, Gordievsky was told to look for tell-tale signs such as the number of lights on at night in government offices and military installations, the movement of key personnel and the meetings of committees. Few KGB officers believed that a first strike was in prospect – that would only come with a major East–West crisis – but the Politburo was pushing Moscow Centre to redouble efforts on the project throughout 1983. The Centre warned that there had been a marked increase in the activities of Western intelligence agencies including disinformation projects, infiltrations and use of *émigrés* against the USSR. Whether or not Soviet fears were justified, fears which only subsided in the summer of 1984, in his privileged post in K Branch where he liaised closely with

MI6 officers, Bettaney was in a unique position to learn about such operations.[14]

Bettaney not only attacked foreign operations, he was deeply concerned about MI5's domestic programme. After being jailed for twenty-three years, he issued a statement through his lawyer which declared: 'In pursuing its domestic policy, the government relies on the aid of a Security Service which cynically manipulates the definition of subversion and thus abuses its charter so as to investigate and interfere in the activities of legitimate political parties, the Trade Union Movement and other progressive organisations.' He was not alone in expressing alarm at these developments.

Cathy Massiter had served in Washington at the time of Watergate. An experienced F Branch officer, her responsibilities included the monitoring of the Campaign for Nuclear Disarmament (CND). She had become increasingly concerned in the early eighties that pressure from above to extend the surveillance of CND was politically motivated. During an interview for Channel 4's *20/20 Vision* programme, Massiter admitted: 'We were violating our own rules. It seemed to be getting out of control. This was happening not because CND as such justified this kind of treatment but simply because of political pressure; the heat was there for information about CND and we had to have it.'[15]

In September 1982, Mrs Thatcher convened a number of highly secret 'liaison committees' at 10 Downing Street which were to concentrate on policy areas that might be vulnerable during the forthcoming election. These included Britain's nuclear deterrent, and a propaganda drive was organised through a series of committees to expose what she termed 'the myths of unilateralism'. A former Tory Party official, Piers Wooley, who took part in the campaign, described the nature of the attack as 'information, disinformation and on many occasions, character assassination'. In March 1983, Minister of Defence Michael Heseltine set up a special counter-propaganda unit called Defence Secretariat 19 (DS19) to combat the unilateralist campaign of CND. It was felt that with a Labour Party committed to unilateral nuclear disarmament, CND would play a crucial role in the approaching general election. Shortly after Heseltine had talks with the director-general of MI5, a senior official from DS19 approached Massiter's boss in MI5.[16]

'I got a message via my branch director [David Ransom]', recalled Massiter, 'that the deputy director-general [Cecil Shipp] was prepared to consider favourably an application from me for a telephone check on a suitable CND target – i.e. a member of the Communist Party who could reasonably be classified as a subversive.' The target was CND vice-president John Cox, even though he did not meet the criteria of a subversive. Massiter goes on: 'We knew from our coverage of the Communist Party that he was not getting up to anything in CND.' However, she was instructed to carry out the operation by Tony Crassweller, who supervised the two sections F4 and F6 which run agents inside political parties and organisations. While acknowledging that technically CND was an internal political matter which in itself did not warrant MI5's attention, senior Whitehall officials concerned with security defended the targeting of CND on the basis that some members of the organisation were 'simply tools of Moscow'. It was a legitimate target because 'you have to think about where their funds come from, whether there's money coming from outside the country, and so you have to look at the CND council and the people involved in the administration.' This was nonsense, as Massiter revealed, but it satisfied the service's 'perverse bureaucratic obsession with regulations' while enabling a 'wholesale disregard for the Home Office rules and the law'.[17]

At the same time as the DS19 approach, a former editor of CND's magazine *Sanity*, fifty-seven-year-old Stanley Bonnett, was recruited as an informant by Special Branch officers, on the instructions of MI5. Informers are often more productive sources than telephone tappings and can be made psychologically dependent on their case officers. Bonnett, with his romantic old-style Communist views, had been out of place in the modern unilateralist movement which covered all political persuasions. His editorship had not been a success. His personal life was also in turmoil. He was easy prey for the Special Branch officers, who paid him several thousand pounds for his information, which was hardly secret. Bonnett admitted that an officer from the Metropolitan Police Special Branch's 'industrial desk' 'turned him over'. 'We had several long conversations. We talked about the different groups who were lobbying for position in CND – the feminists, the Communists and so on.' He also gave them minutes of meetings and lists of CND activists throughout the country. Bonnett said the officers told him that the material would be used for political purposes.[18]

Massiter was also instructed by her superiors to trawl the files and gather non-classified material on any extreme left-wing affiliations of CND's leaders. A report was then passed on to a civil servant, John Ledlie, who was seconded to DS19, who then forwarded it in a briefing paper to Heseltine. A public relations expert, Ledlie, who had worked in the past in Northern Ireland assisting former MI6 chief Sir Maurice Oldfield, passed on MI5's material to Sir Peter Blaker MP, Heseltine's lieutenant in the propaganda exercise. Piers Wooley was also in receipt of MI5 material which detailed attendance at conferences and trips abroad by CND members, especially those linked to the Soviet 'front' the World Peace Council. Blaker subsequently helped draw up a letter which was passed on to the local Conservative Association of Ray Whitney, a former head of the Foreign Office's Information Research Department (IRD) which, until its closure in 1977, had been responsible for propaganda including that of a black variety. On 22 April 1983, as the general election campaign was getting under way, the Blaker/Whitney letter was circulated to prospective Tory candidates. In a *Daily Mail* article titled 'CND is branded a tool of the Kremlin', the reporter acknowledged that 'the Defence Department and Tory researchers have clearly worked hard to establish Communist and Marxist penetration'. The letter included the following passage: 'Within the last few days Stanley Bonnett, editor of the CND newspaper *Sanity*, has been ousted. The secretary of the new editorial board that has taken over is a communist, Paul Nicholls. Mr Bonnett is in a very special position to know what life is really all about behind the gentle mask of the peace movement.'[19]

In the same period, the private anti-communist propaganda group Common Cause, which monitors subversion in industry and the unions, published a pamphlet – *The Communist Influence on the Campaign for Nuclear Disarmament* – which recorded in great detail the communist affiliations of the leading members of CND. It had been allegedly written under the direction of Charles Elwell, an experienced MI5 officer who had retired from the service in 1979. He had headed F Branch when the great explosion in the monitoring of political subversives took place and, as an assistant director, had been responsible for targeting the National Council for Civil Liberties (NCCL) as a subversive group. Elwell was also responsible for writing a research report, *Tracts Beyond the Times*, for the right-wing think-tank, the Social Affairs Unit. Drawing on his past experience as 'a long time student of socialist ideas', Elwell provided a brief guide to 'the Communist or Revolutionary Marxist Press'.

The pamphlet was less interesting for its list than for the glimpse it provided into MI5's view of the political landscape. Communists were defined as 'those who believe in and work towards the fulfilment of Marxist-Leninist aims by Marxist-Leninist means'. MI5 was interested in organisations and individuals 'controlled or influenced' by Marxist-Leninist groups because such groups, 'using revolutionary or parliamentary means or both, seek to introduce an *irreversible* socialist state' (Elwell's emphasis). They would seek to 'utterly vanquish' the bourgeois state and end constitutional opposition.

Treating 'communism' as a kind of virus which spreads through the body politic, Elwell goes on to suggest that through 'fronts' 'Communists are adept at exploiting people's liberal and benevolent instincts as well as their fears and resentments. Grist to the revolutionary mill are those opposed to authoritarian regimes in Latin America, Turkey or elsewhere or to Apartheid in South Africa, those who want to do something for "the wretched of the earth", particularly the alleged victims of neo-colonial exploitation by so-called multinational companies . . .' But those exploited by the Communists are not innocents, they are guilty for associating with them and are to be treated as if they had contracted the virus and are therefore to be classed as 'subversives' on MI5 files.[20]

Elwell was responsible for the decision to open security files on Patricia Hewitt, general secretary of the National Council for Civil Liberties from 1974 to 1983, and Harriet Harman, NCCL legal officer from 1978 to 1982. According to Elwell, 'The CPGB [Communist Party of Great Britain] and the NCCL have always been close to one another since . . . D. N. Pritt, the CPGB's "staunch friend", contributed to its work. Today the *Morning Star* gives generous coverage to the NCCL's activities.' He goes on to say that the 'articulate' Hewitt 'was given an enthusiastic "profile" in the *Morning Star*, for which she writes. [She] collaborates in her NCCL work with a barrister named William Birtles who is a member of Pritt's old chambers . . . Harriet Harman MP, is married to another NCCL activist Jack Dromey, said by the IMG's (International Marxist Group) paper *Socialist Challenge* to have been the architect of the NCCL's "pro-Communist" policy on Ireland. Whether or not this is so, Dromey is certainly very close to the CPGB.' On the basis of Harman's marriage and the fact that Hewitt, who went on to become press secretary to Labour Party leader Neil Kinnock and senior staff member of the Institute for Public Policy Research, was a close friend of Birtles, then a member for the CPGB, MI5 opened files on the pair as 'communist sympathisers'. According to Cathy

Massiter, the deciding factor in putting them on file was Elwell's 'own view that NCCL's attacks on certain institutions such as the police were deliberate attempts to undermine these institutions'.[21]

Following the Massiter revelations about the surveillance operation, both women took their cases to the European Court of Human Rights, which, in 1990, ruled that the files were kept in breach of Article 8 of the European Human Rights Convention which guarantees protection of private life. Although the ruling should have resulted in the destruction of the files, they remain in the possession of MI5 in defiance of the Security Service Act which came into force in December 1989.[22]

Elwell had informed his superiors, on leaving, that he intended working for Common Cause – though a spokesman for the organisation said that 'he went to work for Brian Crozier'. Elwell was employed by Crozier as an editor and researcher on a private anti-communist news sheet, *Background Briefing on Subversion*, which, for a time, was funded by Crozier's friend, the publisher Rupert Murdoch, although Murdoch may not have been aware of the true nature of the publication. Echoing the official line inside the service, its technique against left-wing Labour MPs was to establish 'communist' guilt by association, taking quotations from many left-wing published sources even though the link to communism was tenuous at best. The tone of *British Briefing*, as it became known, was best expressed in its February 1987 issue: 'The march of communism through the trade unions, the Labour Party, local government, religion, education, charity, the media under the leadership of communists who may or may not be members of the Communist Party, is what BB is all about. BB seeks to provide those who have the means to expose the communist threat with clear evidence of its existence.' Among the Labour Party targets were Neil Kinnock, shadow Health Secretary Robin Cook, spokesman for social services Michael Meacher and spokesman for local government

David Blunkett. The Labour MP and author of *A Very British Coup*, Chris Mullin, was singled out for his 'perpetual vendetta against British security arrangements' while Derbyshire MP Harry Barnes was unjustly attacked as 'quite a vigorous Stalinist underminer of British parliamentary democracy'. Several progressive organisations were tarred with the communist brush, notably the charity Shelter for its 'Communist affiliations', the Institute for Race Relations ('effectively controlled by revolutionary socialists') and the World Council of Churches. The newsletter was printed by the anti-Communist trade-union-based Industrial Research and Information Service (IRIS), whose parent body had been Common Cause. Copies were circulated to 'political leaders, MPs, journalists and others', who were requested to treat it as confidential and to refrain from quoting from it.[23]

The anti-CND operation 'was a very important party political issue' which Massiter recognised was 'clearly not a legitimate function because it directly contravenes the charter'. The charter, itself a document, thought Bettaney, 'flawed by considered ambiguity', stated that 'no inquiry is to be carried out on behalf of any government department unless you are satisfied that an important public interest bearing on the defence of the realm is at stake'. The Maxwell-Fyfe directive stated that it was essential that 'the Security Service should be kept absolutely free from any political bias or influence'. Although Home Secretary Leon Brittan admitted that campaigning on unilateralist issues was 'an entirely legitimate activity' and later that 'CND does not attempt to undermine parliamentary democracy', he had, in August 1983, authorised the tapping of the telephone of a leading CND official. In a letter to a fellow Tory MP about Cathy Massiter's claims, Brittan said he was 'fully satisfied' that MI5 was 'absolutely free from any political bias or influence'.[24]

Brittan's strong public support for MI5 was seemingly not as unwavering in private – his backing was viewed as half-hearted by 'the ultras' inside the service. He was not liked, and worse, he was a Jew, who was regarded as being soft on civil liberties and a grudging supporter of the hard-line policies of the Prime Minister. Problems arose following the shooting of WPC Yvonne Fletcher in 1984 outside the Libyan People's Bureau in St James's Square. Brittan had threatened to shake up the Security Service after it had failed to properly evaluate warnings from the CIA on the intentions of Libyan diplomats. According to *Private Eye*, MI5 retaliated by spreading rumours about the Home Secretary's private life, in particular an incident that was alleged to have occurred during the 1983 general election. Someone even went to the trouble of producing small stickers publicising the allegations. The *News of the World* and the *Mail on Sunday* investigated the allegations and both discovered that the smears were totally untrue. But with all smears, however untrue, a stain remains and Brittan was undoubtedly damaged by MI5's campaign.[25]

In November 1979, Mrs Thatcher told the Commons that if MI5's director-general received 'information about a present or former minister or some senior public servant indicating that he may be, or may have been, a security risk', a report should be made directly to the Prime Minister or, indirectly, through the Home Secretary. Two years later, in order to avoid a Profumo-type situation, Mrs Thatcher had asked the Security Service to keep a discreet eye on any potentially embarrassing personal and sexual indiscretions by Tory MPs. Officers in an élite section, allegedly known as the 'Dolly Mixtures', operated from Gordon Street in London, picking up gossip on the social circuit. They may have been behind the monitoring of a guest house run by a brothel keeper in a smart London suburb which, in the early eighties, catered for gays who liked young boys and was apparently frequented by a minister, MPs and members of the right-wing Conservative Monday Club. The guest house was raided by police in June 1982 following the intervention of an MI5 officer, 'JR', who was in contact with the madam. The situation was ironic given that the Security Service was itself breaking Home Office guidelines on the use of sex in entrapment operations. Following the Profumo affair, in which MI5 had been heavily implicated, Prime Minister Alec Douglas-Home had outlawed such operations. The rule was ignored when officers used sexual blackmail against a Soviet defector, Oleg Lyalin, but was reinforced after the 1973 Lambton scandal when it was discovered that a madam involved in the affair had been an informant. However, officers inside the service ignored the warnings and deliberately ran prostitutes who were in contact with MPs. It was an added bonus that some of them were known to be carrying sexual diseases, which provided the service with the potential to blackmail those MPs who succumbed to the charms of these 'ravens'.[26]

The 'Dolly Mixtures' may have been responsible for monitoring the activities of the Royal Family. MI5 apparently opened a file on Prince Charles's relationship with Mrs Camilla Bowles in the late eighties. The service also built up a dossier on the Duchess of York's friendship with the Texan financier, John Bryan, following fears that their liaison might 'threaten the stability of the Monarchy'. Media revelations of MI5 involvement in the surveillance of the royals gave rise to speculation that the tape recording of an intimate telephone conversation between Princess Diana, 'squidgy', and James Gilbey, a close friend, may have been the work of the Security Service. Security experts were sceptical of the claim by retired bank manager Cyril Reenan that he had been responsible for eavesdropping on the mobile telephone with his thousand pound scanner. The quality of the 'Dianagate' tape recording was good and would normally require more sophisticated equipment such as the Celltrack – a desk-top GCHQ – which overcomes frequency changes and locks on to a call irrespective of distance or whether the 'target' is moving. It is widely and secretly used by professional eavesdroppers, the police and intelligence gatherers such as MI5, though why the Security Service would want to damage the Royal Family has not been explained.

Unlike Bettaney, who admits that he discussed his views 'with no one whatever', Massiter and others did express their concern over policy and the general drift to the right. During 1983, Massiter complained to the head of her section, to her assistant director and finally to the personnel section. She told them she 'felt that the work that we were doing was unnecessary and that we were giving in to persistent political pressure. I did feel fairly emotional about it, but they tried to make my reactions the issue.' Thoughtful, likeable and well-read – she had been a librarian before joining the service in 1970 as a secretary – the thirty-seven-year-old Massiter suffered, according to a former colleague, 'from the profound disadvantage for an MI5 operative of thinking about her work'. In consequence, she was sent to see a consultant psychiatrist, who had been given security clearance to deal with officers' personal problems. 'They were obviously not really concerned about my mental health or they wouldn't have let me carry on working.' Senior management did nothing about her complaints. 'The difficulty is that having expressed one's view, there is no way of taking it any further. If your view is not accepted you're simply left with the option of accepting the situation or, of course, ultimately resigning' – which Massiter did in February 1984. The former MI5 officer, who had spent fourteen years in the service, then took part in a Channel 4 documentary on MI5, broadcast of which was prevented by the Independent Broadcasting Authority in the following year. Although Massiter's revelations for television were a breach of her undertakings as a government employee, ministers were loath to prosecute under the Official Secrets Act so soon after the acquittal of former MoD civil servant Clive Ponting, who had been tried for leaking information concerning the sinking of the Argentine cruiser *Belgrano* during the Falklands War. Instead MI5 attempted to discredit the former officer as a 'neutoric betrayer of trust', which Bettaney later suggested from prison was 'standard procedure'.[27]

The resignation of officers and the warnings of Bettaney did little to depoliticise the service, whose senior officers were fiercely loyal to Mrs Thatcher. Between 1983 and 1985 the executive of the Anti-Apartheid Movement was put under close scrutiny. According to a senior MI5 officer in F Branch, a particular target was the City of London Anti-Apartheid Group, which was regarded as the most militant branch of the organisation. 'We were told to investigate it as a front for the Revolutionary Communist Group.' Little evidence was found to justify this view. What information was uncovered from telephone tappings was passed on to officials attached to the South African embassy. 'They said it would help them apply pressure on the families of South Africans living in England.' Other targets included Friends of the Earth, Greenpeace, certain trade unions and prominent Labour Party left-wingers, who had their telephones tapped. With the 1984–5 miners' strike MI5 would sink deeper into the political mire.[28]

3

Antony Duff

> It is an axiom of internal security that there can never be too much intelligence.
>
> Tom Mangold, BBC *Panorama*, 2 March 1981

In 1981, Mrs Thatcher's reluctant climb-down on the issue of the pit closures had prevented a strike by the National Union of Mineworkers (NUM). However, she was not prepared to be defeated in any future conflict by the Conservative Party's *bête noire*. The Cabinet's secret committee, Misc 57, in co-operation with Whitehall's Civil Contingencies Unit (CCU), was ordered to prepare plans to combat any possible industrial action by the miners. Under the chairmanship of the Cabinet deputy secretary, Sir Robert Wade-Gery, blueprints for emergency planning, proposed by Lord Carrington in 1975 and refined by the CCU following the Conservative election success in 1979, were dusted off and presented in a report to ministers in 1982. Haunted, if not obsessed, by Arthur Scargill's success with flying pickets at the Saltley coke depot and the miners' defeat of the Heath government, Mrs Thatcher was determined to win and she was prepared to use whatever resources were available.[1]

A major intelligence 'Get Scargill' operation was put into place during the 1984 miners' strike. Under the cloak of national security – 'saving the country's bacon', as a former head of the CCU put it – Mrs Thatcher's government bent the rules and used a willing Security Service as a political weapon. Britain's GCHQ co-operated with the United States National Security Agency (NSA) in a Europe-wide telephone tapping system, to keep track of the movement of funds directed to the NUM and international miners' trusts by the Soviet authorities. In the process, the operation involved illegally breaching the security of European bank transactions. Go-ahead for the operation against domestic targets had been given by Downing Street based on a code of conduct drawn up with GCHQ, and no warrants were needed for the mass surveillance.

The NSA had broken Soviet international banking codes and was able to track the sending of funds to a Swiss bank. In late 1984, information on the transfer of money to the miners gathered from NSA stations in Europe and the GCHQ satellite station at Morwenstow, near Bude in Cornwall, was passed on to MI5. Soon after, articles on 'Moscow gold' were published in right-wing newspapers. However, the Soviet funds never reached the NUM, having been transferred back to Moscow. In December 1984, Mrs Thatcher raised the matter with Soviet leader Mikhail Gorbachev during a state visit to London, MI6 double agent Oleg Gordievsky, who was the KGB number two at the London embassy, has said that after Gorbachev's visit to Downing Street, plans for transferring money to the NUM were curtailed. Instead, in February 1985, money was sent to the Communist-led Miners' Trade Union International, which controlled an international solidarity fund.[2]

MI5's director-general, John Jones, and the head of F Branch, David Ransom, had both been heavily involved in the miners' strike in the early seventies. In 1984–5, as had her superiors a decade before, Stella Rimington, the head of F2, which deals with trade unions, reported regularly to the Civil Contingencies Unit, whose head, former ambassador to Hungary Bryan Cartledge, also sat on the Joint Intelligence Committee. Rimington provided the CCU with the latest intelligence on the NUM's leaders, their morale, and the progress of the strike. Intelligence gathering was helped by the fact that, during the seventies, F Branch had made a special effort to recruit industrial correspondents with great success, while Special Branch's 'industrial desk' had expanded at an enormous rate, recruiting dozens of informants within the trade union movement, which MI5 had swiftly taken for their own. MI5's industrial desk, which had only two officers in 1970, had by the time of the strike the following year become a sub-section known as FSCN with a staff of seven intelligence officers.[3]

Arthur Scargill and the Scottish miners' leader, Mick McGahey, had been subjected to MI5 telephone tapping operations since the seventies. During the strike, GCHQ officials advised on the telephone tapping operation which involved monitoring NUM headquarters in Sheffield and the telephones of branch secretaries. The multitude of taps created an 'information mountain' within MI5 as key words such as 'picket' triggered the telephone tapping system. One morning, the overload system caused the continuously running tape-recorders to grind to a halt as the tapes ran out. Transcripts were sent to the National Reporting Centre at New Scotland Yard, which organised the deployment of police officers in the coalfields, and to MI5's F2 section. Scargill's visits to the Soviet embassy in London were regularly monitored, and when he turned up with his chief executive, Roger Windsor, a whole posse of Fleet Street photographers appeared.[4]

In 1990, Windsor was the subject of allegations published in the *Daily Mirror* and directed against Scargill and the NUM. This laid – what turned out to be – false accusations about the diversion of Soviet funds to the NUM, a Libyan connection and corruption charges. Before joining the NUM, Windsor had been employed by the trans-national union organisation, Public Services International (PSI). During the sixties a joint CIA/MI5 operation had organised a coup against the Prime Minister of British Guinea, Chedi Jagan. The vehicle used for funding the operation was the PSI. Windsor was paid £80,000 by the *Daily Mirror* for his damaging testimony. Few newspapers took any notice of the release in August 1992 of a legal agreement made by the special investigating office of the Inland

Revenue, which gave the NUM a clean bill of health. The Inland Revenue dismissed claims of corruption, stating that the various secret accounts had been valid trusts which showed no signs of impropriety.[5]

In a Commons motion, Tam Dalyell called on the government to make a full statement 'about the role of Mrs Stella Rimington, in particular in connection with the activities of Mr David Hart, during the miners' strike'. Hart was a wealthy property developer and former bankrupt with an abiding interest in anti-communism. Nicknamed 'Diehard', he had been an unofficial adviser to National Coal Board chairman Sir Ian MacGregor, and gained access to Mrs Thatcher's inner circle, stiffening their resolve against the 'wet' views of the Energy Secretary, Peter Walker, who was willing to negotiate with the NUM. Hart saw the strike 'as a political showdown with the forces of Marxism'. From his suite at Claridge's Hotel, the Old Etonian helped to finance the back-to-work movement, the National Working Miners' Committee, and the breakaway Union of Democratic Mineworkers based in the Nottingham area. His first contacts with the Thatcher government were in the spring of 1981 through Ian Gow, Mrs Thatcher's parliamentary private secretary, a Thatcherite 'ultra' with close ties to MI6.[6]

During the 1983 and 1987 general election campaigns Hart acted as an adviser on speeches and strategy. How close in reality the links were to the Prime Minister's office is hard to judge, but Hart is alleged to have said that he did not need to sign the Official Secrets Act because 'Thatcher's told me so much I could blow her out of the water in five minutes.' In 1988, he took over the responsibility for publishing the robust anti-communist newsletter *British Briefing* from Brian Crozier, which continued under the editorship of Charles Elwell.[7]

The Security Commission's report on the Bettaney affair, published in May 1985, chose to ignore the damaging evidence of Bettaney, Massiter, two former senior officers who gave secret testimony and the junior officers it had interviewed. It noticeably steered clear of criticising Security Service operations. Indeed, the report said that there was nothing to suggest these should be called into question. The Commission concluded that 'Nothing in this report is intended to call in question the professional and operational efficiency of the Security Service.' This alleged 'efficiency' was of a 'high order'. The report avoided dealing with sensitive areas of operations, policy and political guidance. 'Evidence critical of the organisation and management' was omitted and the Commission's detailed recommendations on the internal structure of MI5, which were carried in two long appendices of the report, were not published.

The Commission did produce a highly critical report on MI5 management – Conservative MP Jonathan Aitken called it 'one of the most scathing indictments of the quality of management of any government organisation this century'. It was known that MI5 had not been well managed for a number of years. There had been a lack of a long-term strategy, which had not been helped by the astonishing turnover of four director-generals within a decade and a similar number within the key counter-espionage K Branch. The Commission discovered deep-seated problems over recruitment, vetting procedures and staff morale inside the service and called for the following measures:

- A more open and self-critical style of management in order to counter the necessary isolation of the service and to encourage younger members to express their views.
- A coherent and explicit personnel strategy to be introduced with thorough back-up training for all personnel managers at the Civil Service College, so that accountability and responsibility would be clear-cut, following a thorough-going examination of personnel management practices in the service.
- Those under forty years of age, normally barred from managerial responsibilities, to be trained for management

and substantial devolution of responsibility should be considered.

- The recruitment of 'competent' personnel managers from elsewhere in Whitehall or from 'even wider a field' should be considered and a two way traffic of secondments and cross-postings between MI5 and the Civil Service and the Armed Forces should be encouraged.[8]

In reporting to Parliament on the Commission's recommendations, Mrs Thatcher said that she expected a 'change of style of management' in order to eradicate the significant 'management weaknesses' which had been uncovered. Some interested parties expected more. When in 1983 the Labour Party published its proposals on reform of MI5, *Freedom and the Security Services*, Whitehall sources let it be known that the document ignored 'existing albeit *unannounced* [*sic*] controls on the budgets and the operations of the secret agencies exercised by the Cabinet Office on behalf of the Prime Minister'. The writers of the pamphlet had relied on 'gossip', whereas the 'reality' was very different. However, Jonathan Aitken told the House of Commons that Mrs Thatcher and the Cabinet had promised the tightest ministerial control of MI5 after the Blunt affair in 1979 – as had Callaghan in 1976 – but the Commission's report showed that this had not happened. What the Prime Minister did not reveal was that the change of management style included a change of manager.[9]

Initially, Whitehall sources let it be known that talk of dismissing Jones was 'cloud cuckoo country'; however, Sir John had put up a poor performance when giving evidence to the Commission, who regarded him as being far too complacent. In the spring of 1985, without any publicity, he quietly retired to his new house in the country, where his wife pursued her interest in flower arranging while he improved his golf handicap of eighteen. There then ensued a typical Whitehall in-fight among the five-man committee which had to put forward a recommended choice for the Prime Minister. This must have brought back bitter memories for Commission member Lord Allen, who, in 1972, had failed to impose his own candidate on MI5 against determined opposition.[10]

In 1985, Home Office mandarins had been given assurances that the post of director-general would be kept 'in the office' and would go to their choice, the chain-smoking deputy, Cecil Shipp, MI5's top interrogator in the sixties. Well regarded by the civil servants responsible for supervising the Security Service, the highly experienced Shipp had, in the mid-seventies, served in Washington as a security liaison officer, liaising with the CIA and FBI. However, Home Secretary Leon Brittan was seen as lacking the authority to push for an insider, and there were even fears that under the pressure of the Secretary of State for Defence, Michael Heseltine, MI5 might revert to its original position under the departmental responsibility of the Ministry of Defence with a service chief as its head. This idea was quickly scotched, but Shipp had to be content with a CB and an extension of his time as deputy.[11]

Contrary to popular belief, the eventual choice – the external candidate, sixty-four-year-old Sir Antony Duff – was not the nominee of Mrs Thatcher. She had favoured an intelligence 'insider' and had to be persuaded that the Foreign Office man was a suitable candidate. Sir Antony Duff was part of the Foreign Office team under Lord Carrington which had persuaded Mrs Thatcher in 1979 that the time was ripe for a constitutional conference on Rhodesia. The conference was held at Lancaster House, and during the proceedings Duff and Carrington were fed with intelligence each morning, obtained from Security Service telephone tappings and buggings of hotel rooms of the various delegations attending the negotiations.

Duff served as deputy governor general of Rhodesia and, with Lord Soames, helped organise the peaceful transfer of power to the new Zimbabwe, for which he won much praise. Already past the official retiring age of sixty, he had been brought into the Cabinet Office first as head of the security and intelligence secretariat, which oversees the budgets of the secret agencies. In 1982, he was made chair of the Joint Intelligence Committee, which collates and assesses intelligence from Britain's security services, following the Committee's failure to assess correctly Argentinian plans for invading the Falkland Islands.[12]

Duff was known to keep a low profile and was regarded by the inner circles of the Foreign Office and Cabinet Office as an outsider. Educated, not at Oxbridge, but at the Royal Naval College, Dartmouth, he was by training a naval man with a sound practical intelligence. During the Second World War, aged only twenty-four, he had commanded the submarine HMS *Stubborn* and, during a dramatic incident in which he engineered an escape from the seabed, had shown the cool, methodical thinking for which he became renowned. Duff was never regarded as a Whitehall intellectual; rather he was seen as a dependable bureaucrat.

Relations between MI5 and the Foreign Office have always been frosty. In the past, MI5 did not trust the Foreign Office to be secure, and information – mainly about diplomatic matters – if given, was passed on reluctantly. Additionally the service resented the pressure put on it to gain warrants to bug the Israeli embassy which, according to Peter Wright, 'was easy since the Foreign Office was pro-Arab'. During the Cold War, the Foreign Office was viewed by MI5 as soft on Soviet spying. To expel a known KGB man operating under cover at the Soviet embassy required the approval of the Northern Department Committee of the Foreign Office. The Committee invariably refused permission on the grounds that to do so would upset diplomatic relations and, more importantly, trade deals. Wright believed that its 'main job was stop anybody doing anything to upset the Russians'. The service's 'friends' in MI6 'always worried that the Soviets would throw out their people in Moscow in retaliation'.[13]

There was particular unease about MI5 within the Foreign Office over the case of a British diplomat, Miss Rhona Ritchie.

She had been given a nine-month suspended sentence in November 1982 for passing confidential information to her Egyptian lover, Rifat El-Ansari, while serving in Tel Aviv. None of the material was highly classified and most was made public shortly afterwards. Two years later, the Foreign Office let it be known that they considered Miss Ritchie had been 'both hastily and harshly treated by MI5'.[14]

No doubt the Foreign Office and MI6 used considerable indirect pressure in the hope of imposing a measure of discipline on the Security Service in order to placate the Americans, who were appalled by the lax security within MI5 which the Security Commission had uncovered. Bettaney had been allowed to wander in and out of K Branch's offices in Gower Street without being searched. At night he patrolled the corridors alone with a camera in his pocket, able to photograph numerous files, stealthily rifling through MI5's considerable secrets. Back at his home, sheaves of paper dotted with handwritten accounts of MI5 operations, which Bettaney had memorised, were found stuffed down chairs and hidden inside cupboards. Senior counter-intelligence FBI agents and CIA officers who liaised closely with K Branch, swapping information with their British counterparts, were horrified to discover how easily security had been circumvented.

The 'strong, sensible and quiet' Duff was seen as the 'strong man at the helm' needed to pull MI5 into line. One Cabinet minister thought Duff 'a powerful chap. He will print his personality on MI5 very quickly. He's a gentleman-officer type and people do look up to them when they are, like he is, very fair and firm.' Others were not so sure that a 'gentleman-officer type' was what was required. Sterner stuff was needed. A former Labour minister with experience of the intelligence community thought that Duff would have to be 'tough enough to chop people who get out of hand. The whole nature of a secret agency makes it open to abuse. He'll have to be prepared to be a bastard.'[15]

In a typical example of the deference to the British state

exercised by the British media, newspapers agreed to a D-Notice Committee request not to publish a photograph of the new director-general even though his features had appeared in magazines during negotiations over Zimbabwe. Duff's low profile was to be maintained. Not long after taking up the post in 1984, at a personal briefing with Prime Minister Margaret Thatcher and the Cabinet Secretary, Sir Robert Armstrong, Duff was ordered to 'clean up' MI5. Another outsider, Sir Howard Smith, had been given exactly the same instructions six years previously by James Callaghan. Obviously, Howard Smith had failed. Duff was given permission to enlist officers from other Whitehall departments to help in the process and he was asked to consider and report back on what developments he proposed. It was soon leaked that Duff had completed a savage purge of key personnel inside MI5. It was said that security experts from the Foreign Office and the armed forces had re-screened all MI5 officers. Some senior men had either been 'encouraged' to retire early or had been moved from operational to administrative posts, where they were expected to remain for the rest of their service. Bob Holden was the director of B Branch, which had overall responsibility for Bettaney's vetting, while Martin McOnachie ran B2, which was responsible for personnel management and welfare.[16]

Not long after the briefing Mrs Thatcher announced, in May 1985, the tightening of vetting procedures in the security services in the wake of the Bettaney affair. Vetting arrangements which had applied only to the more senior grades were extended to all staff. It was not only the Bettaney episode which had prompted this decision. In April 1985, forty-seven-year-old Derek Card, a middle-ranking officer in an MI5 vetting section within the MoD, was sentenced to a suspended six months' imprisonment for sex offences against an educationally backward woman. His former employers had stood by him, describing his career in glowing terms. Although Card had faced a 'considerable number of traumas' as a child, he had overcome them to work his way up in the Civil

Service. His twenty-two years' service in vetting had been 'stressful and difficult' and had led to the break-up of his first marriage.[17]

In the same year, another civil servant connected with MI5 turned his 'attentions' to his thirteen-year-old daughter when his marriage became 'empty in all ways'. The assaults on his eldest and youngest daughters grew in 'indecency and severity' over a number of years. In May 1990, the forty-two-year-old senior MI5 electronics expert, working on a project for Saudi Arabia on behalf of Her Majesty's Government, was imprisoned for two years for the indecent assault of his two daughters. Described by colleagues as 'la crème de la crème' for his expertise, he had worked since 1969 for the security services as an expert in telecommunications based in Woolwich, south London.[18]

In addition to better vetting procedures, former security officers felt that what MI5 required was an effective internal security department which, unlike MI6 and the Foreign Office, it did not possess. Within MI5, where security had come under the heading 'personnel', the security risk had been regarded as greater abroad and it was argued that, because the personnel staff possessed an individual's files and handled discipline, they were ideally placed to deal with internal security. However, Duff was said to be considering appointing a special investigator for more decided action on internal security. The investigator would monitor security and check officers under suspicion. He would also work very closely on a day-to-day basis with counter-intelligence officers in both MI5 and MI6, which was effectively K Branch's section 5. Two years later it was reported that little progress had been made in this direction. On the matter of dissenting officers such as Cathy Massiter, the government had been pressed by members of the Commons Select Committee on Home Affairs for a 'proper channel through which they can make their views known'. In the United States the CIA appointed an inspector general to monitor the performance of the CIA and sift complaints about its work. It was felt that such an official was needed in Britain, someone who would become a sounding board for staff discontent.[19]

The new director-general not only attempted to deal with security and personnel problems, but he also set up an internal inquiry to assess targets for the service and future requirements. Noting that reform was urgently needed, Duff ordered a switch in priorities within F Branch from countering subversion to counter-terrorism. A major initiative was launched to recruit informers inside terrorist groups, and this in turn led to recruiting a large number of outsiders to run the agents.

Duff appeared to be different to previous director-generals in that he actually got out of his office and talked to officers, managing to visit each branch and department. This was new, but word soon leaked out that what Duff had discovered was depressing. He concluded that MI5 had failed to keep in touch with the modern world and needed an infusion of younger staff who would bring with them new ideas and more liberal attitudes. He encouraged an existing exchange programme with industry that allowed officers to see a different side of life. Outsiders, such as managing directors, were brought in to hold seminars so that officers could gain insight into the workings of the City, academia and the media. Although former MI5 officers were not as prominent in the City as those of MI6, the Security Service still had its fair share of former officers in key positions. Senior officers had moved into security jobs as consultants with top British firms such as ICI.

Sir John Cuckney, a former 'tough, no-nonsense' training officer, served with MI5 during the fifties. Cuckney told young recruits who asked about MI5's legal status when engaging in burglaries and telephone tapping: 'It hasn't got one. The Security Service cannot have the normal status of a Whitehall Department because its work very often involves transgressing propriety or the law.' He said that MI5's eleventh commandment was 'Thou shalt not get caught'. An intensely private man, Cuckney went on to become a successful merchant banker with Lazards and chairman of the troubled helicopter company Westland after being asked by the Bank of England to sort it out. Admired by Downing Street, Cuckney is one of the 'great and the good', an Establishment figure who straddles the private and public sectors, though one who twitches at 'the astonishing hypocrisy of politicians'.[20]

Duff helped establish clearer links with the media. Editors of the serious newspapers were courted and invited to lecture to junior officers. Duff wanted the service to be able to respond better to any inaccurate statement in the press, though often this meant no more than selectively leaking MI5's version of the story through the usual media conduits. None of these moves was new or particularly reforming, they were just being given a fresh urgency under the Duff regime.

On 29 January 1986, a year after Duff's appointment, a former MI5 officer, John Day, received a reply from Cabinet Secretary Sir Robert Armstrong to a letter he had written on the need for some form of oversight. Armstrong noted that 'more is being done to improve both the management of the service and the degree of awareness that some of us outside have of it than for many years'. In effect, the Cabinet Secretary was admitting that even the people responsible for overseeing MI5 had no clear idea what had been going on. It was reported that Duff felt it was time for MI5 to come out of the shadows and was arguing that some form of oversight of MI5's activities was required to allay the public's fears. In the middle and late eighties the Security Service found itself increasingly in the spotlight over alleged misdeeds and illegal activities.

The government was worried by claims from members of CND and the National Council for Civil Liberties (now known as Liberty) that MI5 had acted illegally in mounting a surveillance campaign against them. The case was being taken to the European Court of Human Rights and it was acknowledged that the court was likely to call for effective oversight to protect the rights of the individual. There were also the Massiter and Wright allegations, which added considerable weight to calls for an inquiry. The government response in the form of increasingly bland statements was met with widespread disbelief. It was realised that some form of complaints procedure would be required to quieten the uproar which continued to build. However, even with a new director-general who had been told to 'clean the stables', MI5 continued to break its charter and directives.

In 1984, Cold War propagandist Brian Crozier wrote a letter to the *Spectator* accusing the American-based liberal think-tank, the Institute for Policy Studies (IPS), of being 'a front of Cuban intelligence, itself controlled by the KGB'. Writs issued against the magazine by the IPS co-director and founder, Richard Barnet, a former aide to President John F. Kennedy, were settled in 1986 when the magazine retracted the statement. However, the case did not go away because Crozier decided to fight the action. It was at this point that MI5 became interested in Barnet's friend and fellow academic Fred Halliday. The Security Service mounted a year-long covert surveillance operation to ascertain whether Halliday, a respected international relations specialist with ties to the IPS, had any links with Soviet officials. MI5 placed Halliday's name on the Suspects Index used by Immigration and Customs officials, who were instructed to inform the Security Service of his movements abroad. Soviet desk officers within K Branch were hoping that, in the event of Halliday innocently coming into contact with KGB officers while on trips to Eastern Europe, MI5 would be able to open a file and mount an official investigation.

At the beginning of 1987, Crozier lost his case and was forced to pay costs. By the autumn of that year, Halliday's name – he had been shown to have no links with Soviet officials – had been removed from the Suspects Index.[21]

At the time of the Peter Wright affair the government came under intense pressure to order an inquiry into allegations that an extreme right-wing faction inside MI5 had conducted a dirty tricks campaign against Prime Minister Harold Wilson in

1974–6. Security Service sources, 'who were very concerned about the activities of others' involved in the smear campaign against Wilson, began passing information to the press and Labour MPs. At the beginning of May 1987, Mrs Thatcher declined to bow to opposition demands, citing the 1977 inquiry ordered by Wilson's successor James Callaghan which concluded that the allegations did not 'constitute grounds for lack of confidence in the competence and impartiality of the Security Service or for instituting of a special inquiry'. The Prime Minister had been advised by Cabinet Secretary Sir Robert Armstrong on the extent of the Callaghan inquiry and had decided early on to block any attempt at a new investigation. Sir Robert was, however, not a disinterested party. During the mid-seventies, when the destabilisation campaign was in progress, he had been Permanent Under-Secretary at the Home Office with specific responsibilities for the Security Service.

The scope of the 1977 inquiry had been narrow and referred to allegations which had appeared in the *Observer* newspaper, specifically that Wilson had been under electronic surveillance. None of the later Wright allegations were investigated. The narrowness of the inquiry can be measured by the fact that Sir Leonard Hooper, the Cabinet intelligence and security co-ordinator at the time, was unaware of its existence and was not consulted about it. In April 1987, former Labour Home Secretary Merlyn Rees said that the 1977 inquiry, with which he had been intimately involved, did not cover any of the later allegations and certainly did not dispose of the affair.[22]

Under growing pressure, particularly from Callaghan, Mrs Thatcher revealed:

> the Director-General of the Security Service has reported to me that, over the last four months, he has conducted a thorough investigation into all these stories, taking acount of the earlier allegations and of other material given recent currency. There has been a comprehensive examination of all the papers relevant to that time. There have been interviews

> with officers in post in the relevant parts of the Security Service at that time, including officers whose names have been made public. The Director-General has advised me that he has found no evidence of any truth in the allegations. He has given me his personal assurance that the stories are false.

Duff informed the Prime Minister that there had been no conspiracy against Harold Wilson and that he had not been the subject of an MI5 investigation nor put under any form of surveillance.[23]

In effect, the Security Service was asked to investigate itself and, naturally, declared itself clean. It soon became apparent that the key figures in the alleged conspiracy had not been interviewed and the man at the centre of the allegations, Peter Wright, had not been approached. Callaghan was far from satisfied by Mrs Thatcher's statement, telling the Commons that she had stubbornly ignored 'suggestions that there should be an independent group who should look objectively at these matters'. Against the advice of members of the Permanent Secretaries' Security and Intelligence Committee, which had counselled that a small discreet inquiry might quell demands for a more radical venture, Mrs Thatcher opposed any such move for fear that it might lead to some form of external control of the security services, a move which she vigorously opposed. There was a growing consensus for such a move, which Callaghan articulated in the House, declaring that he had changed his views since the 1977 inquiry and now suggested that 'an oversight body was needed to review the work of the Security Service, in particular, their targeting, management, structure and staff counselling'.[24]

Duff's proposals on oversight were overruled by Mrs Thatcher, who firmly brushed them aside. She resisted all such talk, and the later Security Service Act, which put the legal standing of MI5 on an official basis, did not include any reference to parliamentary oversight. She gave her own view of security policy to the House of Commons: 'I believe we should continue to enable the security services to run in a secret way – after all, those against whom they operate have the benefit of secrecy.' Against mounting criticism, some aspects of oversight were conceded under pressure from politicians and the courts. However, only the absolute minimum requirement was allowed in what appears to have been a damage limitation exercise. There were some changes in the style of management which were for the better, but the only improvements in ministerial oversight were in the lines of communication. Mrs Thatcher made sure that she took a greater interest in MI5's activities and instituted regular meetings with the director-general which helped to improve the working relationship between Number 10 and the service.

In November 1987, in response to the case of Cathy Massiter, Sir Philip Woodfield was appointed to the new post of Staff Counsellor to consider staff complaints and grievances which fell outside the remit of personnel. Woodfield was regarded as having 'safe hands', for he was something of an intelligence 'insider', having been responsible for MI5 during his time at the Home Office and while he served two terms in Northern Ireland. It was over two years since the Prime Minister had asked Duff to consider 'internal outlets' for MI5 officers' grievances. Tory MP Rupert Allason told the Commons that the 'senior management was brought kicking and screaming to the appointment of Sir Philip Woodfield. That concession was only granted after much discussion.' Former MI5 officer John Day added that the appointment of Sir Philip, who operates from the bosom of the secret state in the Cabinet Office, 'ignores the real issues'.[25]

A line was developed in the press that Duff, an experienced in-fighter in the diplomatic world, was able to force through many of the reforms against opposition from some of his staff who obviously resented the presence of an outsider. However, it was known that the Duff reforms were making little genuine progress. Staff said he had failed to seize the opportunity to clean out the old MI5 hierarchy. He angered staff by promoting officers associated with the widely criticised regime of his predecessor, Sir John Jones. Nine months after his appointment, word leaked out that middle-ranking officers in MI5 were disappointed by the new regime and alarmed by some of the new appointments. David Ransom had been promoted to deputy director-general and Brian Weston, the former head of A1, which was responsible for operations in A Branch, was made deputy of K Branch. Both men were associated with the 'dirty tricks' era of the seventies and early eighties and were seen to be 'favourites' of the deputy, Cecil Shipp, the man who had been bitterly disappointed by his non-promotion to director-general. Officers said there was 'discord and frustration' within the service. Senior Whitehall officials believed that the failure of Duff meant there was a danger that MI5 would again enter the political arena, with consequent calls for oversight.[26]

Essentially Duff's appointment had been a stop-gap measure, a new broom to clean up the service. He was sixty-seven in 1987, way past the official retirement age, and a new director-general would be required. Choosing a successor was to prove difficult and there followed a Whitehall scramble for a suitable candidate. Mrs Thatcher had wanted another outsider to replace Duff and continue with the reforms, it is believed that approaches were made to Sir Brian Cubbon, Permanent Secretary at the Home Office. Cubborn had served in Northern Ireland and was well acquainted with the security services, but he declined to accept the post. The Prime Minister decided to pass over the obvious internal candidates, bypassing those tainted by the Security Commission's report of management mismanagement and failure to detect signs of Bettaney's unstable behaviour. Duff's most likely successors had been his deputy, David Ransom, and the head of K Branch, John Deverell. They, however, had failed to heed the warnings on Bettaney and had to pay the price for Bettaney's treachery. There was no alternative but to skip a generation and put in place someone who was clean and unsullied by the Bettaney débâcle.[27]

4

Patrick Walker

The Official Secrets Act is a law to enable British governments to conceal their mistakes.

Peter Wright

'There has been a rumour going around the service that the person who had the DG's job had a name beginning with W,' said a former MI5 officer. 'But nobody thought of Walker.' The unknown Patrick Walker was appointed in December 1987, following a brief interview with the Prime Minister. Even though Sir Antony Duff had recommended Walker some months before, he had not been the first internal choice. The former MI5 officer added that Walker 'had so little personality I would not have thought it was enough for him to go to the top'. Duff, however, had apparently found an enthusiastic supporter in Walker and believed him to be the person most likely to carry out the reforms which he had set in motion. It was reported that the two had become firm allies against opponents both inside and outside the service.[1]

No photographs of Walker appeared in the British press, and the thin biographies available suggested a naturally shy man to whom publicity was anathema. Fifty-six years old, he was, in words which are music to civil servants, 'sound, responsible and reliable'. Said by friends to be decisive, sharp and to the point, he was a professional intelligence officer who had the air of a middle-class businessman. Soft-spoken with an easy smile, his public school manner was still discernible. Walker was alleged to be a skilled interrogator, a man with a good memory who listened carefully to questions, paused to consider and answered deliberately, in the manner of the media's favourite spook, George Smiley. Unlike Smiley, he reportedly had 'a short fuse' and on occasion a fierce temper. The image portrayed was that of the New Spy who had little to do with the 'buggers and burglars' of the Wright era. It was, inevitably, highly misleading.[2]

Walker was a member of F Branch during the seventies when it expanded its surveillance of subversives at the expense of the traditionally senior K Branch. He was closely tied to counter-terrorist activities which gained more and more prominence within the service. Most senior officers have experience in this area and counter-terrorism is probably now the way to the top. These officers are, in many ways, the hard (wo)men of the service who have seen action on the front line. Although MI5 officers very rarely get their own hands dirty – they use 'cut-outs' in the Army and RUC to do that – Northern Ireland is a dirty war and officers serving there have been party to many 'dirty tricks' operations. Walker had been there in 1980, fighting the IRA as a lowly deputy to David Ransom, on the Liaison Staff which acts as cover for intelligence personnel. He was closely involved in the most turbulent period in recent history: the hunger strikes, supergrass trials and shoot-to-kill controversies of the early eighties.[3]

The Security Co-ordinator in Stormont at this time was a reluctant Sir Maurice Oldfield, who had been persuaded by Mrs Thatcher in October 1979 to accept the post. Oldfield's remit included meshing the four competing intelligence-gathering and security organisations – MI5, MI6, the Royal Ulster Constabulary's Special Branch and Army Intelligence – into a cohesive security machine, steering them away from the infighting which was prevalent before his appointment. Oldfield's appointment caused all the old rivalries between MI6 and MI5 to flare up again. An MI5 man in the province was reported as saying: 'He is a desk man, a paper-pusher who will find it very different when dealing with fast-breaking terrorist operations . . . he is too much to the Left for my taste.'[4]

Oldfield was no liberal. About his time in Palestine in the

late forties, when he interrogated Jewish terrorists, he would talk 'cheerfully about beating them up and pushing people's heads under buckets of water'. A whispering campaign, assumed by friends to be the work of MI5, began against Oldfield almost as soon as he took up the Northern Ireland post. This culminated in the withdrawal of his positive vetting over allegations of homosexual activity as a young man, which he had concealed from the vetters. Oldfield then had to suffer the indignity of being investigated on whether his homosexuality had been exploited by foreign intelligence agencies, by senior officers from the rival service, MI5. In June 1980, Oldfield retired, ill (he believed that he had been poisoned by his enemies). From then on MI5 began to dominate intelligence and security co-ordination in the province. Walker later moved back to London to the counter-terrorism desk, F5, to deal with Irish, specifically Loyalist, terrorism.[5]

At the time of his appointment as director-general, Walker was said to be unsympathetic to those calling for greater openness. However, one of his early tasks was to polish the image of MI5, an image tarnished by the many security scandals of the previous decade. He therefore let his carefully shaped views be known around Whitehall, with the aim that they would eventually reach the ears of the press and the outside world. It was suggested that the blanket of secrecy covering MI5's activities might be lifted a little, and among the ideas floated was one suggesting he should become a public figure able to comment to MPs and responsible journalists on general policy matters. This was a radical step, given that on his appointment the Defence, Press and Broadcasting Committee had warned newspapers against publishing Walker's name. In March 1986, the Committee had issued D Notice No. 6 requesting that 'nothing should be published' on the security and intelligence services without reference to the secretary of the Committee. Typically, the majority of newspapers acquiesced to this form of self-censorship. (As part of its policy of encouraging more openness, in October 1992, the government announced a 'thorough review' of the D-Notice system which is to be completed by the spring of 1993.) It was reported that moves to greater openness were supported by high-flyers within MI5 and by veterans of the service. Former MI5 officer John Day, whose autobiography remains unpublished, said that 'What concerned me is that while some of the criticism of MI5 was undoubtedly deserved, often it was ill-informed. Informed criticism is healthy. If MI5 is moving towards more openness, two cheers.'[6]

Discreet but effective public relations work revealed that Walker believed MI5's reputation of being right-wing was unfair. Relatively few resources were being targeted towards domestic subversion, it was claimed, and the new director-general, with the support of Sir Clive Whitmore, Permanent Secretary at the Home Office, with whom he was said to share a close relationship, favoured some form of oversight. The service has never been subject to real outside control. It has been left to 'get on with it', much depending on trusting the director-general. The Home Office therefore has always aimed to keep security work low-key and in what it has regarded as 'safe hands'. The wish for secrecy has often been a Home Office departmental desire, not always shared to the same extent by MI5 field officers. However, the service's definition of oversight is so far removed from accepted ideas of democratic accountability that Walker/Whitmore's new openness turned out to be no more than window-dressing.

Calls for some form of oversight refused to die down, and during 1988 Mrs Thatcher came under continued pressure from her Cabinet Secretary and the retiring director-general, Duff. This culminated with Lord Donaldson, the Master of the Rolls, in a judicial ruling on the *Spycatcher* affair ruminating that the time had come to 'regularise' the status of MI5. In November 1988, the government sought to allay concern over the operation of the Security Service by announcing legislation to put MI5 on a statutory basis. Here was a chance to propose a form of oversight. Home Secretary Douglas Hurd and other officials were said not to be against the concept, if only for fear that if nothing was done, then pressure for more radical, far-reaching reforms would grow. Better, it was argued, to stifle calls for a fully fledged parliamentary committee by a minimalist proposal: a small oversight committee of senior Privy Councillors who could be relied on not to probe too deeply into the service's operations. Once again, Mrs Thatcher remained stubbornly against. She had little trust in MPs, even Privy Councillors, and they would not be allowed inside the 'barriers of secrecy'. On the advice of intelligence officials, the Home Secretary also came round to the view that the government could not give way to demands on oversight because it might lead to supervision and oversight of the sister service MI6, which officially did not exist. As Rupert Allason noted during the debate on the Security Service Bill, 'this is the sole reason why the Home Secretary has been so obstinate'.[7]

Mrs Thatcher was persuaded that legislation putting MI5 on a statutory basis would help head off demands for independent scrutiny of the service. The highly conservative, restrictive, but also vague nature of the resultant Security Services Act and its complementary Official Secrets Act raised doubts that there had ever been any real conviction behind the proposals for oversight, which had apparently been mooted in Whitehall. The Home Secretary confirmed to shadow home affairs spokesman Roy Hattersley that 'the Security Service wanted the Bill'. In fact, MI5 lawyers had drafted the bill, which was designed as the minimum legal framework that would allow the service to operate much as it had done in the past.[8]

Section 1 of the Act gives MI5 a legal basis, defining its functions, including the protection of national security, in particular 'actions intended to overthrow or undermine parliamentary democracy by political, industrial or violent means'. This was Whitehall's traditional and broad definition of 'subversion', an open-ended concept now abandoned by countries such as Canada, whose security system had been set up and modelled on that of the United Kingdom. A member of the

Canadian Security and Intelligence Service review committee concluded that the word 'subversion' was used 'throughout the English-speaking world to cover a multitude of sins'. Paule Gauthier said in 1988 that the committee 'began to realise that the word subversion, indeed the very concept of subversion, was used most of the time to cover a lack of rigorous thought to camouflage its inevitable result, woolly language'.[9]

In January 1992, Home Secretary Kenneth Baker reaffirmed that MI5's central role was 'the protection of national security'. However, during the passage of the Act the then Home Secretary, Douglas Hurd, declined to enlighten Parliament on what that vague term might mean. Lord Justice Lloyd, responsible for monitoring warrants issued under the Act, noted: 'National security has usually been taken to include threats to the security of the nation by terrorism, espionage and major subversive activities; *but it is not confined to these three matters*' (emphasis added). Without confiding what they were, in his report of warrants issued in 1986 Lord Justice Lloyd added there were cases which did not come neatly within any of the three subheads, 'but which nevertheless fall clearly under the general heading of national security'. What might constitute 'matters' outside 'terrorism, espionage and major subversion' was revealed in the 1985 Home Office White Paper, *The Interception of Communications in the United Kingdom*, which put telephone tapping on a legal footing through the use of ministerial warrants. The White Paper spoke of the issuing of warrants 'in the interests of national security . . . in support of the Government's defence and foreign policies'. As Anthony Bevins concluded in the *Independent*, 'The clear implication is that national security may be equated with support for the defence and foreign policies of the government of the day.'[10]

Earlier in 1988, the press had paid little attention to a question put to the Prime Minister by 'a thorn in the government's side' on security issues, Labour MP Ken Livingstone. He asked Mrs Thatcher 'if she will make a statement on the present definition of national security adopted by her Majesty's

Government'. The reply was really rather odd: 'This term is generally understood to refer to the safeguarding of the state and the community against threats to their survival and wellbeing. *I am not aware that any previous Administration has thought it appropriate to adopt a specific definition of the term*' (emphasis added). Here was the British secret state stripped bare. 'National security' can be stretched to mean anything you want and allows MI5 legally to put anyone under the rubric 'a threat to national security'. The Canadian committee found in their own review of 'subversion' and 'national security' that 'whenever precision was demanded, secrecy was invoked to protect the vague generalities which have sometimes provided a cover for inept, illegal, or simply incompetent activities'.[11]

An attempt by Tory back-benchers to include within the Act a clause stating that MI5 would not threaten legitimate and lawful dissent was rejected by the government. In fact, during the committee stage all amendments were rejected. Instead, ministers engaged in a little public relations work emphasising that the main brunt of MI5's work was the security of the state, in particular countering the threat of IRA terrorism. Less time was now, allegedly, spent on monitoring domestic groups and individuals regarded as 'subversive'. Douglas Hurd told MPs that he saw 'a body of people who, in one way or another, are daily trying to use their ingenuity to protect us from espionage, subversion and terrorism, and the greatest of these threats is terrorism'.[12]

Among the clauses of the Act is 1(3), which states: 'It shall be the function of the Service to safeguard the economic well-being of the United Kingdom against threats posed by the actions or intentions of persons outside the British Islands.' MPs pondered what the clause might mean. In committee, Hurd offered MPs a vague definition of 'economic well-being' – 'a threat from abroad in respect of a commodity upon which we are particularly dependent. One can think of oil as being such an example from the past, though not now.' When

Jonathan Aitken made a few discreet enquiries he was given the impression that the clause had to do with 'offshore oil rigs which needed protection, and about the Channel Tunnel. That would be confirmed by the rather curious reference to the "British Islands".' The fact that the security services were heavily involved in the vetting of workers and were infiltrating the trade unions employed on the Channel Tunnel project gives some substance to this interpretation; though, as we shall see in chapter 21, there were others. Aitken referred to the clause as 'an appalling piece of parliamentary draftsmanship'.[13]

Section 3 of the Act provides MI5 with the legal powers, by warrant, to burgle and bug while having a general duty to obey the law. Section 4 approved the appointment to the Security Service Commission of a judicial officer to review the exercise of warrants issued by the Secretary of State in relation to Section 3. The government was also forced to set up a tribunal of lawyers to consider complaints from the public, following fears that the European Court would find the Security Service guilty of breaching human rights. The court ruling in the 1988 Swedish 'Leander' case found that states were entitled to take broad powers to protect security in secret as long as there was some form of independent oversight. However, under Section 5 of the Act, the rights of individuals who bring specific complaints concerning illegal buggings and burglaries are extremely limited. While the tribunal has to appear independent it also has to remain firmly within Whitehall's 'ring of secrecy'. Also, general complaints about the service's activities are not permitted. It was claimed, at the time, that senior members of the service themselves took the lead in the decision to introduce an element of independent monitoring. It was felt that MI5 could have an 'overt' front without harming its 'covert' operations. This was a sop to service critics who demanded openness. Events had forced MI5's hand, for fear that something approaching real oversight might be imposed from the outside.[14]

One of MI5's most trenchant critics has been the urbane

right-wing Tory back-bencher, now Minister for Defence Procurement at the MoD, Jonathan Aitken. He denied allegations which surfaced during the Peter Wright affair that he had links with the service's rival, MI6, though he has echoed its traditional criticisms of MI5. 'The tone of MI5 is the tone of sound mediocrity, often touched with an inferiority complex about its cousins at MI6.' In the Commons, he pulled no punches in his verbal attack on the Home Secretary:

> The commissioner is a chip for the civil liberties lobby. The tribunal is a chip for lawyers. Sir Philip Woodfield, the staff counsellor, is a chip to the young Turks inside the service who did not like the idea of not being able to report Mr Bettaney, even when he was drunk, as unworthy. The legal status is chip to appease the European Court of Human Rights. It is chips, chips, chips. The Home Secretary is good at chips and cosmetics, but this is not a lasting reform of substance. Parliament will not be gainsaid indefinitely and fobbed off permanently with no oversight.

However, senior officers in MI5 were pleased by the passage of the Security Service Bill. According to informed sources, 'The service feels that with the Act it has come out of the closet. It may now have to take up an increasingly public stance.'[15]

Patrick Walker made vague noises in that direction. Selective leaking and off-the-record lunches with newspaper editors and senior right-wing journalists ensured that sympathetic portraits were painted of the new director-general in the press. They also helped to portray MI5 as a reformed and responsible agency which deserved the support of the people and politicians. This cosy image belied that fact that under Walker's benign directorship, MI5 still appeared to operate in the same old manner. The cock-ups and scandals continued unabated, culminating in the dreadful intelligence blunder over the internment of Arab refugees and asylum seekers during the Gulf War.

In the autumn of 1988, MI5 worked in close co-operation with members of the CIA's London station, in a counter-intelligence entrapment operation against a Cuban intelligence officer. The CIA, following normal procedures, sought clearance from the British authorities before proceeding with the plan. The operation went dramatically wrong and was later described as a 'monumental mess'. Entrapment which relies on threats and inducements often ends in failure, and MI5's only big success appears to have been in the early seventies, with the defection of Soviet intelligence officer Oleg Lyalin.

American State Department pressure had ensured that the British authorities kept the Cuban embassy staff at arm's length. There was politeness in diplomatic circles to members of the embassy but it fell short of friendliness. The ambassador received few invitations to dinner. During the seventies, following the expulsion of the majority of the KGB officers, MI5 kept the embassy under strict surveillance in the expectation that the Cuban intelligence service, the Direccion General de Inteligencia (DGI), would act as a surrogate for their Soviet friends. Whether there was substance to this is not known, since the DGI was alleged to keep few intelligence officers on the embassy roster. However, it did little to prevent the rumour mills grinding out their tales of Cuban intelligence operations.[16]

On the night of 13 September 1988, an MI5 officer was shot and slightly injured when Carlos Medina Perez, a third secretary and commercial attaché at the Cuban embassy in London, fired shots at a car which was trailing him to his flat in Sussex Gardens. Perez and his ambassador were later expelled from Britain. Sitting with the security agents in the car was a Cuban defector to the United States, Florentino Azpillaga Lombard, a former major in the DGI.

Described as 'a significant intelligence figure providing excellent information', the forty-one-year-old Azpillaga had been part of a plot to induce his former friend and colleague, Perez, to defect. Azpillaga had abandoned his duties at the

Cuban embassy in Prague in June 1987 and was then extensively debriefed by the CIA. He specialised in controlling double agents and monitoring secret radio stations operated by anti-communist groupings in the West. The first drips of information revealed that the majority of the CIA's sources recruited by the agency in Havana were double agents. Azpillaga later acknowledged that he had been involved in other CIA operations in which he attempted to lure Cubans to the West.

Some weeks before the shooting incident Azpillaga had approached Perez, who was young and relatively inexperienced – this was his first foreign posting. Spooked by the approach, Perez sent his wife, Marie, home to Cuba for safety and took to carrying the semi-automatic rapid-firing 9mm Browning pistol with which he had been issued for protection. While the CIA and MI5 operation maintained pressure on Perez to defect, unknown to them on the day of the shooting Perez had learnt that his stepson had been drowned in a diving accident. He was naturally upset at the tragedy and still angry at the 'attempt to make contact'. He later told police he had opened fire 'fearing for his own safety'.

The trailing car had contained four people – Azpillaga, his girlfriend, Martha Plasencia, and two smartly dressed minders from MI5 and the CIA. Perez believed that he hit the former DGI major and an MI5 officer, who was seen 'holding a blood-soaked handkerchief to his head'. The government attempted to hush up the affair, but the story leaked out and it was splashed across the front pages of British newspapers. This was not the kind of public outing which the service had planned, and MI5 soon blamed its partner in the operation for the débâcle, claiming that 'it was a classic CIA cock-up'. The CIA retorted that it was 'an MI5 blunder'. An acrimonious inquest took place within the corridors of Whitehall when Home Office officials met with their counterparts from the Foreign Office. An in-house report was prepared for the Joint

Intelligence Committee, the contents of which were never revealed.

There were some minor success stories. In March 1989 a spy who infiltrated British-based dissident organisations for the Czechoslovakian secret service (SFGF) was jailed for ten years after being 'fingered' by a Czech diplomat who had defected to Britain in 1988; the spy had been 'his ticket out'. The true identity of the deep-cover agent, who posed as 'Erwin van Haarlan', a forty-four-year-old Jewish Dutch art dealer, was never discovered. The case involved the first known use of 'DNA fingerprinting' in a spy trial.

'Van Haarlan' lived in the suburbs of North London where he received instructions from Prague by radio, deciphering them with 'one-time pads'. Described in court by an MI5 officer, Miss 'J', as 'a sleeper', he was arrested by Special Branch officers while in the process of taking down a coded message. It was claimed at his trial that it was his two hundred and tenth coded message. Although this was seen as a success for MI5, 'Van Haarlan' had, in fact, remained undetected for a full thirteen years and the radio signals he received had not been picked up by GCHQ in this time. He had been kept under surveillance for two time-consuming years, during which no contacts or accomplices had been identified. At the end of the day it was not clear if he had passed on any intelligence other than that about dissidents and Jewish groups. The threat to national security appeared to be minimal.

MI5 did manage to foil a plot by two unsophisticated amateurs to sell a 'tile', classified only as 'confidential', to the Soviet Union. The pair hoped to sell the tile, used to cover a submarine's hull in order to absorb sonar signals, making it virtually invisible to enemy craft, for £2 million. Joseph Wilson, a former guard at Vickers shipyard, hatched the crackpot scheme with his friend Arthur Price, a taxi driver, at the local Conservative Club in Barrow-in-Furness. Their first telephone call to the Soviet embassy was monitored and the letter with details of the scheme was passed on to the Security

Service. In July 1990, MI5 and Special Branch mounted a sting operation, code-named 'Keyfob', using an MI5 officer with a Russian accent to act as a Soviet buyer for the tile. After three months of negotiation and a surveillance operation involving twenty 'watchers', the pair were arrested and later sentenced to fifteen months' imprisonment.[17]

There were, however, skeletons in the MI5 cupboard of scandals and débâcles which refused to go away. While in the main concerning events which had occurred in previous decades, they were still highly damaging to MI5's reputation and the carefully constructed public relations exercise Walker was undertaking. Peter Wright's tales of moles in the Establishment and within the Security Service itself, and Colin Wallace's insider's view of 'dirty tricks' in Northern Ireland, had been intriguing journalists for most of the eighties.

In 1987, former senior MI5 officer Wright's *Spycatcher* was published in Australia and the United States but not in Britain. Although dismissed as 'old hat' by insiders and left unread by the majority of buyers caught up in the swirl of publicity, *Spycatcher* is probably one of the most important books to be published about Britain since the Second World War. It provided a unique glimpse into Britain's secret state and the way factions and bureaucracies of the permanent government operate in denying citizens the rights and liberties associated with a mature democracy. Although the book contained no threat to national security and betrayed few secrets, it did make – contrary to the views of a number of commentators on intelligence – fascinating revelations about the internal workings of the Security Service. The realisation of this led MI5, according to information from Wright's former colleagues, to compile a briefing paper pointing out, line by line, mistakes in the book. It is not surprising to learn that some initial reviews attempted to rubbish the admittedly hastily edited book by use of a list of minor, and largely irrelevant, factual errors. However, these attempts to discredit Wright came too late; the damage was done. Those who dipped inside

Spycatcher read of a service at times 'out of control', operating outside the law and staffed by bitter individuals who lived in a world of paranoid delusion. A number of potential recruits to the service who bought the book were turned off by what they read.

Although a great deal of heat was generated by Wright's allegations about assassination plots against the Egyptian President Gamal Abdel Nasser and, even more so, about the MI5-backed destabilisation campaign against Labour Prime Minister Harold Wilson, the public was ill served by a Fourth Estate which did little more than regurgitate sections of the book. The lack of sustained in-depth reporting and investigation showed that investigative journalism barely exists in Britain. (While five thousand US journalists belong to the American Society of Investigative Reporters and Editors, no such body exists in this country.) In the United States, Wright's revelations would have produced a series of Senate hearings on the scale of the Watergate investigation. In Britain, they were met by a blanket of official silence and crushing government-inspired litigation.

The eventual bill to taxpayers for this litigation topped £2 million. Even Lord Bridge, by no means a libertarian, was moved to say in a minority decision in July 1987, when a ban on the sale of *Spycatcher* in this country was sought by the government: 'Freedom of speech is always the first casualty under a totalitarian regime . . . Censorship is the indispensable tool to regulate what the public may and may not know. The present attempt to insulate the public in this country from information which is freely available elsewhere is a significant step down that road.' Bridge warned that the government would 'face inevitable condemnation by the European Court of Human Rights in Strasbourg. Long before that it will have been condemned at the bar of public opinion in the free world.' In November 1991, the European Court held that three newspapers which had published extracts from the book had been denied their right to freedom of expression. It added that raising the notion of national security was not sufficient reason for the ban. Even so, the ban on memoirs by former security and intelligence staff remains in place and appears to be more strictly applied than ever before.[18]

In July 1988, an official in the Ministry of Defence discovered a cache of papers relating to the case of Colin Wallace, a former senior information officer at British Army Headquarters in Lisburn, Northern Ireland. In the early seventies, Wallace had worked for the Information Policy Unit, a Foreign Office Information Research Department inspired psychological warfare unit which used black propaganda as part of its weaponry to combat terrorism. The MoD defines 'psyops' as 'planned psychological activities in peace and war directed towards enemy, friendly and neutral audiences, in order to create behaviour favourable to the achievement of political and military objectives'. When MI5 was recruited to the province, Information Policy was also directed to target politicians, in Northern Ireland and on the mainland, who were viewed as opponents of the security forces' hard-line approach. It was Wallace's contention that his refusal to go along with one psyops project, Clockwork Orange, had been one of the reasons for his unfair dismissal from his post in 1975.[19]

On 4 September 1989, Permanent Secretary Sir Michael Quinlan 'burnished his reputation' by advising the MoD boss, Tom King, to reopen the case of Wallace. He told the minister 'it was time to come clean'. The determined Labour backbencher Tam Dalyell had been bombarding Quinlan with letters, articles and questions on the affair. Dalyell had been angry at the treatment he received from government ministers in the House of Commons, having been subjected to 'a load of abuse such as I have not had in twenty-seven years'. Although Quinlan recoiled at his new image of 'Mr Clean', he felt that it had been 'his duty to act'.[20]

Senior Cabinet officials debated long on how to handle the admission that Wallace had been correct in his allegations of dirty tricks in Northern Ireland. The discussion involved

Quinlan's squash partner Cabinet Secretary Sir Robin Butler, former ambassador to Hungary, Leonard Appleyard, and Co-ordinator of Intelligence and Security Sir Christopher Curwen. The intelligence officials, Curwen and Sir Percy Cradock, foreign affairs and MI6 adviser to Mrs Thatcher, argued against confirming Wallace's links to the security services. Cradock allegedly demanded that no further concessions were to be made on 'this damned business'. Butler, who had no wish for a judicial inquiry into Wallace's allegations concerning the Kincora boys' home, agreed and a consensus was reached by the Cabinet sub-committee on a position they could sell to ministers. It was to be a restricted disclosure which would avoid embarrassing the Security Service.[21]

On 30 January 1990, the government admitted that some of Wallace's allegations over the existence of Clockwork Orange were true, after revealing that new documents of 'material significance' had 'now come to light'. The following month, Mrs Thatcher told the Commons that she had been personally misled over the existence of black propaganda operations in Northern Ireland, conceding that Wallace's job included the use of 'disinformation'.

An internal report by senior MoD official David Heyhoe into why ministers repeatedly misled Parliament suggested that the allegations about Kincora and Clockwork Orange had not played any part in Wallace's suspension and the subsequent disciplinary proceedings. Heyhoe's report was a model of Civil Service evasion. He concluded that there was no *prima facie* evidence that individuals were culpable; instead he referred to 'a total discontinuity of collective memory'. A 'more perceptive scrutiny' of the files 'could have led to the earlier discovery of the main papers'. Heyhoe did not refer to the one man who was fully aware of the Wallace–Clockwork Orange connection, sixty-five-year-old legal officer to MI5, Bernard Sheldon. Sheldon, who retired in 1987, had been one of the few officials on the distribution list giving details of Wallace's suspension in July 1975.[22]

The government also set up a narrowly focused investigation into the circumstances surrounding Wallace's dismissal, chaired by fifty-nine-year-old David Calcutt, QC, Master of Magdalene College, Cambridge, who was asked to consider whether compensation should be paid. Calcutt, Whitehall's favourite troubleshooter, has often been called upon when the government finds itself in a tight corner. Dependable, a member of the Interception of Communications Tribunal which has a limited role in reviewing telephone tapping warrants, one of 'the auxiliaries' – those independent members of the 'the great and the good' who help the government, Calcutt was expected to play ball. However, added to this dependability, Calcutt also held a firm belief in the need 'for fair play and protection of the citizen against overweening authority'. When the inquiry was finished he declined Tom King's instruction not to prepare a report but took the view that 'some reasoning, however brief, is needed'.[23]

In September 1990, Calcutt found that Wallace had been unfairly dismissed because unnamed MoD 'representatives' (i.e. MI5 officers) privately communicated with the chair of the Civil Service Appeal Board before Wallace's appeal on 17 October 1975 in an attempt to influence the outcome. The MoD had also failed to give a full job description to the board, thereby misleading it about the extent and importance of his secret work. Calcutt recommended payment of £30,000 in compensation. Despite the evidence of a conspiracy to pervert the course of justice, the Director of Public Prosecutions, Sir Allan Green, advised Scotland Yard not to investigate suggestions of a cover-up by MoD and MI5 officials. The government's refusal to set up a full inquiry into Wallace's allegations prompted shadow defence spokesman Martin O'Neill to allege that Tom King was 'participating in a cover-up designed to avoid political embarrassment rather than safeguard national security'.[24]

Still interested in subversion, MI5 continued its interest in trade union affairs even though successive home secretaries assured MPs that union activities were legitimate and safe from surveillance: 'No trade unionist need fear that he is the object of surveillance by the security authorities unless his own actions and intentions bring him within the strict criteria set out in the definition [of subversion].' However, such 'blanket reassurances' failed to stop operations taking place which had no bearing on national security. As Social Democrat MP John Cartwright pointed out, 'Either the security services have broken their guidelines or they have been used for political purposes.' Blue book security reports on trade union activities 'designed to help ministers and officials judge the political dimensions of industrial disputes' are regularly forwarded by F2 to the Department of Trade and Industry and the Department of Employment. During her term in office, Minister of Labour Barbara Castle dismissed the tittle-tattle on trade union colleagues which was passed on to the ministry: 'The more I read these reports the less confidence I have in our intelligence . . . To begin with the material is always mighty thin and most of it would be obvious to an informed politician . . . Altogether, I really wonder what we pay these people for.'[25]

In 1991, the National and Local Government Officers' Association (NALGO) was advised by 'intelligence analysts' that MI5's F2 section had increased its surveillance on officials of both NALGO and the National Union of Public Employees (NUPE). NALGO, which is perceived to be on the left in employment issues, came under increased surveillance during the union's first nationwide campaign of strikes in 1989. The then Chancellor of the Exchequer, Nigel Lawson, was forced to apologise in October of that year after originally denying that the confidential tax records of two women, both members of the Socialist Workers' Party and involved in the strike, had been handed over to police by the Inland Revenue. During 1991 and 1992, NUPE and NALGO were involved in merger talks, along with the health union, the Confederation of Health Service Employees (COHSE), which would create a 'super union' in 1993, the largest public sector union in Europe. This union would be expected to dominate public services including local government and the health service and would thus pose a threat to the government's attempts at a low-pay policy in the public sector. NALGO's journal, *Public Service*, alleged that MI5's renewed interest included attempts to gain access to 'friendly' union officials, buggings and mail-openings. It was also alleged that attempts were made to place false or slanted information in the media smearing union officials.[26]

Memories of K7 and F Branch dirty-tricks operations against Labour Prime Minister Harold Wilson were revived in 1989. On 25 May, BBC television's Nine O'Clock News programme ran a major smear item claiming that 'senior British sources' had revealed that eleven Soviet officials had been expelled from Britain because they 'were subjecting Labour MPs to blackmail'. The BBC's chief political correspondent, John Sergeant, had been at an 'off-the-record' lunch with William Waldegrave, junior minister at the Foreign Office, who briefed him on the alleged KGB blackmail attempts and links of left-wing MPs with Middle East terrorist states, in particular Libya and Iran. It appears it was MI5 – 'allegations made by British counter-intelligence' – who planted the story on Waldegrave, though they were allegedly furious at the manner in which he then used the 'information'. The Foreign Secretary, Sir Geoffrey Howe, was forced to disclaim any part in the smear and acknowledge that there was no truth in the allegation. Waldegrave, said by Foreign Office officials to have loved the games and intrigues of the intelligence services, dismissed the episode as 'familiar stories of efforts in the past to subvert Labour MPs'.[27]

In October 1991, the draft copy of the Queen's Speech was leaked to John Prescott, Labour's shadow transport spokesman. Such a leak, according to the precedent set under Mrs Thatcher, would have involved calling in MI5 to conduct a leak inquiry. Prescott had been on MI5 files since 1966, when Special Branch kept him under surveillance for his part in the national seaman's strike. According to Prescott, the day after the leak was reported in the newspapers, a computer disc storing the names and telephone numbers of political contacts was stolen from the Commons office of his research assistant. Two other discs were left behind. Prescott told the newspapers: 'It is too much of a coincidence coming so soon after the story about the leak. It is academic to me whether it was Special Branch or MI5.' Seemingly by coincidence, in the run-up to the general election in 1992, Prescott was subjected to a bungled smear campaign when the jilted boyfriend of a former woman researcher at the House of Commons sent a note to the *Daily Mail*. The anonymous note, which was circulated in the Press Gallery in the House, 'suggested that I and others had an affair with a certain person'. Prescott quickly scotched the rumours, declaring the allegation to be 'totally untrue'.[28]

Unlike with previous general elections, in 1992 the media was on guard for any sign of a concerted MI5-inspired smear campaign. There were one or two minor episodes which looked suspiciously like the work of experienced practitioners, but the anticipated surfacing of alleged links between left-wing Labour MPs and terrorist organisations never got off the ground. Curiously, but predictably, the Labour Party played down the bugging of its offices at Headline House, the centre of its fund-raising operation.[29]

Commentators generally failed to notice that these and other scandals and disasters took place following the appointment of Antony Duff, who had been asked to 'clean out the stables', and Patrick Walker, who asked the public to trust him that MI5 was now a 'responsible' agency. It took time for a more truthful portrait to emerge. It was clear that Walker had tried to keep any reforms of MI5 in-house and had refused to concede the need for external oversight. In conversation with suitably tame journalists, Walker refuted the need for 'the most moderate measures of accountability and appeared not to understand the widespread desire for greater openness'. According to one participant, Walker behaved 'like an "outraged lover" when questioned about MI5's past activities, making it clear MI5 had absolutely nothing to hide but reluctant to concede the principle of scrutiny'.[30]

The only known public appearance of Walker while director-general was at the Savoy Hotel for the farewell celebration of his long-time friend Sir David Nicholas, retiring chairman of Independent Television News. It was a brief appearance which left guests bemused. After months of agonised debate, concluding with the Home Secretary Kenneth Baker giving his permission for the outing, all that Walker gave away was his name and rank. It was very proper, very British and hardly the stuff of a new policy of openness. Sir Patrick's two-line entry in *Who's Who* is limited to saying he joined the 'Ministry of Defence, 1963'. As in previous decades, the anonymous Sir Patrick and the still largely unaccountable MI5 were allowed to continue to operate in the same aura of secrecy which, as former MI6 officer Malcolm Muggeridge noted, is as essential to the secret state 'as vestments and incense to a mass, or darkness to a spiritualist seance'.[31]

A serving senior F Branch officer with twenty years' experience in the service forewarned what might happen in the Duff/Walker years. In 1985, 'John Wilson' told the magazine *Monochrome*: 'I think there will be fairly immediate changes to placate Parliament. A well-publicised shake-up will conceal more than it is intended to reveal. Internal security will be tighter, to prevent the recurrence of a Bettaney, but there will be less in the way of public scrutiny. While the old methods of MI5 continue to be effective, there's no reason in the world to change them.'[32]

5

Shoot-to-kill

> They will really be 'killer squads' (though I promise you I won't call them that, with a view to the question in the House).
>
> Sir Gerald Templer

Throughout the Thatcher decade MI5 and other security and intelligence agencies became more and more bogged down in the dirty war in Ireland. The dirtiest and most visible sign of the counter-terrorist campaign was the gunning down of suspected terrorists. Those who accuse the British government of a 'shoot-to-kill' policy in Northern Ireland, in the sense of a deliberate plan of action to assassinate terrorists, tend to portray this as a newly instituted policy. This is not the case. It is not a recent development but a continuation of activities which have been undertaken by elements of the secret state over the last fifty years.

On every occasion that British governments have engaged in counter-insurgency wars, secret undercover units have been created to take on the terrorists. The Security Service and the Army have then dusted down their colonial handbooks and activated a shoot-to-kill campaign of counter-terror, not knowing how else to take on the terrorists. This was admitted by one Ministry of Defence source who told a reporter, after another SAS ambush of IRA terrorists in Omagh: 'There has been no change of emphasis. Covert operations are the cutting edge of the war in Northern Ireland. We have to make use of any opportunities that come our way and use what intelligence we get.' The difference from previous campaigns is that, whereas in the past such actions took place in a far-away country, the current war is enacted in people's living rooms on television. We are much more conscious of events in Northern Ireland, and never before has the secret state had to justify or cover up actions which, to practitioners, based on past history of such operations, appear both inevitable and routine.[1]

Most writers and commentators on the use of counter-terrorism tactics against the IRA tend to refer back to the doctrines of Sir Frank Kitson, commander of the 39th Infantry Brigade in Northern Ireland between 1970 and 1972 and author of the influential study *Low Intensity Operations*. His experience in Kenya with pseudo and counter-gangs, outlined in his 1960 book, *Gangs and Counter-gangs*, have marked him out as the originator of the policy of counter-terror. This, however, is misleading. Such operations have a far longer history and, as Kitson himself has written, 'the United States is well ahead in thinking on the overall direction of counter insurgency and counter subversion operations'.[2]

Pseudo gangs were used as far back as the middle of the last century, during the war against the American native Indian, and counter-gangs, as a direct combat force, were employed extensively during the American campaign against the Huks, in the Philippines, in the 1950s. Screened volunteers were specially trained at secret training camps where they were given a permanent alias, cover stories and were subjected to intensive instruction on guerrilla tactics, ready for covert operations. 'Targets, which were only tentatively set in advance, might include the killing of top leaders or the destruction of their organisation. They would also create incidents to cause divisions in the guerrilla ranks.' The major object of the exercise was to effect close contact with the enemy and to gather intelligence.[3]

British ideas and responses to terrorism have been conditioned by experience gained during the Second World War, when the shadowy Special Operations Executive (SOE) helped train and arm resistance groups, some of which later evolved into post-war liberation movements, guerrilla and terrorist groups. The British, for instance, had trained the Jewish Haganah 'Special Night Squads' which later turned against their former friends in Palestine. The widely respected military historian John Keegan, in a review of SOE's history, wrote that the organisation 'dirtied the British government's hands'. The implication being that Britain's counter-terrorism strategy against the IRA had been compromised from the beginning by adopting the use of terrorist methods developed by SOE during the war. Britain could not claim the high moral ground. 'Means besmirch ends,' wrote Keegan. SOE's most influential leaders, such as Colin Gubbins, had spent a good deal of time studying the methods of IRA leader Michael Collins, admired for his cunning and planning in terrorist operations.[4]

The true origin of the police-type 'shoot-to-kill' policy which has operated in Northern Ireland can be traced back to Britain's war against Jewish terrorist groups in Palestine in the forties, where special forces personnel were to be found in abundance. At the beginning of 1947, the British authorities came under pressure to hit back when terrorist gangs increased their attacks on security personnel. In response, Assistant Inspector-General Bernard Fergusson proposed the use of 'special operations', which have been defined as 'unexpected strokes of violence usually mounted and executed outside the military establishment of the day, which exercise a startling effect on the enemy'. In February 1947, Fergusson submitted his plan for a system of special squads who would engage in unorthodox police activity with the aim of creating 'situations likely to result in armed clashes'. The squads would be made up of 'a small number of officers, who have technical and psychological knowledge of terrorism, having themselves been engaged in similar operations on what may be termed the terrorist side in countries occupied by the enemy in the late war'.[5]

Given the necessary political go-ahead, Fergusson proceeded to recruit Alistair McGregor, a former soldier and MI6 officer (in some accounts an SOE officer), who had experience of resistance groups, and Roy Farran, a highly experienced SAS (Special Air Services) officer who had fought alongside SOE in the Balkans. Farran has said that 'Fergusson was right in the basic principle that an underground war can only be fought by counter-terrorist forces, who are prepared to mix with the enemy in his own environment. Small groups can counter other small groups.' The Palestine 'killer squads', as they became known, grew out of a unit called the Police Mobile Force, and one of their Trojan horse operations involved the use of a laundry van as cover. In a curious historical parallel, the Military Reconnaissance Force (MRF) also used a laundry van in Northern Ireland in the early seventies as cover for covert operations until it got 'blown'.[6]

Although Fergusson denied that these were assassination squads, the units did operate on the borderline of legality. The squads were used 'to exploit existing intelligence to capture or kill insurgents'. Farran admitted that the squads, which included at least five SAS war veterans, were given powers to operate as they pleased. Members understood that they had been given 'a free hand for use against terror when all others were so closely hobbled'. Counter-insurgency expert Richard Clutterbuck estimates that Farran's small squad 'eliminated' as many terrorists as a battalion employing normal cordon and search operations. The squad was able to use methods close to those adopted by the Jewish terrorists, but such methods quickly became a political embarrassment. In October 1947, a general court martial acquitted Farran of a charge of murder in connection with the disappearance of Alexander Rubowitz, a young member of the Stern Gang. Farran, who went on to become Solicitor-General of the Canadian province of Alberta, came to regard the Fergusson initiative as a failure because there was no political end in view. 'I would have done better not to have tried.'[7]

As David Charteris notes in his study of this episode, control and discipline are the keys to these types of operations, because they can so easily degenerate into 'private armies' and thus become a law unto themselves. The British experience suggests that this is the norm, since the higher authorities, fearful of public exposure, never fully integrate these paramilitary units into the normal command structure. When operations do go wrong, the authorities deny the powers given to the squads and the members are usually hung out to dry, disowned by the officials who set them up in the first place. This was the case in Palestine, where the spotlight of the world's press was particularly strong. In other countries, the same tactics were employed with barely a murmur of dissent.[8]

Many of those who worked in Palestine found their experience and skills were required in other counter-insurgency campaigns. A small and tight band of security personnel were to have a disproportionate effect on British counter-terrorist policy. The police and Kenyan regiment based 'Special Force' used counter-gang tactics with great ferocity against the Mau Mau. Quietly and efficiently, they dispatched five hundred to a thousand tribesmen employing a range of methods from shootings to multiple stabbings and strangulation with piano wire. Kitson's apearance on the scene added to the noise and fuss as the less experienced army personnel tried the same tactics of counter-terror.[9]

Security experts who made their way to Malaya became known as the 'Palestine mob', while MI5 and police personnel were dubbed the 'Malay Mafia'. The Ferret Force, made up of former SOE Force 136 personnel, inflicted heavy losses on the guerrillas. During the emergency, Field Marshal Sir Gerald Templer, who was both High Commissioner (civil administration) and Director of Operations (military administration), let it be known that he proposed 'to use special squads of jungle fighters . . . they will really be "killer squads" (though I promise you I won't call them that, with a view to the questions in the House). They will be at the disposal of the Special Branch . . . to use on any good information which comes in. We have always set our face against the use of "killer squads" in infantry battalions of the police generally, since it has a bad effect on the fighting morale of all those who are not in the "killer squads" since they never get a proper crack.' This is the first, and last, time a senior official has admitted that they were 'killer squads', but the concept did not change for the next forty years.[10]

The arrival in Northern Ireland of the Army's leading counter-insurgency theorists, Brigadier Frank Kitson, in 1970, led to the implementation of familiar policies and operations which he had seen developed in other parts of Britain's former empire. Field Marshal Lord Carver later acknowledged the existence of 'surveillance operations by soldiers in plain clothes . . . initiated by Frank Kitson when he commanded the brigade in Belfast, some of them exploiting ex-members or supporters of the IRA, of which I was aware, and for which I had obtained Ministerial approval'. Before he left the province in 1972, Kitson had put into place a system of élite mobile surveillance and 'reaction' squads, which operated at the height of the campaign of sectarian assassinations, with a degree of uncontrolled independence. A covert Army Intelligence unit attached to Kitson's 39th Infantry Brigade, the Military Reconnaissance Force (MRF), has been acknowledged to have been a 'counter-gang'. There seemed to be an amateurish quality about the unit which harked back to Farran and Palestine. One officer told the press that 'the unit is part of the normal chain of command' but went on to say that 'he would like to retain the benefit of some doubt in the matter'.[11]

The MRF operated out of the Palace Barracks at Holywood on the outskirts of Belfast, under the guise of civilians, often in civilian cars. The four-man 'Special Duties Teams' were trained by SAS personnel in the use of weapons, surveillance and counter-insurgency methods. Members were encouraged to think like the IRA and to train in the use of IRA weapons, particularly the Thompson sub-machine gun. Run by Captain James McGregor, the MRF used flats and offices in Belfast and ran the Four-Square Laundry service whose distinctive van was used for surveillance. Additional intelligence came from the Special Detachment of the MRF – 'turned' IRA terrorists, known as 'freds', who were driven in great secrecy around Republican and Loyalists areas, identifying suspects. The MRF units, however, went beyond surveillance operations and some of their personnel took to shooting 'suspects' from passing cars. At the trial of one member of the MRF, accused of attempting to murder three men at a bus terminus, Sergeant Clive Williams identified himself as the commander of a unit of the Military *Reaction* Force, which more accurately described the MRF activities.[12]

Another undercover surveillance unit which served as a cover for infiltrating SAS and SAS-trained soldiers into the province was the 4 Field Survey Troop, located at Castle Dillon as part of a genuine engineers' regiment. Former Military Intelligence officer Fred Holroyd has revealed that the troop had a second level of cover – as the Northern Ireland Training and Tactics team (NITAT), which was created as a secret intelligence-gathering unit when the Army discovered, on arriving in the province, that 'Intelligence was generally piss poor'. Around 1979, NITAT changed its name to the Intelligence and Security Group (NI). The 4 Field operations were highly secret, using their own specially adapted 'Q' cars and specialised firearms, while their accommodation was guarded by MoD police. The government continues to deny that such a unit existed.[13]

The SAS had worked closely with the SOE during the Second World War and afterwards fought numerous official and 'deniable' counter-insurgency campaigns in Borneo, Malaya, Oman, Kenya and the Yemen. In Aden, the SAS 'took to the streets, dressed as Arabs, and armed with the Browning automatic pistol, which has remained one of their favourite weapons, fought with the assassins with their own methods – just as they are doing in Belfast today'.[14]

In the late sixties, a number of senior SAS officers formulated ideas on the future direction of the regiment, which they believed had lost its way. Major-General John Strawson, official biographer of the SAS, has written that 'It was becoming clear to those responsible for certain intelligence and security matters in this country that there was a need for a kind of armed branch of MI5 and MI6, a military back-up to such organisations, which could be called in as necessary both at home and abroad.' The change came in 1972 when the British secret state reorganised its response to internal threats in the wake of the miners' strike and the emergence of Arab terrorism. Colonel John Waddy of 22 SAS drafted a blueprint for the regiment which recognised its central role in counter-terrorism. The most visible sign of this reorientation in the regiment's capability took place in May 1980 when SAS troops stormed the Iranian embassy in Prince's Gate, London.

The government's response to the seizure by Arab terrorists of hostages inside the embassy was co-ordinated by a secret crisis committee known as COBRA (an acronym derived from the Cabinet Office Briefing Room). Chaired by the Home Secretary, its fifteen members included junior ministers from the Foreign Office and the Ministry of Defence, senior civil servants, representatives of MI5 and the SAS. COBRA was backed up with the support of twenty or more specialists who were on twenty-four-hour standby. The SAS became involved on their own initiative almost as soon as the hostage-taking operation began, when a former SAS NCO, Dusty Gray, who was a police dog-handler outside the embassy, telephoned SAS headquarters at Hereford. They were officially called in by the Joint Operations Centre within the MoD, which acts as a clearing house for special operations. It includes members of the regiment, the Foreign Office, the Home Office and the security services. The Counter-Revolutionary Warfare unit from B Squadron 22 SAS was ordered by the Prime Minister to mount a siege on the embassy after negotiations failed and the terrorists executed one hostage. Technicians from MI5's A Branch were employed to place microphones and insert small cameras in the walls. However, it was something of a failure as the walls proved to be too thick to penetrate. Since then, the SAS has built up its own intelligence database on portable computers of key buildings and potential targets such as commercial aeroplanes.[15]

Controversy surrounded the siege, during which five of the six terrorists were killed by the SAS assault squad. The order was 'shoot to kill', as the government did not wish to have terrorists in prison, risking the possibility that they might then become the target for another hostage operation by their terrorist friends and colleagues. An MoD source told James Adams, 'There would have been a degree of awkwardness about too many survivors.' The SAS men involved were given assurances that whatever the outcome there would be no sanctions taken against them. They were, in effect, given a free hand. Hostages alleged that the SAS executed terrorists after they had surrendered, with some who had disarmed being shot in the back. One had eighty-two bullets in his body. SAS men were yelling, 'Who's a terrorist?' as a few of the hostage takers had mixed in the general group of people in an attempt to escape. 'They were sitting with the group so [an SAS man] asked one man to stand up and then shot him.' According to witnesses others were killed 'where they sat with their backs to the centre of the room, and their hands on the wall'. The one terrorist to be arrested survived only after a struggle between a policeman and a SAS man who tried to take him back inside the embassy. This 'successful' action became a model for similar SAS operations.[16]

In the last decade, the officer-class spirit with its nod towards the concept of 'aristocracy', engendered by the regiment's founder David Stirling, appears to have vanished from the modern SAS as it increasingly relies on recruits from the Parachute Regiment, with their passion for physical fitness and use of brute force. These 'hard men' of working-class origin with their macho dress and demeanour, which curiously apes certain homosexual styles, are in the acscendancy if not in control of the small four-man patrol operations where officers are deliberately excluded. Those who serve in Northern Ireland have been described as 'warrior-janissaries who worshipped at the high altar of violence'.[17]

Although there are examples of the SAS capturing rather than killing IRA terrorists, they are rare and provide a stark contrast with RUC and Army figures. According to Mark Urban in an illuminating article on the modern SAS, between 1978 and 1983 the regiment 'killed nobody in Northern Ireland because of high-level decisions that Army ambush-type operations should be stopped'. However, in the following five-year period, while the Army killed only three IRA terrorists, the SAS was involved in the shooting of twenty.[18]

Accurate intelligence is essential for the SAS planned ambushes which are euphemistically called 'hard arrest'. The SAS is not an intelligence-gathering unit; instead it works alongside soldiers from the 14th Intelligence Company, an élite reconnaissance unit which engages in undercover deep surveillance and provides detailed reports on terrorists' movements. This secretive unit, known locally as 'the Detachment', which appears to have grown out of the 4 Field Troop, draws men from the intelligence corps and is trained by the SAS at Hereford. The unit recruits bright soldiers in their mid to late twenties who display 'resourcefulness and psychological strength', though, as with the SAS, there has been a shortage of suitable candidates. Divided into detachments of around twenty soldiers, 14th Int. operates under the control of the Army but includes MI5 advisers in its hierarchy. Since 1987, 14th Int. and a small element of SAS troops permanently stationed in the province have been under the administrative control of the Director Special Forces (DSF), Lieutenant General Sir Michael Wilkes, a former SAS soldier. The two undercover units are known collectively as the Intelligence and Security Group (ISG), and more commonly as 'The Group'. The Group has little to do with the pen-pushing units of the same name stationed on the mainland and in Germany. The activities of the Group and RUC Special Branch specialist units, which on occasions supplement the surveillance reports on which the SAS act, are integrated by the Tasking and Co-ordination Group.[19]

In his book *Secret Armies*, James Adams, recipient of many briefings from MoD and SAS spokesmen, dismisses talk of an assassination policy and instead writes of 'isolated incidents of killing IRA men who could easily have been taken into custody'. There have been too many killings involving under-cover units in ambush-type situations for these to be totally uncoordinated and unrelated. The Army's Land Operations Manual points out that the SAS squadrons are specifically equipped for counter-revolutionary operations in insurgent-held areas which include tactics of infiltration, sabotage and assassination. The SAS has never been trained to arrest people and its members do not carry handcuffs. It is understood by senior Army officers at the Ulster headquarters 'that no prisoners will normally be taken in SAS ambushes'.[20]

The early eighties version of the Army's manual on Counter-Revolutionary Operations states that 'An ambush is a surprise attack by a force lying in wait upon a moving or temporarily halted enemy.' Soldiers formed into 'killer' groups are to be positioned so as to be able to fire into a 'killing area'. No warnings are given. The manual reveals that 'the aim of an ambush is thus usually achieved by concentrating heavy accurate fire from concealed positions into carefully selected killing areas which the enemy have been allowed to enter, but from which their escape is prevented by fire and possibly obstacles'. In the eighties political sensitivities forced a cosmetic change from the term 'ambush' to the more ambiguous 'Observation Post/Reactive (OP/React)'.[21]

As the then Northern Ireland Unionist MP Enoch Powell pointed out in 1988, without a declaration of war the ambush is illegal, and you cannot declare war on anything less than another state. Therefore the secret state is constantly obliged to fabricate cover stories. The one thing that cannot be admitted is ambushing. In that sense, the concept of 'shoot-to-kill' is something of a distraction. Whether X aimed above or below the waist is neither here nor there if X is in place for an ambush with a machine-gun. British Army manuals define a successful ambush as one in which all the enemy are killed. As one Army veteran told *The Times*, what the SAS do is 'kill terrorists'. Former senior officials within the Northern Ireland Office at Stormont believe that on a number of occasions the SAS soldiers have administered the final *coup de grâce* to their victims with a single shot through the temple. To use the SAS is to acquiesce to a shoot-to-kill policy.[22]

During the secret struggle against the IRA, the Northern Ireland Office has had no real control over the actions of the covert groups. Too often in the secret state, senior officials and politicians avoid responsibility for operations, being content to administer broad policy. 'Real power is exercised', suggests Mark Urban, 'by those who are not responsible to parliament or the electorate who, in turn, shield those who *are* responsible from painful decisions.'[23]

6

Stalker

> It is impossible to make an omelette without breaking eggs.
>
> James Anderton on anti-terrorism

> My anger in this case stemmed from the denial that things had gone wrong, that no eggs were broken even though the omelette was there to see.
>
> John Stalker

On 27 October 1982, three Royal Ulster Constabulary (RUC) officers were killed in an Irish National Liberation Army (INLA) bombing. It turned out to be a significant incident in a black year for the security forces. An RUC spokesman said that the bombing 'raised the temperature'. There were later reports that RUC officers were 'hyped up' and 'very angry' about the killings. The *Independent* was moved to admit that the events which followed 'looked unpleasantly like revenge'.

On 11 November 1982, three unarmed Provisional IRA men, Gervais McKerr, Eugene Toman and Sean Burns, were killed at a roadblock on Tullygally East Road, near Lurgan, by members of the élite Headquarters Mobile Support Unit (HQMSU). An RUC spokesman said that the men were shot trying to escape. The police had fired 109 bullets into their car. Thirteen days later, another HQMSU unit poured automatic fire into an isolated hayshed. The RUC officers later alleged that two young men, Michael Tighe and Martin McCauley, had pointed rifles, which turned out to be sixty years old, at them from inside the building. McCauley was wounded by the hail of bullets, while seventeen-year-old Tighe, who had no paramilitary connections, was killed. On 12 December, two unarmed members of the INLA, Roddy Carroll and Seamus Grew, were killed by nineteen bullets fired into their car on the outskirts of Armagh. RUC officers from the HQMSU unit involved went on to lie at the subsequent trials, partly to conceal the fact that members of Special Branch had been involved in an illegal cross-border operation. It would appear that 14th Int. surveillance operatives were also involved in the events leading up to the Carroll/Grew killings.[1]

At one stage, when RUC Chief Constable Sir John Hermon overruled a chief superintendent who recommended that murder charges be brought against several RUC officers, the Northern Ireland Director of Public Prosecutions (DPP), Sir Barry Shaw, threatened to resign if the charges were not instituted. Hermon expressed fears that force morale would suffer and RUC informants might be exposed in court. When an internal inquiry failed to resolve the matter to Sir Barry's satisfaction, the Deputy Chief Constable of Greater Manchester, John Stalker, was asked to head an outside inquiry. His remit was to investigate the circumstances surrounding the fabrication of evidence and false statements following the series of killings, which were seen by many people as evidence of a 'shoot-to-kill' policy.

Stalker appeared to have the necessary qualifications and safe hands with which to undertake the inquiry. By 1983 he was a 'high-flyer', attending a year-long course at the Royal College of Defence Studies on the challenge to preserving stability in the face of violent change through the threat of military power. In part, the course dealt with internal subversion – with Northern Ireland serving as a case study. Stalker seemed an ideal candidate for what was bound to be a difficult and controversial job. As Peter Taylor points out in his book on the Stalker affair, it was unlikely that MI5, whose C3 section had responsibilities for vetting the police, would have allowed him to get this far if there had been a skeleton in his cupboard.[2]

The principle of 'police primacy' had been policy since 1976 following the introduction of 'Ulsterisation', which had been outlined in a Labour government document, *The Way Forward.* This revealed that the RUC would gradually assume the leading security role as troops were slowly withdrawn. The initiative for the undercover operations remained with the Army and the Security Service, but following the election of the Conservative government, which had promised a tough line on terrorism, the distinction between military and police operations was allowed to become blurred. When, in 1979, former MI6 chief Sir Maurice Oldfield became co-ordinator of the security services in the province, he made it clear that the government wanted to see an extension of the covert war.

Oldfield set up the Joint Operations Planning Committee at Castlereagh, comprising the RUC Special Patrol Group Bronze section, RUC Special Branch, MI5 and MI6 and an SAS Special Tasks team called 'Whiskey'. A Special Security Directorate was created to prevent leaks from the different agencies. Additionally, between 1981 and 1982, the RUC Special Branch set up the HQMSUs to 'take on' the IRA. Sources within the RUC claimed that the go-ahead for these operations was sanctioned at a very high level in London, probably through the Joint Intelligence Committee. Close friends of Oldfield believe that he was against an assassinations policy and this may have led MI5 to agitate to have him removed from Ulster. Likewise the Permanent Under-Secretary of State at the Northern Ireland Office, Sir Philip Woodfield, is believed to have voiced doubts about setting up the RUC units.[3]

In 1981, James Prior, Secretary of State for Northern Ireland, stated: 'What we need to do is to use the methods the terrorists use in order to overcome [the IRA].' This was a well-received view in sections of the RUC where more militant officers were heard to suggest that 'The Provies can be defeated. We should declare war on them. We know who they are. We could stiff the clatter out of them tomorrow, if we were given a free hand.' Since 'a freer hand' was given in 1981, forty IRA terrorists have been shot dead by undercover soldiers. Few of these incidents have resulted in a prosecution because the 1967 Criminal Law Act allows 'such force as is reasonable in the circumstances'. This vague concept means in practice that soldiers only have to demonstrate that the target was a terrorist.[4]

Responsibility for the operations of the HQMSUs was held by the Assistant Chief Constable, Trevor Forbes, who was head of the RUC Special Branch. The two HQMSUs each had around twenty-four officers with a Special Branch inspector in charge of each unit. Smaller groups of three or four men operated from undercover 'Q' cars. The undercover men, whose average age was twenty-eight, were trained by the SAS at Hereford and were 'rushed through the formalities of police training' – shades of Palestine. SAS personnel were critical of some of the recruits, who seemed 'overly committed, gossipy and passionate in their fight against the terrorists'. James Adams notes, without a trace of irony, that the SAS later heard 'through their own sources that the men they had trained had taken the law into their own hands'.[5]

Officers of the HQMSUs were trained to respond with 'firepower, speed and aggression'. The object was simple, namely 'to eliminate the threat'. It has been repeatedly said by government spokesmen that there is no alternative to aiming to kill the victim. The officer with overall responsibility for the units was quoted as saying that HQMSU officers 'were not trained to fire at people's legs but at their bodies to put them permanently out of operation'. SAS soldiers dismiss outright the notion that it is possible to disable terrorists by shooting at their legs. Former Hong Kong Commissioner of Police Roy Henry has said of his force's tactics in the use of firearms: 'You never use automatic fire, of course, and you never deliberately aim to kill. You aim at the knee. And you give clear and distinct warning first.' This makes an interesting contrast with the HQMSUs' methods. Although the

HQMSUs were a counter-terrorist unit and not riot police, they were a police counter-terrorist force and as such a significant step was taken by bringing in the method – aim to kill.[6]

Within the RUC Special Branch, designated E, a number of specialised units aided the HQMSUs, E1 dealt with Administration while E12 was responsible for Legal Services, E3 (Intelligence) and E4 (Operations) were responsible for liaising with the Security Liaison Office at RUC headquarters which was staffed by MI5 field officers. E5 involved working with the Special Military Intelligence Unit (SMIU). The HQMSUs were activated by E4 on the basis of intelligence fed to it by the most secret departments E4A (A for Action) and E4B, C and D, which carried out physical and technical surveillance. Success depended on the intelligence provided by these units, which also collated additional intelligence provided by the Army and MI5. A degree of control over most of the operations was held by MI5, which insisted on its technicians planting bugs and on the supervision of their use. The most important and sensitive information came from that provided by informers or 'touts' and CTs (converted terrorists).

The E4 unit fed its intelligence to the RUC's Tasking and Co-ordination Group (TCG) based at Gough Barracks, in Armagh, which works closely with MI5 and controls anti-terrorist operations. The TCG is chaired by a senior Special Branch officer with the Army's liaison officer from either the SAS or 14th Int. in attendance, joined by MI5 officers once an operation is in progress. The TCG 'tasked' the HQMSUs on specific operations which were tightly controlled by senior Special Branch officers, who then debriefed members of the HQMSUs after the operation's conclusion and provided cover stories. They also interpreted the status of those killed in the broadest terms, labelling some 'wanted' or an 'on-the-run terrorist', which was not always the case. Seventeen-year-old Michael Tighe was labelled as a known 'republican' in a dossier prepared after Tighe's death based on a non-existent informer. 'Too often', Stalker found, 'that word meant nothing more than "slightly suspected", but had the effect of raising the stakes unacceptably.'[7]

The intelligence forming the basis for the Tullygally East Road and the hayshed ambushes came from a very active informer known as 'the mole' who was in receipt of large amounts of money, sometimes in the form of 'incentive payments', i.e. payments by results. 'The mole' made over £30,000 in a relatively short time. Payment throughout was administered by MI5, which is responsible for funding the monthly payouts to agents made through mainland banks, from its allocation of the Secret Vote made by Parliament. 'The mole' was believed to have been recruited by Army Intelligence prior to 1976 and then handed over to the RUC Special Branch, E3 and E4 being most closely involved as his handlers. Stalker was disturbed by his activities but never learned his identity.[8]

Stalker soon discovered that, within the RUC, the Special Branch wielded immense power. Unusually, it was staffed not by short-term placement officers, but by 'career' officers who controlled much of what went on inside the unit. Other sections of the RUC were resigned to the all-pervading power of the Special Branch and were conditioned not to ask awkward questions. Decisions within the unit were made on the principle of a 'Chinese Parliament' which meant that no one took individual responsibility for what were alleged to have been collective ones. In addition, the threat of prosecution under the Official Secrets Act was used to keep questioning officers in line. Once the killings had become a matter of public controversy, just as had happened to Farran in Palestine, the unit was 'abandoned and isolated by a police force that . . . used them and then cut them adrift'.[9]

Sir John Hermon was against Stalker's inquiry from the beginning and 'privately regarded it as unnecessary'. When the two met for the first time, Hermon warned Stalker about the 'jungle' he was about to enter. The Chief Constable had expected the inquiry would be narrowly focused and would merely 'review' the in-house CID inquiry. This hope disappeared when it became clear to Stalker's team that CID officers had 'showed a lamentable standard of professionalism in their enquiries'. When Stalker refused to back away from a full investigation of the circumstances surrounding the killings, the RUC Special Branch became obstructive. This was particularly so when the inquiry threatened to intrude into sensitive areas such as the use of informers. Stalker's team met with hostility from the middle and senior ranks, setting off all kinds of 'panic bells'. They came to believe that 'the mole' had been involved in serious criminal offences and that there was a common thread behind the killings which might lead to similar incidents which, hitherto, had been hidden away. There was a suspicion that an *agent provocateur* had been at work and that much of the information forming the basis of the ambushes was bogus.[10]

Knowledge that the Security Service had played a key role in the surveillance operation which led up to the killings may have produced further pressure for non-cooperation. The RUC was aware that it was likely to lose out in any dispute with MI5. It appeared that MI5 had deliberately blocked a high-level RUC investigation into allegations of homosexual abuse at the Kincora boys' home in East Belfast by people in contact with the security services. The RUC was repeatedly refused permission by MI5's executive head of legal services, Bernard Sheldon, to question a senior MI5 officer, Ian Cameron, who had been told about the abuses in the mid-seventies but had declined to pursue the matter. The report into Kincora by the Chief Constable of Sussex, Sir George Terry, was published in October 1983. It was noticeable that there were no references to the co-operation of MI5. It was only later that Sir John Hermon personally discovered the way his force and colleagues had been treated by the Security Service. According to reports, he was 'absolutely livid'.[11]

In a similar vein, in December 1984 the *New Statesman* revealed that a two-year RUC investigation into Army 'dirty tricks' in the province during the mid-seventies had been obstructed by MI5. Insufficient evidence was produced by RUC detectives to warrant prosecutions following the claims of former Military Intelligence officer Fred Holroyd. MI5 and MI6 refused to co-operate with the inquiry and evidence from a similar MoD investigation was not passed on to the RUC. It was claimed that MI5 was particularly worried that the Northern Ireland DPP, Sir Barry Shaw, was 'regarded as a less tolerant legal figure' than those with which MI5 normally dealt. In late 1983, MI5's legal adviser, Bernard Sheldon, approached the MoD's Secretariat 6, which is concerned with Northern Ireland operations, and asked for its help in blunting the RUC inquiry. Sheldon also saw officials at the Northern Ireland Office, who later advised Sir John Hermon 'to curtail his investigation in the national interest . . . agents' lives would be at risk if the police investigated the criminal offences which Holroyd had revealed.'[12]

It is entirely possible that a conspiracy to remove Stalker evolved as soon as his appointment was announced. Special Branch officers did not want a 'witch-hunt'. Within two months of his appointment, a police informer in Manchester, who had helped the RUC with information about the IRA, was making wild and unsubstantiated allegations about Stalker. Even a journalist as pro the security services as James Adams admitted that Special Branch officers 'once their actions were discovered . . . decided to thwart any outside investigation. The suspicion remains that some members caused the allegations to be made in order to muddy the waters.' Michael Prince, in his biography of Manchester Chief Constable James Anderton, alleges that within one week of Stalker's appointment a senior Special Branch officer arranged a secret meeting with MI5 and MI6 colleagues at the Crest Hotel in Liverpool. During the ensuing discussion it was proposed that MI6 should 'remove' a key witness, the wounded Martin McCauley, while 'poison ivy' – false evidence – should be planted to smear him.[13]

The inquiry took on a new and, for Hermon, potentially

damaging turn when Stalker and his team discovered that the hayshed where Tighe had been killed had been under electronic surveillance. In October 1984, it was denied to Stalker that the hayshed had been bugged; however, Army officers were willing to confirm the installation. A bug had been planted by MI5 and recorded by a police and Army technical team. 'The tape was to become the rope in a bitter tug-of-war between those who believe that methods of intelligence-gathering should be protected at all costs and those who regard the tape as possible evidence of murder committed by police, and therefore belonging in a wider arena.'[14]

The head of RUC Special Branch, Trevor Forbes, told Stalker, 'You will never be able to hear it.' Hermon said that he could not further the investigation of the tape without the authority of the Security Service. On 28 January 1985, Stalker travelled to London where he saw Bernard Sheldon and was told that MI5 had no objections to him pursuing the matter. Hermon blamed MI5 for the inaction, claiming that they 'had the most powerful interest in the tape'. On 15 May, Stalker saw MI5's Director and Co-ordinator of Intelligence (DCI) in Belfast, who said that the way was now open to 'complete consultation' but subject to 'unspecified safeguards' after MI5 had assessed the content of the tape. With rising anger, Stalker refused to accept the conditions, complaining that the 'labyrinthine processes through which I had been groping' had brought him back to the same position he had been at five months previously. 'It was obvious to me that much midnight oil had been burned.'[15]

The following month, Stalker was back in London, meeting Sheldon and the DCI, who stated that they were prepared to release all the information but were 'very reluctant to discuss the authority for the use and installation of the device'. Stalker was asked to accept that 'everything was politically and legally in order'. The significance of this request passed over Stalker's head. He had been told that permission had been granted 'under the general authority of the previous Northern Ireland

Secretary, James Prior'. In fact, MI5 had bypassed Prior and sought authority from a well-disposed Home Secretary, William Whitelaw. The DCI had only informed Prior of the bugging operation *after* the bugs were in place. MI5 were hiding many things from Stalker.[16]

An MI5 technical officer from A Branch inserted two devices in the hayshed at the end of September 1982. Special Branch had been wary of using a bug and thought that human surveillance, though dangerous, would be more reliable. In this they were proved to be correct. The apparent failure of the bugs led to the removal of the explosives hidden in the hayshed going undetected. The explosives from the hayshed were to be used in the bomb which killed three RUC officers on 27 October – the incident which became the springboard for the killing of the six men by the HQMSUs. 'The mole' was able to name three of those killed – McKerr, Toman and Burns – as being responsible for the bombing. MI5's technical operation had clearly failed and was a great embarrassment. Furthermore, the tape's existence was not revealed to the Attorney-General, who undertook the prosecution, which later collapsed, of officers involved in the shootings of Tighe and McCauley.[17]

On his return to Belfast, Stalker was shocked when Hermon denied him the tape, telling him dramatically, 'Never, I am afraid. The tape has been destroyed but a transcript exists.' Stalker thought that 'this revelation came as a surprise even to the senior MI5 officers'. Not so, for once again MI5 officers had lied. It was claimed that the bugging was a routine operation and that the tape had been destroyed – this being 'policy'. According to Peter Taylor's sources, 'under these strict and top secret rules [drawn up by the Joint Intelligence Committee], all surveillance tapes are physically destroyed, not just wiped, once transcripts have been made of them to harvest material of intelligence value', the reason being that they are protecting 'systems that have been refined and protected over many years'.[18]

There were over forty tapes covering the period of the surveillance operation. The crucial ten-minute tape – Tape 42 – featuring the killing shots was handed by an RUC Special Branch constable, who monitored the shooting, to his senior officer at the Tasking and Co-ordination Group. It was sent to Belfast for transcription by women police officers – known by the macho Special Branch officers as the 'Bitch Squad' or 'Henhouse' – and was then destroyed. However, a clandestine copy of the missing tape was made by an Army officer, who was monitoring the hayshed, as 'a macabre souvenir'. The tape was locked away in a safe in Belfast, where it was available to at least half a dozen MI5 officers and provided them with valuable ammunition in gaining RUC co-operation as it held evidence of unlawful killing. A senior MI5 training officer visiting Northern Ireland out-stations heard the tape and is believed to have been the person who informed the inquiry.

An 'interim' report from Stalker was finally delivered to Hermon on 18 September 1985, excluding the relevant section on the tape. Although long overdue, it took five months for the report to be delivered to the DPP in Belfast, Sir Barry Shaw. On 4 March 1986, Shaw insisted Hermon give Stalker greater co-operation. Hermon did not meet Stalker for twelve weeks and appeared to pay little heed to Shaw's instructions. Stalker realised that after eighteen months of trying to obtain the tape it was still no nearer to being in his grasp. On 28 May 1986, Stalker was busy in his garden when an official from the Greater Manchester Police Authority telephoned to inform him that he was under investigation by a team led by West Yorkshire Chief Constable Colin Sampson. The various insubstantial allegations centred around his relationship with a local Tory businessman, Kevin Taylor. They were largely based on the uncorroborated testimony of a known criminal and liar, David Bertlestein (alias Burton), who had died in prison in March 1985. Stalker would later learn that Sampson was also to replace him on the Northern Ireland investigation.[19]

Stalker had been misled by what he termed MI5's 'essentially neutral stance'. MI5 was reluctant to talk about the authority for the placement of the bug for fear that Stalker might discover MI5 had also bugged the car in which McKerr, Toman and Burns were killed. According to BBC reporter Chris Moore, 'the security forces involved in the covert surveillance operation were able to listen to the conversation going on in the car'. As Sampson tried to gain access to the clandestine hayshed tape MI5 field officers ordered its destruction. Sampson later recommended the prosecution of a number of MI5 officers for conspiracy to pervert the course of justice for this deliberate act.[20]

On 23 March 1987, the final section of Sampson's report was delivered to Hermon and Shaw. In January 1988, Attorney-General Sir Patrick Mayhew told the House of Commons that because of 'considerations of national security' no charges would be brought against any of the seven named RUC officers in the Sampson report, including charges of conspiracy to murder, nor against the MI5 officers involved in conspiracy charges. Revealing his 'deep anxiety', Mayhew added, 'I have had to balance one harm to national security against another.' The British government was worried that prosecutions would have removed the top echelon of the RUC, emasculating 'its main bulwark against terrorism'. Two senior officers were suspended but were later reinstated. RUC officers said in private that if prosecuted they 'would disclose all'. The Attorney-General's statement to the House of Commons, wrote Duncan Campbell, 'officially sanctioned four years of fabricated evidence, cover-up, obstruction and delay' in investigating the six killings.[21]

Clearly, the government had been uncomfortable when Stalker had initially proposed charging RUC officers because it knew any further investigation would lead 'to the top of the force and beyond, exposing the philosophy, strategy, and tactics behind covert security operations in Northern Ireland'. Indeed, the main pressure to stop the charges appears to have come from MI5, which was deeply involved in operations on both sides of the border and wanted to protect its 'national assets' and covert operations. In February 1988, Stalker told *The Times*: 'I never did find evidence of a shoot-to-kill policy as such. There was no written instruction, nothing pinned on the notice-board. But there was a clear understanding on the part of the men whose job it was to pull the trigger that that was what was expected of them.'[22]

The secret state's descent into mimicking the actions of the terrorists had lost the government its claim to the moral high ground. In consequence, Northern Ireland increasingly took on the characteristics of a Balkan state.

7

Gibraltar

SHOT DOWN LIKE DOGS

The *Sun*

Politicians who authorise the use of the SAS do so in the knowledge that they are employing a deadly weapon which lacks an adequate safety-catch.

Editorial, the *Independent*, 10 September 1988

In February 1942, there occurred an incident which echoes down the years. The British authorities in Palestine were determined to entrap thirty-four-year-old Polish-born Avraham Stern, leader of the most notorious terrorist group, Fighters for the Freedom of Israel. Stern was tracked down by CID officers acting on a tip-off to a top-floor apartment in Tel Aviv. What happened next is still a matter of controversy. In his autobiography, the most senior policeman present, Assistant Superintendent Geoffrey Morton, writes that Stern 'made a mad rush towards the open window leading to a flat roof . . . I had no reason to disbelieve his oft-repeated threat to blow up himself and his captors . . . Stern could not possibly get away for the house was surrounded and he knew it. What, then, was his object? I could only conclude that he had some infernal machine rigged up and that he was making a desperate attempt to reach it. None of the police in the room could get to the window before him, so, in order to prevent another shambles, I shot him dead.'[1]

Forty-six years later, on another piece of the British Empire, Gibraltar, two leading Provisional IRA members, thirty-one-year-old Mairead Farrell and thirty-year-old Daniel 'Butch'

McCann, were walking past a Shell service station when a soldier, who was following directly behind them on the footpath, shouted a warning. Immediately, an SAS colleague fired from the road, hitting Farrell in the face. She raised her hands to the superficial wound but was hit again in the head. Stunned, shocked and in extreme pain, she turned away and began to fall to the ground. More bullets ricocheted off the petrol pumps. McCann, moving quickly to assist Farrell, was shot twice, once in the face and then in the top of his head. The other SAS man moved forward and, from a distance of three feet, fired three shots into Farrell's back. The bullets exited from the front, her heart shot to pieces. He then moved across and fired two more bullets into McCann as he lay face down on the ground.

A third IRA terrorist, twenty-three-year-old bomb-maker Sean Savage, ran towards the town, pursued by a man running awkwardly with a gun in his left hand. Suddenly and without warning, the pursuer opened fire. Savage fell as the first shot hit him in the back. A 'frenzied attack' then began. Robyn Mordue, a British holiday-maker on the Rock, saw the victim bleeding. Frightened, he hid behind a car and was violently sick. He heard, but did not see, the shooting which followed. Five bullets ripped into Savage's back. His body arched backwards 'bouncing on the floor' as six shots hit his front – his chest, arm, leg, hand and shoulder – the force of the impact breaking a leg and an arm. As Savage lay 'corkscrewed to the ground' his killer, an SAS soldier, standing at his feet, fired the fatal bullets, the *coup de grâce*. He fired two shots from his Browning pistol into Savage's head, the cartridges ejecting four feet to the right. Three more shots caused 'extensive brain damage' and 'multiple fractures to the skull'. Sixteen to eighteen bullets resulted in a total of twenty-seven wounds.[2]

At the subsequent inquest, anonymous SAS soldiers testified that they had been briefed by a senior officer who informed them that MI5 intelligence believed the terrorists would be carrying a remote-control device to trigger a car bomb placed in the town. This intelligence turned out to be entirely false. Soldier B testified that he opened fire because 'I believed that she was going for the button . . . we were told it was 100 per cent certain to be a button job.' He added, 'I thought mad McCann was going to go for the button.' Offering to surrender by shouting out 'stop, stop, I surrender' was not an option left open to the terrorists. 'I would have carried on firing. He may well have said that and pressed the button at the same time.' Soldier D said that 'only a shot in the brain guarantees immobility'.[3]

In September 1988, with unprecedented world-wide media coverage, MI5 officers and SAS soldiers were forced to justify their actions at the inquest held into the deaths of the three terrorists. However, too much was at stake to allow a full disclosure of Operation Flavius and a full cover-up was put into place. The autopsy of the victims was a sham. There were no X-rays, and photographs of the bodies and wounds were not made available. The pathologist was not shown forensic and ballistic reports to help him reach a proper conclusion. Evidence from witnesses was subject to blatant manipulation, while the witnesses themselves were smeared or frightened off from testifying. One security source revealed that the delays in holding the inquest had been 'really helpful'. The dirty-tricks team, he went on, 'had plenty of time to go in and nobble the credibility of the key witnesses'. Cross-examination was restricted by the use of government Public Interest Immunity certificates forbidding questions which strayed into 'sensitive' areas. Statements from the SAS soldiers had been taken nearly three weeks after the event, leaving plenty of time to coach government witnesses with a collective account of the shootings. The well-rehearsed testimony left many with the impression that some of the government witnesses simply lied.[4]

As early as 1985, the British authorities had received intelligence about IRA suspects who were mixing with

British and Irish holiday-makers in Mediterranean resorts. By November 1987, when McCann and Savage flew into Malaga airport on a reconnaissance mission, Spain's International Terrorism branch had established an extensive network of police surveillance with British Special Branch help on the IRA Active Service Unit's (ASU) activities. There was close collaboration with MI5 (code-named 'Snuffbox'), which had a senior officer from the F5 desk installed at the British embassy in Madrid to oversee the operation. MI5 intelligence on the ASU appears to have been extensive and of a high order. MI5 realised that the unit was planning a major bombing on the Continent and conceived Operation Flavius – named after the Roman senator who published rules of legal procedure – to thwart the bombers. The assessment was that the likely target was Gibraltar and the date the traditional changing of the guard by the Royal Anglian Regiment on 8 March 1988.

The operation was masterminded within MI5 by the new director of T Branch responsible for counter-terrorism (not Stella Rimington as given in some reports). Input also came from the Northern Ireland Director and Co-ordinator of Intelligence, Lieutenant-Colonel John Burgess, an experienced intelligence officer who had commanded the Special Military Intelligence Unit (SMIU) in the province in the mid-seventies and later the Intelligence Corps depot at Ashford in Kent. The head of T Branch was a key figure in co-ordinating the planning through the top-level committee, the Current Intelligence Group (CIG), responsible for Irish terrorism. The CIG, which includes members of MI5, MI6, GCHQ and Special Branch, was backed up by the Joint Intelligence Organisation which, in turn, reported to the Joint Intelligence Committee (JIC). Within the Cabinet Office a high-security network code-named 'Codin' linked the key ministries, the Metropolitan Police Special Branch, MI5, MI6 and other security agencies. Weekly assessments from CIG were sent to Prime

Minister Margaret Thatcher and selected members of the Cabinet.[5]

The CIG on terrorism is in turn linked into the European Community Trevi group through the Home Secretary. Flavius was an example of the new co-operation on terrorism as security officials and organisations communicated via coded fax machines installed by security services throughout the European Community via the Trevi communications network, Corea.[6]

On Wednesday, 2 March, acting on intelligence from MI5 that the bombing was imminent, the JIC alerted the Joint Operations Centre. The JOC, in turn, contacted the joint SAS–SBS (Special Boat Service) Headquarters Group which had been established earlier in the year, bringing together the various undercover units including the Intelligence and Security Group, responsible for surveillance and intelligence operations. The HQ, under the command of an SAS Director of Special Forces and an SBS deputy, was ordered to deploy a full SAS Special Projects Team of sixteen men which is available on standby at Stirling Lines, Hereford, for operations outside of Ulster. Anxious to have political backing for their actions, they consulted the Prime Minister, who has to agree to military actions, security and anti-terrorist measures overseas involving military personnel, at an early stage, and it was Mrs Thatcher who gave the final decision to commit the SAS. The team flew out to Gibraltar the following day and in effect became an instrument of MI5 although still technically under the command of the MoD.[7]

The rules of engagement were specifically tailored for the operation, but in case anything went wrong a lawyer accompanied the team to iron out any difficulties. This proved to be unnecessary; according to one SAS soldier, the regiment 'is the only agency whose job is to go out and zap people'. This was an experienced SAS squad and the outcome, said another SAS man, was 'hardly surprising, given the people who were sent'. Duncan Campbell suggests that 'Army and intelligence officials had long been keen to see the deaths of the three experienced IRA members'. He believes that the original intention was to move against the terrorists in the middle of the Rock's airstrip, well away from independent eyewitnesses and all the ensuing embarrassment. Panic set in when the fourth member of the team, the watch-keeper, was lost by the surveillance team.[8]

The senior MI5 officer, Mr 'O', who organised the operation from London, had spent seven and a half years on the Provisional IRA desk. His linkman on Gibraltar was not called at the inquest because he would have been 'instantly recognisable and was too important to risk'. It has been suggested that this was Air Chief Marshal Sir Peter Terry, Governor and Commander in Chief of Gibraltar. On 18 September 1990, Terry was shot and seriously wounded by the IRA at his home in Staffordshire. The Police Commissioner, Joseph Canepa, was appointed by Terry and was responsible to him. 'O's assessment of the tactics of the IRA unit was given to the Deputy Commissioner of Police, who passed it on to the fifty or so people involved in the operation around midnight on Saturday, 5 March.[9]

Mr 'O' admitted three intelligence mistakes in the briefing he prepared for the SAS soldiers, the Gibraltar Commissioner of Police, military officers and the colony's Governor. Although he later said that 'almost invariably all that is known are fragments and we have to put forward an assessment of the likely course of events', the version of the final briefing as given to the inquest was much more definitive – so much so that Mr 'O' rejected other interpretations of the evidence. The three 'mistakes' were believing that the car brought on to the Rock contained a bomb, that it could be exploded by a remote-control detonating device and that the IRA trio would be armed.

Special Branch and MI5 officers were in place at Malaga airport when the terrorists arrived in Spain on 4 March. The fact that the ASU travelled to the Rock on the Saturday, 5

March, should have indicated the use of a blocking car, particularly as parking is a permanent problem in the small colony, where there are over five hundred cars for every mile of road, but this assessment seemed not to interest MI5.[10]

Although the first official briefings on the alleged car bomb referred to a timing device, Mr 'O' told the Coroner's court that his assessment of the bomb was based on a car found in Brussels on 21 January 1988 which contained about 110 lb of Semtex explosive and a remote-control detonating device. 'This was much the safest way of exploding a device. The bombers had a better chance of getting away.' The only problem was that none of the scientific experts or officers from the SAS and MI5 could recall a similar instance of the IRA using a remote-control device where they were not in visual sight of the bomb.

SAS soldier 'G' told the court that 'at the briefing we were given, we were told that the aerial-controlled car bomb and the radio-controlled elements of it were going to be similar to the Brussels find – I know that a transmitter was part of that package.' This appears to have been a *post hoc* invention. This cover story had first been aired in the *Sunday Times* in May 1988 when the Insight team reported that Belgian detectives had found 'a sophisticated remote control device'. However, this turned out to be 'an integrated circuit from a domestic television set, for building into the circuitry of bombs'. Unfortunately for the Insight team, Belgian detectives linked the find of the Semtex to the IRA on the basis that the detonating device was *not* of the remote-control type.

Spanish newspapers later reported the Spanish police's 'certainty' that the three terrorists had entered Gibraltar without a bomb and said they had informed the British authorities of this fact. However, Soldier 'G', an SAS explosives 'expert', declared that he believed the car had contained a bomb when he made his on-the-spot assessment. This was disputed by Colonel Styles, a retired bomb disposal officer of great renown. He told the inquest that even those with limited experience could tell by simply looking at the car suspension whether it carried a bomb or not.[11]

No attempt was made to arrest the three IRA terrorists as they crossed into Gibraltar from Spain, which could have been done peacefully and successfully. To explain this, the MoD concocted a story that the Spanish police, responsible for surveillance on the Spanish side, had lost the trio on Friday, 4 March. Pressure was put on the Spanish authorities ensuring that no Spanish Special Branch or police officers appeared at the inquest. Spanish government sources claimed that the British ambassador, Sir Nicholas Gordon-Lennox, had urged senior Spanish officers involved in the IRA surveillance to keep quiet. A 'statement' was prepared from the head of the Malaga Special Branch, Tomas Rayo Valenzuela, who was not called to the inquest. It was not sworn before a lawyer, as is the custom and gave rise to considerable controversy. Valenzuela was head of the Anti-Terrorist Brigade of the Malaga police, but was not directly involved in the surveillance operation controlled by Brigada Exterior, the Spanish sister service of MI5. He later told reporters: 'I deny emphatically ever signing a document of this type, not only because I lacked the authority, but also because it is written in English, a language which I neither speak nor understand . . . It's an absolute lie and I don't know where it came from.'[12]

The British defence at the inquest relied on the theory that the MI5/SAS team had been caught off guard by the sudden appearance of the three terrorists in Gibraltar. However, journalists had spoken to the Spanish police officers who had followed the car to the border post. The Spanish Interior Ministry also released a communiqué on 9 March 1988 which confirmed this fact. The actions of the British security forces on the day give credence to the idea that they knew exactly what was happening. Special Branch officers were in place by 8 a.m. and the MI5 and SAS teams were *in situ* at noon, just thirty minutes before one of the trio, Sean Savage, crossed the border. The head of the Gibraltar Special Branch told Chief

Inspector Joe Ullger that there was no intention of making an arrest at the border crossing.[13]

At meetings at the MoD and 10 Downing Street the decision was made to commit the SAS special projects team. In Gibraltar a high-level joint force committee, with MI5 steering, worked out the details of the operation with the Commissioner of Police, Joseph Canepa. The ambush was set for the Sunday morning, 6 March. As the terrorist trio entered Gibraltar they were picked up by a Watcher team of MI5/SAS personnel. At 3.40 p.m., Commissioner Canepa handed over control to the SAS. This was the exact time Inspector Joseph Revagliatte, the officer designated in charge of Firearms Team One, arrived at the Shell garage and set off his siren. It was also the precise moment at which the SAS and Revagliatte's Firearms Team began to close in on the suspects. The sudden blare of the siren caused the terrorists to look around – individually, making 'sudden unexplained jerky movements'. Within seconds, the SAS soldiers opened fire. At 3.41 p.m., the three IRA terrorists were dead.[14]

According to James Adams, a post-action analysis of Flavius by MI5 and the SAS concluded that little needed to be changed in either training or operational methods. The Security Service had, according to this account, worked effectively with special forces. Flavius was considered 'a successful operation'.[15]

8

The Gulf War detainees

> Those who are able most effectively to undermine national security are those who least appear to constitute any risk to it.
>
> Lord Donaldson, February 1992

In the first week of January 1991, during the opening rounds of the Gulf War, the British government, in response to Iraqi President Saddam Hussein's threat to 'extend Iraq's battle to the whole world', issued to government departments a 'terror alert'. It was reported that 'British Intelligence believes targets in this country are high on the list'. Officials feared that resident Arabs might well be used to carry out terrorist actions and, in a climate of suspicion, the security services rounded up ninety-one Iraqis and Palestinians for detention and eventual deportation.

What followed would later be described by senior Foreign Office officials as 'the worst intelligence débâcle for years'. Home Secretary Kenneth Baker was said to have been shocked when he discovered the flimsiness of the intelligence on which MI5 had based its case. At the end of the war none of those who contested their deportation orders was subsequently expelled and no one was put on trial. Angry that, following the war, diplomatic relations in the Middle East would inevitably be damaged, the Foreign Office called for an inquiry. Further, it seized the opportunity to claim that MI5 was ill-equipped to deal with international terrorism, a subject which it said was better dealt with by MI6, the service over which it formally exercised ministerial control. Sources suggested that MI6's greater knowledge of the *modus operandi* of Arab terrorist groups might have helped to avoid the blunder.[1]

Over the years there have been a number of similar secret inquiries and, in general, the conclusions and remedies have been identical. A slap on the wrist is delivered to the director-general of MI5 prior to Parliament being informed that management and ministerial control has been tightened and the public being assured that the Security Service is abiding by the directives which govern its operations. Calls for a public inquiry are always rejected in the interests of secrecy and security. That this game is allowed to be played out is an example not only of the British disease of secrecy and the permanent government's desire to avoid the responsibilities of a true democracy, but also of the politicians' ignorance of the intelligence world and contemporary history. Fifty years ago, the British secret state instituted the same system of detention when Churchill demanded that MI5 'Collar the lot'. The same bit players – only their names were different – and identical organisations acted in a similar intelligence débâcle. Within days of the detention of Iraqis and Palestinians an *Independent* editorial referred back to Churchill's policy and said: 'We must avoid repeating such injustices'. Nevertheless, that is exactly what did happen, no one having learned the lessons of history.

At the beginning of the Second World War, during the 'phoney war', a hysterical atmosphere had been generated by sections of the press who created an imaginary 'fifth column'. Even though MI5, in private, was 'very much inclined to doubt' whether a fifth column existed, it fed the Joint Intelligence Committee (JIC) with security reports on German and Austrian subjects, including a list of alleged fascist sympathisers among Italian residents. The subsequent JIC policy of 'panic alien restrictions' and internment was opposed by the Foreign Office, which was concerned that retaliatory action might be taken against British citizens living abroad.[2]

On 27 June 1940, Richard Latham, deputy head of the Foreign Office's refugee section, bitterly denounced the Security Service: 'MI5, charged with the examination of the loyalty of individuals and with investigation of the bona fides of refugees, has adopted the rule of thumb that any person of foreign nationality is to be presumed to be hostile.' There was anger about the arbitrary fashion in which victims of the internment policy were reviewed for release. The procedure had 'complete reliance' upon MI5's own assessments, and the service was able to turn down applications if it felt that release would result in 'immediate or potential danger'. MI5 officers remained immune from questioning about their decisions. Latham wrote that he could not 'stress too strongly the danger of accepting blindly the recommendations of MI5 or even the facts stated in MI5 reports [whose work] discloses a notable incapacity for weighing evidence and a tendency to conceal this incapacity by unnecessary recourse to secrecy'. Latham went on to attack the service's 'stupidity and poor organisation' and 'the lack, in most of the personnel of MI5, of a political background adequate to enable them to judge the cases where evidence is indirect'. MI5 had merely imposed 'arbitrary rules of thumb which led to injustice and chaos'. At the heart of the matter, Latham charged, was MI5's 'secret and largely irresponsible status'.[3]

Criticism reached a peak in July 1940, following the tragic sinking of the *Arandora Star* on its way to Canada packed with internees. Possibly as many as 650 people – Germans, Italians and British – were lost at sea. Harold Farquhar, a Foreign Office Member of the Home Office Aliens Advisory Committee, asked senior MI5 officers Guy Liddell and Jack Curry for an explanation of the selection procedure. They tried to pass the buck, blaming the Home Office, but Farquhar was unconvinced. 'MI5 have no properly constituted dossiers . . . It is with them a question of hit or miss.' At the conclusion of his inquiry into the sinking, Lord Snell reported in secret to the Cabinet on 27 November 1940 that 'among those deported, were a number of men whose sympathies were wholly with this country. I cannot regard this lack of discrimination as satisfactory.' However, he did not consider the errors 'a cause for serious criticism'. In response, Farquhar minuted Foreign

Office colleagues: 'The Whitewash has been laid on very thick.'[4]

Powers of detention without trial are available to the Home Secretary in peacetime. Today, at any one time, over one hundred people – mainly asylum seekers – are held under the 1971 Immigration Act. Those whose cases are deemed to involve 'national security' can be detained and deported under a rarely used section of the Act. In 1988, Palestinian journalist Nasri Hajjaj was deported. The only evidence against him was that he had met with senior members of Sinn Fein, a legally constituted political party. Although the resultant interview was openly published, MI5 claimed that his meeting suggested a link between the Palestinians and the IRA – something which the Home Secretary apparently accepted.

In the run-up to the Gulf War with Iraq, although the press never engaged in the hysteria which had been prevalent in 1940, it did help to set the scene for the disastrous policy of detention and deportation by its assessment of a likely terrorist response from Iraq's President Saddam Hussein. Stories abounded about possible terrorist actions. The *Sunday Times* reported that 'Intelligence units fear that terrorists could use biological weapons, perhaps even poisoning a city's water supply.' However, the same report revealed that five months of intensive surveillance by the intelligence services had 'produced little of value' with 'few signs that dozens of terrorists have infiltrated Europe'.[5]

In the *Sunday Telegraph* Christopher and Valerie Elliott – who, as did James Adams of the *Sunday Times*, appeared to have remarkable security service sources denied to other journalists – informed readers that 'MI5, MI6 and Special Branch have started a bout of activity greater than at almost any time during the Cold War. Their work is co-ordinated by Sir Percy Cradock, chairman of the Joint Intelligence Committee, through the Cabinet Office, and is the backbone for Cabinet threat assessment.' A former experienced Foreign Office diplomat, Cradock had been appointed by Mrs Thatcher as her personal representative on the JIC in 1988, before becoming chair. Special Branch and MI5 were ordered to step up their surveillance and monitoring of Iraqis and Palestinians. As 'a precaution' the Home Office expelled eight Iraqi diplomats and sixty-seven other Iraqis living in Britain, even though there was no evidence 'that attacks were being planned'. This was described by one official as 'a very useful pre-emptive strike'.[6]

Prime targets of the expected terrorist campaign were believed to be commercial airliners, and security was intensified at all major British airports. Armed police were seen for the first time at the regional airports, while troops in armoured cars patrolled Heathrow. Another addition to the intelligence community, the newly expanded Security Inspectorate (SI), extended its monitoring of airport and maritime security. The number of inspectors was quickly increased from five to sixteen. These included former detectives, Customs officials and Army personnel from the Intelligence Corps, who are trained to test out security arrangements, sometimes carrying replica guns and radios stuffed with imitation plastic explosive. A new post of Chief Inspector, with responsibility to the Transport Secretary, was appointed in 1990 in the wake of the bombing of the Pan Am aircraft over Lockerbie. The first Chief Inspector, Hal Doyne Ditmass, was a former senior MI5 officer who had served in Washington in the early sixties, liaising with the CIA and FBI. Doyne Ditmass had extensive experience of counter-espionage as a case officer in the old D Branch and was a veteran of A Branch's Movement Analysis which involved computerising the Watchers' records of the movements of KGB officers stationed in London. Before retiring from the service he had been in 1985 Director and Co-ordinator of Intelligence (DCI) in Northern Ireland, where he was responsible for introducing Movement Analysis to the battle against the IRA. He was awarded a CB in the 1988 Queen's birthday honours list.[7]

From the start of the security operation, Home Office

sources emphasised that the deportation orders had been served only on those who presented a genuine risk to national security and that it was not internment by another name. Security sources insisted that the detentions were 'intended to avert terrorism, were selective and precise and that all those detained were "either activists or sleepers"'. Detainees were given a pro forma letter from the Home Office stating that a decision had been made to detain them pending deportation under the 1971 Immigration Act. 'The reasons for the Secretary of State's action [are] national security . . . and your known links with an organisation which we believe could take terrorist action in support of the Iraqi regime makes your presence in the UK an unacceptable security risk.' Other Whitehall sources said that the detention operation was 'a panic reaction' based on 'speculative accusations' of links with terrorist organisations. MI5 acted 'on the hoof', basing its judgements on 'third-rate intelligence'. The Home Office had just accepted the recommendations of MI5, according to one civil servant, because 'there was no one to blow the whistle'.[8]

The list of ninety-one Arabs regarded as potential terrorists had been drawn up by three MI5 middle-ranking F Branch officers working with outdated files from the Arab section of the Registry. Much of the information went back nearly twenty years, some supplied by the Special Branch. A section of twelve Special Branch officers keeps permanent watch on Iranians, Iraqis, Palestinians and Libyans, relying heavily on contacts with MI5 and political exiles living in the United Kingdom. According to sources, libraries have been used by Branch officers to trace the ideological interests of Arab students. The Branch had supplied MI5 with gossip from its sources on university campuses and from surveillance of pro-Iraqi demonstrations. This included details on students who had been coerced to take part by the Iraqi embassy. Security sources admitted that none of those detained was guilty of any acts of terrorism. They came under suspicion because of a distant relation connected with terrorist activities or past associations with 'clubs' or 'societies' regarded as 'suspect'. No guns or bomb-making equipment were ever discovered, nor were the suspects' homes searched.[9]

While the use of guilt by association and lack of hard evidence were an abuse of civil liberties, neither constituted a breach of MI5 guidelines. Foreign Secretary Douglas Hurd, who was at the forefront of criticism of MI5's intelligence operation against detainees, had, when Home Secretary in 1985, revealed that government grant aid was refused to a number of seemingly innocuous community and voluntary groups in Northern Ireland because they were suspect. They were deemed to have 'sufficiently close links with [terrorist] organisations to give rise to a grave risk that to give support to those groups would have the effect of improving the standing or furthering the aims of a [terrorist] organisation'.[10]

The detention operation also involved the imprisonment of a number of Iraqi students as prisoners of war. Thirty-five prisoners of war were held at Rollestone military prison camp on Salisbury Plain, behind two perimeter fences of barbed wire guarded by one hundred armed troops from the Devonshire and Dorset Regiment. The inner compound where the Iraqis were held was dubbed 'the cage' by soldiers. The camp had been set up under royal prerogative powers to detain 'enemy aliens'. However, as a solicitor for the students said in preparing her case for the High Court, there had been 'no royal proclamation, no order in council and no emergency legislation passed by Parliament. The only justification for this behaviour is a First World War court case which ruled that a German civilian could be treated as a PoW because all Germans were dastardly and could not be trusted.' A further thirty-three Iraqis were held in Full Sutton jail, near York.[11]

The Home Office refused to explain why the Iraqis had been classified as PoWs, but leaks to the Elliotts at the *Sunday Telegraph* provided a security justification for the operation. 'One of the men detained was the head of the British-based branch of the Iraqi secret police, the Mukhabrat. He had enrolled as a student but was pursuing activities from a pair of houses in West London.' An Anti-Terrorist Squad officer claimed that Abu Nidal terrorists might be recruiting Iraqi students to carry out bombing or assassinations. A week later, again according to their 'intelligence sources', the Elliotts revealed that 'a number of foreign nationals detained . . . were attempting to arrange arms shipments to Iraq. Those involved were linked to the Iraqi military but posed in Britain as having abandoned such connections.' The *Sunday Telegraph* claimed that 'intelligence information against the thirty-five prisoners of war is considered hard'. It was based on 'a list held by a Iraqi military attaché which was obtained by MI5'. It was later disclosed that the list, which contained the names of thirty-three PhD students studying in Britain, had been sent to the Bank of England in October 1990. It had been passed on by the Bank, where an official liaises with the security services, to MI5. It soon became clear that the students had no military connections but had been merely trying to ensure that they continued to receive funds while Baghdad's assets were frozen. That the grants had been administered by the military attaché at the Iraqi embassy was enough for MI5 to treat all thirty-three as military personnel.[12]

At an emergency meeting of the Trevi group of European security ministers (see chapter 14 for the background of Trevi) in Luxembourg on 22 January 1991, an exchange of information between security agencies was agreed. This exchange allegedly revealed that the countries were dealing with terrorist 'networks'. 'If we get a few in one country, we get more in another,' said a security source. The Germans were anxious that former members of the East German Stasi might be involved with Middle East terrorist groups. It was also feared that Palestinian groups might be using terrorist groups based in Europe for operations. The security ministers agreed to a tightening of border controls, focusing on what were seen as the 'softer' countries, Italy and Greece and based on fears expressed by Home Secretary Kenneth Baker that these countries 'might find difficulty in screening out potential terrorists'. Although no country except Britain set up a similar system of detention, there was a massive security operation throughout the European Community. Greece did deport twenty suspected Iraqi-sponsored terrorists, and in Italy seven Iraqis were expelled for 'irregular activities', while two hundred Iraqi navy personnel were interned on board their warships. Germany carried out raids on the homes of a number of Arabs, and a French operation called Vigipirate included searching 10,000 cars on the Franco-Belgian border. The head of the Dutch security service later called the Trevi-organised Europe-wide initiative 'the biggest security operation since World War Two'. Britain, it was admitted, had been at the forefront of the security arrangements and the hard-line policy of detention.[13]

On 20 January, two days before the Trevi meeting, the *Sunday Telegraph* referred to 'seven Palestinians' being expelled and reported that the intent of the operation was 'to nip plots in the bud'. Although there was 'cautious optimism that the Iraqis have little capacity for mainland terrorism . . . acts by surrogates and by terrorist organisations such as Abu Abbas [Palestinian Liberation Organisation] cannot be ruled out'. Even a responsible paper, the *Independent*, was willing to publish dubious information: 'Police have smashed a Palestinian terrorist network planning attacks on . . . British targets.' It alleged that 'Detailed plans were discovered last week by German police when they arrested four men in raids on dozens of houses in Berlin. Seized documents described plans to carry out the attacks on allied targets demanded by Saddam Hussein . . . it is understood the German discovery led to the arrest of seven Palestinians . . . in London.' Under agreements made by the Trevi group, German security has responsibility for collating intelligence on Arab terrorist suspects in the EC and this would have been passed on to MI5. However, while the *Sunday Times* reported that the raids by German security on the homes of Arab radicals had 'produced no new information', other newspapers reported allegations from 'intelligence sources' which claimed that those arrested 'have links with Middle East groups. One is related to Abu Nidal, one of the most notorious terrorist leaders.' The German head of the Institute for Terrorist Research and former director of the Hamburg office of Germany's internal security agency the BfV (Verfassungsschutz – Protection of the Constitution), Hans Horchem, helped kindle terrorist mania when he warned that 'over one thousand Iraqi hitmen lurked in every corner of Europe'.[14]

One of those detained on 17 January on grounds of 'national security' was forty-seven-year-old Abbas Sheblak, a part-time researcher at Kingston Polytechnic and senior information officer at the Arab League. He had lived in London for the previous sixteen years and the week before his arrest was advised by the Home Office that his British citizenship papers were being processed. Like other Palestinians in Pentonville prison, Sheblak was opposed to Saddam and was a member of the anti-Saddam Arab Human Rights Committee. 'For the first two days we had not even an inkling of what lay behind our detention. But on the third day we read a leak to the newspapers that the security services had broken a cell of seven Palestinian terrorists planning bomb attacks in Europe. I realised suddenly that we were these seven.'[15]

Another detained Palestinian, opposed to Saddam Hussein and terrorism, was computor salesman Ali el-Saleh. He had lived in Britain for twenty-one years and had been granted permanent residence. The 'detailed information' used against him failed to include the existence of his two children. His only known political activity had been his presidency of the moderate General Union of Palestinian Students in 1971–5. His wife, who was also on the list of those to be detained, until the discovery of the children, was allowed to report to her nearest police station. 'If they think I'm a terrorist, then why do they let me move about? If they thought Ali was a terrorist why did they give us permanent residence in this country and British travel documents?' The intelligence against el-Saleh was out of date and the main 'link' appeared to be a false accusation from the Jordanian government that he had been a member of the People's Front for the Liberation of Palestine. A Home Office source confirmed that the reason for his detention was that his 'wife's sister's husband's uncle was the terrorist Abu Nidal'. Sheblak also learned that the Home Office considered that he was in some way connected to Nidal.[16]

A third Palestinian, known as Mr 'B', was detained because he was the nephew of the 'infamous terrorist' Abu Nidal, leader of the Fatah Revolutionary Council. The thirty-one-year-old married engineer had met Nidal once at a family meeting in the Lebanon in 1976 but had already disowned him following the death of his parents. Information from Jordanian intelligence appeared to be the basis of the accusations against him. Mr B came to Britain in 1977 and 'was gradually able to put the past behind him', said his wife. 'He now sees his past coming back to haunt him . . . he sees the prospect of being persecuted for the rest of his life because of an accident of birth.' All three Palestinians had on entering the country been vetted by the security services before they were allowed to stay.[17]

Justice Simon Brown gave Mr 'B' leave for judicial review, saying there was 'an urgent need to decide whether this is internment by the back door or a proper use of powers by the Secretary of State'. However, the court's willingness to defend citizens' rights soon crumpled in the face of the national security question. Justice Simon Brown in effect washed his hands of Mr Sheblak. Having slept on the matter overnight, the next day he refused an application by Mr Sheblak, saying he had 'erred' the previous day and that the challenge was 'misconceived'; he now thought that the Home Office's claim of a national security risk did not require elaboration. A letter read out in court, but not available to Mr Sheblak or his lawyer, revealed the reasons for his deportation. Mr Sheblak had 'known links with an organisation' which might, in the present circumstances, take terrorist action against 'unspecified Western targets', which made him an 'unacceptable security risk'. Mr Sheblak denied having any links with anything remotely resembling a terrorist organisation and was told by the judge that it was 'manifestly more appropriate' for detainees to challenge deportation notices by appealing to the Home Office appointed advisory panel set up for that purpose.[18]

The 1968 Wilson Committee on Immigration Procedures recommended that 'security' deportations should not be exempt from the fundamental principle that 'any administrative decision should be subject to scrutiny and appeal before execution.' However, under the 1971 Immigration Act there is no right of appeal 'against a decision to make a deportation order . . . if the ground of the decision was . . . in the interests of national security'. Instead, detainees were allowed to appear before a Home Office advisory panel, the members of which had been appointed by the Home Secretary. The 'three wise men' system was set up by Home Secretary Reginald Maudling in 1971; it was not until 1977 that it came to prominence over the deportation 'in the interests of national security' of American radical journalist Mark Hosenball and CIA defector Philip Agee. Panel members were also known as the 'three blind mice' because its pretence at any kind of justice was a disgrace.

The 1991 panel included Lord Justice Lloyd, who had worked with MI5 as a member of the Security Commission since 1985 and as the commissioner responsible for monitoring the Interception of Communications Act, and was said by security sources to enjoy a relationship of 'mutual admiration' with them. The second member, Sir Robert Andrew, Northern Ireland Permanent Secretary until 1989, served in intelligence before joining the Ministry of Defence in 1963, where he rose to become assistant secretary. At the Home Office as deputy secretary he was responsible for the department which administers detention and deportation orders and had acted as liaison with MI5. The third member, David Neve, a former chair of the Immigration Appeals Tribunal, was described by those who had experience of the panel as 'a bit dour' and 'not very sympathetic at all'.

The hearings wereheld in camera and legal representatives were barred, though detainees could be assisted by a 'friend'. Despite the Wilson Committee's recommendation that 'there could be no question of withholding from the appellant particulars of what is alleged against him', that is in fact what happened. Home Office lawyers defended the procedure on the basis that the allegations supplied by MI5 against the detainees could not be detailed, so as not to compromise the sources. It would be too dangerous even to say with which organisation a person had connections. Detainees faced McCarthyite questioning about their political views on the Gulf War, the United States of America, Iraq and members of the Iraqi Ba'ath Party. Some of the questioning suggested that Israel's intelligence agency, Mossad, had supplied information to the British authorities, a view confirmed by the BBC's Paul Reynolds, who was told that Israeli intelligence might be getting its own back against moderate Palestinians. The questions were often angled from a preconceived view that the accused belonged to organisations which advocated violence. At the end of the process, the recommendations of the panel were merely advisory ones which the Home Secretary could choose to ignore. Andrew Puddephatt, general secretary of the civil rights organisation Liberty, said the hearings highlighted the dangers inherent in the British state's attitude to national security. 'Much of our legislation uses this term as a blanket justification for the suppression of human rights.'[19]

Even so, the panel found that the majority of detainees posed no threat to national security. On 8 March 1991, the Home Secretary announced that there would be no more deportations. A number of those detained were later recognised as Iraqi dissidents and given refugee status by the Home

Office. Discomfort in Whitehall was acute when a number of those wrongly detained threatened legal action to seek compensation for wrongful imprisonment. The Foreign Office was said to be 'furious at the Home Office round-up'. The Home Secretary, Kenneth Baker, came under pressure in the Cabinet from Foreign Secretary Douglas Hurd, who said that the irresponsible manner of the detentions was damaging Britain's reputation abroad. (One of the detained Palestinians, Abbas Sheblak, was well known to Hurd.) Diplomats claimed that Britain risked 'losing the peace' after the Gulf War and that 'the last thing Britain needs in this crisis is to be seen as an Arab-hater'. The Home Office had disregarded Foreign Office objections because 'the Foreign Office is always being accused of consisting of a bunch of Arab-lovers'.[20]

The Home Office began a top-level internal inquiry under Sir Philip Woodfield, who in 1987 had been appointed Staff Counsellor for the security and intelligence services. The inquiry's brief included examining the whole process of deportations planned on security grounds, with special reference to those deemed to be security risks. It also looked at the work of the 'three wise men'. Once again, an inquiry into an MI5 intelligence blunder was to be kept in-house. MI5 had shown an extraordinary ineptitude in assessing the evidence, while the Home Secretary and his officials had ridden rough-shod over suspects' rights. Turning a blind eye to this abuse of power, when the injustice was exposed, MI5 sought protection behind the traditional veil of secrecy.

In 1940, Foreign Office official Richard Latham had lambasted MI5 because of its 'incapacity for weighing evidence', the use of 'arbitrary rules of thumb which led to injustice and chaos', and 'stupidity'. At the heart of the matter, Latham claimed, was 'a tendency to conceal the blunders by unnecessary recourse to secrecy'. Latham joined the RAF and was shot down in 1943, not living to see MI5 confirm once more its record of incompetence and unprofessionalism in vetting internees. When he delivered his report to the Home Secretary in

December 1991, Sir Philip Woodfield cleared the Security Service, accepting MI5 'arguments that it was right to err on the side of caution' when drawing up lists of suspects. He decided that Special Branch and MI5 should not be condemned. Once again, the whitewash had been laid on thick.

A few weeks later it was revealed that news of one of the detained, Abbas Sheblak, had been reported in a London-based Saudi newspaper during the Gulf War. The paper had wrongly suggested that Sheblak was a terrorist and supporter of Iraq. Using the newspaper report as evidence, shortly after Kuwait was liberated the Kuwaitis executed a man named Sheblak whom they accused of collaboration with Iraq. This man was a distant relative of Abbas Sheblak. MI5's cavalier use of outdated information had led to the death of a totally innocent man.[21]

9

Stella Rimington

> She was a tall, big-boned woman with a surprisingly quiet voice and a slight, almost undefined lisp that some men found very appealing. In the tough and masculine world in which she had competed and won, she had sacrificed femininity for function . . . She had an outstanding brain, fast and analytical.
>
> James Adams, *The Final Terror*

In February 1992, a woman was appointed director-general of MI5, the first female head in its eighty-three-year history and the first of any major security and intelligence organisation in the world. Much to the surprise of Home Office officials the appointment, which normally warrants a small article in the quality newspapers, attracted a great deal of interest in the tabloid press. Although the media were encouraged that, for the first time, the appointment of a new head had been officially announced in a press release, little information was forthcoming. Journalists were left to scratch around for the thin profiles of Stella Rimington which appeared in the newspapers. It was hardly the policy of glasnost.

In the former communist countries of Eastern Europe, journalists are used to a greater openness in covering the activities of the security services; it is now possible to telephone the press office of the KGB, for example. Such openness does not prevail in Britain, nor should we expect it. A Home Office spokesperson from F6 Division, which administers the 1989 Security Service Act, explained that the naming of Mrs Rimington was merely due to the fact that MI5 had been put on a statutory basis by the Act and this was therefore in line with the service's changed status. Her naming seemed to be simply another symbolic gesture of openness, rather than any genuine willingness to make the service accountable – a typical Whitehall tactic which lets as little light into the secret world as possible, while brushing aside the need for accountability and oversight. When asked what the chances were of a television documentary being made about MI5, a Home Office spokesperson said: 'It wouldn't get very far . . . The status quo hasn't changed.' She had been inundated with requests for interviews with Stella Rimington but none had been granted.[1]

On her appointment, Stella Rimington released her own statement which, while welcome, was far from illuminating: 'Despite the changes which have taken place in the world in recent years, the service continues to have a difficult job to do. I am very pleased to have been given the responsibility of leading the service in facing up to the challenges which the coming years will bring.' It fell far short of the confirmation process which citizens might expect in a democracy, for a post which carries such heavy responsibilities and deals with the sharp end of civil liberties. She did not have to submit to questioning by democratic representatives, as did Robert Gates, before Senators, when appointed director of the CIA. A taxpayer might also like to know more about a post with the rank of second permanent secretary which carries a salary of £77,500. Home Secretary Kenneth Baker declined to meet MPs to discuss Mrs Rimington's appointment and responsibilities, informing them that he had no intention of departing from tradition by revealing the budget and payroll of MI5. Although he had sponsored a Freedom of Information Bill in 1979, Baker said these matters were 'closely associated with the Security Service's operations which must remain secret'.[2]

Stella Rimington's promotion was a clever but glib move by the Home Secretary, for the appointment appeared to implement the Prime Minister's dormant policy of enhancing the role of women in society. A man with a self-confessed 'pretty thick skin', Baker was often to be seen exuding confidence in the face of more bad news. At fifty-nine, Baker was lucky still to be in the Cabinet after what a Whitehall source called 'a year of unmitigated horrors'. (He was replaced following the 1992 general election.) Background leaks gave substance to the view that Rimington had been promoted purely on merit, but that was only partly true. In reality, MI5 lacked a generation of high-quality senior officers from which to choose a new head. A number had been passed over because of their part in the Bettaney débâcle. John Deverall had to be content with a CB in the 1992 honours list, a reward for his role as deputy director.

The many women in the service, some of whom have risen to top posts as heads of Branches, have, in the main, achieved this distinction on merit. There are a small group of highly competent women officers within the service, among them MI5's former security liaison officer in Washington, a graduate of Lady Margaret Hall, Oxford, Elizabeth Manningham-Buller. It is clear, however, that the service's failure to recruit high-flyers has acted as a form of unofficial positive discrimination. While employment policies and habits for top jobs actively discriminate against women, even during the recession men have sought higher salaries and better promotion prospects in the City. Stella Rimington's success was a sign of the deep problems facing the Security Service.[3]

Stella Whitehouse was born in 1935 in Croydon, the daughter of a mechanical engineer. Her family moved to the Midlands, where she attended Nottingham High School. Little is known of her school and university days, as the 'weeders' have been busy taking out photographs and records from the files. Not among the academic élite, she fluffed her interview for Oxford and graduated from Edinburgh University in 1958 with a second-class degree in English. In 1959, she moved to Liverpool, where she trained as an archivist, an occupation which stood her in good stead for her intelligence-gathering activities. Four years later, aged twenty-eight, Stella married John Rimington, a contemporary at Nottingham, who worked for the old Board of Trade. After a period abroad in India, she joined the Security Service in 1969 as an executive high-flyer.[4]

Like all new Fast Stream Entrants to the service, Stella Rimington began her career in F Branch, monitoring the activities of political subversives. Within the first five years of her career she had two daughters, though motherhood did little to hinder her prospects. She quickly gained a reputation as an astute political researcher and analyst who was 'very efficient' and able to 'get the job done'. For a period, she worked on Northern Ireland; although not a field operative, she did in later years make occasional visits to the province. In F5 she worked closely with Military Intelligence, collating and analysing the data collected on Irish terrorism. She was not a specialist, but gained 'wide experience in all areas' of the service's brief.[5]

Meanwhile, her husband had been appointed director-general of the Health and Safety Executive in 1984. Mrs Rimington was known to be ambitious and was willing to work all hours regardless of domestic commitments. When a photograph of her was published in the left-wing magazine *New Statesman* in December of that year, she was so taken aback by this breach of security that the family were forced to move house. This strained an already fragile marriage and the couple separated in 1986, though they remain 'excellent friends' and have not divorced. Did the Home Secretary ask Ms Rimington about her marital arrangements? When Percy Sillitoe became director-general, Prime Minister Clement Attlee warned him that 'under no circumstances should he commit himself to discussions with his wife on secret matters'. In fact, Sillitoe frequently ignored this demand and his wife 'went to her grave knowing a lot of top secret disclosures'.[6]

Although described in the newspapers as not being 'a hard-liner' Stella Rimington's career record belies that description. In 1984, as head of F2, which is responsible for monitoring trade unions, she played a key role in the miners' strike. This was an important and influential post in that she was responsible for the collation and distribution of the Box 500 reports which are circulated weekly to key ministers. Any material which has been obtained illegally is excluded and given extra security to protect MI5 from discovery. 'During the years Ms Rimington has been with MI5 they have stumbled from one disaster to another. And she was party to some of those decisions such as bugging CND members and Union leaders. And all the time we were haemorrhaging secrets.' In the mid-eighties, Ms Rimington was promoted to the influential post of director of K Branch and then, in 1989, after the bombing of the Deal barracks, head of counter-terrorism, dealing with the IRA as well as Arab terrorism in the UK. She was said by a colleague to have 'a dramatic ability to read the terrorists' intentions and second-guess them.' In 1990, she was appointed senior deputy director-general, working closely with Sir Patrick Walker on the fifth floor of MI5's Gower Street headquarters.[7]

Although she has been described as 'a person with very little personal charm', a former colleague knew Stella Rimington, who was referred to as 'Mrs R' inside the service, as a 'smashing person with a formidable grasp of her work'. Another officer said she was 'a person of incredibly clear brain, very broad and imaginative, very incisive in argument and extremely quick to pick up the weak point in anybody else's argument – extremely good in committee'. The assessment of her as 'a good organiser and administrator' appealed to her Civil Service supporters within the Home Office. Her brief as director-general is to provide value for money from the recently increased budget, which is between £300 and £500 million per annum. She is also to put a stop to some of MI5's maverick activities and repair the damaged relationships with other agencies. However, insiders claim that she is still surrounded by 'less able hardliners'.[8]

A civil servant who had contact with the service in recent years described MI5 as 'a dinosaur filled with yesterday's men [and women] beavering away at nothing very much'. A vigorous public relations campaign conducted over the past couple of years has tried to counter that notion, presenting MI5 as a service in tune with the needs of the nineties.[9]

Journalist James Adams, a regular recipient of Home Office and MoD handouts and unattributable briefings, suggested in a puff piece in the *Sunday Times* that the old-boy network centred on the gentlemen's clubs of London, which had dominated the Security Service, had given way to a much more cosmopolitan influx which better approximated the social mix of contemporary Britain. He illustrated the different atmosphere at Gower Street by referring to the changes that had taken place in the fifth-floor executive dining room. It now employs a female Cordon Bleu chef who has taken off the menu the steak and kidney pie beloved of the public school men and replaced it with quiche and salad for the new Young Turks. It is true that policy changes on recruitment have helped to draw in a wider cross-section of the British populace, with the net widened as officers are taken increasingly from the red-brick universities and less often from Oxford and Cambridge. However, MI5 PR exercises should not obscure the fact that the service has arrived at its present composition more by default than design.[10]

There has, over the last decade, been a decline in the idea of public service in the security services. *Spycatcher* and other security scandals have put paid to much patriotic zeal and, with the end of the Cold War, the moral basis of the profession has to some extent disappeared. The insider's view of 'that mediocre world' in the novels of John le Carré and the caustic revelations under his real name David Cornwell destroyed any lingering romanticism: 'Our senior officers hated each other for reasons we were not allowed to know. They hated our sister service even more.' MI5 was a service where 'everyone seemed to smell of failure . . . Great ability rubbed shoulders with breathtaking incompetence and when you were new you never knew which to expect.' No longer is there the allure of secrecy, while the image of James Bond appears outdated and morally reprehensible. As one careers officer put it, 'How they get anyone at all to join up now is a mystery to me.' Recognising this to be the case, Patrick Walker called in an outside management consultancy agency to advise MI5 on where it would be going in the nineties and to help present a better image to the world.[11]

Throughout the last ten years, MI5 has suffered problems of recruitment. There are applicants and it is easy to fill posts, but the calibre of recruits is not there for a sophisticated modern service increasingly reliant on computers for assessment. In the seventies, John Grayburn, who went on to head K5 which was responsible for Soviet bloc and Chinese agent recruitment, and another officer, Christopher Saunders, had been recruiters at Oxford. 'They wanted intelligent people. You had to have at least a 2:1,' according to a female officer who joined straight from university. On-the-nod recruitment still goes on at Oxbridge by well-placed dons; however, there appears to be a decline, as top graduates go into better-paid professions rather than consider intelligence work. MI5 no longer attracts the academic high-flyers. Although all recruits are graduates they tend to have average or poor degrees. A career in the Security Service is usually considered only after all other avenues have been closed. Michael Bettaney failed the Home Civil Service exam but was considered good enough for MI5.[12]

In the early eighties, Robert Holden, head of the personnel department, B Branch, and Keith Thomas, responsible for recruitment through B1, and a former deputy head of F Branch, extended the reach of recruitment by cultivating contacts in the careers advisory boards of the red-brick universities. The careers officers are occasionally invited to seminars at MI5 headquarters, where they are told what the service is seeking. However, they complain that obsessive secrecy means they are never given a clear idea of the service's needs: 'To be honest I know more about what the student might end up doing by reading what is written about it than by listening to these people. They just talk about the fact that they need people to analyse information. I am just left with a vision of people sitting in small rooms looking through piles of files. It all sounds even more bureaucratic than other bureaucracies.'[13]

In 1989, before the recession blighted graduate employment, universities reported 'almost no interest at all' in the security services. It had been the same for three or four years. The alternative for MI5 was to make do with the second-rate. A number of recruits have been former policemen or Special Branch officers and members of the armed forces. 'Loyal and effective though they may be, brainpower is not necessarily their strong suit.' This prompted Walker to engage the services of a private employment agency – rumoured to have been Saxon Bamfylde – to advise him on recruitment policy.[14]

The service also tried securing the right calibre of recruit by indirect advertising. In March 1983, the secretary of the Association of County Councils wrote to chief executives asking for candidates for a career in 'an unspecified branch of the Civil Service'. The post might include 'one or two accompanied tours of duty in Northern Ireland or outside the United Kingdom'. Details were sought on people aged between twenty-eight and thirty-six with an honours degree 'who find themselves blocked for promotion'. They were to be articulate and literate with an analytical and questioning mind. The job would require 'unusual persistence and attention to detail and the ability to mix well with men and women of all kinds and backgrounds'. Written before the arrest of Michael Bettaney, the letter revealed that 'immaturity or tendency to emotional instability are key disqualifying factors'. Those employed by the security services are classed by psychologists as loners of the 'stable introvert' type.[15]

During 1989, discreet and disguised advertisements were placed in the national press by a head-hunting firm trying to attract top-class lawyers. The new Security Service Act required that MI5's legal department under its new head, David Bickford, should handle actions expected under the Act. The service also needs lawyers to deal with operational problems concerning such things as illegal entry. The firm agreed to absolute secrecy and was asked not to name the client in advertisements or the initial interviews. Lawyers with an aptitude for 'logical and lateral thinking' were offered an initial £30,000 starting salary. One thirty-two-year-old applicant was told that the job would involve working for the Ministry of Defence on the new official secrets legislation. 'I soon realised who my real employers would be.' Asked 'a lot of questions about my background and family', he also sat an intelligence test described as 'about eleven-plus standard'.[16]

On receipt of an invitation from the MoD, suitable applicants for the fifteen annual vacancies attend a preliminary interview at 14–17 Great Marlborough Street, a bland sixties building. The hour-long discussion with the head of personnel and another senior member of MI5 centred, in the mid-eighties, on events in the news and current government policy. This included their attitude towards Arthur Scargill, the miners' leader, the Labour MP Tony Benn and the deployment of Trident. Today it might include attitudes on Ireland, the Gulf War and animal rights. At no stage are candidates given a hint about the nature of the work. At a second interview at MI5 headquarters in Gower Street, the applicant is positively vetted by officers – mostly with armed service backgrounds and entrenched conservative views and values – with detailed questioning on their background and lifestyle, including sexual history and orientation. The process known as EPV also entails checks against records, credit checks and interviews with those who know the individual. Successful entrants have to have British parents and grandparents. Having relatives inside the service also helps and is usually a guarantee of success in the vetting process. Entrants no longer have to suffer the indignity of the polygraph. The machines, which Washington security liason officer Martin Flint brought back from the United States manufacturers, Stoelting, in 1983, proved to be totally ineffective for security screening on the eighty-five staff who were tested.[17]

Former MI5 officer David Cornwell has written that 'the secret world I went into, and which served as a metaphor for the last bit of our history, was a man's world and infused with that homosexuality which is peculiarly English and regimental.' He adds that 'the Cold War was an all-male party'. Although homosexuals were banned from intelligence work because of the risk of blackmail, they were tolerated, unless they became entangled in an embarrassing incident. However, homosexual relationships had been officially treated as an absolute bar to positive vetting (PV) clearance. In 1988, a twenty-two-year-old data processor at GCHQ, Andrew Hodges, was suspended after openly admitting he was a homosexual. This was rather bizarre and tragic given that a senior MoD official agreed in 1983 that 'the crucial element is the desire to conceal . . . that is what makes a man blackmailable'.[18]

During 1990, the issue was brought to the fore by a number of senior civil servants who, having openly declared their homosexuality, were denied PV clearance and promotion. The government decided to lift the automatic ban on homosexuals serving in the security services 'in the light of changing social attitudes'. MI5 recognised that concealment made people more vulnerable to blackmail, and admission of homosexuality at a security vetting was no longer made a bar to access to highly classified material. However, the government's new policy outlined in an August 1991 confidential memorandum, 'Homosexuality and Security Vetting', contained a catch-22. Having been encouraged to 'come out' for the sake of honesty and openness, officers have been warned that they may still be sacked for 'past deliberate falsehoods and untrustworthiness'. This will be tested by the 'extent to which an officer is open about his or her sexuality, lifestyle and relationships'. There are as yet no recorded instances of MI5 officers disclosing their sexual orientation since the lifting of the ban.[19]

In recent years, MI5 has heavily recruited women, motivated not by desire for equality of the sexes but by sheer need. Many men have been unwilling to do what new recruits soon discover is a mind-numbingly dull and routine job, consisting of sifting scraps of information, communications, surveillance reports and newspaper clippings, trying to spot interesting developments and changes in patterns. Although salaries were raised to a decent level under the Duff reforms, there is still much grumbling. Promotion prospects, with the three basic grades of officer, senior and director, are limited and bright people are still likely to be more attracted to better-paid jobs in the City, commerce and academia.

Britain's traditional seats of power remain stubbornly male-dominated. Fewer than one in two hundred senior board directors are women. Body Shop's Anita Roddick is the only female managing director out of the 1,300 quoted companies. Until recently, the all-male Cabinet set the trend for board-rooms everywhere. *Crawford's Directory of City Connections* for 1992 noted that women's success in climbing to the top in the limited areas where they do, seems to be largely confined to 'female areas'. That, it would seem, now includes the Security Service. Out of the 2,300 personnel in MI5 (1500 in administration), more than 50 per cent are aged under thirty, and more than half of those are women. As with a number of other professions such as the probation service and the social services, the percentage of women could grow even further as men seek better prospects elsewhere.

Before the war and for a time after, upper-crust males occupied most of the best jobs in MI5, recruited by personal recommendation and invitation. People tended to invite people similar to themselves; the class system, therefore, operated within the service and was obeyed on all levels. 'The people at the top', recalled Peter Wright, 'all suffered from the extraordinary belief that the upper classes were trustworthy in matters of security and the lower classes were not . . . the received wisdom was that their own sort was loyal and that everybody else was potentially disloyal.' In wartime, by necessity, the rules were different and a number of people entered on merit, but these recruits tended to leave once peace was secured. It was only much later that officers were recruited because they had specific skills. 'It was an upper-class club,' claimed a former female officer. 'And I hated it.' The service remained until very recently a male-dominated organisation with special ties and cufflinks. 'Nothing female,' recalled the officer. 'I can remember being annoyed about that on principle.'[20]

It took longer for women to be put on an equal footing. Many upper-class females were recruited to work in the Registry and were known as the 'Registry Queens'. They were often friends of members of the personnel department, who 'tended to know this sort of girl. None of these girls needed a job. They were all just filling in time before getting married and becoming Lady So-and-So . . . Cynics said that girls rarely lasted more than nine months in the Registry.' In contrast, those given the more responsible jobs were middle-class women with specific skills, who secured the post on merit. According to Peter Wright, there were two sorts of women who joined the service, 'chorus girls and nuns'. 'The former flitted around the edge, never really becoming involved at all, while the latter dedicated their lives to it a way few men would do.' The 'nuns' were easily spotted since they 'wore sensible shoes and spoke in strong, measured tones'. A high percentage of those who have made it to the top have either been unmarried or divorced. It appears that little has changed from the days when David Cornwell was an MI5 officer. 'Institutional loyalty of the kind they cling to really precludes the absolute love that, particularly in middle age, they begin to look for. Success in love – I don't think the British believe in that at all, really. Certainly not the administrative classes.'[21]

Women have traditionally been posted to dull but essential secretarial work and the transcription of telephone tappings. The secretaries were mostly recruited from upper-class families as a matter of policy. Vernon Kell, the longest-serving director-general, is alleged to have said, 'I want all my girls to be well bred and have good legs.' They were not regarded as security risks, though Chapman Pincher has claimed that many of his scoops came from titbits given to him by secretaries in MI5. In the early seventies, women officers rebelled against the poor pay and conditions of service. A delegation made representations to the director-general about discriminatory practices. In 1975, women in the Intelligence Corps were integrated into the career structure on an equal footing with men. Inside MI5 women are increasingly employed as information processors in the computer-led service where they compile and cross-reference in minute detail the mass of data which the service collects. This is now the main occupation of officers. One estimate suggests that it constitutes 90 per cent of the work in counter-intelligence. 'This may explain why MI5 has been so keen on women, perhaps believing they have the patience to listen to interminable conversations between insignificant trade unionists.'[22]

Male commentators have suggested that women are more psychologically suited to intelligence work than men, being better able to cope with life in the secret world. This seems to be the same kind of nonsense which previously excluded women from senior positions. Stress is endemic to intelligence work and gender seems to be no barrier to its effects. A study among Home Office executive officer civil servants found that women were increasing their consumption of alcohol faster than their male colleagues. Particularly vulnerable were single women in stressful jobs.[23]

As part of the graduate training programme, new recruits spend time at the Government Communications Headquarters (GCHQ) at Cheltenham, where they learn to use MI5's sophisticated filing system based on the service's computer, R2. Although it is no longer 'a paper world', the service still 'marches on its files. I was one of the infantry', recalls David Cornwell. It is official policy that a new file cannot be opened unless the subject is a member of a subversive group. 'Still Life', membership lists of targeted organisations, which are often obtained by clandestine means through burglary, infiltration and informers, are thus the 'most valuable single source on subversives'. If an officer comes across a new name he/she will hand an action slip to the Registry staff, who will check it against the alphabetical index held by Registry, which is where the dossiers on 'subversives' are kept.

Trainees spend two to three years in F Branch, bunched up in a big open-plan room, four or six to a desk, three desks to a room, tediously clipping and filing obscure, mostly left-wing periodicals, recording the results on the computer. Those expecting something more glamorous soon become bored with F Branch and the fallout rate among new recruits is high. 'It's a bloody awful job, people hate it,' according to one former MI5 officer. 'It is like working in insurance.' Another admitted that 'the work is desperately dull . . . It's bloody boring wading through people's phone taps. People talk about how the dog is getting on or they bought some potatoes today.'[24]

A hint of excitement comes when the A Team, the professional cracksmen of MI5, teach the new recruits how to break into houses and offices, 'leaving without a trace' and without being caught. Pairs of trainees select a suitable target and then submit plans which are scrutinised and generally pulled apart by the professional locksmiths and burglars of A1(D) and A1(A). 'We had to note how busy the street was, whether the neighbours were out during the day, whether there was a nosey cleaning lady or workman around and where the best escape routes were.' Occasionally, as in Operation Margarita, the exercise takes place abroad. Two agents arrived at the Gulden Hotel in Mechelen, Belgium, in June 1990 for 'practice in the use of tradecraft, clandestine rendezvous, dead letter drops, all kinds of contacts, photography and detection of surveillance'. After the three-day operation, 'David' and 'Henry' were debriefed by a senior officer and returned to Gower Street.[25]

The closed style of management in the service, defended by strict adherence to the need-to-know principle, means that the junior ranks are excluded from any involvement in the overall operation and policy making of the service. This is in spite of the fact that such action is, as MI5 trainee Miranda Ingram recognised, potentially destructive. 'Suddenly at the age of twenty-four you have to decide whether to open a file on a fellow citizen. Your vetting assessment may ruin somebody's career.' It was a world Cornwell would recognise: 'I toiled from morning and often till late into the evening at the dossiers of people I would never meet: should we trust him? Or her? Should their employers trust them? Might he be a traitor, spy, lonely decider, a suitable case for blackmail by the unscrupulous opposition? Thus I, who seemed to have no understanding of myself, was being asked to sit in judgement of the lives and loves of others. I was not versed in the ways of the real world, only my own.'[26]

In the old days, new 'indoctrinees' were taught from the moment of entry that they were 'crown servants' and not 'civil servants'. This distinction was regarded as important since, in the service's view, its role left it independent of parliamentary accountability. New recruits were lectured by MI5's legal adviser, Bernard Sheldon. Asked if the service's burglars were bound one day to be caught in the act, Sheldon told them that 'they had always got away with it up to then'. Sources close to MI5 argue that today things are different and that the cavalier attitude to the law is gone.[27]

The political complexion of MI5 is also alleged to have undergone a transformation. In the House of Commons during the debate on the Security Service Act, former Conservative Prime Minister Edward Heath spoke about MI5 officers 'who talked the most ridiculous nonsense and whose whole philosophy was ridiculous nonsense. If some of them were on the tube and saw someone reading the *Daily Mirror* they would say: "Get after him, that man is dangerous, we must find out where he bought it".' During the John Jones era, MoD civil servant Clive Ponting was alarmed to have to deal with senior MI5 officers who were 'utterly reactionary, tucked away in their own little world of their own'. In the same period, junior MI5 officer Miranda Ingram found that some of her colleagues 'thought that people who wore jeans were potentially subversive'. The overall tone was 'right-wing'. Even those majority of officers who 'are content just to do their job . . . the politically uninterested' are 'inevitably conservative, and probably Conservative'. Is this still the case?[28]

The resignation of officers such as Cathy Massiter and the arrest and conviction of Michael Bettaney, who had joined the Labour Party, probably limited the scope for views outside of a very narrow band. It would seem that deviation from government – Conservative – policy is generally not tolerated. In February 1984, Sir Clive Whitemore, Permanent Secretary at the MoD (currently the Home Office), headed an *ad hoc* committee which investigated 'what guidelines existed for managers on the policy to be adopted towards servicemen who belonged to or sympathised with organisations promoting policies fundamentally contrary to those of the government, but which were neither extreme right- or left-wing'. As a result of the review, regulations were amended so that 'service personnel are not to take an active part in the affairs of any political organisation, party or movement'. The last tag, which was deliberately left ill-defined, presumably referred to groups such as CND. It is highly likely that the regulations for service personnel also apply to MI5 officers.[29]

The staff remain predominantly middle class, but a good deal of effort has gone into portraying the new breed of officer as being more in tune with the needs of a modern service and the concerns of the citizen. More liberal-minded, they are 'analytical and careful', not seeing reds under every bed and more tolerant of the activism on the Left. Increasingly, the threat of subversion is played down, with MI5 officers arguing that 'the kind of excesses alleged by Peter Wright would be impossible today, as the staff themselves would not allow it'. An example given is that of the widespread use in the early eighties of telephone tapping against CND. 'We simply wouldn't get away with that kind of thing today. The climate inside the service and in society at large is completely different.'[30]

These claims ring a little hollow. The catalogue of errors under Patrick Walker, culminating in the horrendous treatment of the Gulf War detainees, provides little comfort. That episode starkly illustrated that a 'murky cluster of practices' remain firmly embedded inside the service. As any student of bureaucracies would know, it could not be otherwise. Long-term practices of secrecy and deceit, if left unaccountable, are likely to lead to abuse. When secrecy is joined to power – MI5 has immense power from hoarding and controlling the flow of information – the danger of the spread of abuse increases. Concealment of past mistakes by internal inquiries which avoid embarrassing explanations adds to the problem.[31]

MI5 is akin to a secret society whose officers are united by one purpose, which is secrecy itself: belief, methods and membership. Sissela Bok in her book *Secrets*, has suggested that for those individuals who 'live with secrecy day in and day out' and are 'trained to give up ordinary moral restraints in dealing with enemies', working in an intelligence-gathering organisation is 'an experience that isolates and transforms the participants'. It gives 'insiders a stark sense of separation from outsiders'. According to those who have been through the process: 'New recruits are given no cover story to help them keep the nature of their work secret. They are told simply to say that they work for the Ministry of Defence and, if pressed, to say that the work is secret. It is made clear that it will be frowned upon if they slip up and let someone know what they do.' The psychoanalyst Carl Jung, while recognising that a degree of secrecy is essential for mental health, believed that the 'maintenance of secrets acts like a psychic poison, which alienates their possessor from the community'. Officers find themselves at one remove from their fellow citizens. They grow accustomed to being guarded in their relationships, and eventually discover that the only people they trust are their colleagues. Gradually they are moulded into shape. Individual expression within the service is discouraged and dissent is stifled.[32]

Once trainees have finished their probationary period on general duties, juniors are transferred to specialist areas within the service, including counter-espionage in K Branch and, increasingly, T Branch and counter-terrorism. The latter is the most popular with probationers, who discover that counter-subversion work is 'not nearly as exciting as popular fiction would suggest'. One female officer, who left because of a general unease about how she was earning her living, recognised that while 'Northern Ireland was dangerous', it was 'real, an exciting post which people wanted to do'. There was no moral ambivalence attached to the work. 'It was perfectly clear what the job was. It was the same with the Middle East desk – the threat of terrorist bombs and so on.'[33]

Though there is little evidence that the Provisional IRA has ever contemplated assassinating members of the Security Service, Stella Rimington will have to live with the potential threat while she remains in office. She will be shadowed day and night by SAS-trained armed bodyguards, including two women who are crack shots. The one place where she may be able to relax is at the Reform Club, a short chauffeured drive from Gower Street. The club happens to be the haunt of a number of former spooks – John Bruce-Lockhart, Christopher Herdon, Roger Horrell and John Longrigg – from the rival service MI6. Embarrassingly, the Reform is the club where, in 1951, traitor Guy Burgess filched a book before he eluded his MI5 watchers and defected to the Soviet Union.

The Reform aims to provide 'a social club for reformers'. Will Stella Rimington turn out to be a reformer?[34]

10

MI5: The Branches

> The work of an agent in the Intelligence Department is on the whole extremely monotonous. A lot of it is uncommonly useless.
>
> Somerset Maugham

The Security Service, which served Mrs Thatcher well, has been generously rewarded for its close relationship with her during the eighties. In 1993, MI5 will move out of the eight buildings scattered around the capital that it currently occupies, into new £100 million premises on Millbank. The 'imperial neo-classical' Thames House, designed by Sir Frank Baines in 1928, has been converted – in great secrecy and at great expense, £130 million – into its new headquarters. The arrangements for the move into Thames House, which will provide office space for 2,300 people and parking for 800 cars, will be a top priority for director-general Stella Rimington. Until then, MI5 officers will continue working in the rather faceless, Eastern European looking tower block in Gower Street.[1]

Gower Street, once the centre of K Branch's counter-espionage activities, is now shared with the other branches, a brick in the wall of K Branch's declining influence. Former MI5 director-general Sir Percy Sillitoe once remarked that 'counter-espionage was the most dreary, uninspiring and over-rated occupation imaginable'. He believed the 'mystery and excitement of cloak and dagger operations was more in the public's imagination than to be found in fact, and stemmed from a natural awe of the unknown'. The public have, in the main, taken their view of the counter-espionage world from the novels of John le Carré and his character George Smiley, who seems imbued with an almost mystical ability to solve the overly intricate plots, which he unpeels layer by layer. Indeed, within the service K Branch was portrayed as being at the cutting edge of the intelligence game, deserving the sobriquet 'the élite'; few officers, though, knew what really went on inside the department. As Sillitoe soon discovered, within the service 'its popular reputation for excessive secrecy was in no way exaggerated'.[2]

Kim Philby, in reviewing one of le Carré's books, said that the plots had become too complicated; the reality was much more banal. We now know from recent revelations and interviews with KGB officers that all the talk of a 'hall of mirrors' in the counter-espionage game was, in itself, an illusion. The KGB never did use false defectors. The majority of their operations were remarkably simple and straightforward. 'We expect Intelligence officers', David Cornwell has written, 'to be brighter than they are. I've invested mine with far more intelligence than they possess. The reality was terribly tiresome.' We also know that MI5 claims of massive recruitment by the KGB in Britain were completely false. Vladimir Kuzichkin, who defected from his post in Iran to MI6 in the early eighties, told his debriefers that KGB officers were instructed not to recruit Britons in their own country but to 'concentrate their attention on representatives of third countries'. This is supported by the earlier defection of Oleg Lyalin in London in 1971, when two Greek Cypriot brothers, who did not have access to sensitive material, and a Malayan called Abdoolcader, who was able to supply the KGB with the numbers of cars used by MI5, were arrested for spying. 'The agents of residencies abroad could be counted on the fingers of one hand,' claimed Kuzichkin. In his time the KGB's S Directorate had 'only two agents in Iran' and in Japan, 'a round zero'.[3]

For many officers, counter-espionage has probably lost the edge it had during the Cold War. It no longer holds the position within the service that it once had, though there are still attempts to raise the old bogey. In December 1991, with the collapse of the Soviet state and the formal ending of the Cold War, Foreign Secretary Douglas Hurd was still threatening the mass expulsion of Soviet spies from Britain. K Branch estimated there were up to fifty KGB and GRU (Soviet Military Intelligence) officers working in London, though some were believed to be acting as a law unto themselves. It was admitted that the espionage was as much directed at economic targets – such as industrial, scientific and technical targets – as to defence. The Foreign Office itself believed that the KGB's First Chief Directorate activities in Britain, now controlled by the Foreign Intelligence Service under Yevgeny Primakov, would be curtailed owing to domestic political and financial pressure. It was a view shared by senior KGB officers, who complained that their expense accounts no longer stretched to taking out contacts to lunch at the Ecu de France. They now had to make do with a coffee at McDonald's. K Branch officers are increasingly concerned with the surveillance of Middle East espionage networks.[4]

Behind the greying net curtains of Gower Street, much of an F Branch officer's time is spent compiling files on individuals, based on information gathered by clandestine means – though some of it will come from published sources. 'You would be surprised how much information is publicly available,' reveals a former MI5 officer. 'The trick is knowing where to look.' A first contact may be made with the General Records Office in Southport, with its central confidential register of local general practitioners' records of the ninety million people who have lived in Britain since the Second World War, which will provide basic information. Eventually the officer will seek the assistance of S Branch, which runs the support services – the computer centre, known as the Joint Computer Bureau, and the huge Registry and library of paper files in Curzon Street's Leconfield House, which was constructed during the Second World War as a citadel able to protect its occupants, including, occasionally, the Royal Family, from aerial bombardment.[5]

Located on the first floor of Curzon Street is the vast hall containing R3, the Registry, where the personal and information files are stored in four hundred large ceiling-high storage bays. The twelve computer-controlled automated file storage and retrieval systems, known as conservatrieves, were installed in 1976. At the beginning of the Second World War, the service allegedly held four million paper files, during Peter Wright's time two million, and today around one million on those considered subversives or a potential threat to national security. In reality there may be far more, since MI5 no longer destroys files 'on the basis that they are the key to their work and they cannot accurately predict when files will ever be needed again'.[6]

Computerisation of the service's records began in 1971. During the mid-seventies, MI5 commenced building its extensive computer network, based on massive ICL computers featuring Virtual Machine Environment software. In the late seventies, the service used outside employment agencies to recruit between sixty and a hundred experienced computer programmers for 'creative analysis work at one of the most advanced installations in London . . . our clients have a considerable volume of new projects on hand'. By 1980, the Security Service had set up what was, at the time, the largest computer centre in Europe. In January 1984, a new and more powerful twin ICL 2980 system with 'gargantuan' storage was ordered on behalf of MI5 by the MoD. The main computer, known as R2, is situated on the ground floor of Curzon Street.

An 'on-line' service gives officers instant access to R2. The R2 computer is believed to operate a Free Text Retrieval (FTR) system. The Lindrop Committee on data protection found that this presented 'new dimensions of unease'. FTR systems, said Lindrop in 1978, provide 'an easy method of browsing through collections of information [and] are well suited to surveillance requirements such as the preservation of national security . . . They are ideally suited to the retrieval of every occurrence of particular items of information from a large mass, and for discovering the relationship of one piece of information with another.' The Data Protection Committee felt that FTR systems presented 'special problems of definition and control'. The 'unstructured files place virtually no constraints on the quantities or type of data which may be stored'.[7]

The Security Service has a country-wide network of two hundred satellite terminals linked to the mainframe database, which holds information equivalent to the amount contained in 50,000 medium-sized books and has room to hold basic data, if required, on twenty million people. The last estimate is that R2 holds registered 'permanent security files' (PF) on around one million people; however, files necessarily refer to many more persons than those named on the file heading. R2 also holds a list of between 10,000 and 20,000 names, compiled for the War Book, of 'subversives' who might be considered for internment under Defence regulation 18b in time of war.[8]

One desk in A Branch has the specialised task of recruiting civil servants who will pass on data without the knowledge of their superiors; this, though, is often unnecessary. In 1953 a government directive instructed the director-general of MI5 to 'establish a comprehensive set of security records. In order to do this you will arrange that all government departments and agencies submit to you for inclusion in your records all information bearing on security which may be, or come into their possession.' This directive was specifically excluded from the provisions of the Data Protection Act, thereby allowing the service freedom to trawl through the state's record systems with no restraining safeguards in place. If necessary, information can be secured from other government departments by more informal means. R2 is linked into several large government computers as part of a network initiated in 1972 called 'MoD-mult'. Computer industry sources revealed, in the early eighties, that a secret Government Data Network (GDN) interconnecting several important data banks was under active development linking Home Office, Customs and Excise, Inland Revenue, Health, and Social Security computers and eventually the police computer. All this is taking place in the absence of standard procedures governing exchange of information. The development is believed to have been brought into existence under the supervision of Brigadier John Spackman, Under-Secretary and Director of Social Security Operational Strategy, DHSS, 1983–7, and former chief of the Information Systems Division at SHAPE.[9]

All Department of Social Security (DSS) and Inland Revenue files are computerised; the DSS Departmental Central Index at its Newcastle computer complex lists all of Britain's fifty-four million inhabitants. It was Rupert Allason, in his book on the Special Branch, who first revealed that MI5 utilises DSS records. 'By assessing the information relating to a person's contributions, it is possible to learn his place of work, if she or he has one, or the area in which the individual lives.' Specific information can be obtained from the special liaison office at Newcastle (special section A, records B). According to a DSS spokesperson, what can be transferred to MI5 was 'one of these awkward questions' she was not prepared to answer. Although other countries have outlawed the use of the National Insurance number (NINO) as a universal Personal Identification Number (PIN), Britain appears to be moving in the opposite direction. The Security Service uses the NINO as a PIN for its computer files.[10]

If information is not available from official sources then it may be sought by clandestine means. 'A' Branch is responsible for field surveillance and, more particularly, 'dirty tricks' – buggings, telephone tappings and burglaries. The head in the mid-eighties was the enthusiastic 'eccentric' Royd Barker; beneath him – responsible for A2 (Technical Support), was 'Mr Phonetapper', Jeffrey Blackburne-Kane, who received a knighthood on his retirement in 1985.

According to former MI5 officers, lawbreaking within A

Branch was 'absolutely routine'. The sole purpose of the offshoot section, A1a, was to break and enter property. Officers who undertook these burglaries say that 'it's not just private homes, they'll do offices; they'll do banks; they'll do diplomatic property; no holds barred, it doesn't matter'. Officers can call upon the Resources Index to help them in their operations if they are in need of specialist expertise, which may include plumbers and locksmiths. Piano tuners have apparently proved useful in the past, and even ballet dancers have been recruited for operations, though in what context is not known.[11]

The main call on A Branch comes from its involvement in bugging and telephone tapping, which is undertaken in close co-operation with British Telecom. In May 1992, Lord Justice Lloyd reported that there was no basis whatsoever for the 'speculation' that many perfectly innocent citizens are subjected to telephone tapping. Back in the real world, Granada Television's *World in Action* revealed that the Security Service had tapped the telephone of Lieutenant Robert Lawrence, the Falklands War hero whose story was told in the film *Tumbledown*, and his father, Commander John Lawrence. Whitehall had been concerned that his demand for compensation from the MoD might cause 'political embarrassment'.[12]

A telephone tap begins with a request from a Branch desk officer in charge of a target, who prepares a file including name, telephone number and a supporting justification for the tap. Approval is sought from the officer's section chief and MI5's deputy director. Those targets with the highest priority are selected and forwarded to the Home Office. According to Cathy Massiter, 'an application for an intercept warrant will be minuted with a one paragraph summary of two or three sentences known as the "short reason" which provides the justification for a warrant which is usually all that the Secretary of State and the Permanent Secretary will see unless they request more'.[13]

Within the Home Office the requests are processed by a section of F4 Division, though effectively the decision to authorise a warrant is made by the Permanent Secretary, who consults with MI5. Home Secretary Leon Brittan informed Parliament that 'the process is not a straightforward one . . . Unless there is urgency, there is much interchange between the agency and those who advise the relevant Secretary of State. An application might not be made formally if it is made clear that it is unlikely to be granted.' By law, warrants – which can run for six months – are required to be issued by the Home Secretary. However, in theory any Secretary of State can carry out this function – and the government did not deny this during the debate on the Security Service Bill – which means, for instance, that a Secretary of State for the Fisheries could authorise a warrant. In other instances, if the Home Secretary happens to be away from the office, as long as he is informed of the reasons for a warrant being issued, a civil servant of under-secretary status or above can sign the warrant, which will be valid for two days. In the past, there has certainly been collusion between F4 officials and MI5 to backdate applications of taps which were already in place. 'A kind official at the Home Office brushed aside the usual red tape.'[14]

One warrant can cover a whole organisation, allowing dozens or even hundreds of lines to be tapped. Labour MP Merlyn Rees told journalists that when he was Home Secretary and responsible for signing warrants, while there were 250–400 warrants in force, in actual fact two to three thousand lines were tapped. A few years later, aware that he had let slip figures which had remained hidden from scrutiny, Rees greeted a Government White Paper's rather smaller figure 'with an almost audible sigh'. When Liberal MP Clement Freud asked a Conservative Home Secretary whether 'the number of interception orders is cumulative – that is to say, those currently in force – or is the number given simply that of the new orders that have been published?' he did not receive an answer. As Duncan Campbell pointed out, the cumulative number of warrants in force could be rather more than that implied by the yearly total published. Old warrants are said to be renewed with 'effortless ease'.[15]

Despite attempts to reassure the public on the matter, there has been a huge increase in the number of telephone-tapping operations in recent years. Official reports conceal more than they reveal. Modern technology means that telephone tapping, which currently costs the government £15 million per annum, is a cheap way of gathering intelligence. Official warrants cover only a small proportion of the total of official taps, of which three out of four are believed to be for security purposes, and may cover a multitude of sins. Some taps, such as those of foreign embassies, are semi-permanent. Northern Ireland warrants may also include mainland targets. Merlyn Rees informed the Commons in 1985 that 'some taps continue for a long time . . . they are blanket taps'. John McWilliam, MP, a former British Telecom engineer who knows a great deal about the subject, said in the same debate that 'certain official tappings do not require warrants'. This derived from 'an institutional relationship' between British Telecom and the security services. In practice, MI5 is treated differently from the police, who, in the main, adhere to the guidelines. BT engineers admit that 'when the tap is being made for the security services, we never see the warrant'.[16]

Through the summer of 1981, the Home Office convened a series of meetings of an *ad hoc* Feasibility Study Group, made up of BT and security services personnel. The group agreed to retain the close working arrangement in force between themselves on telephone tapping. This relationship was formalised when the government wrote into the 1984 Telecommunications Act, Section 94, which allows a Secretary of State to issue BT, regardless of the wishes of shareholders and the scrutiny of Parliament, with directives 'as appear to be requisite or expedient in the interests of national security'.[17]

The telephone-tapping operation, Tinkerbell, employs BT's

'secret squirrels', known by the code AS 314 2W, who operate from 81 Newgate Street in the City. The specially hand-picked and vetted engineers, whose numbers have increased by more than 75 per cent in the last ten years, are paid from a secret Home Office payroll.

In co-operation with MI5, BT compiles its own political blacklist of 'subversives' for 'reasons of national security'. It covers employees whose job titles have nothing to do with security work. The blacklist is compiled by the Security Division (Sec D) of the Security and Investigation department, which deals with vetting of employees and liaison with MI5. Below Sec D is the Corporate Personnel Services department, whose activities are said to be even more clandestine, including a unit known as CP7 which furnishes executives with detailed dossiers on the political affiliations of trade unionists. In the mid-eighties, BT's head of the personnel department was Michael Betts, previously responsible for MI5 vetting arrangements at the BBC.[18]

Tinkerbell's estimated 35,000 tapped telephone calls are relayed to the ninth floor of BT's Gresham Street HQ; there are other smaller tapping centres around London. More than one hundred transcribers, mainly women, are employed to type out the huge volume of taped conversations captured from the voice-activated tape-recorders. Blue and green MI5 vans pick up the 'product' and deliver it to customers, although a large and growing proportion of taps are now relayed over secure lines direct to MI5. A transcription clerk who joined MI5 in 1978 'went to work in MI5's industrial room with seven other women, transcribing the tapes of telephone calls which had been tapped. Each morning, I'd collect the actual tapes from a room on the fifth floor which contained banks of recorders operating twenty-four hours per day.'[19]

In 1991, the Commissioner responsible for overseeing the issuing of warrants put to rest one myth when he revealed what had unofficially been known for some time – that, contrary to popular belief, telephone taps are silent. 'Neither the connection of the device itself, nor the interception of communications by such means, is audible in any way to the subscriber.' Tales of blips, clicks, poor lines and crossed lines are part of the mythology of having a tapped line. Engineers generally make sure that tapped lines are free of 'squawks and farts' to enable transcribers to hear the conversation clearly.[20]

MI5's needs require the service to keep abreast of the latest technical advances, ensuring that no means of communication escapes their attention. Portable telephones can be tapped 'in the interests of national security' and sophisticated technology allows telephone boxes to be identified and tapped. 'Treeing' enables not only telephone calls from A to B to be monitored but also those from B to C – 'instantly'. BT's System X allows for metering information which will be available to everyone, including MI5. In many ways, this obviates the need for expensive and time-consuming telephone tapping and does not require a warrant. Since MI5 has so often in the past based its files on nothing more than guilt by association, a list of telephone contacts will serve just as well as a full tap. By the mid-nineties, System X and other developments will enable engineers to tap telephones without physically interfering with individual lines or company switchboards, from a new high-security installation, the National Network's Central Operations Unit at Oswestry. Telephone-tapping technology is a growing industry, and the privatised BT has been anxious to improve its service to the government as part of a profitable business. The government pays BT £10 million annually for its telephone-tapping operation.

Officers from MI5's A Branch, backed up by the BT engineers, are sometimes used in an operation to break and enter private homes and premises to plant listening devices. More often, engineers place taps on lines, without warrants, under the guise of carrying out telephone repairs. A technique known as Radio Frequency Flooding enables the monitoring of conversations in a room by an improperly hung-up telephone receiver. Although the sound quality is not high it was used extensively in the seventies. In 1985, the BBC TV paranoic thriller *Edge of Darkness* offered a high degree of accuracy when it revealed the code-names of the various bugging operations carried out by MI5. 'Azure' – a conventional bug in a room; 'Cinnamon' – a Special Facility (SF) bug planted in a telephone junction box and able also to pick up conversations in a room; 'Towrope' – the raw product gathered from a telephone tap. Whether these remain the same is unknown, though in the world of intelligence old habits tend to linger on. Peter Wright revealed that, in his time in the service, for convenience Claridge's Hotel had all its rooms permanently bugged, while top waiters at leading London restaurants would also be in MI5's employ and help with the bugging of tables.[21]

The use of bugs by the Security Service does not come within the remit of the Interception of Communications Act and is one of those grey areas regulated by the Home Office. An indication that control was not as tight as the government suggested was partially revealed in a June 1985 statement by the Home Secretary, when he released details of new rules governing the use of surveillance equipment. Leon Brittan included the comment that 'the criteria for the authorisation and use of listening devices and of certain types of visual surveillance are *considerably tightened*' (emphasis added). Home Office guidelines on 'the use of equipment in police surveillance operations' give senior officers wide discretionary powers. Those same largely unregulated powers are available to the Security Service. Private security 'debuggers' claim that 'increasingly we are finding equipment with MI5's trade mark all over it. MI5 is extending its monitoring of firms which do business abroad.'[22]

In the early eighties, the Department of the Environment had responsibility for the Special Electronics Section in Grosvenor Road, where workshops carried out work for government departments. Hidden within its activities was a special section which prepared bugging devices for use by MI5.

Bugging equipment is also provided by the Metropolitan Police's own laboratory at Grove Park, Camberwell, while research is carried out by a joint MI5/police station at Sandridge, near St Albans.[23]

Mail opening is conducted by a 'Special section' of the Post Office's 300-strong Investigation Division. In London, letters were taken from a local sorting office to Union House in St Martin's-le-Grand, near St Pauls. Methods have changed little in decades – steam from a kettle is still used – though there are now special sprays which make envelopes temporarily translucent and electronic scanning machines which can read some mail unopened. Care is taken not to leave signs of opening; Peter Wright advised that Sellotape remains impenetrable to mail openers. Contents of letters are photocopied then passed on to interested parties. Until the mid-eighties, mail intercepts made at the receiving end were known as 'Phidias', and at the sender's end as 'Ratcatcher'.[24]

Another source of intelligence is that derived from physical surveillance. The Watchers, who were run in the mid-eighties by a woman, Julia Faux, are, according to Peter Wright, 'just ordinary chaps doing a job which is most of the time very dull, but which requires a lot of skill and intelligence, as well as patience and a phenomenal memory'. One of their main jobs is manning Static OPs (Static Observation Posts) in houses overlooking the entrances to embassies. Faces are checked against 'a mug book' containing thousands of pictures of foreign intelligence officers. When Wright left in 1975, there were 250 Watchers operating out of a house in Regent's Park and later from the Euston Tower building. The Watchers spend their time 'sitting in drab rooms equipped with binoculars, telephoto camera, and log book and an overflowing ashtray'. The alternatives can be worse – 'sitting in a car, watching for something to happen. Usually, nothing happens at all.' Today there are many more women employed: couples appear more natural on surveillance operations. There have, though, been complaints in the past from wives who feared that this might lead their husbands into temptation.[25]

Following people on foot is acknowledged to be difficult; the Soviets, in particular, were very adept at losing their 'tails'. According to Wright, it was a bigger problem by car, even with the benefit of souped-up engines and special suspension. Watchers have dispensation for going through red lights and breaking speed limits. During the eighties, cars – paid for by the Department of Transport – were equipped at a garage in Streatham High Street, officially a garage for the Department of the Environment. Inside the garage, protected by security cameras, MI5 mechanics reassembled the cars in the manner of James Bond's Aston Martin with two-way mirrors, bullet-proof glass, false number plates and video, including infra-red cameras, hidden in the headlights. VHF aerials were disguised as driving wing-mirrors, with UHF aerials fitted into a small fin on the rear shelf of a car. Radio messages were disguised as taxi and ambulance calls. Servicing was undertaken at the 'very private' Crawford Street garage, guarded very securely by its own uniformed government security officers.[26]

The one Branch new recruits hope to avoid being posted to is the lowly C Branch, responsible for protective security. Its officers are often former policemen or ex-Army officers who join the service late in life because of the military's early retirement policy. Ambitious officers do not like being side-lined into the mundane work of C Branch, which involves implementing regulations covering those civil servants with access to security information. This includes 'vetting, education in security, rules for handling classified information and the physical protection of information, locks, safes, guards etc'. Computer terminals within government departments are now regularly checked for possible eavesdropping by hostile agencies who may be able to monitor the radiation emitted from the screens. The Branch also takes the lead on leak inquiries. While some resources and sections have been directed into other areas such as counter-terrorism, the humdrum work of vetting still finds favour with the security-conscious Conservative government.[27]

While the Branch does not carry out the vetting of civil servants – this is undertaken by the MoD's Personnel Security Investigating Unit (PSIU) – it does have overall responsibility for the system which covers Whitehall, the armed forces and the police. C Branch acts as a 'post box passing on information from one service or agency to the government department that is making the vetting enquiry'. Nearly 66,000 posts with access to classified material are considered sensitive enough to warrant formal positive vetting (PV) procedures, although classification of the material may have been 'for its political sensitivity as much as for its subject matter'. The PSIU PV investigators come from similar backgrounds to their counterparts in C Branch and have been described generically by one security official as 'retired majors with emotional problems'. They share the same conservative philosophy which 'militates against the more liberal official approach' promoted in recent years.[28]

In 1990, the Personnel Security Committee in the Cabinet Office approved a simplified, tiered approach to vetting, which it is hoped will reduce the numbers subjected to these checks. The 'first rung' negative vetting, which involves a trawl through MI5 and Special Branch records, has now been replaced by Reliability Checks. There are also Counter-Terrorist Checks for those applying for jobs in the public sector and in companies involved in sensitive government work. PV(S) is aimed at those with regular access to secret material. The process is unwieldy in that it can take up to three months, slowing down the recruitment process. The political views of those vetted can play a crucial role in the outcome, particularly when they do not accord with government policy. One Civil Service applicant who supported a welfare rights group was rejected for a post in 10 Downing Street because her 'sincerely-held beliefs' would place her in 'an agonising dilemma in such a sensitive post'. However, she was told that 'under a different government, she would pass the procedure'. PV(TS), which includes checks on credit-worthiness and interviews with friends and relations, covers those people with regular access to 'top secret' information. The same checks though in greater detail (EPV) are required for security and intelligence staff and those associated with such work.[29]

Complaints about vetting made to the new Security Service tribunal have all been rejected, with no reasons given. This may be explained by Lord Justice Stuart-Smith's comment that C Branch 'does not and has no opportunity to check the veracity of the information' which it supplies – a remarkable defence which the Commissioner appears to accept. A number of complaints are now the subject of a challenge at the European Commission on Human Rights.[30]

C Branch, which for many years was run from offices above the art galleries of Cork Street, is also responsible for the vetting of personnel and security of the 2,000 companies in the defence-related field which feature on MI5's 'List X'. A 'secret aspects letter' is sent to companies prior to acceptance of a government contract, listing the requirements for the security criteria laid down by MI5. Companies have no choice but to accede to the security demands if they wish to keep the contract. MI5-trained company security officers, known as 'controllers', supply a list of employees to the special advisers from C Branch. The names are initially checked by C3 against files held by Registry, for membership of subversive organisations. The actual vetting process is undertaken by F2, which monitors trade union activity and subversion. The Branch also seeks information on personnel who make visits to politically sensitive countries. Discreet inquiries are made, followed by formal interviews. Occasionally, this can lead to recruitment of staff as a valuable source.[31]

There has been an unchecked rise in character assessments of employees based on 'lifestyle checks'. Seamen contracted to work on ships carrying nuclear waste for British Nuclear Fuels Ltd (BNFL) were ordered to reveal who they had been living with for the past five years, including failed and broken relationships, or face the sack. This followed from an October 1990 change in government policy which BNFL said required the vetting of 15,000 employees in the interests of 'national security'. A 1982 Security Commission report revealed that the PV process within the nuclear industry was the result of agreements made with the United States, which insists that PV is undertaken on persons with actual or potential access to atomic secrets. The assessment grade runs from A (clearance) to D (negative). The recommendation is passed on to the MoD's Security Division, which decides whether or not the employee should be allowed to work for the company.[32]

It is only in recent years that the veil over the seamless web of secret vetting in the public and private world, which the Security Service has controlled and organised over the last fifty years, has been lifted. The BBC used a security liaison officer, in Room 105, who submitted the names of applicants to C Branch, which in turn passed the names on to F7, which looked at political extremists in the media. MI5 recommendations to the BBC's Personnel office were rarely overruled. A smaller number (150) of journalists and staff within the BBC, who will have key roles in the event of war breaking out, are now vetted by MI5. All permanent staff at the British Library, including cleaners and counter staff, are secretly vetted by MI5 and Special Branch in a process which involves checks on the political affiliations of people applying for jobs or promotion. Management at the library appears to accept MI5's judgement as final.[33]

The eighties saw an astonishing growth in the field of private vetting by a service industry which may involve as many as 100,000 operatives in commercial espionage. One company, the car manufacturer Rover, set up its own secret vetting unit, B.G. Research Service. With extensive contacts with other security units in Europe, its screening network was described by one security source as 'the best in the country and probably in Europe'. The official security services may come to rely increasingly on this type of private agency as budgets are tightened, with targets and resources switched to other areas.[34]

Despite hints from ministers and official spokespersons that vetting is now undertaken only where absolutely necessary, the evidence suggests otherwise. Indeed, more and more occupations appear to come within the vetting net. In 1990, the government was apparently 'hot' on the idea of a massive extension of vetting under a new system of vetting by a National Criminal Records Agency which would cover thousands of people in posts of public trust, from social workers to private security guards. While some areas may warrant vetting, the move has to be set against the increased surveillance which now extends to quite ordinary citizens and a process wherein job applicants are kept in the dark. It has been estimated that as many as one million public and private posts are subject to some form of security vetting. The personnel of C Branch have become increasingly important in a society which appears to be becoming more, not less, secretive.[35]

11

The Special Branch

Once the Special Branch had been established, there was no lack of work for it.

Sir John Moylan, Scotland Yard, 1934

There remains some confusion over precisely when the Metropolitan Special Branch came into existence. It is generally assumed to have been in March 1883 when the Irish Bureau was formed in response to the Fenian campaign for Irish independence. However, it was not until February 1887 that a secret department entitled the 'Special Branch' was formed with a cadre of four police inspectors. What distinguished this body from the Irish Branch, and marks it out as the precursor of its modern namesake, is that it not only monitored Irish terrorism but also took on the responsibility for the surveillance of foreign immigrant groups and anarchists from Eastern Europe. The Special Branch is still actively concerned with immigration.

Considering Mrs Thatcher's admiration for Victorian values, it is interesting to note that the mid-Victorians never had an equivalent of the Special Branch. In fact, a large percentage of the ruling liberal élite were genuinely opposed to the suggestion of spying agencies being employed. Erskine May asserted: 'The freedom of a country may be measured by its immunity from this baleful agency.' The creation of an organised spying system happened to coincide with the beginning of Britain's long, slow economic decline and the loss of imperial power.[1]

The Special Branch remained, until the First World War, primarily concerned with violent criminals, such as terrorists and bomb-throwing anarchists. It was not until the spectre of Bolshevism hovered over Britain that the Special Branch began to show an interest in the Labour movement and soon developed a close relationship with anti-communist vetting groups based within indusry, in the belief that subversive elements were at work in the munitions factories. It also took on counter-espionage duties and was routinely called upon to do leg-work for the recently formed MI5. In 1909 the Special Branch had only thirty-four officers; by May 1913 the number had grown to over seventy-five. At the end of the war the Branch had constituted itself as the political police force that we know today.

During the Second World War the Special Branch's staff swelled to well over one hundred officers. In the forties, Labour Prime Minister Clement Attlee sanctioned an increase in its size and activities to combat what was perceived as communist subversion in the docks and industrial disputes. It was also tasked with producing a list of members of the Communist Party of Great Britain. In the early sixties, the Campaign for Nuclear Disarmament became a significant target of SB surveillance.

At the time of its reorganisation in 1961, the Special Branch had 200 officers but was still just a section of the Metropolitan Police. The restructuring of police forces which accompanied the 1964 Police Act brought about, for the first time, the formation of regional Special Branches. By 1975, every provincial force had established its own full-time Special Branch. Although in theory each force was independent, all activities were co-ordinated by Scotland Yard. Each of the fifty-two separate police forces have Special Branch officers, though the smaller county forces may have only a handful. There are 600 Special Branch officers in the Metropolitan Police, with around 2,000 Special Branch officers in England and Wales, covered by an annual budget of £24 million. There has been a sixfold increase in personnel in the last twenty years. In Scotland, excluding civilians and support staff, the number of SB officers doubled during the Thatcher years, perhaps reflecting the nationalist and left-wing drift in the eighties and the lack of support north of the border for Mrs Thatcher and her government.[2]

A major change in the direction and emphasis of the Special Branch came in 1968, the year of the student riots and the emergence of the New Left. The autobiography of the anarchist Stuart Christie is amusing for its account of the bumbling Branch officers who were clearly at a total loss as to how to differentiate between the many varieties of Trotskyist and Maoist organisations that had suddenly sprung up. Branch officers, who had hitherto been used to the clear-cut politics of the Communist Party, relied on 'a grossly inaccurate' book by an American author, George Thayer, *The British Political Fringe*, for their distorted information on the new groupings.[3]

In late 1968, Special Branch numbers were substantially increased by the Labour Home Secretary, James Callaghan, to meet the threat of the 'far and wide left'. In July 1970, official backing for the change came in a secret report from Lord Helsby, former head of the Civil Service. The report of the Committee on Protective Security, which passed its recommendations on to the Official Committee on Security (OCS), MI5's oversight body, had sought views on the measures necessary to assess the reliability of Civil Service staff who might have access to protected information. While recognising the traditional position that 'the Communist Party has a fundamental interest in subverting the State, and constitutes a threat to the security of protected information,' it also, for the first time, targeted Trotskyists and Maoists as potential threats to security. The OCS recognised that these groupings would need to be monitored to cover the requirements of the newly introduced vetting arrangements. This dramatically widened the SB's information-trawling activities, which were now extended to students and university campuses.[4]

At the same time, in consultation with MI5 and the Home Office, the Association of Chief Police Officers (ACPO) issued terms of reference which 'guide the work of Special Branches in some detail'. In December 1984, a revised set of these guidelines, *The Work of a Special Branch*, was issued, clarifying in particular the Special Branch's relationship with MI5. 'A Special Branch assists the Security Service in carrying out its tasks of defending the Realm against attempts at espionage and sabotage or from the actions of persons and organisations, whether directed from within or without the country, which may be judged to be subversive to the State. A Special Branch provides information about extremists and terrorists to the Security Service.' In effect, the Special Branch acts as MI5's front office. Special Branch officers, who are sworn constables, act as the law enforcement arm of the Security Service, being responsible for arrests of spies and those who have contravened the Official Secrets Act. MI5 divides the country into nine regions and employs senior police officers – for instance, a retired local Assistant Commissioner who has had responsibility for the Special Branch in the area – to liaise with the police liaison officer.

The Special Branch acts as an extension of MI5's intelligence-gathering capability. Often it is MI5 which requests the Special Branch to target a particular individual. The service will also use local Branch officers for its own surveillance operations. Informal meetings between the Special Branch and MI5 officers will co-ordinate the intelligence effort (MI5's A3 section which was responsible for liaison with the Special Branch appears to have been closed down), the results of which are forwarded to London, Box 500 – the code for MI5. Chief Constables are often left in the dark about Special Branch activities and are informed on a need-to-know basis. If they oppose MI5 interference in local SB activity, persuasion will, if necessary, come from higher levels within the service, even from the director-general if need be, to enable MI5 to obtain what it wants. When an A1 officer carries out a burglary in the provinces, the help of the local Special Branch will be sought. It is an operational requirement that MI5 does not break the law by stealing anything during an authorised burglary and, therefore, a Special Branch officer will normally be on hand to play the role of the thief. This is done on the basis that if anything goes wrong, the officer is more likely able to sort out any problems with the local police.[5]

Although the relationship between the Special Branch and MI5 is closer than many people realise, it is also true that there remains on the ground a great deal of friction. MI5 officers show little respect for provincial Special Branch officers and, according to a member of F Branch, 'tend to look upon Special Branch officers as second rate and patronise them. This irritates the Special Branch, especially because they know there's nothing they can do about it.' Conversely, Special Branch officers 'do cultivate contacts with MI5 agents, because it's a mark of prestige to have one'.

The F4 division of the Police Department of the Home Office does not simply give the Special Branch a target list of groups and organisations considered subversive; instead, in consultation with senior MI5 officers, the head of the Metropolitan Special Branch and the leaders of ACPO, it provides brief and broad guidelines. However, this policy is limited and may lead to local initiatives and abuse. There is little direction for supervision of the provincial Special Branches, which, it has been claimed, may mean officers protecting their position by watching as many different groups as possible, in case a senior officer suddenly asks for information about one of them. MI5 officers accuse some Special Branch officers of being 'over-zealous' in their campaigns against local activists. 'They harass them until the targets start to complain to their local MP, and then approach MI5 to bail them out.'[6]

The 'basic' role of the Special Branch 'arises from the chief officer's responsibility for the preservation of the Queen's Peace. Its work is to assist the chief officer in discharging this responsibility.' This entails 'the acquisition of intelligence related to public order'. 'Such information will enable the Branch to provide assessments of whether marches, meetings, demonstrations and pickets pose any threat to public order.' Home Secretary William Whitelaw explained to Parliament that this would 'require information to be kept on individuals who are active in a political movement, not because of the views they hold out but because the activities of the group could be such as to encourage public disorder'. Although countering Irish terrorism is a prime Special Branch concern, 50 per cent of officers are involved with 'political' targets, including trade union affairs. A 1974 leaked copy of SB 'general orders' made it clear that local police have to inform the SB of all known political and industrial meetings and demonstrations; shorthand writers for these meetings are provided by the SB. Any information obtained, which is often based on contacts with employers, is passed on to MI5.[7]

Government guidelines require the Special Branch to restrict diplomats and foreign officials to certain boundaries and it is responsible for monitoring those who attempt to travel beyond the permitted radius around London. Officers also protect the Royal Family and other public figures, though this is a role which they are likely to lose in the future. The closest the public come to seeing SB officers is usually at public meetings, the well-groomed, restless men, bulges in their sharp suits, who hover behind ministers. A high percentage of officers maintain surveillance at airports and seaports. They also deal with immigration and naturalisation enquiries. There is a National Joint Unit which co-ordinates information and enquiries when a local SB arrests or questions individuals under the Prevention of Terrorism Act and it then expedites orders under the Act.

The Special Branch also monitors the extreme Right. Half a dozen London officers concentrate on infiltrating fascist groups, but it is certainly the case that such activities have been in decline since the early eighties. MI5 had information on all members of the National Front National Directorate, much of which, according to MI5 officers, was obtained by the Special Branch. A Special Branch officer working within the National

Front also infiltrated the paramilitary Column 88. Branch officers have also attempted to infiltrate animal liberation groups. Information they gather is collated by a team of detectives operating the Animal Rights National Index (ARNI), set up in 1986 under the auspices of the SB.[8]

The Metropolitan Special Branch, situated on the eighteenth and nineteenth floors of New Scotland Yard, comes under the command of a Deputy Assistant Commander in 'C' Department, John Howley. Below him are three Commanders in charge of the main sections – administration, ports and operations. The Special Branch is no longer a short-term posting; officers regard their membership as a career with which they will remain for the whole of their service – twenty or thirty years. Candidates are culled from recommendations made by senior police officers. They will face a general knowledge test on current events and a written test. Ideally a candidate will be between twenty-three and twenty-five years old, a uniformed constable with at least two years' experience as a qualified officer. He is expected to show maturity and a degree of political awareness and, increasingly, know a foreign language. Many are the brightest officers, often from public schools; however, the expansion of the SB has inevitably resulted in the recruitment of less able officers. Applicants are positively vetted by a Home Office unit liaising with MI5. The number of females is said to be over 10 per cent, and there are a number of black and Asian officers.[9]

During a probationary year, recruits will receive training from MI5 on security matters and in firearms training, becoming proficient in the use of small handguns and, occasionally, Heckler and Koch sub-machine guns, as favoured by the SAS. The initiation course includes seminars on terrorism and the IRA, the Official Secrets Act and the 'acquisition of intelligence related to public order'. New officers will also receive more detailed lectures on subversion, run by the Security Service which will outline classic case histories. MI5 training officers will also teach them how to develop contacts and run informers.

The Metropolitan Special Branch carries out its traditional role as the national liaison and record-keeper for MI5. Much of the work of a Special Branch officer is painstakingly dull, filling in reports and, along with many of the one hundred civilian staff, helping to keep records up-to-date in the registry. A considerable amount of the information is retrieved from government records, with officials prepared to relax the rules. In 1974, the registry included an index of 1.1 million names with accompanying files; this quickly rose, on the introduction of computerisation, to 1.4 million. Today, it is believed to be nearer to 2 million. Each of the names is included on the basis of one of twenty-seven 'areas of interest'. Some 350,000 are tagged with 'pink slips' and are subject to special 'dockets' containing extra surveillance material. It is estimated that there are 2.5 million individual files in the Special Branch's system, including 'intelligence' data on suspect activities and associations. They are consulted, on average, 300,000 times per year. Many records are still on paper, but since 1973 they have been increasingly computerised.[10]

Special Branch officers also have access to the Police National Computer (PNC2) – the largest police intelligence system in Europe. If a police officer requests information from the PNC2 on an individual who happens to have been targeted by the SB, a bell will ring in Special Branch headquarters to alert them. When gathering 'soft' intelligence, local SB officers will have access to collators' files. Since 1966, all police forces have been required to appoint local intelligence officers, whose task it is to assemble a 'memory databank' on anyone who 'comes to the notice' of the police with the help of informants. The Lindop Committee on Data Protection noted the difficulties this kind of intelligence presented for civil liberties. It distinguished between 'information' which it said was factual data, such as name and date of birth, and 'intelligence', which may be speculation and hearsay.[11]

The Special Branch computer is also linked into Immigration, Drugs Intelligence and Fraud Squad files. There is, further, a terminal at Heathrow Airport containing 7,600 names of persons of special interest on whom a rapid response is required by SB officers when an individual leaves or enters the country. While SB officers have access to all records belonging to these sections, the reverse is not the case. Access to SB data is strictly controlled and often withheld from other sections. The SB computer at New Scotland Yard is shielded against electronic snooping by a costly process known as 'Tempest'. The security surrounding access to the computer is so intense, with passwords and other restrictions, that 'some security routines are said to take more than half-a-day to complete'.[12]

Even the *Police Review* has commented that while 'much of the information is valid intelligence. A substantial proportion is unchecked bunkum.' The 1985 report by the House of Commons Home Affairs Committee was a heavily circumscribed investigation of the Special Branch; it refused to consider specific cases – this would probably have proved too embarrassing. A classic example of a Special Branch abusing its remit occurred in 1981 when Madeline Haigh wrote a letter to her local paper, the *Sutton Coldfield News*, protesting against the siting of cruise missiles, and was monitored by the local Special Branch on the basis that 'she might be a person prepared to support or get involved in public protests of a nature likely to become violent'. Despite the 'unprofessional' methods of the SB inspector involved, he remained in the Special Branch and was defended by the West Midlands Police chief, Sir Philip Knights, who said that the enquiries 'fell within the terms of reference of the Special Branch'.[13]

The only Chief Constable to undertake a serious review of local SB files, John Alderson, told the Home Affairs Committee: 'I found that officers, often with the best of intentions, had made records of things which I thought unnecessary. They had nothing to do with criminal affairs at all but in their view were sufficiently of interest to the Special Branch and probably the security services to warrant being recorded. A very high proportion of the records were either out-of-date or of the kind one would not want to keep.' When he began to weed out the Devon and Cornwall Special Branch files, he found that out of several hundred he reviewed as few as twenty were considered relevant. Alderson said later: 'A lot of it was rubbish . . . The left were given disproportionate attention.' What Alderson did not realise at the time was that some of the files he ordered to be weeded out were sent to MI5. 'In the end you can't do anything about MI5; nobody can do anything about it.'[14]

In November 1984, the House of Commons' influential Select Committee on Home Affairs did conduct a limited inquiry – described by one participant as 'a once in a lifetime affair' – into the Branch but it was oppposed from the start by the Home Office, which successfully curbed its scope. The government also used the lobby system to brief journalists with unattributed stories attacking critics of the Special Branch. Individual witnesses and Special Branch officers, interested groups with evidence of Branch wrong-doing were not called and the Committee refused to accept what was deemed to be sensitive information. In its final conclusion the Committee divided on party political lines following a bitter row in which Tory members made plain their unwillingness to countenance criticism of the Special Branch's work. It concluded that 'there were no grounds for public anxiety'. Labour members disassociated themselves from the Committee's findings, declaring the report 'a whitewash', and instead called for an independent investigation into the the role of the organisation. However, a glimpse of Special Branch work was made public, and the guidelines to police forces on its activities were published for the first time. Home Secretary Leon Brittan's request to Chief Constables to 'weed unnecessary information from their files' and 'publish as much as possible about Special Branch work' has gone unheeded.[15]

In the last thirty years, in a period when it also employed substantially more civilian staff and shed many of its tasks to other organisations, there has been an eightfold increase in the number of Special Branch officers. At the same time, the number of officers specifically engaged on domestic intelligence-gathering and anti-subversion work has increased five-fold. This has taken place without a single debate in Parliament. The Special Branch is supposed to be as accountable as ordinary police forces to local police authorities, but this is clearly a fiction. No Chief Constable or Home Secretary would countenance enquiries into Special Branch activities. The Special Branch remains outside of democratic control and is one more element of the secret state which escapes an effective form of oversight.

12

Oversight

> It is dangerous and bad, for our general national interest, to discuss these matters.
>
> Harold Macmillan

The above quotation was used by Harold Wilson to preface a chapter on 'The Prime Minister and National Security' in his 1976 book, *The Governance of Britain.* In one of the shortest chapters ever written, Wilson wrote: 'The prime minister is occasionally questioned on matters arising out of his responsibility. His answers may be regarded as uniformly uninformative. There is no further information that can usefully or properly be added before bringing this Chapter to an end.' Critics have generally taken this to be an example of Wilson's toadying to the Establishment. On the other hand, I think it entirely plausible that Wilson wrote the passage with tongue firmly in cheek. When the book was published, the former Prime Minister was privy to a good deal of information about the MI5-backed plots against him. Wilson knew from first-hand experience that the whole edifice of governmental oversight of the security services, and in particular MI5, was a sham.

Another Labour Prime Minister, James Callaghan, admitted as much in an extraordinarily confused and rambling statement to the Commons Civil Service Committee, which was enquiring into the accountability of the security services. 'I am not sure what its accountability is to Parliament. I am not sure about Ministers. I find it a difficult question to answer, I really do . . . I am going to give you a very unsatisfactory answer, I do not know.' Callaghan was only able to suggest that a great deal depended on the interest of the Home Secretary. 'Some Ministers do not want to know . . . others want to know a great deal about what is going on.' He appeared to suggest that in the absence of accountability, trust was the only available option. 'I am certain there must be a very high degree of responsibility among those who serve in MI5 or MI6 because they have very great powers, considerable powers, and I think the ethos of those services is as important as the degrees of accountability that can visit upon them.' However, as he admitted, 'I am very, very mixed up about this.'[1]

The Conservative government appears to have no such doubts. During the debate on the new Security Service Act in November 1988, Home Office minister John Patten informed the House of Commons that oversight of MI5 was practised and worked well. The director-general of the Security Service remained personally responsible to the Home Secretary for the work of the service. The policy had changed little since 1951, when Conservative Home Secretary David Maxwell-Fyfe 'jotted his five points down on a napkin when he was away from the office for lunch for an hour'; or when later the Cabinet Secretary, Lord Normanbrook, without reference to the politicians, issued an additional directive which informed the service that the director-general could 'turn to a senior Permanent Secretary for advice and assistance on the policy aspects of his work' – thereby legitimising the role of unelected officials in directing the service. However, experience suggests that Acts and directives have contributed little to accountability. In 1972, MI5 director-general Sir Martin Furnival-Jones told the Franks Committee, which was looking at ways of reforming the Official Secrets Act, that a directive was 'a very un-English thing'.[2]

Patten told a largely sceptical Commons that the 'Home Secretary, of course, has a very thorough knowledge of the priorities of the service' – though this did not appear to extend much beyond 'ensuring that the resources it needs to carry out its work' are available and satisfying himself 'that those resources are used effectively'. The Home Secretary attends regular meetings at which he is 'informed and consulted about matters concerning the management and work of the service'. Additionally, the director-general presents an annual report to the Prime Minister and the Home Secretary 'covering the whole range of the service's activities' which 'always produces a full discussion'. The Prime Minister remains responsible for overall security policy to which MI5 contributes and 'again there are regular meetings'. The director-general may have direct access 'on major security issues affecting the safety of the country' and, according to Normanbrook, on 'matters of supreme importance and delicacy'. But as George Young, a former intelligence officer experienced in the ways of Whitehall's secret bureaucracies, pointed out in his book *Subversion and the British Riposte*, 'Although the Director-General has a right to direct access to the Prime Minister, he does not lightly go over the heads of permanent under-secretaries for fear of creating future problems.'[3]

The simple truth is that the Home Secretary does not really know what is going on inside MI5. The service does not appreciate exterior control. One security source told journalist Nick Davies that the role of the Home Secretary is considered ineffective. 'He hasn't got a clue what is going on. If he comes around, you lock away any sensitive files and set up a display file specially for him to look at – a spoof file on some imaginary subversive with lots of exciting material in it. He's not going to know any better.' Former senior MI5 officer John Day acknowledged that 'experience has shown that the Home Secretary on his own simply cannot carry out oversight of MI5.' This was principally because 'accountability depends on accurate, timely information, and it is questionable to what extent this has been available to ministers in the past.' Former Labour Home Secretary Merlyn Rees largely conceded that this was true. 'What is going on is generally kept away from the Home Office and only the Home Secretary and one official are involved. At the moment the system is fragmented and, therefore, mistakes are made.' The service comes under the wing of the Home Office's F4 Division, which is responsible for departmental policy on 'counter-terrorism, security liaison and subversive activities'.[4]

The Home Secretary does not direct long-term planning or become involved in short-term operations or even the service's budgeting. He is fed information on a need-to-know basis according to criteria decided by civil servants. Often, the information is of little use to ministers. 'In my experience,' Roy Jenkins told the Commons, 'the organisation wastes a great deal of ministers' time in dealing with its own peccadilloes, which detracts from any benefit which it provides.' While the Prime Minister will be given a brief summary on any case requested, it will be without any operational details. He will not be allowed to know any of the intimate details of MI5's work. This 'studied ignorance' is by 'mutual agreement'. The policy works on the principle that the less you know the safer it will be if you are questioned in the House of Commons. However, this means that senior ministers do not really understand how the service operates.[5]

Even within the arcane world of Whitehall, the Security Service appears to occupy a unique position. In its 1985 report, the Security Commission recognised that MI5 is 'a self-contained and substantially autonomous organisation'. The service clearly believes itself to be so. In a semi-official briefing to *The Times*, it confirmed its status as 'a semi-autonomous' organisation outside normal lines of control. The Commission added that MI5 was unusual for its 'comparative isolation', implying that, within MI5, management lacked the self-critical attitude necessary to keep the service under review. James Callaghan was vague about the accountability of MI5 when he was asked by a Commons committee whether the service had been 'out of control' during the seventies. He told the Committee that he did not know what the term meant. 'If it means do they take initiatives of their own kind without clearing everything with a minister, the answer is yes . . . They sometimes put to a minister actions which they think he will regard as repugnant but nevertheless they hope he will agree and the answer will be yes. Then it depends on the minister, whether he is sufficiently alert to say no.' And if they think he will say no, there are, according the late George Young, deputy chief of MI6, ways around the problem. 'There is a curious convention in Whitehall – you can inform the Prime Minister without telling him. The Cabinet Secretary can wait for "an opportune moment" which "may never come".'[6]

If ministers do decide to take an interest in security matters they will be actively discouraged, with obstacles being put in their way. 'When a recent junior minister, John Stanley, took an unusual interest in security operations, his persistent intrusions were not welcome, even though he was about the last man who could be suspected of unhelpful motivation.' As Hugo Young noted, while this 'may bring operational benefits', it has 'some dubious consequences. The abdication of ministerial control has been accompanied by an unfailing ministerial tendency to justify everything the security people get up to.' Labour ministers have also been made aware of the powerful position MI5 holds as keeper of the files. Discreet security surveillance is maintained over MPs and peers of all parties. Information is passed to the government about the personal lives and politics of all likely appointees to office. After a general election, the director-general of MI5 is the third person to see the new Prime Minister, when the files are called up from Registry and reviewed. Most information concerns the appointees' intimate private lives and has little to do with national security, but it does put the Security Service in a very powerful position. Senior MI5 officers may be 'hesitant' in informing a minister if they consider him to be 'a security risk'.[7]

The key figures linking MI5 with the Prime Minister and the Home Secretary are the Cabinet Secretary, Sir Robin Butler, and the Permanent Secretary at the Home Office, Sir Clive Whitmore. Both sit on the powerful Permanent Secretaries'

Committee on the Intelligence Services (PSIS), which 'discusses general priorities, potential political embarrassments or scandals, and the budgets of the security and intelligence agencies. It reports to the prime minister but it is not concerned with operations.' Financial briefs are passed on to the Ministerial Committee on Intelligence (MIS), which is chaired by Prime Minister John Major, but the MIS, which was recently unveiled as a Cabinet committee, is little more than a rubber-stamp committee. Within Whitehall are a number of other bodies, including the Official Committee on Security, the Personnel Security Committee, the Security Policy and Methods Committee and the Electronic Security Committee, which deal with security matters 'such as positive vetting, leak inquries, the classification of documents, the physical security of buildings and the protection of sensitive information held on computers'. These committees of officials are served by the Cabinet Office staff, whose accountability, such as it is, is to the Cabinet Secretary and finally, though rarely exercised, to the Prime Minister. There are no parallel committees of ministers. It would be wrong, however, to suggest that these committees have real control over MI5 since, in practice, adequate supervision has never been exercised. Through Butler and Clive Whitmore, the Permanent Secretary at the Home Office, the director-general 'would be aware of the government's general area of concern as regards security matters'.[8]

Senior civil servant Sir Finlander Stewart produced a report for Prime Minister Clement Attlee in 1947 which said of the post of director-general: 'The appointment is one of great responsibility, calling for unusual experience and a rare combination of qualities. But having got the right man, there is no alternative to giving him the widest discretion in the means he uses and the direction in which he applies them.' MI5 is a highly hierarchical organisation with the director-general and the two deputies being responsible for determining the direction and priorities of the service. They link through their

Secretariat to other intelligence services and their own officers abroad. Below them is the board of branch directors. Even so the director-general will be largely in the dark about what really goes on in all corners of the service. Broad guidelines are set, but it is left to senior officers how they obtain their information.[9]

Without the benefit of real oversight and aware of pressure from the European courts for effective safeguards, ministers assure the public that the judiciary will protect citizens' civil liberties and provide the necessary watchdog role over the Security Service, ensuring that it operates within the law. This is a delusion. The courts have very rarely challenged the executive on matters of national security. Lord Fraser, the senior law lord, stated in 1984: 'The decision on whether the requirements of national security outweigh the duty of fairness in any particular case is for the government and not for the courts. The government alone has access to the necessary information, and in any event the judicial process is unsuitable for reaching decisions on national security.'[10]

In 1985, following the Massiter revelations, the government asked Lord Bridge to investigate whether the Home Secretary had ever improperly authorised telephone taps. The scope of the inquiry was deliberately narrow, avoiding the possibility that MI5 had undertaken unauthorised tappings. Bridge, having studied 6,129 telephone-tapping applications in three days, reported that all warrants between 1970 and 1984 had been correctly authorised. This bizarre and incredible conclusion elicited the response from the former Labour Home Secretary Roy Jenkins that Bridge had 'made himself appear a poodle of the executive'.[11]

Following the introduction of the new Official Secrets Act, the government appointed Lord Justice Stuart-Smith as the Security Service Commissioner, with responsibility as chair of the Security Service Tribunal, to investigate public complaints against MI5. In his early sixties, the cello-playing Stuart-Smith is regarded as a 'dull dog'; according to one prominent QC, 'if he is not of the Establishment, he faces it on the periphery. I would not think he knew how to think other than in terms of the Establishment.' Stuart-Smith said of his role that he would 'probably be a reactor rather than an initiator in this context'. A legal colleague thought that he would 'not be looking for a case to strike at the Establishment, but if it floats across his snout he will sniff harder'. So far, Stuart-Smith appears not to have sniffed anything unsavoury. In the year up to December 1990, fifty-five complaints were laid before the tribunal, and in 1991 the number was nineteen; not one was upheld.[12]

Home Secretaries have refused to give any details of the work of the tribunal. David Waddington said that 'It was up to Stuart-Smith in consultation with the members of the Tribunal to determine what information might be included in his annual report to the Prime Minister.' Since the Commissioner has defined his remit in the most conservative manner, the government has little to fear from disclosure of the tribunal's work and MI5 activities. The tribunal's deliberations have taken on a Kafkaesque quality. Stuart-Smith has conceded that complainants alleging improper burglaries by MI5 will not be told if their property was searched in the case of the tribunal finding that the search was justified.[13]

The limitations of the tribunal were further exposed when it was revealed that it will not investigate files MI5 opened on individuals before the end of 1989, even though this information may be used against them and could form the basis of applications for warrants – and even though MI5 admitted to Stuart-Smith that 'its general policy is to retain records of suspected subversives indefinitely in case they are of relevance at any time in the future'. This would include those containing false information, those made in error and those with illegally generated material. The tribunal's attitude has not been constructive. In May 1992, it gave approval for MI5 to retain these records in order to 'enable the tribunal to carry out its investigations'. However, since it will only investigate information collected after 1989, it leaves MI5 with decades of uncorroborated information on file.[14]

The judiciary have, in the past, turned a blind eye to MI5 misdeeds, even though Lord Denning claimed in his report on the Profumo affair that 'members of the Security Service are, in the eyes of the law, ordinary citizens with no powers greater than anyone else'. Douglas Hurd, the Home Secretary who guided the Official Secrets and the Security Service Acts through the House of Commons, appeared to suggest that this was correct, admitting that MI5 had never had any powers to bug communications, open mail or enter premises. 'There have been no statutory provisions giving the Security Service special powers in this respect.' Hurd was not telling the whole truth. As Lord Donaldson admitted during the *Spycatcher* litigation, 'It is silly for us to sit here and say that the Security Service is obliged to follow the letter of the law, it isn't real.' In the past, prerogative powers protected MI5 from prosecution and enabled Peter Wright and his colleagues to 'bug and burgle our way across London at the State's bequest, while pompous bowler-hatted civil servants in Whitehall pretended to look the other way'. Donaldson said that while 'the Security Service is bound by the strict rule of law' there is always 'a prerogative power not to pursue criminal proceedings'. It was essential that any 'wrongdoing' did not 'deprive the Service of the secrecy without which it cannot possibly operate'. In the 'public interest' MI5 officers would occasionally have to break the law, and this was acceptable.[15]

MI5 has always justified illegal telephone tapping by claiming that it was operated under the royal prerogative. In 1952, Sir David Maxwell-Fyfe told left-wing Labour MP Sidney Silverman that MI5 was authorised to tap telephones on his authority under a 'power which been used by every Government of whatever political faith since the telephone was invented and is a Prerogative power'. Five years later, Lord Birkett, whose committee was investigating telephone tapping, was told that such actions had developed from 'an ancient power . . . derived from the actions of the monarchy when seeking to safeguard the realm'. In effect, the prerogative allows the Crown to do anything it pleases except where the power has been limited by statute. This power invoked by MI5 and ministers is not, Neal Ascherson has written, 'something outside the unwritten Constitution but on the contrary, is its inner backbone. It is simply the State, wearing a paper crown, doing as it pleases.'[16]

As we have seen in chapter 4, it was Donaldson's comments that persuaded the government to introduce the Security Service Act which places MI5 'within the law'. This made a mockery of Lord Denning's grossly naïve statement that the Security Service 'cannot enter premises without the consent of the householder'. In effect, the Act gives authority in law to MI5 to break into the homes of 'ordinary citizens', tap their telephones and open their mail. Stuart-Smith's reports have offered little protection to the citizen. He admitted that the Home Secretary was 'dependent on the accuracy of the information contained in the application and the candour of those applying for it. This is, of course, essentially a question of integrity and quality of the people involved in the security service.' MI5's record on warrants, such as those based on erroneous information during the campaign against CND, provides no basis for such trust.

Lord Justice Lloyd is the commissioner responsible for monitoring telephone tapping and mail openings by the security services. In his first annual report on the operation of the system, Lloyd refused 'in the public interest' to disclose the number of search and burglary warrants. Instead, he cited the 'comparatively small number' and the now restricted purpose for which they are granted. He gave the warrants a clean bill of health. However, there are many caveats to his report, which, for instance, omits tapping warrants issued by the Foreign Office and the Northern Ireland Office. Lloyd did acknowledge that one warrant can cover more than one telephone line and noted that new tapping techniques 'added greatly to the efficiency of interception'. At the end of the day, there is no effective sanction against illegal tapping, since the tribunal has no way of finding out about taps placed without a warrant.

Unfortunately, Parliament has not given the courts a role in the operations of the Interception of Communications Tribunal or the Security Service Act. Decisions of the tribunal 'shall not be subject to appeal or liable to be questioned in any court'. In February 1992, during a failed application for judicial review by Harriet Harman and Patricia Hewitt, Mr Justice Kennedy in the High Court questioned the wording of the Act and suggested that in certain circumstances the courts certainly would have jurisdiction to intervene. However, even if this did happen it is unlikely that it would make a great deal of difference. In March 1992, the Court of Appeal dismissed an appeal against a conviction in which telephone intercepts, made from a cordless telephone, were not backed by a warrant and were thus illegal. Commenting on the Section 1 provisions of the 1985 Interception of Communications Act, Lord Justice Steyn said that 'it would usually be perfectly proper for the Crown simply to decline to say whether a warrant was or was not issued'. In the particular case before the court, Steyn claimed that 'the police officers were local officers who might not have been very familiar with the Act. It was not suggested that they deliberately contravened the 1985 Act.' All that mattered, claimed Steyn, was 'the quality and content of the recordings'. It would appear that ignorance of the law is now an acceptable defence for MI5 officers engaged in illegal activities.[17]

Oversight of the security services is limited to a very tight circle within the secret state. Ministers are tolerated, primarily, because they are Privy Councillors and 'the oath they take when achieving that honour is sufficient security cover'. They agree to 'keep secret all Matters committed and revealed unto me', from which, as Peter Hennessy points out, 'Like the Mafia's system of omerta, only the grave can bring release.' It is accepted that members of the Privy Council have been, in effect, positively vetted. However, power over the Security Service is mostly concentrated away from lines of ministerial responsibility, ensuring a lack of parliamentary scrutiny. At the end of the day, MPs, whose oath of allegiance is not regarded as sufficient security cover, are not trusted by the service. Questions in the House of Commons about MI5 have traditionally been blocked by the Table Office on the grounds that they refer to matters 'of their nature secret'. The rules on such matters are made by a committee of unelected Commons clerks, which has in the past included former members of the security services – Arthur Martin (MI5) and Ian Milne (MI6).[18]

In January 1992, a small step forward was made on this issue. In a surprise move, following the announcement by the Home Office of Stella Rimington's appointment as director-general, the officials who vet MPs' questions to ministers indicated their willingness to allow, for the first time, enquiries on 'certain matters' about MI5, although this would not cover operations or individual cases. It will be interesting to see whether this will yield any worthwhile information; on past precedent the promise is likely to be unfulfilled.

Part of the problem has been that apart from a few isolated individuals in Parliament, most notably back-bench Labour MPs Tam Dalyell, Dale Campbell-Savours and, before he turned from poacher to gamekeeper, Conservative MP and now minister at the MoD Jonathan Aitken, the accountability of the security services, except in the case of major security scandals, has aroused little interest or concern. The main reason for this has been the failure of the Labour front bench to give a lead and to help exploit the government's weakness on the issue. It has been said that Neil Kinnock's desire to do just that was tempered by his close advisers, who were concerned by the ability of the Conservative Party and its allies in the press to turn security issues into ones of national security where the Labour Party's patriotism is questioned. Official security briefings for the Opposition leaders made 'behind the Speaker's

Chair' in the House of Commons can be used to bring them within the 'ring of secrecy'. They find themselves in a privileged position and any secrets revealed 'on Privy Council terms' cannot be passed on to colleagues. In the belief that they are privy to special information, they can 'adopt a suitably patronising attitude towards their humble backbenchers'. Criticism is thus effectively blunted.[19]

Within Parliament the Select Committee on Home Affairs is entitled to investigate those activities of the Home Office which are paid for from public funds, and there appears to be nothing in standing orders to prevent it doing this. The Committee has on occasion edged around the question whether it should investigate security service issues. Each time, by using the whips and their majority on the Committee, the government has made it clear that it would be a waste of time because ministers are not prepared to answer questions and the inquiry would make little progress.

Parliament has little idea of how much is spent on the security services. During the eighteenth and nineteenth centuries MPs made repeated attempts to make the governments of the day account for the money spent under the 'secret service vote'. It was only in 1977 that Parliament repealed the 1782 Secret Service Act, which limited expenditure on the security services to £10,000 per year; successive governments had been illegally overspending for two centuries. In this century, the Public Accounts Committee has examined the issue only twice in the last fifty years, with little success. The annual Public Expenditure White Paper includes a figure for the 'secret service vote', which in 1992 totalled £185 million. However, this is a small proportion of the total expenditure, over £1,000 million, which is estimated to have increased by 100 per cent during thirteen years of Conservative rule. The true figure is hidden in the budgets of other departments, most notably the Ministry of Defence, the Home Office and the Foreign Office. In 1980, MoD Permanent Secretary Sir Frank Cooper told a Commons committee that such 'laundered' payments were legitimate, having been given in 1946 the permission of the Public Accounts Committee. The covert use of MoD funds for MI5 activities were, Cooper claimed, 'fully accountable in every sense of the word'. A number of MPs have disagreed but their requests for fuller information continue to be turned down. In December 1988, the Financial Secretary to the Treasury, Norman Lamont, told the Commons: 'In the interests of national security, successive governments have declined to publish the information requested.'[20]

The Security Service budget, more than £300 million per annum, is accounted for by an unelected civil servant, the Cabinet Secretary, who, on behalf of ministers, forwards a certificate to the head of the National Audit Office, assuring the Comptroller and Auditor General that the money is being spent properly. The Comptroller, who acts as Parliament's watchdog over the government's finances, is formally appointed by the Queen, following a joint decision taken by the Prime Minister and the chair of the Public Accounts Committee. Many of the staff have been vetted and may be given sensitive information. Before he retired in 1987, the Comptroller, former Treasury mandarin Sir Gordon Downey, said that he would, if there were to be some oversight of the security services, be willing to help Parliament scrutinise their budgets. However, he said that MPs were generally 'apathetic'; thus Whitehall escaped real accountability. Downey was replaced by an 'insider', John Bourn, who had worked in the MoD and the Northern Ireland Office, alongside Sir Maurice Oldfield, playing a key role processing information and documents from informers and whistle-blowers. In March 1993, Bourn indicated that he had a 'free hand' to investigate funds MI5 derived from other government departments.[21]

Following the 1992 general election, Prime Minister John Major, who holds overall responsibility for the security services, established a Cabinet sub-committee to examine the principle of oversight. It agreed to establish a committee with cautious supervisory powers. The Cabinet sub-committee, which included Home Secretary Kenneth Clarke and his predecessor Douglas Hurd, now Foreign Secretary, had considered 'highly confidential papers', almost certainly submitted by the Cabinet Secretary, Sir Robin Butler. Although not a right-winger, Sir Robin is seen by colleagues as a conservative with a small 'c' who would want to do only the minimum required on areas such as constitutional reform. In late 1991, in preparation for the possible election of a Labour government, Butler visited Canada and Australia to see how those countries operate the oversight of their security services. In the event, the files prepared on this and a Freedom of Information Act were not required, but reform remained on the agenda, if only to stem the tide of growing criticism at the lack of movement on the issue.[22]

Major's sub-committee agreed that a Commons Select Committee should not be allowed to enquire into the work of the Security Service. Instead, a committee of parliamentary monitors would be set up to assure the Commons that security operations were being conducted within the rules; this would not involve rank-and-file MPs. The provisional plan is for a small committee of Privy Councillors, MPs and possible peers, to have limited access to information, including budgets, and to monitor policy matters. Julian Amery, an old imperialist who knows a great deal about the secret world, told the Commons during a debate on oversight for the Security Service: 'I amused myself in the bath this morning thinking of the Privy Councillors who might be selected . . . Some of them are rather old, and some have dubious pasts.'[23]

When Kenneth Clarke took over as Home Secretary shortly after the General Election, he told reporters that MI5 was 'amazingly accountable'. He quickly back-tracked from that statement and explained that what he had meant was, 'compared with what used to be'. While the current plans are welcome, they are half-hearted and are designed solely to prevent independent democratic oversight of the service. A Home Office spokesperson appeared to acknowledge that the government's attempts at oversight were feeble, when she informed one inquirer: 'We release a report under the Interception of Communications Act 1985, then there is the annual report of the Commissioner and another annual report under the terms of the Security Service Act. They are very thin documents.'[24]

The absurdity of the present system has best been illustrated by the latest report of the Commissioner, Lord Justice Lloyd. He revealed that during 1991 the Security Service had not sought a single telephone tapping warrant for a subversive, defined as being 'a major threat to parliamentary democracy'. We can either accept that this statement is true – there are no subversives in Britain worthy of a telephone tap, which begs the question, why do we spend millions on a service whose raison d'etre is the defence of the realm – or, are MI5 employing thousands of telephone taps without a warrant? In either case something is very wrong.[25]

In January 1993 the Home Affairs Committee robustly defended its right to scrutinise the role of MI5 in order to 'help protect against any possible abuse of power'. Brushing aside well-worn arguments that oversight would weaken the effectiveness of the service because it was impossible to distinguish between policy and operations, the Committee – which has queried police policy – concluded that 'vital areas' should not bypass Parliamentary scrutiny simply because of 'administative decisions that former policing matters should become matters for the Security Service.'

Committee members, who were denied the opportunity of questioning Mrs Rimington but were allowed to dine with her at Gower Street, asserted that 'ability to respect security is not limited to Privy Counsellors'. Committee chair, Sir Ivan Lawrence, said that while 'abuse of power flourishes' an oversight committee of Privy Counsellors would be seen as 'a creature of the government more than a creature of Parliament'.

13

Ireland

An adventure playground for secret agents.

Kevin McNamara, Labour Party
Northern Ireland spokesperson

Despite the objections of its senior officers, MI6, which officially operates overseas, was put into Northern Ireland in late 1970 by the Conservative government, 'The arrival of [MI6] did have one crucial effect,' according to the service's chronicler, former defence correspondent Anthony Verrier, 'this was to mean that the mounting of covert counter-intelligence operations could be justified as requirements by the overriding necessity to find a political solution.' He goes on: 'From 1971 onwards, [MI6] officers came to believe that the Provisional IRA was a political organisation which could be outwitted, not merely a terrorist organisation which must be destroyed.' An intelligence 'supremo' drawn from MI6 was seconded to the Northern Ireland Office at Stormont with a senior MI5 officer as his deputy.[1]

After the imposition of direct rule in March 1972, MI6 was involved in arranging talks with the IRA and at the same time provided support to the middle-ground politicians. The political moves eventually foundered, partly because of disputes between MI6 and the Army, which, along with MI5, favoured concentrating on a military solution. MI6's presence was eventually reduced after a series of 'cowboy operations' were blown by the Irish government in Dublin. The celebrated cases of the Littlejohn brothers, who organised MI6-backed bank robberies, and MI6 officer John Wyman, who ran agents in the Republic, were exploited by MI5 disinformation as part of the bitter struggle for power in Northern Ireland. In late 1973, London decided to withdraw MI6 control and put MI5 in overall charge of the intelligence effort in the province. Senior MI5 officers took over the posts of Director and Co-ordinator of Intelligence (DCI) and the Intelligence Controller at Army headquarters at Lisburn.[2]

In the early seventies, intelligence collection and assessment were recognised to be extremely poor, and something akin to chaos reigned in the British counter-insurgency efforts in Northern Ireland. The Royal Ulster Constabulary were distrusted by British intelligence officers, who thought the force was too closely aligned with the Protestant cause. In 1973, a member of the 'Malay Mafia', Jack Moreton, who had reorganised the Malayan Special Branch in the fifties, was brought out of his recent retirement from MI5 and sent to Northern Ireland to do the same to the province's RUC Special Branch. He also helped set up the MI5/Army computer database on the terrorists, which relied heavily on old records from the IRA border campaign of 1956–62, during which Moreton had operations. Thus by 1974, when MI5 was beginning to assume control, a classic counter-insurgency campaign was in place with various undercover units, Army Intelligence, RUC Special Branch, MI6 and MI5 all jockeying for position.

The bitter rivalry between MI5 and MI6 in the mid-seventies ended with MI5 in the ascendancy. On the recommendation of Sir Maurice Oldfield, who had never been happy with the Secret Intelligence Service operating on what he thought was 'home territory', MI6 reduced its role in Northern and Southern Ireland, though it still conducted operations on the Continent and in the United States against arms supply. There is still a small contingent of MI6 officers in Northern Ireland who are attached to MI5, though officially they are seconded to the Home Civil Service.

The tried and tested techniques, honed through use in many undercover wars across the globe, which had succeeded in Malaya, and to a lesser degree in other colonial campaigns, were eventually found to be wanting in an urban setting where the terrorist retained a substantial bedrock of support. A 1979 Defence Intelligence Staff document, 'Future terrorist trends, 1979–83', drawn up at the request of the Ministry of Defence in consultation with the MI5 DCI, was pessimistic about defeating the IRA. It concluded that the IRA had the 'manpower they need to sustain violence during the next five years'. The Provisional IRA were not 'merely mindless hooligans' but 'intelligent, astute and experienced terrorists' who were 'sufficiently cunning to avoid arrest'.[3]

Nevertheless, boxed in by the stubborn belief in a military solution, which senior Army officers and commanders admitted was not achievable, MI5 dug in for the long war of attrition. Surveillance techniques were refined, the databases grew dramatically and the tiny territory was saturated with hundreds of intelligence and security experts – all to little avail. It is now clear that the IRA threat has been contained, but the political process has not moved an inch forward since MI6's brave attempt at a political dialogue with the Provisionals in the early seventies. Perhaps that does not matter to MI5. By the late seventies, the Security Service was firmly entrenched in the province, and to have worked there had become a necessary career move for ambitious officers. If the 'war' should end, MI5 would lose one of its prime roles and find it hard to justify its existence.

The Director and Co-ordinator of Intelligence (DCI), under cover of the Permanent Under-Secretary for Security Policy, with a group of MI5 officers controls Security Service activities in Northern Ireland from an office at Stormont, known as 'the Department'. Although he is a powerful figure within the security world – he sits on the MI5 board in London – the DCI has no authority to compel the RUC or the Army to undertake operations. In the early days, the DCI was 'effectively impotent' as he was 'caught between feuding organisations'. According to Mark Urban, his power largely derives from his role as an unofficial security adviser to ministers at Stormont and the fact that unlike his counterparts on the mainland he is responsible to the Secretary of State for Northern Ireland and not the Home Secretary. MI5 teams in the province are responsible for intelligence gathering and assessment, running agents and specialised technical surveillance. Security liaison officers are attached to the Northern Ireland Office, RUC headquarters, Knock, and Army headquarters at Lisburn.[4]

Army manuals insist that intelligence is 'the key to success' in counter-terrorism. A Whitehall team which reviewed intelligence-gathering activities in the province in the middle and late seventies was 'surprised and shocked' by what it discovered. It came across 'phenomenal cock-ups' and there was 'over-confidentiality and secretiveness in the management of the work' especially in the field of informers. Information was not shared, with the result that people died. In consequence, in 1978 and 1979 a series of changes was instigated in security circles, resulting, eventually, in the direction and co-ordination of intelligence-gathering activities by the Royal Ulster Constabulary Special Branch. Although MI5 and Army Intelligence still play a major role in the intelligence-gathering process, the system is largely centralised under the RUC, which accepts daily co-operation with the other agencies with varying degrees of success. Additional intelligence is collected by GCHQ and the Royal Corps of Signals.[5]

While there have been extraordinary advances in technology, the recruitment of 'touts' is the security services' most important weapon in their fight against the IRA – much more significant than information gained through telephone tapping and electronic surveillance. Supergrasses are no longer used, their death knell having been rung in the mid-eighties when the Court of Appeal in Northern Ireland acquitted eighteen men jailed for a total of four thousand years following convictions on the evidence of IRA man Christopher Black. The steady flow of information from informers involved with the paramilitaries allows the RUC Special Branch to keep 'half a step ahead of the IRA'. Four out of five attempted terrorist actions are curtailed by the RUC acting on intelligence; however, 'when the flow is interrupted, violence erupts'.[6]

RUC Special Branch runs the majority of informers and, with the exception of one highly secret unit controlled by the Army's HQ Northern Ireland, has tried to stop military units running their own touts. The feeling among security officials at the Northern Ireland Office at Stormont has been that much of the RUC still leans towards the Loyalist community and is still tainted with sectarian bias. It is therefore useful to allow more than one agency to run informers – especially among the Loyalist groups. Similarly, the RUC believes that its touts could not be transferred to a different agency since many would distrust English handlers.

MI5 is still involved in agent running[7] and under Antony Duff there was an increase in the number of outsiders taken on by the service to help run agents in Northern Ireland. A number of officers and 'support staff' were recruited from the province, including officers from the RUC Special Branch and some who had served there with the Army. RUC sources suggest that these included a number of officers forced out of the RUC for their part in various operational blunders. They were subsequently recruited by MI5 in acknowledgement that they had taken the blame for what were Security Service mistakes. One RUC officer recruited in the late eighties, named Brown, was responsible for liaison with the Special Branch E4A section which provided raw intelligence for the Headquarters Mobile Support Units and MI5.[8]

Michael Bettaney was one of the officers who ran MI5's training programme for new recruits on Ireland, Operation Banner. This is based at the 'non-national' Joint Intelligence Training Centre at Ashford, Kent, which is used as a talent-spotting centre, providing MI5 and MI6 with an entry into the spy service of every English-speaking country. The JITC provides courses on rapid-response exercises with various weapons, manufacturing explosives, agent penetration and deep interrogation. Bettaney was a Catholic who, while supportive of counter-terrorism, was critical of the service's understanding of Ireland. In 1989, Jonathan Aitken told the House of Commons that on MI5's Irish terrorism desk 'there is some indication that there is little education in the true history and the politics of Ireland which would give the Security Service official the breadth of knowledge needed to grasp the dimensions of the problem.' New officers in the province are not always held in high regard by those who have worked alongside them. 'Some of them were laughable.'[9]

The activities of the different intelligence agencies are discussed at regular meetings of the integrated intelligence centre known as the Tasking and Co-ordination Group (TCG). The regional TCGs play 'a critical role in what security chiefs call "executive action" – locking together intelligence from informers with the surveillance and ambushing activities of undercover units'. Relations between the assistant chief constable of E Department, which controls Special Branch, and MI5's operations director in Ulster are termed 'cordial and excellent'. The Special Branch controls almost 95 per cent of intelligence and is said to be trusted by MI5. Officers involved in agent running are trained by MI5 and, according to informed sources, 'have begun to teach the teachers'.[10]

However, MI5 still holds considerable sway in co-ordinating informer operations. As long as MI5 continues to have control of the finances for touts, requests from the service will always be treated sympathetically. In 1985, the Northern Ireland Office reported that £1.5 million had been spent on resettling informers and ensuring their safety over the previous seven years; the annual cost of this service is substantially more today. The security services have not found any difficulty in paying out large inducements. In a few cases, informers have been offered upwards of £75,000.[11]

The 1979 Defence Intelligence Staff (DIS) assessment noted the central role that informers would play in intelligence gathering. It was a period when 'some security chiefs saw the entire campaign to isolate the IRA from the community in terms of the contest for informers'. However, the DIS assessment also recognised that the reorganised IRA was 'less vulnerable to penetration by informers'. This would lead to a dirty war in which the IRA would 'increasingly seek to eliminate those involved'. According to journalist Kevin Toolis, the RUC informer strategy is to 'spread its intelligence net wide. Almost everyone from the nationalist community who could be a source of information is regarded as potential informer material . . . The most casual contact with the police can result in a recruitment attempt.' The RUC will then use every means available, including money and coercion, to blackmail the mainly young members of the terrorist organisations to inform. 'But these agents,' believes Toolis, 'soon become mere tools. Their lives are cheap.' Once an informer has passed his first piece of information to the RUC, he is trapped. If he withdraws co-operation he can face 'nutting', IRA slang for killing touts.[12]

MI5 officers can make their careers on the basis of one high-grade source. According to Fred Holroyd, who as a military intelligence officer ran informers for MI6 in the middle seventies, MI5's policy when running informers was 'basic and shortsighted'. MI5 officers were prepared to use any means, 'legal or illegal', blackmailing the source into 'acting out of fear for his or her safety'. Those running the 'national assets', as MI5-run agents are known in recognition of the service's role as guardian of the realm, were told 'to carry out operations which cannot be traced back to the handler'. Holroyd soon discovered that this meant that 'instead of running a network full of mutual trust' they were 'embittered and fragmented' operations in which 'no one could afford to turn their back'. MI5 was prepared to be much more ruthless than the Army in its quest for short-term successes, resulting in a series of unnecessary casualties. Over the last twenty years, more than forty Republican informers have been assassinated by the terrorists, victims of the intelligence 'dirty war'. While security sources claim the identities of 90 per cent of terrorists are known, through the developments of informer networks, this intelligence has been of only limited use in convicting terrorists. Perhaps because of this fact, informer-derived intelligence has often been used for mounting SAS-style ambushes.[13]

Attempts to develop informer networks on the British mainland and on the Continent have achieved few successes. At the end of the seventies, following the bombing of a number of Army barracks in West Germany, which the IRA discovered to be easy targets, the security services stepped up their recruiting drive among the Irish community in Europe. This was undertaken through the British Services Security Organisation (BSSO), a joint MI5/Ministry of Defence unit made up of civilian intelligence specialists, with headquarters at Rheindahlen, West Germany. Its chief, Terry Gough, liaised with MI5 and MI6 officers in London and at the Bonn embassy, while the Cologne branch, under Tim Coke, liaised with its West German equivalent the Bundesamt für Verfassungsschutz (BfV – State Office for the Protection of the Constitution). On sensitive operations against terrorist groups which do not involve the military, MI5 has direct communications with BfV's Section 7. A Berlin BSSO station, under Gilbert Hughes, was also running jointly with MI6 an extensive surveillance operation involving telephone tapping on German territory.

Over these operations sat a series of co-ordinating committees. Under the chairmanship of a senior diplomat from the Bonn embassy, the MI5 counter-intelligence officer at the Bonn embassy, code-named CX, the chief military policeman in Germany and the MI6 chief of station at Bonn sit on the Joint Intelligence Committee (Germany). This meets occasionally to discuss strategy against the IRA in Germany and levels of security awareness. The JIC(G) is fed by assessments on the IRA terrorist threat made by the Joint Security Group, which relies on intelligence from MI5 and the BfV.[14]

The chief of the Army Intelligence and Security Group (ISG)

in West Germany, Colonel W. C. Deller, had suggested recruiting sources run in Northern Ireland who were travelling to Germany for the purpose of 'penetrating the Irish community, as a means of obtaining some forewarning of a PIRA attack'. It was, however, recognised that there were difficulties about running an intelligence-gathering operation among Germany's civilian population when the agents might be subject to German jurisdiction. Ignoring these constitutional and diplomatic rules, it was decided in 1979 by the ISG(G), based at Rheindahlen, to recruit five informants within the Irish community. The ISG, an Army Intelligence Corps sub-unit, chose not to inform the other security agencies of the operation.

By coincidence, during 1980, members of the intelligence and assessments staff of the Cabinet Office Intelligence Unit (UKI) discussed with John Deverell, the head of MI5's F5 section which deals with Irish terrorism, the possibility and feasibility of 'steering' agents into the Irish community in West Germany. Unbeknown to ISG, MI6 had already begun a similar operation. Scream was a UKI operation controlled by the Joint Irish Section of MI5 and MI6 but run primarily by MI6 using 'offensive penetration' agents working in Germany. Informed about the details of Scream, ISG admitted to MI5 that it was running agents and, in November 1980, Lieutenant-Colonel Small of the ISG told the BSSO of the five informers that had been recruited.

The MI6 chief of station at the Bonn embassy suggested that the Army be used to 'talent spot and then to pass to [MI6] for recruitment of potential agents'. The BSSO agreed that the ISG's activities needed to be 'severely harnessed'. The JIC approved Operation Ward in 1981 and it was given the sanction of Dr Meier, president of the BfV, with the stipulation that the director of the BSSO had a duty to exercise 'professional judgement [and] ensure that the operation was properly controlled'. By that summer a special Ward Control Group was in place at Rheindahlen, meeting every two months to approve operations and monitor progress. The five Army informants were turned over to British intelligence in 1981. Co-operation with the German authorities was always less than total, and though a 'number of the Group's contacts were declared' to a West German counter-terrorist officer, other Army ISG agents were never revealed to the BfV.

The whole operation was beset by confusion and rivalry over control of intelligence. There was also the secretive way each agency operated in defiance of the rules. The BSSO was furious. R. C. Cullen, head of the BSSO security branch, charged that senior MI6 officer Michael Moore had been 'sowing the seeds for uncoordinated action, duplication, etc.'. The forty-six-year-old chair of the Ward Control Group had received an OBE in 1981 in recognition of his work in the Middle East but had little experience of European operations. The BfV was not amused on discovering that, without the knowledge of the others, three different agencies were keeping the same individual under surveillance, each with the intent of recruiting him. BfV feathers were 'ruffled' and the Germans had to be 'talked around'.[15]

In December 1982, the director of the BSSO eventually went straight to C/UK (either Sir Colin Figures, chief of MI6, or Sir Antony Duff, Co-ordinator of Intelligence and Security) and demanded that Moore be ordered to stop using Operation Ward to steal Army Intelligence agents. BSSO also put MI5 under pressure to terminate Ward. The BfV was infuriated by an operation which increasingly violated German constitutional legal proprieties. It had been surprised to discover that an Army Intelligence unit, Section 28, whose official duties were to tail Soviet military liaison officers, had also been employed. The operation lacked professionalism and the Germans insisted on greater access to information on the agents. It was only later that the BSSO and the BfV realised just how unprofessional the operation had been. One agent, 'Bedford' had been recruited to supply information not only on the Irish community but also on the domestic German political scene. The BfV was never informed. Instead, the Army ran 'Bedford' as a joint agent with the local German security agency, the Landesamt für Verfassungsschutz (LfV), behind the back of the BfV. The LfV was not informed about Operation 'Ward'. In another twist, by the end of 1983 'Bedford' was suspected of being an agent for Irish groups and the BSSO ordered the Army to 'disengage' and leave the LfV in charge.

One reason for the failure by the British to inform their German counterparts was that the network had no real intelligence to impart. The use of labourers without work permits led to the arrest of one, code-named 'Flint', and another, 'Elgin', was charged with involvement in 'lump' activities. Of the sixteen original Ward agents 'only two can be said to be active in the sense of reporting at all'. 'Malta' had been 'compromised' and 'Glasgow' had lied to his handler. After five years' planning and three years in operation, Ward had failed to produce 'any worthwhile intelligence'. What was more astonishing was that Ward was the only such operation then in progress in Germany. It was allowed to continue with an agreement to meet with the Germans every two years.[16]

Ward was a catastrophic failure. The collapse of the joint MI5/MI6 informer network in 1984 enabled the IRA to regroup and reopen the conflict in Europe. It would appear that leaked Top Secret BSSO intelligence documents on the Ward and Scream operations, exposing the informer networks, enabled the IRA to restructure its terrorist operations and play the counter-intelligence game itself, turning the recruited agents back against the British agencies. The IRA were thus able to launch a series of highly visible terrorist actions in Europe without interference from the security services. In March 1987, the IRA exploded a 300 lb car bomb at Rheindahlen, home of the BSSO. The Active Service Units were only stopped when counter-intelligence agencies were able to apprehend a number of IRA terrorists in France and Holland. Following the publication of the secret BSSO documents in

October 1989 an extensive, but in the end fruitless, leak inquiry was undertaken by MI5 and the Army in Germany. The IRA later claimed that the papers had been taken not from the BSSO headquarters in Rheindahlen but from a British intelligence office in Sennelager, where a joint intelligence centre is used by a German special border police force, GSG-9, and the SAS.[17]

With the end of the Cold War, an agreement was made in September 1990 between West Germany, the United States and France to shut down Allied intelligence installations in Berlin. BSSO was closed down in June 1991, though some of its operatives were left in place until September to evaluate files remaining in Germany. It is believed that a number of its personnel were incorporated into MI5 expansion into Europe. Security sources have suggested that MI5 has used its enhanced financial muscle to penetrate the IRA at a high level. However, in the light of the Ward failure, claims that MI5 has developed an effective network of agents on the Continent, something which impressed Home Office officials, deserve to be taken with a pinch of salt. Much more productive have been the well-placed informers recruited in Northern Ireland in recent years, the most important and controversial being a Loyalist, Brian Nelson.[18]

Nelson's exposure resulted from an outside investigation by John Stevens, Deputy Chief Constable of Cambridgeshire, into leaks of intelligence material on terrorist suspects to Loyalist groups. Nelson's activities as an informer and recipient of intelligence dossiers came to light when the Stevens inquiry unexpectedly strayed into Military Intelligence territory. It was an inquiry which is generally believed to have been ineffective, fuelling 'the perception that all outside inquiries into the province's secret "dirty war" are nobbled'. Military Intelligence, which ran Nelson, is believed to have withheld vital evidence of collusion between the security forces and the Ulster Defence Association from the inquiry. Members of Stevens's team remain convinced that the mysterious fire which damaged their computer records in January 1990 was not accidental.[19]

The security services and the Army avoided a deeply embarrassing public exposure of their methods and activities when Brian Nelson pleaded guilty and therefore avoided a lengthy trial. The case was sufficiently important to have been discussed in Cabinet. In a behind-the-scenes deal, Nelson was sentenced to ten years' imprisonment for his role in conspiracy to murder and some twenty other charges. The charges to which he pleaded guilty show that he repeatedly broke the rules, acted beyond his brief as an informer by taking part in illegal activities, and did so with impunity. His handlers knew this, yet took no action to prevent it happening.

Brian Nelson took risks in his undercover role as chief intelligence officer of the Loyalist terrorist group, the Ulster Defence Association (UDA), while also playing a secret role as an informer for Military Intelligence. Nelson's mother had been a member of the peace movement in the seventies, while his father, a tolerant man, had a number of Catholic friends. In the sixties, Nelson joined the Black Watch regiment and then, in 1972, the UDA. In his twenties, he was imprisoned for a 'sectarian offence'. For the next eleven years Nelson worked for the UDA, moving up the ranks and gaining the confidence of his colleagues in the paramilitary organisation.

Nelson claimed to journalists that he was a double agent throughout this period. One prime source for recruitment has been former soldiers who return to civilian life in Northern Ireland and become involved with the paramilitaries. It is said that, by 1985, Nelson had had enough of his stressful post and was sickened by the sectarian murders. A highly strung man who lived on his nerves, Nelson left the province to make a new life in West Germany, where he set up a flooring business. While in Germany, Nelson maintained his contacts with both the UDA and Military Intelligence. In the light of our knowledge of Ward, it is possible that Nelson was part of the follow-up operation. In January 1987, he was approached by his old handlers and asked to return to Northern Ireland. On his way back to Belfast he was interviewed by an MI5 officer in London. MI5, which traditionally has responsibilities for monitoring Loyalist activity on the mainland, told him that he was needed to fill 'an intelligence vacuum' in the agent coverage of Loyalist paramilitaries in Northern Ireland, by once more infiltrating the UDA.

Once in the province, Nelson was run by the most secret unit in Military Intelligence, the FRU – Field Research Unit – known locally as 'the Detachment'. In one version of the Nelson operation, MI5 allegedly opposed his being run by the FRU. In 1980, the Commander of Land Forces, Major-General James Glover, centralised Army informer handling with the FRU at HQNI, Lisburn. Its personnel are mostly drawn from the Intelligence Corps briefers, who are known by Army slang as the 'green slime'. Inside the UDA, Nelson's main task was to collate masses of information acquired by the organisation from leaked Army documents. He built up the intelligence dossiers on IRA suspects, whom the UDA then attempted systematically to assassinate. At the same time, as a 'patriotic agent', Nelson was secretly leaking these plans to his half-dozen handlers in the Army, who were attached to the 14th Intelligence Company. For his information, Nelson was paid around £30,000 by the British taxpayer.[20]

Military Intelligence is only allowed to run agents in Northern Ireland on the strict understanding that informer operations are made known to the regional Tasking and Co-ordination Groups. Any intelligence gathered is to be shared with the RUC, in writing, on 'contact forms.' However, Military Intelligence only passed on limited amounts of Nelson's information, in verbal form, to the Special Branch liaison officer. RUC Special Branch later complained that it had been deliberately cut out of the 'take'. RUC officers came to believe that Nelson's handlers were inept, though they also suspected that there might have been a more sinister reason for the failure to share intelligence. Had his handlers allowed murders and bombings to be carried out? During his time as the UDA intelligence collator, the paramilitaries carried out seventeen murders, most of them on the basis of information collected by Nelson. He was also involved in a bombing campaign organised by the Loyalist paramilitaries. This raised the suggestion that the Army had 'nominated' certain Republicans whom they were happy to see 'out of the way'.[21]

In one 'nominated' case, Cameron Hastie, a corporal in the Royal Scots, passed an Army document to Joanne Garvin, a member of the Ulster Defence Regiment. This was undertaken in the knowledge that she would, in turn, leak details of a 'Declan McDaid' to the UDA. The document then fell into Nelson's hands; he, in turn, passed an index card and a photograph of McDaid on to Winkie Dodds, a UDA assassin. Dodds had asked Nelson for suitable 'targets' for assassination. In May 1988, thirty-year-old Terry McDaid was shot and killed in his home when he was mistakenly identified as his brother, Declan. Although he claimed to have warned his Army handlers about the expected murder, it was Nelson who triggered the killing. Nelson also targeted Pat Finucane, who was shot dead in February 1989 with the full knowledge of Nelson's handlers. Finucane, a prominent solicitor, had represented many Catholics and nationalists, which had prompted Home Officer minister Douglas Hogg to state to a House of Commons committee, only a month before Finucane's murder, that certain solicitors in the province were 'unduly sympathetic to the cause of the IRA'. The security forces, armed with Nelson's information, made no apparent effort to prevent the killing. The RUC Special Branch were also outraged by Nelson's successful targeting of Brendan Davison, who was murdered in 1988 after working in the IRA's internal security unit and as a Special Branch informant.[22]

One FRU officer did believe that Nelson was 'out of control' and lodged a memo to this effect with his superiors in Military Intelligence. They not only turned a blind eye to the allegation and to corroboration from the handler's reports but, later, went out of their way to defend Nelson in court. The colonel who commanded Military Intelligence in Northern Ireland from 1986 to 1989 'gave the impression, by his demeanour and in his lavish tributes to Nelson, of believing, strongly, that no charges should have been brought'. He said that given the nature of the work, the strain he was under and the risk of death which surrounded him day-to-day, any mistakes Nelson may have made were 'all very understandable'. The colonel, who was described by a senior RUC officer as 'a liar . . . with no integrity in his approach', was awarded a 'meritorious service award' for intelligence work in Ulster.[23]

The presiding judge at the trial, Lord Justice Kelly, poured scorn on this defence of Nelson's actions. 'Our system does not create for the agent an "in-between" category that lies somewhere between guilt and innocence. The agent is prosecuted and punished for crimes as an ordinary criminal.' While recognising that there might be extenuating circumstances, in that an informer might find it difficult to maintain the line between lawful co-operation and criminal offending, he went on to say that Nelson had crossed the line from penetrating the UDA and gathering intelligence to partaking in the activities of murder gangs.

However, the security services were not about to allow this to pass; too much was at stake. The colonel attacked the Home Office 'armchair rules' for handling informers which insist that they do not become involved in criminal activities. 'In my opinion the guidelines are more appropriate to the criminal fraternity of the East End of London than to paramilitary groups. Brian Nelson is a victim of the system to which he was actually very loyal.' As part of its campaign to wrest control of counter-terrorism from Special Branch, MI5 was pressurising the Home Office to give immunity from prosecution for informers who might be involved in terrorist and criminal activity. A former MI5 undercover officer, with obvious deep knowledge of Nelson, broke the new Official Secrets Act and went public in the *Daily Telegraph*. He acknowledged that it was difficult to 'maintain the line between what is lawful and what is not', as Lord Justice Kelly suggested when sentencing Nelson. The anonymous officer admitted that he 'was guilty of conspiring to commit some minor offences. But if murder or bombs had been mentioned I could have made an excuse and left. But where the targets are involved in day-to-day killing such nicety is impossible. Any lack of enthusiasm would be an instant pointer for men already alert for infiltration. The agent must, if discovery is to be avoided, join enthusiastically in the activities of the organisation *even if they are seriously criminal*' (emphasis added).[24]

The MI5 officer related his own experience of agent running: 'A deep-cover agent has one link to the sane world – his controller. There has to be complete trust between the two . . . But that trust extends to believing that behind the controller is the support of the State.' He believed that the determination to prosecute Nelson was 'incomprehensible' as it sent out the 'signal to any agent left in Northern Ireland that the State does not have the courage to stand by him'. He concluded that the Nelson case left intelligence gathering in Northern Ireland 'in tatters'.[25]

It was against this background that, in February 1992, ministers ordered a senior MI5 officer to Belfast to assess how the intelligence gathered from informers run by the RUC Special Branch, the Army and MI5 is used and might be put to better effect. The officer also reviewed the way the three services operate and whether agent running should be left in the hands of one agency. Security spokesmen in Northern Ireland had claimed that the differing agencies had been co-operating well together and had not been hampered by traditional rivalries; the Nelson affair exploded that notion.

Military Intelligence is generally regarded as the poor relation when it comes to MI5 and MI6, but it has built up its own pool of informers in Northern Ireland. The Army has often been aggressive in its attempts to set up its own networks. Military Intelligence personnel were known to 'poach' RUC informers with offers of instant cash, and they controlled access to information on the basis that 'the military always knows best'. The Army responded to RUC charges by suggesting that its recruitment strategy is more imaginative and that it has fewer time-serving agents peddling worthless information.

In the mid-seventies, the Army and MI5 built up a huge intelligence-gathering operation producing a massive databank of information. In 1987 the Army 125 Intelligence Section of 12th Intelligence and Security Company at Lisburn took delivery of a super computer code-named 'Crucible'. In a major development away from just storing information on individuals, Section 125, along with senior MI5 officers such as Hal Doyne-Ditmass, introduced 'movement analysis', which is able to help plot the movements of suspected and known terrorists in the province. This had first been developed by the Canadians and was used extensively by MI5 to track the movements of Soviet intelligence officers in London. Information is fed into the system from the numerous computer terminals in the province at roadblocks and from general intelligence gathering. Older intelligence hands doubt whether the immense amount of time and effort required in feeding the never-ending appetite of this system brings any great success. However, it is unlikely that the Army or MI5 would be willing to relinquish control of such intelligence.[26]

Despite these disagreements, security sources suggested that as a result of the inquiry the Army and MI5 would be allowed to run their own agents, though Army rules would have to be brought into line with RUC practice. Given that the inquiry was undertaken by an MI5 representative, it was bound to appear rather unbalanced – especially when it was revealed that part of the remit was to examine the role of Director and Co-ordinator of Intelligence (DCI) and whether it should remain in the hands of MI5 or be passed to another agency. More importantly, the review included a recommendation for a new 'Director and Co-ordinator of Security', similar to the role given to former MI6 chief Sir Maurice Oldfield in 1979. The new post would not be advisory but would have executive powers to direct operational resources and make policy decisions affecting the police, Army and security services. The essential difficulty for any integrated counter-insurgency campaign in the province has always been that civil arms of the state have been unwilling to surrender their powers to the Army. The creation of such a post would meet stiff resistance from those in the RUC, who resent outside intrusion into their activities. Since 1976 the police have held primacy for security and intelligence affairs over the Army and would see themselves as the prime candidate for the new post.[27]

As a result of the review, in July 1982 a new body was created, the Provincial Executive Committee (PEC), with authority over all security operations. This appears to have been a triumph for Hugh Annesley, Chief Constable of the RUC, a force which has never taken him to its heart. Born in Dublin, albeit to a Protestant family, Annesley has not been in favour with the mandarins at the Northern Ireland Office, though he has nevertheless managed to reorganise the RUC towards a planned approach instead of a reliance on fire-fighting operations. The PEC consists of the Commander of Land Forces, Major-General Ian Freer; the newly appointed RUC Deputy Chief Constable (Operations), Blair Wallace; the head of RUC Special Branch; and the MI5 DCI. Wallace will have responsibility for security operations and will concentrate exclusively on co-ordinating the work of the security forces. Intelligence assessments, which had recognised that the IRA could 'orchestrate' terrorist acts province-wide, had prompted the creation of the new post, while the framework of the PEC was laid down in 1990 when police, district and Army brigade boundaries were redrawn to coincide for the first time.[28]

The new proposal, while sensible, hardly seems a step forward, but rather a nostalgic retreat to the period in Malaya when Templer had complete control over security policy with almost dictatorial powers. Whether such a policy would solve anything after twenty-three years of intense security and intelligence operations, which have resulted in a failure to defeat the terrorists, is highly unlikely. Perhaps it is time for the 'sensible chaps' in MI6 to resume their political initiatives.

14

Europol

I did not join Europe to have free movement of terrorists, criminals, drugs and illegal immigrants.

Margaret Thatcher, 18 May 1989

The detention of refugees during the Gulf War should not be seen in isolation, but rather as a trial run for the much more serious prospect in Europe of coping with widespread immigration from the disintegrating former Soviet empire and the Third World. The operation was a test for the co-operation of the Europe-wide security agencies. Viewed in this light, it was a great success.

European security officials have warned that the expected wave of mass immigration might herald a flood of terrorists, drug-traffickers and international criminals seeping into the European Community (EC) under the guise of asylum seekers. Scare stories have bludgeoned willing interior ministers into making new policies and pursuing initiatives with an unjustified haste. With little debate and virtually no democratic sanction, a quiet revolution has been taking place concerning security policy inside the EC.[1]

There is an obsessive fear among EC governments of future threats from outside of national borders when internal frontier controls are relaxed in 1993. The European Commission circulated a paper in October 1991, for the Maastricht summit, which sought agreement on policies to stem the 'ever-swelling tide' of asylum seekers. There is also an increasingly hostile view taken of those rejected as 'economic migrants', with a 'fast track' approach to the deportation of 'refugees in orbit'. The abolition of internal frontiers will go hand in hand with increased vigilance at external borders, and may lead to extra controls over the freedom of movement of visa holders. It is into this area that MI5, Special Branch and sections of the future FBI-style police force have moved with plans for a EC-wide exchange of resources and information on potential subversives.[2]

While there is, at present, no master plan, and most initiatives are fragmented, as the decade progresses harmonisation within the EC on practices and policies must increase. The implications for citizens (and for the future direction of MI5) are potentially enormous. In 1989, an EC spokesman told a House of Lords inquiry that 'those countries which do not currently do so may wish to consider changing their internal surveillance into a tighter system'. In a breach of traditional secrecy, the Metropolitan Special Branch, which is heavily involved with duties at ports of entry and airports, informed the same committee that it would require greatly increased powers to check for the presence of terrorists and 'undesirables'. This might include 'a significant increase in our surveillance capability' and a radical 'easing' of extradition arrangements between states. The Special Branch argued that there 'could well be strong pressure for the introduction of some form of national identity card, extra police powers of "stop and search", enhanced anti-terrorist legislation and more stringent registration of non-EC nationals'.[3]

Legal experts have asserted that Britain's secretive system for dealing with asylum seekers branded as national security risks falls well short of the 1951 United Nations Convention on Refugees (to which Britain is a signatory), which provides safeguards for genuine victims of persecution. The UN has said of Home Office criteria: 'The impression conveyed is one of bias against asylum seekers.' It is a view with which Britain's courts have reluctantly agreed.

In August 1990, forty-three-year-old Karamit Singh Chahal, who had lived in Britain for twenty years, was detained for deportation though it was likely he would suffer persecution and possibly torture if forced to return to India. The 'three wise men' panel, much in evidence during the Gulf War, advised him it had proof that he was linked to terrorism – though the panel refused to reveal any details. The case was seen by the government as part of 'the international fight against terrorism'. Mr Chahal had played a key role in campaigns by the secessionist International Sikh Youth Federation (ISYF), which called for the setting up of the independent state of Khalistan in the Punjab. He appealed to the High Court against deportation, during which hearing the Court was informed by the Home Office that Mr Chahal had been 'centrally involved in the organisation, financing and planning of terrorism'. Money collected through a network of Sikh temples was allegedly sent to India to finance terrorist operations. The activities of the ISYF were closely monitored by the Indian embassy and, on a visit to India in 1984, Mr Chahal was tortured, losing his hearing in one ear. Mr Chahal denied the allegations of terrorism, saying the case against him was based on 'disinformation' supplied by the Indian government.[4]

Mr Chahal's deportation would appear to breach Article 3 of the European Convention of Human Rights, which warns against placing an individual at risk of 'inhuman or degrading treatment'. The Home Office argued that the law allowed ministers to deport 'a national security risk' refugee even if the move rendered him vulnerable to torture. However, Mr Justice Popplewell said that he felt 'enormous anxiety' at the decision of Home Secretary Kenneth Baker. In a similar case, involving a Zairean seeking political asylum, the Home Secretary was judged to be in contempt of court for failing to halt his deportation. Baker's successor, Kenneth Clarke, turned down the appeal of Mr Chahal, who had been held in prison for two and a half years.[5]

The Treaty of Rome, which set up the EC, failed to give the Community clear authority to deal with such matters as immigration, border controls and asylum seekers. As a result, these matters have been held to lie outside Community 'competence' and therefore have largely been discussed by unelected inter-governmental bodies not bound by Community rules. The relevant committees, which meet behind closed doors, are not obliged to consult with the EC and national parliaments are kept in the dark about their deliberations. This has been a situation which has suited Britain, with its traditional disregard of parliamentary scrutiny of security policy. When the Commons Home Affairs Committee looking at practical police co-operation within the EC requested, from the Home Office, a document drawn up by interior ministers in Dublin in June 1990 covering new areas of co-operation, the Committee was deliberately snubbed. In the same month, a convention from the EC, determining which state is responsible for dealing with asylum applications, was 'laid before Parliament'. Because it required no change in domestic legislation, Parliament was allowed to debate it but not to prevent ratification by the government, which invoked the crown prerogative. Even new Home Secretary Kenneth Clarke expressed astonishment at this lack of democratic accountability. In July 1992, Clarke told the *Guardian*: 'We must have given Parliament something to scrutinise . . . I'm amazed that British ministers have been allowed to get away with it for so long.'[6]

At the Luxembourg summit in June 1991, John Major said that Britain remained unwilling to abolish all border checks on travellers from within the Community, though he hinted that the position could be relaxed if the 'perimeter fence' around the Community were tightened sufficiently. The concept of a 'ring fence' surrounding what has been dubbed 'Fortress Europe' has come to dominate the thinking of EC governments and security officials. Major did agree to proposals for 'institutional machinery' to link national police forces aimed at combating serious crime, terrorism and drug-trafficking and supported calls for a EC-wide system for exchange of information within a European police force, Europol.

The British government, which has always baulked at moves which might undermine the ability of the state to control security policy, claimed that the 1991 Maastricht treaty did not 'affect the exercise of the responsibilities with regard to . . . the safe-guarding of internal security'. The Home Office fears that the removal of internal borders could make it easier for terrorists to enter Britain from the Republic of Ireland. British ministers have battled with their European counterparts to retain immigration and passport controls on EC citizens at ports of entry, though this will remain open to challenge through the European Court. The sovereignty issue is at the heart of Home Office policies, which is not surprising as it remains Whitehall's 'most unreconstructed department'. The government has constantly vetoed any intrusion by the EC into Home Office affairs and has, instead, supported *ad hoc* approaches to increased co-operation between police forces and security agencies in the EC.

Some interior officials and British senior police officers would like to see more informal co-operation and the development of the European desk at the International Criminal Police Organisation (Interpol), which remains outside the remit of EC officials. This is the view of the Commons Home Affairs Committee, which is opposed to setting up new institutions and 're-inventing the wheel for the sake of political innovation'. However, Interpol has no powers of investigation, being no more than a clearing house for national police force information on international criminals and a forum for discussion. There is also a good deal of national jealousy over its functions.

British officials did not like the fact that since 1956, when the constitution stated that the head of Interpol should come from the organisation's host country, the agency has been largely dominated by the French. Arrangements have changed in recent years. The Secretary General is ex-Scotland Yard Special Branch officer Raymond Kendall, whose links with the agency go back twenty years while another seconded Yard officer, Detective-Superintendent Stuart Cameron-Walker, heads the European Secretariat, which liaises with police forces both inside and outside the EC. The inclusion in Interpol of countries from the former Soviet bloc and China make it, in the eyes of the British authorities, vulnerable on security matters. The shared view of senior police officers throughout Europe has been that 'by disproportionately increasing its number of members, Interpol has paralysed itself'. American police officials have claimed that the agency has 'such poor security' that it is 'a liability, not an aid'. Drug-traffickers in league with corrupt officials had, the Americans claimed, tapped into Interpol's intelligence records. A Special Branch spokesman told the Home Affairs Committee in 1988 that 'Interpol staff are not experienced in affording proper protection to classified material, do not possess the requisite security clearances, and the politics and motives of some of its members are, to say the least, questionable in the context.' This was odd, given that the agency was headed by one of their own. The real concern lies in the fact that, despite its exemption from French data protection laws, Interpol's rules for the protection of individual civil rights regarding retention of information are relatively stringent, while those for the Special Branch are non-existent. Furthermore, Interpol's use of the 'theory of predominance' in collating intelligence on terrorism means that it is more inclined to deal with 'violent' crime than target 'political' terrorism. This means that its guidelines on information gathering are drawn too narrow for Special Branch and MI5, both organisations being notoriously cavalier in their definitions when compiling files on suspects.[7]

Senior British security officials are happier dealing with the informal groups which meet outside the framework of the Treaty of Rome and the competence of the EC. Here, their discussions are particularly well hidden from public scrutiny and democratic accountability because their deliberations are on 'operational' matters. The Commission is given only observer status at meetings of the Trevi group of ministers, the Nordic Accord, the Heads of Capital Cities Conference, the Pompidou Group, which embraces twenty European nations and deals specifically with drug-trafficking, and the even more secretive 'Ad Hoc Group on Immigration', set up in 1986 to 'end abuses of the asylum process'. Policies are developed through these groups by civil servants, police officers, Customs and Immigration officials, with input from the security services. In Britain, this includes the Home Office, MI5, the Association of Chief Police Officers and the European Liaison Section of the Metropolitan Special Branch.

The most important group is Trevi, named after the fountain in Rome. It was set up in 1975, largely on the initiative of British and Dutch interior security ministers. British security officials have a high regard for the Dutch intelligence service, Binnenlandse Veiligheidsdienst (BVD), which was developed by the government-in-exile in London during the Second World War in close co-operation with MI6. Trevi co-ordinates working groups on terrorism, public order, organised crime and a wide range of policing issues. In the last five years, its remit has been extended to include immigration, police and security co-operation, and the exchange of information. It has a semi-permanent secretariat and, in the past, MI5 officers including Michael Bettaney have been seconded to Trevi. Plans are in hand for Trevi liaison officers to be stationed in all the EC countries, with some posted abroad to gather and exchange intelligence. MI5 plays a central role in co-ordinating operations, meeting with a group of senior officials in section F4 of the Home Office who set policy and report to ministers. The British see Trevi's 'distinctive strength' as lying in 'the informal, spontaneous and practical character of its discussions'.

Trevi, which meets every six months, is split up into four working groups whose proposals are sent to the K4 Committee for implementation:

- Group 1 exchanges information on the institutional and legal framework and analyses the terrorist threat in Europe and from outside the EC. It includes officials from F4, MI5 and the police.

- Group 2 discusses training, forensic science and equipment.
- Group 3 deals with drugs and organised crime, with input from the Customs and Excise and the London Central bureau of Interpol. This group developed proposals for a European Drugs Intelligence Unit (EDIU) to gather intelligence on organisations such as the Colombian drugs cartels and the Mafia. European Customs services are developing a system called SCENT (Systems Customs Enforcement Network).
- Group 4 considers the need for a common information system.[8]

Trevi works closely with other EC security groupings. In 1979, the Dutch Centrale Recherche Informatiedienst organised a conference in the wake of the assassination by the IRA of the British ambassador to The Hague, Sir Richard Sykes. The ambassador was acknowledged to be a 'security expert responsible for an internal report on the safety of British diplomats following the killing of Christopher Ewart-Biggs [a Foreign Office diplomat with responsibilities for the secret services]'. Co-operation between Britain, Belgium (Groupe Interforce Antiterroriste, GIA), Holland and Germany rapidly developed into the Police Working Group on Terrorism, which was later approved by Trevi. Another offshoot, the Group of National Co-ordinators on the Free Movement of People, set up in 1988 by EC ministers, produced the 1989 Palma Document which agreed to the exchange of information and the central collection of intelligence on terrorism. In 1988, a coded facsimile system (Corea) for the rapid transfer of photographs, fingerprints and documents had already been set up for anti-terrorist units in the EC plus Finland, Sweden and Norway. The agency which distributes the codes is the European Liaison Section of the Metropolitan Police Special Branch. One of the first uses of Corea was in 1988 during Operation Flavius, against IRA terrorists on Gibraltar. It was again in use in June 1990 when three IRA suspects were identified in Holland and Belgium.[9]

The Maastricht Treaty, signed in February 1992, called for the extension of existing co-operation by member states through the Trevi group in areas of common interest, citing 'asylum and immigration policy and policy regarding nationals of third countries' (countries outside the EC). Home Secretary Kenneth Baker had already discussed the development of a 'fast track' policy with regard to dealing with supposed bogus asylum seekers, at a meeting of Trevi. The ministers agreed on a list of fifty-three countries whose nationals would require a visa for entry into the EC and a common list of 'undesirables'. It was also agreed that grounds for exclusion would include 'national security' and 'aliens considered likely to compromise public order'. The proposed Asylum Bill was very similar to EC proposals for handling refugees whereby cases involving asylum seekers would be speeded up, denying them basic legal rights. In an editorial, the *Observer* called Baker's policy squalid and discriminatory: 'Let us be blunt: it is racist.'[10]

At Luxembourg, John Major outlined the arrangements of the Schengen frontier-free convention as being appropriate for the whole Community. These include setting up a central computer and provisions to allow national police forces to engage in 'hot pursuit' of suspects into the territory of other EC countries. The Schengen Agreement, which was formally recognised in 1985 by Germany, France, the Benelux countries, Italy, Portugal and Spain, approved the abolition of their internal border controls ahead of the rest of the EC. They share an information system which lists those 'undesirable aliens' who will be denied entry to the countries in the group. This is backed up by the Schengen Information System (SIS), based in Strasbourg, which will include information on refugees, asylum seekers, crime, firearms and people under surveillance. This 'switching system' will give access to National Information Systems (NADIS) containing some seven million entries on a total of 800,000 individuals. The group have agreed to increased policing of external borders, and citizens of non-EC countries will be subject to particularly stringent checks. Refugees will be expelled if they are deemed to pose a threat to 'public order, national security or international relations'. Asylum seekers will be given only one chance of entering a country and may enter only one country within the group. In August 1992, Britain took advantage of this rule to expel victims of 'ethnic cleansing' attempting to stay in the country to avoid the Yugoslavian conflict.[11]

Because Britain does not want to see an end to border controls, it currently remains outside Schengen; however, the new Police National Computer (PNC2) will have an interface with the Schengen Information System and intelligence will be shared. The Home Office remains wary of too close an involvement with SIS, since the safeguards laid down for the storing and use of information on the computer are much stricter than are found in Britain. There are firm rules for exchanging 'name-linked data', and asylum seekers will have the right to see the relevant information and have it corrected or erased, a facility denied to people in Britain. Schengen's meticulous rules on data protection are well in advance of Britain's. 'Sensitive data' – details on racial origin, political views, religious or other beliefs – are not allowed to be incorporated into the computer. There is also oversight of the system which is to be monitored by a 'technical support organisation'. However, problems may arise over the exchange of information concerning 'threats to public order or security' as there are considerable variations of the term 'public order' within the countries of the EC. While Home Office officials support the desire to 'harmonise' security policy and the need to construct an accurate database on EC citizens and those who pose a threat to internal order, the exchange of information with all these safeguards on political subversives presents a problem. A Chief Constable told a House of Lords committee that it would be extremely difficult to explain 'to a European mind our thinking at this end on what we regard as a threat'.[12]

Although in 1981, following the Council of Europe Convention for the Protection of Individuals, Britain agreed to set up the Data Registrar, it refrained from following the wider options of the Convention. This allowed for the inclusion of manual records which are still used by private vetting agencies such as the Economic League. Additional conditions disallowed the transfer of data to 'private bodies' without the consent of the subject. This is particularly important in the field of private and public vetting, which each year becomes a bigger and more unregulated security industry. The British government also declined to implement the Convention's recommendations on sensitive police data and the compiling of files reflecting political views and membership. A Council guideline stated that such data should not be collected simply in order to compile a file 'on certain minority groups whose behaviour or conduct is within the law'. Section 27 of the Data Protection Act gives a blanket exemption on the signature of a minister to the provisions of the Act in cases of 'national security'. In such cases, the existence of the files is not even required to be passed on to the Data Registrar. Even registered data may be exempted on the signing of an appropriate certificate by a minister. Britain is the only member to oppose the recommendations.[13]

Proposals before the EC seek to go beyond these provisions which, in the case of 'national security' files would require the data protection authority to check the records on behalf of the person concerned. Britain is also opposed to restrictions on the interconnection of government data-banks which, once again, is illegal in a number of EC countries.

Proposals for restrictions on the movement of asylum seekers and increased surveillance within the EC's internal borders have led to calls for the introduction of a universal identity card. The Home Office opposes compulsory identity cards, not as matter of principle but on the grounds of cost.

Kenneth Baker believed that the introduction of a voluntary system was the best option. In truth, there is no such thing as a voluntary scheme. Beginning in 1984, the government issued to new Social Security applicants the National Insurance Card, which contains a universal identification number. It also carries a magnetic strip capable of holding 200 characters, the purpose of this has not been revealed. In addition, talks which have taken place on improving the security of credit cards with the addition of photographs appear to be taking us down the road of an identity card system by default.

In the United States, plastic fake-proof computer-coded driving licences based on computerised image compression include digital photographs, fingerprints, tamper-resistant type and magnetic strips from which police using computers can verify the holder's identity. A similar system is used in the security systems of Buckingham Palace, the House of Commons, and Windsor Castle. At Britain's insistence, the UK version of the new EC passport includes computer-readable characters. Internal Home Office papers reveal that 'one of the major benefits of an automated machine readable system is the potential for performing automatic SI (Suspects Index) checks'. There are said to be 20,000 names, including those of drug-traffickers, terrorists and 'subversives', on the Index available to immigration officers at 500 terminals at ports and airports, enabling details of movement to be logged automatically by the computer. The Immigration Service is developing its own 'new and fast growing' intelligence system, alleged to have over 300,000 entries on illegal immigration on its 'Ivan' computer at Harmondsworth.[14]

Britain's data registrar has warned of the implications of these moves. 'A national identity card offers the opportunity not only to determine that this individual may be who he says he is but to record information about him. This opportunity is enhanced if, as seems likely, the card is designed to be machine-readable.' This would 'open up the possibility of linking collections of information about individuals'. He called the possible introduction of a national identity card 'a step with potentially serious privacy implications for all United Kingdom citizens. From a privacy and data protection viewpoint the arguments suggest that the step should not be taken.'[15]

The Security Service has been operating closely with its European partners for a number of years in the counter-terrorism field and has used the connection to compensate for the diminution of counter-espionage work following the fall of the Soviet empire. It has been undertaking its own form of bureaucratic empire-building. However, increasingly it is the police and the Special Branch which are establishing the institutional framework for security policy and co-operation within the EC. The Association of Chief Police Officers (ACPO), representing chief constables, is now a powerful body with increasing influence in policy areas concerning the EC. It is linked to Trevi through its sub-committee, the International Affairs Advisory Committee, responsible for overseeing contributions to international discussions. Clearly there are connections between calls in the EC for the creation of a European police force, Europol, which was given the formal go-ahead at Maastricht, and similar developments in Britain for a national investigative police force.

While, to begin with, Europol will be an intelligence-gathering agency, it is expected, in the medium term, to co-ordinate 'investigations, search operations and identify investigative approaches'. This is as far as some British officials would like it to progress. However, the head of Germany's international bureau of the Bundeskriminalamt (BKA) said in April 1992: 'We feel that eventually Europol will become an investigative agency . . . The drugs unit [EDIU] is simply the first phase of Europol, to which counterfeiting will be added next March, and other types of organised crime over the next couple of years, so it will be complete by 1994.' In September 1992, France and Germany, 'in what looked like a pre-emptive putsch to whatever emerges', opened a Europol secretariat in the same building as the Schengen Information System headquarters, perhaps as a prelude to full integration of the two agencies.[16]

In recognition of the changes taking place within EC security circles, in 1989, Sir Peter Imbert, Commissioner of the Metropolitan Police, with the support of senior Whitehall officials, called for the establishment of a national detective agency to combat increasingly sophisticated international crime. Imbert was perturbed by the need to combat crime which knew no borders by a police force which was highly fragmented. He said that in the early eighties a surge in drug-trafficking had led to the formation of a national intelligence unit. He pointed out, however, that there was no central unit officially established 'to receive and process non-drug intelligence from abroad . . . There has been a lack of investment, a slowness in developing an overall intelligence strategy.' He subsequently proposed the setting up of an FBI-style national police unit to oppose the new threat.[17]

Imbert received support from the Labour Party, which called for a national intelligence unit with its own operational arm. This would be, suggested home affairs spokesman Barry Sheerman, 'the best way of dealing with the new problems presented by European integration and the opening up of boundaries in 1992'. Labour's proposals went further than government plans, giving responsibility for combating drug-trafficking, terrorism and other organised crime at international and national level to the new unit. It would also have a remit to liaise with forces in the EC. The effective way to deal with terrorism, Sheerman said, 'was good policing and good intelligence'.[18]

Imbert's proposals were received critically by some senior police officers and the civil liberties lobby, who feared the centralisation of police power and the loss of local control. To appease the critics, the proposals were subsequently watered down and instead a step-by-step approach was adopted without, at this stage, an operational capability. The new, but less all-embracing, FBI-style force would, according to John Dellow – then president of the ACPO – give 'the same benefits without legislation and without upsetting chief constables unhappy about a national force'. For the moment, new initiatives are restricted to the collection and dissemination of information.

The biggest and most comprehensive computer network for intelligence on major crime in the United Kingdom has been proposed by the new National Criminal and Intelligence Service (NCIS, pronounced Ensis). The computer, known as NIX, will have a very powerful analytical capacity and will include 'intelligence' and 'hearsay' on organised crime, drugs and money laundering. Unlike other EC states, people in Britain will not be informed of the full extent of the data held on them. NIX, which will not come on stream for a number of years, will be linked to the new Police National Computer (PNC2), which officially contains only 'fact-orientated' information. The PNC2 will give regional police forces instant access to a database of about 5 million criminal names, 40 million vehicle owners, 450,000 missing vehicles, 135,000 missing persons and 1,160 'extremist crimes index'. The PNC2 has been built with Siemens hardware and software supplied by Software AG, making it compatible with European systems, in particular the Schengen Group, whose powerful computer system was also developed by Siemens. The NCIS computer will include the indexes from the National Identification Bureau (the old Criminal Records Office), the London Central Bureau of Interpol, the Animal Rights Index and the Special Branch. It is also absorbing the National Drugs Intelligence Unit formed to co-ordinate police and Customs intelligence on drug-trafficking. Many of the Customs officers from the 100 strong unit will joint the NCIS. The new computer will aim to create a 'one person, one record' with intelligence on one database, initially, targeted at fifty professional criminals earning over £100,000 per annum.[19]

The first head of the 400 strong NCIS was the former Chief Constable of West Mercia, fifty-eight-year-old Tony Mullett, a man with a very low profile and regarded as being 'a safe pair of hands'. The mild-mannered Mullett was responsible for organising the setting up of the NCIS information system, which went 'live' at the end of 1992. There are five regional 'branch offices' with local CID operations able to 'buy into' the new database, which will be 'working with information, collating, analysing and discerning patterns and passing it on'. The NCIS is currently recruiting some of the best operational officers from around the country. It has also improved the network of drug liaison officers in Eastern Europe and has taken over the British desk of Interpol. Mullett was forced to retire in December 1992 because of ill-health as a result of a punishing travel schedule. It is likely that the true scope and character of Britain's newest intelligence agency will not be known until a longer-term head is in post.[20]

A number of senior police officers criticised the formation of the NCIS and warned of a 'hidden agenda' which would lead to a national police force. The real hidden agenda may be very different. The creation of the NCIS and other *ad hoc* units provoked a serious debate in Whitehall about the future and relevance of MI5, whose recent track record in its counter-intelligence role had not impressed senior civil servants. In private, senior police officials expressed the view that police agencies such as the NCIS might lead to the demise of MI5, an agency to which, traditionally, they have been hostile.

The more erudite and responsible senior policemen have always been critical of MI5's policy of collecting intelligence on the basis of suspicion and potential for undefined future behaviour rather than for the prosecution of a court case. They argue that this led to the excesses of political interference which have characterised MI5's operations. This may seem a hypocritical view in the light of the release of a number of people wrongly imprisoned for terrorist offences and other well-publicised miscarriages of justice, but the potential for creating a security agency responsive to the needs and requirements of a democracy probably lies in the use of traditional police methods. Under the control of the Home Secretary, there would be an opportunity to bring parliamentary accountability to the various *ad hoc* groups and provide the Home Affairs Committee with the opportunity to undertake oversight of the police and the new emerging intelligence agencies.[21]

During 1990 and 1991, some of these ideas were floated by senior police officers. It was agreed that police reorganisation would continue throughout the decade and that an FBI-style agency with full operational powers would emerge. Such an organisation would most probably include the incorporation of the currently fragmented and still localised Special Branch, which former Home and Northern Ireland Secretary Merlyn Rees suggested should become a national force responsible to the Home Secretary. It was felt that if this did happen – and the odds were thought to be stacked in its favour – then it would begin to impinge on many of MI5's traditional areas of activity. Increasingly, MI5 looked like an organisation from a different era which had little relevance in the post-Cold War world. MI5 had spent so long in the wilderness of mirrors with a mind-set and *modus operandi* which mistook speculation and prejudice for fact that it was no longer reasonable to expect that it could be reformed. Naturally, senior Security Service officials were alarmed by what they were hearing. So began a bitter, intense turf fight.

15

Counter-terrorism

MI5 are a bloody menace.

Senior police officer

Commentators are currently awarding terrorism the special status accorded to espionage during the Cold War. It should be considered, however, that it is entirely possible that the terrorist threat is just as exaggerated as was the danger from Soviet espionage. In fact, over the last two decades the number of people in Britain who have died as a result of terrorism is relatively low when compared to, say, the number killed by reckless drivers.

The threat from domestic terrorist groups on the Continent has reduced sharply over the last ten years and, with the possible exception of the IRA, remains at the level of a minor irritant to both the general public and governments, discounting the occasional spectacular actions which move it for a day to the front pages. Likewise, despite outrages such as Lockerbie, terrorism from the Middle East is substantially lower than it was in the early seventies. While some statistics from think-tanks on terrorism claim a rise in the level of activity, official statistics show that during the whole of 1991 there were only fifty-nine terrorist-related incidents on the British mainland, ranging from the trivial to the major. Incongruously, the Security Service has chosen this moment to move into the counter-terrorist field. While this move might fill the void which exists following the collapse of communism, the policy has little logic and is full of dangers.

It is debatable whether terrorism poses a real threat to the realm. Spy-writer Nigel West (Conservative MP Rupert

Allason) has noted, with dismay, MI5's move into counter-terrorism. 'With the best will in the world, Irish terrorists are not a threat to the realm. They are a nuisance to Christmas shoppers, and they are murderers, but they are a job for Special Branch, not intelligence.' 'West' appeared to modify this in the House of Commons; 'Counter-terrorism is a very important, very specific and very professional activity and it has never been an activity in which the Security Service has been involved. It has traditionally been left to Special Branch and the Anti-Terrorist Squad . . . the role of the Security Service is simply to gather information and supply that information to the relevant quarters.' MI5 is not in a position 'of supplying witnesses and that is why it has not indulged in counter-terrorism in the past'. Former senior MI5 officer Charles Elwell agreed. He expressed the view that the 'intrusion of MI5, which is specifically a counter-espionage organisation, is absolutely wrong. MI5 has nothing to do with terrorism which is a crime. It should be dealt with by the police.'[1]

Until recently, MI5 gathered intelligence on Protestant terrorism in Britain and on the IRA in the Irish Republic and on the Continent. The Royal Ulster Constabulary is still responsible for countering the Provisional IRA in Northern Ireland, while MI6 and GCHQ monitor activities from their bases abroad, in particular the Middle East. There has been intense rivalry between these different agencies, with MI6 and MI5 squabbling over their respective roles in Northern and Southern Ireland. Ministers, meanwhile, have privately expressed the view that competition between agencies is healthy as long as they are willing to exchange information.

Combating terrorism on the British mainland has been in the hands of the police, who believe that terrorism can only be countered by using the same techniques and methods as those used against violent crime. The police have, at the back of their minds, the knowledge that hard evidence is required to bring an arrest and conviction, while the security services have tended to blur the lines and make no distinction between relevant intelligence and speculation. Elements within the security services tend to exaggerate the terrorist threat to national security and this can lead to trawls for information which often have little to do with the crime in question.

The dilemma presented by allowing secret, unaccountable agencies to operate in this field was noted by the 1975 Royal Commission on Environmental Pollution, which reported on nuclear power. The Commission warned that the 'plutonium enemy' might mean the 'secret surveillance of the public and possibly of employees who may make "undesirable" contacts. The activities might include the use of informers, infiltrators, wiretapping, checking on bank accounts and the opening of mail.' These 'would be practised on suspected members of extremist or terrorist groups or agents . . . we regard such activities as highly likely and indeed inevitable'. The Commission, under the chairmanship of Sir Brian Flowers, added that 'no doubt' these methods were already in use against 'certain small groups that are regarded as dangerous'. A year later, the Atomic Energy Authority Constabulary, the special force which guards nuclear installations and has close ties to sections of MI5, was given the right to carry arms and to engage in hot pursuit of anyone believed to have taken 'nuclear material'. Whether the Constabulary, which appears to be under no form of democratic accountability, ever employed these clandestine methods is entirely unknown. Whilst the accountability of the police is flawed, we do have a fair idea of their activities.[2]

On the British mainland the 100-strong B squad of the Special Branch (SO12) is, in its own words, 'the national intelligence collation agency for Irish republican terrorism in Great Britain'. The Anti-Terrorist Squad (CO13), which collates evidence, as opposed to intelligence gathering, has the power to direct Special Branch activity, including the surveillance of suspects. Working closely with the intelligence gatherers of the Metropolitan Special Branch (SO12), the Squad stays in daily contact with its commander. Its head reports directly to the deputy assistant commissioner New Scotland

Yard, who is also responsible for the Special Branch. According to Home Office guidelines, 'Special Branch provides information about extremists and terrorist groups to the Security Service (or, in the case of Irish Republican extremists and terrorist groups, to the Metropolitan Police Special Branch).' The Special Branch and the Anti-Terrorist Squad viewed the Irish terrorism section of MI5 as only one of several agencies involved in counter-terrorism, and both organisations pride themselves on their close links to European security agencies – SB officers are stationed in The Hague, Wiesbaden and Paris – and the Irish Garda.

Metropolitan Police Commissioner Sir Kenneth Newman had originally insisted that no one should hold the post of head of the Anti-Terrorist Squad, formed in the early seventies out of the Bomb Squad, for more than four years. The post is exceptionally demanding, involving a high degree of personal risk. The constant rotation of staff, Newman argued, would lessen the risk of creating an élite force. However, organisations tend to have their own inertia; fifty-three-year-old George Churchill-Coleman, who joined the Metropolitan Police in 1960, has been the longest-serving commander of the squad. Commander from 1985 to 1992, he was held in the highest esteem by Downing Street and the Home Office, though his image was tarnished by the squad's failure to capture the IRA Active Service Units currently operating on the mainland and responsible for a string of bombings and assassinations. A man who 'adapted well to new technology and open management', he is a senior member of his local Manor of St James masonic lodge. Although 'a member of the inner cabal of the ever growing and confused intelligence industry', Churchill-Coleman wanted it to be known that he was a policeman – 'an old-style detective' – and not a spook. According to a senior colleague, 'He is typical of that type. He has an ingrained suspicion of the security services, the military and all foreigners.' That suspicion was probably confirmed by the manner of his going, which came as a surprise, and the attempt to make him a scapegoat for security failures. In September 1992 word of his 'axing' as head of the squad was leaked to the *Sunday Express*. Yard sources suspected the Home Office, while others accused MI5 which had crossed swords with Coleman-Churchill. The new head is the modest and largely anonymous fifty-one-year-old David Tucker. He had been in charge of SO11, a backroom unit, rarely publicised, which is responsible for the collection of criminal intelligence and the establishment of surveillance operations.[3]

Although there are weekly meetings between the different security agencies at New Scotland Yard, where information is pooled, old suspicions surface when 'intelligence is hoarded rather than shared'. Information is power, and there appears to be a reluctance to co-operate fully by handing over the agencies' greatest asset. Rivalries persist and operations have been hindered by a reluctance to swap information for fear of compromising sources. MI5, in particular, has been singled out by the police, the RUC and the Army for failing to co-operate and for its lofty dismissal of the other agencies' work. MI5 tends to see itself as a professional agency among a group of amateurs. 'Special Branch officers don't get a broad enough vision. Some have developed superior attitudes and got out of touch.' In turn, the Army has claimed that the Special Branch on occasions denied it detailed assessments of the terrorist threat against bases in England and on the Continent. The RUC and Garda Special Branches have also criticised their counterparts on the mainland for not passing on 'the precise information that we gave them. They put their own spin on it and condensed it as they saw fit.' In the end the RUC passed its 'unadulterated' intelligence straight to provincial police forces.[4]

Even between the Anti-Terrorist Squad and the Special Branch there is occasionally some friction. Squad officers often consider their Special Branch colleagues too aloof. These disputes came to a head in the mid-eighties when Sir Kenneth Newman cut the specialist squads by 10 per cent, with the

Special Branch suffering particularly heavily from the move. Senior Branch officers pushed the case for disbanding the Anti-Terrorist Squad and transferring its duties to the Special Branch. Squad officers responded by claiming that SB officers had been unwilling to pass on all the relevant information to which they had access. They also resented the Special Branch's role as an internal watchdog, 'spying on us as much as on the terrorists'.[5]

It was around this time that Sir John Cradock, deputy secretary at the Ministry of Defence, reviewed intelligence-gathering and counter-terrorism operations. There had been a proposal, presumably from MI5's director-general, Sir Antony Duff, and his advisers, to transfer the Special Branch's counter-terrorist duties to the Security Service. Cradock rejected the move.

Despite all these rivalries, as Richard Norton-Taylor noted in the *Guardian*, on the ground police forces, when fighting terrorism, have in general co-operated well with their partners throughout this country and the EC. Problems developed when the secret agencies became involved. 'Investigations into the Lockerbie disaster have been stymied not by police forces but by national security and intelligence agencies which are influenced by political and diplomatic considerations.'

The world's biggest murder inquiry took place following the bomb explosion aboard Pan Am flight 103 which claimed 270 lives over the small Scottish town of Lockerbie on 21 December 1988. As soon as it became known that this was a terrorist bombing there began a typical bureaucratic struggle over control of the investigation. In the early stages, the police had their hands full with the rescue and clearance operation, and it was obvious that the Strathclyde police force had no experience of dealing with a major terrorist case. Senior intelligence officials pressured Prime Minister Margaret Thatcher and Home Secretary Douglas Hurd to impose a national body, such as the Metropolitan Police, to oversee the inquiry. Special Branch officers arrived at Lockerbie expecting to take over, but they were not welcomed by the local police. 'They were easily identifiable. They always wore expensive Italian suits,' Scottish police officers told *Sunday Times* journalist David Leppard. 'They were very condescending towards the rest of us. They tried to attach themselves to the people from the Security Services. But MI5 didn't want to know.' Since the deaths included local Scots, the local force had to undertake the inquiry. Members of New Scotland Yard's Anti-Terrorist Squad were reportedly 'pretty pissed off with that'. Eventually, the London Special Branch boys were ordered to leave and the local Branch organised liaison duties. Crucial help came from Detective Superintendent Chris Bird of the Anti-Terrorist Squad, an acknowledged expert on Middle East terrorism.[6]

The police inquiry, centred on the Lockerbie Incident Control Centre, was housed in a local school. On the first floor was the Joint Intelligence Group (JIG), working closely with the security services. John Armstrong, deputy head of the Strathclyde Special Branch, was the link man with MI5 and MI6, which retained their liaison roles with the foreign intelligence services and which were to prove vital in the massive international inquiry. The most important information came from the CIA's counter-terrorism unit at Langley, Virginia. Intelligence collected by agents in the field and from electronic surveillance was passed on by the director of the unit, Vincent Cannistraro, to the MI5 liaison officer in Washington. He in turn forwarded the intelligence to MI5 headquarters in London and finally to the JIG.

Only the Chief Constable of Strathclyde, three detective superintendents and John Orr, one of Scotland's most experienced detectives and head of the inquiry, were allowed to see the secret material forwarded by the security services; however, even this was sanitised and the raw intelligence data was kept to a small circle excluding Orr. As part of the bureaucratic compartmentalisation, Orr never had direct contact with the security services. Although the Special Branch officers of the JIG liked to create a mystique about their activities, police officers were amused to note that instead of using the sophisticated 'Holmes' computer to collate and analyse the information, they 'spent their working day writing out cards, making up written files and indexing everything manually'.[7]

According to Leppard, 'As the inquiry progressed, some officers began to suspect that the intelligence agencies were deliberately withholding information. The prospect would later cast a sinister shadow over the incident centre.' At first it was the German BKA and then the CIA which appeared to be blocking progress on the inquiry. Later, suspicions grew about the regular anonymous visitors from the security services, a senior officer from MI6 and his red-haired woman colleague, who signed themselves in as civil servants from the MoD.[8]

The inquiry came under acute political pressures, which were channelled through the security services. The Cabinet Office's Joint Intelligence Steering Group was troubled by rows with the Germans concerning when and where the suitcase bomb had been put on board the aircraft. MI5 was concerned that the row might jeopardise its close relationship with the BKA in its pursuit of IRA terrorists on the Continent. Later, it became apparent that the governments of the United States and Britain were pursuing a policy of rebuilding relations with Iran and Syria, the prime suspects for the bombing. The security services were also under pressure because of their failure to act on warnings.[9]

When, on 8 December 1988, the Department of Transport (DoT) received photographs and a description of a radio cassette recorder bomb, it was 'frustrated by the lack of any assessment of the area of threat from the security services'. A 'Helsinki' warning, alleging that a bomb would be placed on a Pan Am flight 'within the next fortnight', was received by the DoT and was passed on to the security services on 12 December. DoT officials took the lack of any response to imply that the threat was unimportant. An assessment from the security services was passed to the DoT, but not until 23 December 1988 – two days after Lockerbie. When Dr Jim Swire, representing relatives of the flight victims, tried to raise this matter at the Fatal Accident Inquiry he was met with 'an electric silence'. The performance of the security services remained a closed book. Swire believes that 'where there is total freedom from accountability there is unlikely to be great efficiency'.[10]

The police inquiry was naturally hampered by dead ends and false leads but also by the deliberate muddying of the waters. It was discovered that the passenger list included a number of American intelligence personnel, returning home for Christmas. The CIA was distressed to discover that four American intelligence officers were aboard flight 103, and dispatched sixteen of its agents in the aftermath of the crash to retrieve secret documents among the debris. The CIA failed to recover the documents, which detailed the activities of a secret United States Middle East Collection Ten (MC10) unit. The unit had been working for the Defence Intelligence Agency (DIA) in Beirut and Cyprus in a Drug Enforcement Agency (DEA) controlled drug sting called Operation Khourah. This episode was later linked to the murder of three CIA officers in a Berlin hotel in February 1991. The three had apparently been waiting to see a Palestinian informant about information on the four agents killed at Lockerbie. It was little wonder that the Scottish police 'felt that they were fighting a losing war against the encircling secrecy'.[11]

In March 1989, Transport Minister Paul Channon, at an off-the-record lunch, told a number of political correspondents that the inquiry had targeted the terrorists responsible and that arrests were imminent. On 29 March, the police inquiry team concluded in a report that 'There can be little doubt that Marwan Khreesat is the bombmaker for the PFDLP-GC [a Palestinian terrorist group] and there is a possibility that he prepared the explosive device which destroyed PA-103. As such he should not be at liberty.' Judicious leaks ensured that the 'full facts' of the case were reported in the *Sunday Times*, which laid the blame squarely on Iran and Syria. CIA terrorism chief Cannistraro had concluded that 'From an intelligence point of view this case has been solved. There is a lot of evidence which puts this at the doorstep of the Iranian government.' State Department officials said that 'analysis leads logically to Ahmed Jibril's Popular Front for the Liberation of Palestine–General Command who carried it out under the umbrella of Syria on behalf of Iran in revenge for the shooting down of an Iranian airbus over the Gulf in July 1988.' However, United States President George Bush and Mrs Thatcher had reportedly spoken to each other in March 1989 and privately agreed that they would 'low-key' the whole affair.[12]

By the summer of 1990, with the *rapprochement* with Iran in full swing, the inquiry was in danger of stalling and the police had to rely increasingly on titbits from the CIA to push the investigation forward. It was now that attention began to focus on a Libyan connection. The CIA revealed details of a meeting held at the headquarters of the Libyan Intelligence Service which had planned the bombing. The CIA apparently passed on details of this meeting to MI6, but it was dismissed as one of dozens of warnings which crossed the Libyan desk at Century House. The Gulf War was changing the political scene in the Middle East and the coalition forces were desperate to keep Syria on board, with Iran remaining neutral. Truth, it would appear, was about to be sacrificed on the altar of political expediency. Even the *Sunday Times* was moved to note that 'an official cover-up has been mounted by London and Washington to sweep under the diplomatic carpet the role of Syria and Iran in the Lockerbie bombing.' The two former 'terrorists states' were officially cleared just a few days before the last of the Beirut hostages were released.[13]

In November 1991, arrest warrants were issued in the United States and Scotland for two Libyans, Abdelbaset Ali Mohmed Al Megrahi and Al Amin Khalifa Fhimah, who were held to be responsible for placing the bomb on board Pan Am flight 103 in Malta. The evidence for this came from a defector, Abdu Magad Jiacha, an alleged Libyan intelligence officer in Malta who worked undercover as the assistant manager at the Libyan Arab Airlines. Jiacha, whose evidence is disputed by Maltese officials, defected to the United States for 'financial reasons' at the end of 1991. In an effort to build up his credibility, British sources let it be known that a Libyan 'hit team' was on his trail. The accused Libyans are regarded by investigators as 'low-level technicians' in an operation ordered and carried out by others. By January 1992, the head of the State Department's office of counter-terrorism had reversed its previous assessment and announced that there was no evidence linking the PFDLP-GC to the Lockerbie bombing.[14]

The Lockerbie inquiry was a bitter experience for many of the senior policemen involved. Traditional police methods had achieved a great deal, but this success had been frittered away by meddling and obstruction from largely unaccountable secret services. This had a corrosive effect on police perceptions of international security agencies and their desire for co-operation. To many Lockerbie officers, 'The idea that Europe's police forces will be able to harness their collective resources in the interests of a combined European fight against terrorism appears naive.' Likewise, in Britain the police found themselves in a turf battle with the Security Service over control of counter-terrorism. The idea that the various agencies might drop their long-developed antagonism to each other to combat the upsurge in IRA terrorism also appeared naïve.[15]

16

The Turf Battle

MI5 do not live in the real world.

Senior Special Branch officer

In 1990, intelligence assessments made by the Joint Intelligence Committee (JIC) reported that the IRA presented a greater menace than at any time in the past two decades. This appeared to reflect not so much the reality – bombings and killings had been substantially higher in the early and mid-seventies – as a general pessimism that counter-terrorism tactics had failed to defeat terrorism. According to the JIC, the IRA had bounced back with renewed vigour and deadliness.

When asked in July 1991 about prospects for combating the IRA, Hugh Annesley, Chief Constable of the Royal Ulster Constabulary, said: 'The immediate outlook's grim. We are facing at the moment probably the highest threat in the last two years.' An IRA military strategist warned that his organisation had both the means and the stamina to continue its campaign of violence into a third decade and beyond if necessary. 'We want to stretch the enemy, both materially and in terms of their nerves.' Senior security sources saw there was a grain of truth in this propagandist statement. 'Without any doubt, they are the most professional terrorist organisation in the world today.' In the absence of political solutions the security services could do little more than commit themselves to the long haul in the battle against the Provisional IRA.[1]

Generally, Northern Ireland intelligence on the IRA is believed to be good, with all the main players identified. Informers within the IRA have provided the security forces with enough hard intelligence to stop the majority of bombers getting through to their target. Good intelligence has also meant that the IRA has had difficulty in planning campaigns on a long-term basis in any detail. IRA Active Service Units (ASU) are increasingly given more autonomy to pursue their campaign, and this inevitably leads to mixed results. However, there is a limit to what counter-terrorism can achieve against a well-organised group which still has a substantial bedrock of support among a section of the nationalist population, estimated at 10 per cent. There is a constant supply of recruits and collaborators and the IRA appears to have a strong financial infrastructure. With substantial arms supplies from Libya stockpiled, the IRA will always be able to mount operations.

Most commentators agree that everything which can reasonably be undertaken against the IRA has been done. In the words of an Army Intelligence officer, 'in a democratic society, there is only a certain amount you can do'. To go beyond the present security arrangements and intelligence-gathering methods would endanger the civil liberties of a wide section of the populace and provide the terrorists with the propaganda weapon they seek. Even the police have baulked at proposing further draconian measures. Head of the Anti-Terrorist Squad, Commander Churchill-Coleman made the point in April 1992; 'We've got to keep a measured view. It's all very well to adopt draconian measures, but what do we move to – some sort of police state?'[2]

The IRA has been fairly successful in its campaigns in England. It has mounted a series of nightly small bomb attacks in London, a news-making mortar attack on Downing Street and a spectacular bombing of the Baltic Exchange, which resulted in three deaths and the withdrawal of insurance cover for terrorist damage. There may be as many as five ASUs operating, with some security sources suggesting that a sixth, and possibly more, was put in place during the summer of 1992. Whereas RUC intelligence in Northern Ireland is of a high quality, the police on the mainland have been hampered by a total lack of hard intelligence. Though there have been criticisms of the Special Branch and the Anti-Terrorist Squad, it is unlikely that any other agencies could achieve faster results in tracking down the bombers.

The IRA has clearly learned from past mistakes and has regrouped into a cell structure, with minimum contact between one cell and another. Volunteers are increasingly drawn from Southern Ireland. Young, highly educated and outwardly respectable, the Southern Command recruits, known as 'lilywhites', may spend years undercover before being activated for operations on the British mainland or in Europe. In England, the IRA has avoided using sympathisers within the Irish community, knowing that this is the first place Special Branch will look to recruit informers. It is believed that 'ghosts', agents who are officially dead and are therefore not on security files, have been reactivated on the mainland. To combat this sophistication, the call has been to give MI5 the lead in the fight against the IRA.[3]

When MI5 director-general Sir Patrick Walker began to shift resources from counter-subversion to counter-terrorist work he attempted to persuade successive home secretaries to allow the Security Service to move further into mainland operations. In the event they would not agree to a change of policy. However, the tiny group of Whitehall officials who come into contact with senior MI5 officers were convinced of the need to do just that and began to argue the case behind the scenes for a greater role for the Security Service. As early as February 1990, informed sources were letting it be known that, with the demise of the Cold War, senior Home Office officials were considering taking overall responsibility for intelligence gathering on terrorism away from the police and the Special Branch. Exploratory talks had taken place between Home Office officials and members of the Northern Ireland Office on reform of the security response to the IRA.

A similar call came from terrorism 'expert' Paul Wilkinson, Professor of International Relations at the University of Aberdeen and Director of Research of the Institute for the Study of

Conflict and Terrorism. Wilkinson called for the reorganisation of the 'ramshackle' agencies working in the area and the establishment of a powerful centralised command control and co-ordination unit. Also required would be the 'complete computerisation of all intelligence into a standard system for sharing by the various intelligence agencies' and the introduction of computer-reading identity cards. Such a unit, it was argued, would require the control of computerised intelligence at a national level and would need the specialist skills of MI5. Wilkinson took as his model West Germany and its centralised operations based on extensive computerisation. However, a close look at Germany's counter-terrorism record, which was good in the seventies, shows a distinct lack of success in tracking down terrorists in the eighties. The counter-terrorist agencies did not manage to bring the Red Army Faction to justice. One lawyer suggested that the 'so-called third generation of the RAF terrorists appears to be an invention of the security agencies'.[4]

Other thinking centred on creating a single counter-terrorist force modelled on the lines of the FBI, which would co-ordinate all intelligence and a range of operational matters as well. This would cut across traditional boundaries and remove several bureaucratic layers which were thought to hinder full co-operation between the different agencies. While Europe was moving towards this kind of co-operation, Britain, it was suggested, was still stuck with old rivalries and attitudes. However, critics failed to mention that in the majority of EC countries police primacy rules with regard to counter-terrorism. In 1990, Sir Christopher Curwen, Co-ordinator of Intelligence and Security in the Cabinet Office and former chief of MI6, was asked by the JIC to conduct a limited review of these areas. In the event, Curwen decided against transferring counter-terrorist duties to the Security Service, though a number of centralising changes were made.

In late 1990, following the murder by Irish terrorists of Tory MP Ian Gow, a Home Office Central Unit of officials was set up to exchange information on the Provisional IRA and issue warnings to people who might be at risk. Further moves were made in October of that year, to enhance co-ordination on anti-terrorist operations between disparate police forces across the country. It was said that operations had been hindered in the past by disagreements between regional police forces. In particular, there had been squabbling in 1989 between the Kent police and members of the Anti-Terrorist Squad, following the bombing of the Royal Marine barracks in Deal. A new national anti-terrorist unit, chaired by the Metropolitan Police assistant commissioner responsible for special operations, was given particular responsibility for counter-terrorism by Home Secretary Kenneth Baker. The Home Secretary let it be known that he was satisfied that there was good co-operation between the different agencies, as well as a determination to combat terrorism.[5]

A good many changes were also taking place within the Security Service, largely as a result of the reorganisation put in place by Antony Duff and then by Patrick Walker, which made terrorism the number one priority. Resources were diverted from F Branch, now down to forty officers, into the new Counter-Terrorism T Branch. Sources suggest that only 15 per cent of the service's time is taken up with counter-subversion work. According to Mark Urban, T Branch 'is a burgeoning empire which is sucking up other parts of the organisation'. Sections taken over included the old F5, responsible for monitoring Loyalist terrorism; F3, dealing mainly with Middle East terrorism; and C4, dealing with security matters in government departments concerning counter-terrorism as well as running exercises with the SAS. The new T Branch is also believed to have a role in vetting arrangements for the new counter-terrorist checks, which were introduced in the summer of 1990. Counter-terrorist checks are made on those people applying to take up posts involving 'proximity to public figures at particular risk of attack by terrorist organisations' or individuals with unescorted access to likely terrorist targets.

They will be checked to establish whether they are connected with or 'may be vulnerable to pressure from terrorist groups'. Changes to vetting policy in October 1990 also required employees of certain industries to be subject to 'lifestyle checks' which included questionnaires about sexual partners over the previous five years. This information was required in the interest of national security, 'in particular to counter the threat of terrorist attacks'.[6]

Ministers agreed that the only way forward was the gathering of intelligence and decided to boost the numbers of intelligence officers monitoring the IRA. Since the mid-eighties, the service has recruited an extra 300 staff and officers have been posted to France and Germany for liaison duties. A number of MI6 officers with intelligence-gathering expertise are believed to have transferred over to the Security Service. There has been some extension of MI5's role 'by the back door'. An MI5 officer and a senior civil servant were drafted into Special Branch to oversee its intelligence gathering on the IRA, while a special unit within the Home Office/MoD has tried to place a number of MI5 people within the Anti-Terrorist Squad. MI5 also set out to expand into other fields of terrorism, setting up a special desk to deal with extremist Islamic groups in this country which might use violence on orders from abroad. The desk apparently includes recruits from Asian families. Special Branch are already responsible for monitoring the activities of Islamic fundamentalists.[7]

MI5 has had particular expertise in monitoring the funding of the terrorists, with one officer, over a period of thirteen years, being solely responsible for keeping track of IRA finances. The new specialist Terrorist Funding Unit, set up in the Northern Ireland Office, and the RUC's special department C13 – the anti-racketeering squad – are designed to deal with the financial structure and funding of terrorist organisations, though the latter is said to lack officers with the necessary skills to counter fraud and racketeering. C13 has recently been enlarged with state-of-the-art surveillance equipment computerised intelligence banks and additional legal powers. The 1991 Emergency Provisions Act authorised the summoning on the instructions of the RUC and with the consent of the Northern Ireland secretary of any person to account for his financial activities. Operation Whiplash, started in 1991 following the seizure of a mass of documents from Republican clubs, led Special Branch and Department of Trade investigators to suspect that the IRA had employed money to buy into a quoted industrial firm which was subsequently used to launder terrorist funds. This turned out to be pure disinformation. The chief executive of the company, Wace, resigned after stock market rumours that his company was linked to the IRA. An internal investigation failed to produce any evidence of such a link and absolved the executive of any involvement.[8]

Almost unnoticed, early in 1991 it was announced that MI5 was put in charge of world-wide agent running against the IRA. The position had been that while the Security Service undertook intelligence gathering on the IRA in the Republic of Ireland, where it is helped by a small contingent of MI6 officers, and in Europe, MI6 had responsibility for intelligence gathering abroad. Earlier, ministers let it be known that, with the Cold War over, MI6 agents based in Eastern Europe and the old Soviet Union could be deployed to help in an expanded operation to tackle the IRA. The new policy stated that MI5 'has the lead responsibility for intelligence work . . . against Irish republican terrorism overseas'. While retaining responsibility for non-Irish terrorism overseas, the Secret Intelligence Service appeared to have lost out in this particular turf battle with its old rival.[9]

MI6 suffered from its failure to detect the shipment of arms and explosives from Colonel Gadafi's Libya to the IRA. Evidence of Libyan involvement emerged in October 1987 when French Customs seized an Irish-crewed freighter, the *Eksund*. It was carrying nearly 200 tonnes of arms including Kalashnikov assault rifles, ground-to-air SAM-7 missiles, a million rounds of ammunition and more than 2 tonnes of

Semtex. Security sources said they were 'shocked' by the seizure. This was the fifth shipment to Ireland since August 1985, when a yacht, *Casamara*, delivered 10 tonnes to an isolated beach forty miles south of Dublin. Another ship, the *Kula*, smuggled 14 tonnes in October 1985, while the *Villa* landed a further 80 tonnes in July 1986. The RUC estimated that the IRA received a total of 6 tonnes of Semtex, twenty SAM missiles, 1,500-plus AKM rifles, 1.5 million rounds of ammunition, fifty RPG-7 rocket launchers, ten flame-throwers and a quantity of general purpose and heavy machine-guns. Only about one-third of this massive arsenal has been recovered. This was a major intelligence blunder, all the more damaging because GCHQ was assumed to have Libya and its shipping lanes under constant electronic surveillance.[10]

In June 1992, the Libyan government agreed to give information on the shipments to Edward Chapman, the British chargé d'affaires at the British mission to the United Nations in Geneva. This followed international pressure on Libya to 'contribute to the elimination of international terrorism' following its alleged involvement in the Lockerbie bombing. MI5 and MI6 gave the Libyans a shopping list of questions, the answers to which were thought initially to be 'a stunning coup'. The material contained names of IRA contacts – according to Libyan sources long dead or no longer involved in operations – and details of the weapons shipments. Officials described the information as containing 'positive elements which may prove helpful'.[11]

These various bureaucratic moves were not enough to stifle further criticism from politicians following the failure during the summer of 1991 to capture the IRA ASUs operating on the British mainland. Once again, security sources called for the setting up of a central body to handle intelligence. As head of the Anti-Terrorist Squad, Commander Churchill-Coleman was appointed national police co-ordinator in the fight against terrorism on the mainland. The squad, assisted by a central computer intelligence system, was to be responsible for monitoring and directing operations by local CID chiefs.

However, a formal interdepartmental review of MI5's role in the post-Cold War world, launched in 1991 on the order of the Joint Intelligence Committee, helped to re-focus opinions. Added to which, the IRA campaign continued to achieve successes while the police were hamstrung due to the lack of hard intelligence provided by the Special Branch. 'They are supposed to have this strong network of people on the ground,' said a security source. 'But actually they are thin on the ground and their people are low grade.' The lack of highly trained and skilled experts to co-ordinate and interpret the available intelligence had created additional problems. Attempts had been made to cultivate more informers, increase agent penetration, improve arrangements to collate and analyse intelligence and improve joint operational capability between the various police forces, but the changes required considerable time to bear fruit.[12]

The bungled Special Branch operation at Brixton Prison, which led to the escape in July 1991 of two IRA suspects, Pearse McAuley and Nessan Quinlivan, proved to be the catalyst for a wide-ranging review of counter-terrorism on the mainland. The Staffordshire Special Branch had used a prison officer as a paid informant to extract intelligence from McAuley and Quinlivan about the attempted murder, at his home near Stafford, of Sir Peter Terry, former Governor of Gibraltar, in 1990. The officer had first made contact with the Special Branch when he trained with the SAS reserve squadron in the area. Friends of the officer claimed that he also worked for the Security Services. He was asked to play along with an escape plot, based on the successful escape of Victor Dark in 1990, and had discussed bringing in a gun before panicking and moving from the jail in February. The Staffordshire Special Branch had later informed the Metropolitan Special Branch of some of the details, but not all, and the informant had been dismissed as a 'Walter Mitty' character. The scheme backfired when the men broke free using the method the Special Branch had suggested. Police sources suggested that this was, in fact, an MI5 bungled operation. The Security Service, which directs many Special Branch operations, had failed to give full details to the department at the Home Office which acts as a two-way clearing house for information of potential use to the prison service, preferring to let the escape bid develop in the hope that it might lead to a possible intelligence coup in uncovering further Provisionals. 'They are a bloody menace,' a senior police officer said. 'We catch two IRA men and our own side lets them out.' Whatever the truth about MI5 involvement, police chiefs used the opportunity to tell the Home Office the undercover war against the IRA should be left to the Special Branch.[13]

A second review, completed in September 1991 by Sir Christopher Curwen, once again decided against giving MI5 a greater role in the fight against the IRA. Ministers let it be known that there was a new determination to increase resources, manpower and effort to counter the IRA and terrorism in general. There would be a new drive against the IRA, with particular emphasis on improving intelligence gathering in the Republic of Ireland. More MI5 officers were sent to Belfast to help in the intelligence war.[14]

The Security Service, however, was not going to allow matters to rest there after putting so much effort into refocusing the role of the agency. Stella Rimington was said to be intending to remotivate the service and equip it for a tough new drive against the Provisional IRA. The 'Director-General to be' visited Northern Ireland as part of a diplomatic and strategic bid. She and her deputy, Christopher Davey, lobbied ministers and delivered a paper to the JIC on proposed MI5 plans to take over responsibility from the Special Branch for all counter-terrorism activities and 'take the lead' in mainland operations. The stakes were high; failure in this enterprise would expose the service to the threat of disbandment. It had nowhere else to go. According to David Rose's sources the lobbying achieved its first success in November 1991 when the Prime Minister, John Major, convened a meeting to discuss the Curwen review with the Home Secretary, Kenneth Baker, Defence Secretary Tom King, Metropolitan Police Commissioner Sir Peter Imbert, representatives of the Cabinet Office and MI5, and Brian Johnson, president of the Association of Chief Police Officers. Instead of endorsing the report, as expected, the Prime Minister rejected the recommendations and announced yet another review. John Major is considered by insiders to be a weak, ineffectual Prime Minister, at the mercy of his advisers. Presumably, therefore, he had been strongly steered in a particular direction by those close to him.[15]

The Home Secretary, in consultation with the Prime Minister, set up an *ad hoc* committee including Tom King. The Whitehall committee was chaired by Ian Burns, deputy permanent secretary at the Home Office. According to initial reports, 'Burns comes with a reputation for frankness at his previous job at the Northern Ireland Office, and by all accounts is not being intimidated by the different interest groups.' MI5's recent track record on counter-terrorism had not impressed Whitehall observers. Burns was asked to report with recommendations to the JIC in early 1992.[16]

The Burns inquiry led to a typically fierce bureaucratic war in which police sources openly voiced their criticism of MI5's competence and accountability. Brian Johnson served on the Home Office working party and put the case for expanding the police's role. There was, however, some disagreement between senior police officers about the rôle of the Special Branch, which exposed its isolation both inside and outside the police force, even though Police Commissioner Sir Peter Imbert had served in both the Special Branch and the Anti-Terrorist Squad. The disagreement led ministers to order a further assessment of the way that Special Branch carried out its duties in the counter-terrorism field. William Taylor Assistant Commissioner of the Metropolitan Police and chair of

ACPO's anti-terrorism sub-committee, submitted a minority report favouring the creation of a national anti-terrorist unit set up on the same basis as regional crime squads but which would be kept outside of the the new National Criminal Intelligence Service (NCIS), which, while it handles confidential information, does not at present collate classified intelligence.[17]

Burns also had a series of meetings with representatives from the MoD and the JIC, the MI5 director-general and her deputy and senior MI5 officers, who presented a series of position papers at the round-table talks. It was leaked in February 1992 that Burns's initial report recommended only some 'fine-tuning' in responsibilities for counter-terrorism. Full-scale reform was judged unwise in a period when the terrorist threat was deemed by the JIC to be high. Final decisions were to be held over until after the general election. This allowed MI5 to undertake another round of lobbying. In an astute move, Stella Rimington met with shadow Home Secretary Roy Hattersley, before the election. She was no doubt aware that the Labour Party had been particularly sympathetic to the police arguments on this issue, with Labour leader Neil Kinnock indicating that he saw no reason for the Special Branch to lose its primacy. After the general election, she followed this up with a series of meetings with the new Home Secretary, Kenneth Clarke. The talks served only to emphasise the lack of clout the police have inside Whitehall; the JIC includes MI5 but not the police. Stella Rimington was becoming an increasingly influential figure within Whitehall.[18]

The police suffered a further embarrassing blow when, on 21 April 1992, highly sensitive minutes of a Metropolitan Police Policy Committee held on 10 December 1991 were leaked to the *Irish Times*. According to the document, William Taylor, in his role as Assistant Commissioner for Special Operations, reported that the one thing needed to combat the terrorist threat was intelligence, 'of which there was little at this stage'. While Taylor 'unequivocally rejected' any idea that the document had been leaked by MI5, other senior officers saw the leak as part of a 'black propaganda' campaign by the Security Service as part of its campaign to wrench control of counter-terrorism from the Special Branch. For some observers, the leak showed that a 'cancer of distrust' still existed between the police and the Security Service.[19]

It would appear that MI5 had used its muscle to get its way. Those who have seen the Burns Report describe it as 'a peculiar document', which while echoing the reservations of the earlier Curwen review and stating the known drawbacks to greater MI5 involvement in police operations, drew conclusions which were the opposite of the main body of the report. 'It came up with the recommendation which the person who commissioned it wanted in any event.' In May 1992, Kenneth Clarke announced some 'far-reaching and significant changes'. MI5 would have the 'lead responsibility' in gathering intelligence on the IRA in mainland Britain, taking over that role from the Special Branch. In an interview with the *Daily Telegraph*, Clarke said that 'it had been important to end the uncertainty . . . otherwise relations between the Security Service and the police Special Branch might have started "festering"'. Clarke told the Commons that 'Operations on a wider basis, including the collection of evidence and the arrest and prosecution of those suspected of terrorist offences, are plainly essential in dealing with terrorism. Those wider responsibilities must rest with the police.' There would be more resources, he added, in tracking down the IRA.[20]

This success for the Security Service, described as a 'brilliant coup', was a blow to the status and pride of the Special Branch. Unionist MPs and RUC sources rejected the move, saying that it was a move away from police primacy. They said that there was no real understanding of the IRA among the 'Whitehall Warriors', who falsely believed that there is a security solution to the problem.

Police sources expressed their doubts about the policy

change, fearing that it would have grave consequences for civil liberties. 'The only extra tactics which MI5 could employ would be illegal. We are a great deal more open and accountable than MI5.' While recognising that MI5 officers 'are brilliant as analysts . . . it is questionable whether they would do the job as the public want it to be done'. Having down graded subversion, which often involved gross invasions of privacy and bending of the rules, the launch into terrorism might just lead down the same road, computers bulging with ever-expanding files, with only a tenuous link or relevance to anti-terrorist work.[21]

The police were concerned with the implication that terrorism might be redefined and broadened to suit the Security Service and be given the label 'political', as the IRA has always claimed for its bombings. The police have defined terrorism as 'politically motivated *crime*', which means that the activities of groups such as the Animal Liberation Front are investigated by the police Special Branch. However, the Animal Liberation movement has now been mentioned as a suitable target for MI5. There is no clear definition of terrorism, which creates some confusion and a potential for abuse. According to the 1974 Prevention of Terrorism Act, terrorism is 'the use of violence for political ends, and includes any use of violence for the purpose of putting the public or any section of the community in fear'. In 1992, the British government agreed to the Trevi definition: 'The use or attempt to use violence by an organised group to achieve political goals'. The definition of violence remains unclear and could, conceivably, refer to direct action by political groups. In the Netherlands, the definition has been broadened to include violence against property, while in Germany similar legislation is being used to convict 'supporters' of terrorist groups.[22]

Following its victory, MI5 may also begin to encroach on the operation of the Prevention of Terrorism Act (PTA) – a particular target being the National Joint Unit at New Scotland Yard, which, staffed jointly by provincial Special Branches and the RUC, co-ordinates the use of detention and exclusion powers under the PTA. In practice, the PTA is used as an intelligence-gathering aid and not for securing prosecutions. In the last eighteen years, during which the PTA has been in force, 86 per cent of those held were released and only 3 per cent charged with terrorist offences. In the last three years, while 500 people have been detained only three have been convicted of serious acts of terrorism. Under the PTA, even though a person may have been detained and released without a charge, his file will remain on Special Branch and MI5 computers, containing a photograph, fingerprints and personal details. Under the provisions of the PTA, files are exempt from destruction. The file may also be used in the counter-terrorist checks and be used to flag that person's movements if he or she leaves or enters the country. The Attorney-General's decision in April 1992 to invoke the PTA to force Channel 4 to reveal confidential sources on a programme about collusion between the security forces and members of the paramilitaries was possibly, the *Guardian* suggested, a harbinger of 'other poor days to come as the security services move full-heartedly into counter-terrorism and an Official Secrets Act burnished for the Cold War adds to the Irish problem'.[23]

Home Office security officials have made the claim that back-up controls given to Special Branch officers under the PTA have effectively curbed the movement of terrorists and weapons between Britain and Ireland. This is odd given the evidence that six or more IRA ASUs are operating on the British mainland. The Home Office boast is largely directed against the EC adopted policy of open borders beginning in 1993, which will necessitate a rethink by Whitehall on its Irish border policy. It is seen by some officials as a golden opportunity to introduce an identity card system into the United Kingdom as part of a counter-terrorist strategy. According to a report in the *Sunday Telegraph*, the Home Office has already commissioned a study of the new technology which includes the indexing of fingerprints and screening at immigration points. There are also calls for an extension of powers under the 1971 Immigration Act to demand a passport from any member of the public as a check against terrorism and for an amendment of the PTA to remove the requirement for 'reasonable grounds' when the commission of an offence is suspected.[24]

Lothar Jachmann, second in command of the German security service in Bremen, the Landesamt für Verfassungsschutz (LfV), said in a seminar in March 1992, 'In my thirty years, experience [in counter-terrorism] I have not come across any real new means.' MI5's predicted response on the British mainland will be to increase the use of infiltrators and informers, but police have been dismayed that this might lead to immunity for terrorists. Subtle pressure and moral blackmail play a role in recruiting informants. 'Sometimes the position is created for a man so that MI5 can come along to help him – a bit like breaking a man's leg so you can offer him a crutch.' The same coercive tactics used in Northern Ireland to blackmail people to inform have, on occasion, been practised on the mainland. The Special Branch under the direction of MI5 threatened one young Sinn Fein activist in Birmingham with an exclusion order and separation from his children if he refused to co-operate. Trying to infiltrate tight cell structures as well-planned and maintained as the ASUs currently operating on the British mainland is difficult, if not impossible. (Northern Ireland is a profoundly different area of operations.) In a similar situation, operating against the Red Army Faction and other terrorist cells, Lothar Jachmann, with all his experience, found that the use of the infiltrator method in counter-terrorism 'led us nowhere'.[25]

Although terrorism is in overall decline, the last few years have seen a rise in the number of applications for warrants for telephone taps against terrorist targets. This is likely, with MI5 involvement, to increase and open the way to further abuse. Already, following a terrorist incident, there is often a concentration of telephone taps without the use of warrants. Standard practice appears to include the wholesale monitoring of telephone boxes across a whole district, especially in well-known Irish areas.[26]

The police did manage to wring some concessions out of the defeat. One proposal, for the Home Secretary to chair a 'standing committee' which would consider all the intelligence gathered before deciding which agency would act on it, was scrapped. It was agreed that MI5 intelligence would be shared with the police. Whether this will happen is another matter. In the view of one senior Special Branch officer, 'MI5's agenda is built around counter-espionage, a slow process, keeping information for themselves long after it has squeezed things dry'. Often intelligence flowed to the police far too late, when it was no longer relevant. It was also agreed that the SAS would not to be used on the mainland, because the police normally carry out all armed operations. However, while there are to be clear lines drawn between 'intelligence', which is MI5's domain, and 'operations', which are entrusted to the police, the lines will inevitably become blurred.[27]

MI5 officers have already moved into Special Branch offices at New Scotland Yard and have been monitoring its intelligence-gathering methods. This is the thin end of the wedge, according to some Special Branch officers who fear a loss of jobs. MI5 is being given a new role within the criminal justice system. The Special Branch is helping to train MI5 officers in the preparation and presentation of court evidence. MI5 officers could regularly appear in court and run operations leading to prosecution.[28]

'The outcome, if MI5 gets its way,' complained a senior policeman, 'could be the creation of a sort of FBI, but by the back door.' That does appear to be the hidden agenda of some Whitehall insiders and one in which the Security Service would have the upper hand. Sources told the *Telegraph* the current moves could lead to the creation of a new national counter-terrorist unit which would involve MI5 and Special Branch sharing headquarters, with the Anti-Terrorist Squad being brought in as an investigation arm of the new unit. While agreeing to the idea of a centralised police force with a national counter-terrorist unit, in a lecture to the Police Foundation in July 1992, RUC Chief Constable Hugh Annesley challenged the policy by indicating that he would like to see a *police*-based operational unit. Annesley, who in 1987 was head of Metropolitan Special Operations and London representative of Interpol, had in 1985 spent time at the FBI academy in the United States.[29]

'If they get terrorism,' a senior policeman warned, 'drugs will be next.' Despite official protestations, buoyed by its success, MI5 does hope to expand its interest in intelligence gathering by moving into drugs, money laundering and major fraud and increasing its role in Europe. MI5 officers are already seeking briefings outside their traditional remit. The new National Criminal Intelligence Service (NCIS) and access to its computer would appear to be in its sights, but this is bitterly resented by police officers who believe it will 'undermine' the new agency. 'With NCIS and its computer you would not be far away from Orwell's Big Brother,' said one senior police officer.[30]

The changes represent another example of the general centralising tendencies of the present government creating new and untested bureaucratic structures. Will they succeed? The Home Secretary has said that the 'quality of personal relationships' is particularly important in cross-agency activities. A new senior MI5 post to advise Chief Constables on the new arrangements has been set up, while MI5's deputy director-general, Christopher Davey, has had several meetings with senior Special Branch officers, 'horse-trading'. Meanwhile, Special Branch and MI5 officers are said to be working together through new liaison arrangements, 'albeit with some tension', and areas of friction and rivalry remain. Given their past record, this is not a marriage made in heaven. The enforced fusion, which officially began on 1 January 1993 but which went operational at the end of 1992, is just as likely to exacerbate as end the traditional turf battles. Valuable time is likely to be wasted in trying to make it work while the active service units carry on undetected. In August 1992 a major surveillance operation on an ASU, which was monitored collecting thirteen tonnes of explosives from a lorry park in Brent, North London, involved four separate New Scotland Yard departments and a surveillance team from MI5's A4 department. The operation proved to be a disaster as the IRA suspects escaped. The 'miscalculation', according to police sources, owed a great deal to poor communications between the units and the non-compatibility of radios and computers. As Annesley points out, 'If we want good quality intelligence in five years' time we have to put in the resources and effort now.'[31]

Interestingly, while the Security Service won this particular fight, it lost the propaganda war. The editorials of the leading Sunday newspapers were resolutely against the move. The *Observer* worried about the 'dangers of allowing free rein to a secret, non-accountable organisation'. *The Times* had advised before the decision was made public that 'No branch of government can so blind an inexperienced minister as the security services.' It counselled against change on the basis that 'something must be done' to combat the IRA, arguing that 'there is no reason to think that the involvement of MI5 would improve matters'. Once the decision was made, *The Times* said, it was a 'mistake'. 'Mr Major's decision is also a crude comment on the better "class of mind" (or class of person) the MI5 offers to susceptible ministers.' It thundered: 'Britain's anti-terrorist law, the Prevention of Terrorism Act, is already draconian and illiberal. On top of it has been piled an edifice of costly hyper-security which does little but boost the ego of the terrorist. The IRA threat neither needs nor deserves yet further boosts by calling in new agencies to counter it.' The editorial, finally, while recognising the need to redefine roles, called into question MI5's entire reason for existing. 'The role of internal surveillance, in a healthy and well-policed democracy, is more questionable.'[32]

17

Mysterious Deaths, Deniable Operations and Private Spooks

> Some circumstantial evidence is very strong, as when you find a trout in the milk.
>
> Henry David Thoreau

Do the security services carry out assassinations? The simple answer is, we do not know. Rumours circulating during investigations into the Supergun affair suggested a unit of former SAS soldiers, employed by private security companies, was used by government agencies for assassinations, but no evidence was produced. Certainly, during the Second World War MI6 did order the assassination of a number of people, as did its American-based offshoot, the British Security Co-ordination, the latter employing the services of Mafia members, a forerunner of the Mafia-backed CIA plots against Fidel Castro. Likewise, the covert Special Operations Executive had the capability to undertake such operations, and it is believed that this expertise was transferred to MI6 at the end of hostilities.

During the forties, assassinations did take place, mainly among the exile groups in the displacement camps in Germany, by surrogates of the intelligence services. It has been alleged that, by 1950, such options were no longer considered politically acceptable and the practice was curtailed. However, on the orders of Prime Minister Anthony Eden, MI6 was told to put 'thuggery' back on the agenda and, during 1956/7, planned a number of assassination plots against the Egyptian President Gamal Abdel Nasser. Poison gas, German mercenaries, SAS execution squads and exploding electric razors were all part of the failed plots used during the period and known within the service as 'the horrors'. Since then, there has been little evidence of any assassination planning though, given the ultra-secrecy such a policy would attract, we should not expect any.

The publicity given to accounts of the 'twenty-five mysterious deaths in the Defence Industry' during the early eighties raised the spectre of security-service-backed assassinations in Britain. However, the evidence available remains pitifully thin and only one or two cases should ever have produced any suspicions. Brian Worth, former Deputy Assistant Commissioner of New Scotland Yard, concluded in an internal report for the defence contractors Marconi that in all probability the suicide verdicts on the scientists working in the electronic warfare field were correct. 'Whether the incidents are looked at singly, collectively or in groupings, there is no evidence of a commonality of purpose or design; nor indeed a pattern of deliberate outside influence.' Excluding Northern Ireland (dealt with in chapters 5 to 7), the number of deaths which might suggest evidence of assassination on the British mainland can be counted on the fingers of one hand. The murder in the seventies of Special Branch informer Kenneth Lennon remains unresolved and deeply troubling. In the eighties, the deaths of two anti-nuclear protesters led to a spate of rumours, but were they assassinated?[1]

The crashed car of sixty-one-year-old Scottish lawyer and vice-chair of the Scottish National Party (SNP) Willie McRae was found on a hillside on the A87 road from Invergarry to the Kyle of Lochalsh on the morning of 6 April 1985. At first it was believed he had simply died in a car crash on the way to his holiday home at Dornie. Then medical evidence was released which suggested suicide. It was later revealed that McRae had died from a shot to the head fired from his own Smith & Wesson .45 revolver. It was two days after the incident that the gun was found. Although the fingerprints on the gun were McRae's and the bullet was found to come from the same gun, many questions remained unresolved, fuelling suspicions that McRae had been murdered because of his involvement in extreme nationalist politics. Not least of the questions raised was why had the gun been fired twice? A whispering campaign began to strengthen the suicide theory; it suggested that McRae had 'his own sexual preferences' and that he was a 'dissipated old drunk', although the autopsy found his body had contained no alcohol. There does appear to be some truth in Procurator Fiscal Aitchison's quoted remark of 16 June 1985 that 'all sorts of factors were coming into this'.[2]

McRae was a member and associate of a number of nationalist groups which would be classed by the authorities as 'terrorist'. There was speculation in nationalist ranks that McRae was the 'mastermind' behind Operation Dark Horse run by the mysterious Scottish Civilian Army, which had deposited parcels of anthrax spores on the mainland to publicise the poisoning of Gruinard Island. Certainly, McRae was a thorn in the side of the nuclear industry and was a leading campaigner against the Atomic Energy Authority's attempts to dump nuclear waste in the Highlands. He was proud to be a member of Siol Nan Gaidheal (SNG), an uncompromising but largely romantic direct-action group on the fringe of the SNP in the early eighties, some of whose supporters went on to take part in terrorist actions with its military wing, Arm Nan Gaidheal, and others with the Scottish National Liberation Army (SNLA). One SNG project involved a travelling caravan which became the gathering point for a number of militant nationalists including David Dinsmore, who became the national organiser of SNG and a member of the SNLA. The caravan became 'the nursery school for "tartan terrorists"'.[3]

McRae 'had dealings' with the SNLA and was a close friend of Dinsmore, with whom he had been in contact three days before his death. On 16 May 1983, Dinsmore was charged with sending a letter bomb through the post, with intent to cause an explosion and injury to Lord Mansfield. At a later trial on 24 January 1984, a Special Branch informer disclosed that Dinsmore had uncovered direct links between the SNLA and the Irish National Liberation Army, and that the Irish terrorist group had funded an escape route with safe houses in Dublin. This discovery was unconnected with the fact that Dinsmore had fled to the Irish Republic. The disinformation continued in the press when the *News of the World* claimed that the IRA had smuggled Dinsmore out of Scotland. On 26 August 1984, the newspaper attributed a whole series of terrorist actions to Dinsmore. Nationalists described the allegations as 'totally fabricated'. Over the Christmas period, the Special Branch used the Prevention of Terrorism Act to raid homes of supporters in a trawl for information.[4]

All these groups and activities attracted the attentions of the Special Branch. It is known that in this period MI5's F Branch took a particular interest in lawyers and had a desk monitoring Scottish nationalism, so it would be surprising if McRae had not been on their files. McRae was under twenty-four-hour surveillance by Special Branch officers from Strathclyde, and there is strong evidence that he was followed, certainly on the day before his trip north. He told friends that he had been trailed to his holiday home (to which Dinsmore had a set of keys) on a previous trip. In August 1984, at the height of the scare stories concerning Dinsmore, his house was burgled.

Among the odd features of the crash and subsequent inquiry were the following:

- Only a couple of miles before his car ran down the hillside, McRae had changed a tyre and, for some reason, put the punctured tyre on the back seat of the car. Is this the action of a man about to commit suicide?
- The car was found to be facing back up to the road. Although it was said to have somersaulted on its way down the hillside the car keys were found in McRae's lap. There was no evidence of broken glass inside the car, and damage to the car was inconsistent with the alleged violent collision with boulders on the hillside.

- McRae's files and briefcase, which he always carried with him, were missing.
- His gun was eventually found twenty yards away from the car. Even the Solicitor-General, Peter Fraser, admitted that 'it was certainly further away than it would have been if it had just fallen from his grasp and it is unlikely, given his head injury, that he could have thrown it.'
- About fifteen yards from the car was discovered a neat pile of items containing papers which had been 'meticulously ripped up', a credit card and his smashed-up watch.
- On the morning of McRae's death, a group of hitch-hikers, twenty miles south of the incident, were startled when they saw a man get out of a red Ford estate car and fire a high-velocity rifle in their direction.
- Police carried out an internal inquiry into the conduct of the McRae case, the findings of which were never revealed.[5]

McRae's strange death came only a year after the brutal killing in Staffordshire of another anti-nuclear campaigner. For ten weeks during the spring of 1985, Assistant Chief Constable Peter Smith of the Northumbria force led an independent inquiry into the way the murder investigation into the death of seventy-eight-year-old Hilda Murrell was handled. Miss Murrell had been found dead in a copse outside Shrewsbury, six miles from her home, in March 1984. She had been stabbed and beaten but had actually died of hypothermia after being abducted. It took three days to discover her body. In July 1992, the police finally released vital information that semen had been found on Miss Murrell's body. This evidence, which might have suggested a sex attack, raised more questions than answers. Why did the police take eight years to release information which, on the surface, might have silenced those who claimed Miss Murrell had been assassinated by agents of the state? Perhaps there really was more to her death than first impressions indicated.[6]

Miss Murrell's house had been burgled in what appeared to be an expert way. The telephone had been disconnected in such a manner that a ringing tone was heard by callers but the telephone in Miss Murrell's house did not ring out. 'The cutting of the green lead to her home telephone', revealed a senior MI5 officer, 'is a textbook technique known to most operatives. Similarly the damage done to the capacitor [of her telephone in her cottage at Llanymnech] could have been done with a hard blow with a hammer.' He believed that the methods betrayed the mark of the security services. In 1980, in what was planned as a 'pre-emptive strike', MI5 had authorised the burglary of the home of Dr Jenny Martin, a senior pathologist who was researching into the effects of 245–T, a chemical used in pesticides but banned in the United States. The British government had become anxious about the amount of bad publicity being created by the use of the chemical. All of Dr Martin's research was stolen during the burglary. The break-in remained unsolved until 1985, when a MI5 officer revealed the involvement of the Security Service.[7]

Two theories began to develop about the Murrell murder. The first was that Miss Murrell had been accidentally murdered following a bungled burglary carried out because of her anti-nuclear stance. Her nephew, Rob Green, who began to investigate the murder, was told by 'sensitive' sources that the murder was connected with the nuclear industry. The second theory was that it was linked to Green himself; he had been a Naval Intelligence officer at the time the Argentinian cruiser *Admiral Belgrano* was sunk. Labour MP Tam Dalyell believed that the murder was tied to the Thatcher administration's concern about leaks over the decision to sink the *Belgrano*. Dalyell went as far as to claim in the House of Commons on 19 December 1984 that an intelligence source had informed him the burglary involved two intelligence officers and that the decision to search the house had been taken at a fairly low level. He also said that Miss Murrell's name appeared on Special Branch files.[8]

Special Branch officers investigated claims that a network of private investigation agencies might have been involved in the surveillance of Miss Murrell. As one private operator claimed: 'Something went badly wrong and it involved officialdom. Now everyone is running around in ever-decreasing circles, trying to plug the gaps.' The Special Branch appeared to be particularly interested in those agencies with links to the Security Service.

In January 1983, Peter Hamilton of Zeus Security Consultants had asked Barrie Peachman of Sapphire Investigations Bureau in Norwich to provide him with names of objectors – 'subversives who were agitating' – at the Sizewell B public inquiry into the construction of a pressurised water reactor nuclear power station on the Suffolk coast. Miss Murrell had presented a document to the inquiry in September 1984 and was, at the time of her death, 'polishing and correcting' the paper for the inquiry, which drew to a close in March 1985. There is no evidence that Miss Murrell was one of those investigated. Hamilton later said that he was acting on behalf of an important client in the City of London, whom he refused to name. His enquiries ceased in May 1983. Peachman later told Gary Murray, a fellow member of the Institute of Professional Investigators (IPI), that Hamilton's request 'was a secret government operation'.[9]

This was also the view of another private client of Hamilton's, David Coghlan, who was regarded as the best 'buggist' in the business. He had been employed by Hamilton to bug the meetings of those opposed to the building of a new reactor. He was told that this legitimate, loose coalition of greens, anti-nuclear protesters and local people were 'sinister subversives who were controlled from behind the Iron Curtain'. Another freelance operative employed indirectly by Hamilton in the surveillance work was a Libyan electronics engineer, Hassab Assali, who was later imprisoned for making bomb timers. Assali claimed that he supplied bugging equipment to Zeus as well as to the MoD and the Central Electricity Generating Board, the body constructing the Sizewell reactor. It was inconceivable to Coghlan that the operation was anything other than an MI5-sanctioned one. 'Who else would be interested?' A senior F Branch officer thought it likely that 'most major groups involved in the Sizewell inquiry would have been monitored'.[10]

Hamilton was a sixty-five-year-old former Military Intelligence officer who had served with the British Army in many trouble spots throughout the world in counter-insurgency campaigns. In 1953 he was awarded the MBE (Military) whilst on the staff of Field Marshal Templer in Malaya during the emergency. In the late fifties and early sixties, Hamilton was posted as a security officer to Cyprus and Rhodesia before joining Chubb as a security consultant. A long-time member of the IPI, he admitted that he had 'spent much of his life in the Security and Intelligence world', while Gary Murray asserted that Hamilton was linked 'to the highest echelons of British Intelligence'. Company documents stated that Zeus aimed 'to provide security services of all kinds to Government and other authorities'. It was also able to legally operate electronic bugging equipment on behalf of government departments.[11]

Seemingly without Hamilton's knowledge, Peachman farmed the project out to another investigator, Victor Norris, who ran Contingency Services and had a natural flair for covert operations. Peachman, though a successful businessman, was not a trained investigator and often used Mr Norris. Norris claimed to be involved in running campaigns against CND with a team of 'imitation lefties' and to have undertaken operations for the Home Office which were 'a bit too precarious or dirty' to be done directly. A right-wing extremist with a criminal record for sexual and violent offences, Norris had previously boasted of his security links. There is some evidence that he may have been involved in acts of provocation on behalf of the security services against the Left in the late sixties.[12]

As president of the IPI, Barrie Peachman was under pressure following breaches of security and misappropriation of Institute funds by fellow members. Two private eyes had handed a 28-page dossier to New Scotland Yard's anti-corruption squad, CIB 2, outlining a number of allegations including evidence that a network of private detectives and police officers were obtaining highly confidential information illegally from the Police National Computer. They were found guilty in January 1989 and given suspended sentences. Peachman was also concerned that the Sizewell project might be unravelled by the media. On 17 April 1984 he shot himself, probably as a result of difficulties over the affair with his mistress, his administrative director and assistant in the Sizewell surveillance. She received and dispatched information to and from Zeus and helped in other sensitive assignments.

The police investigation concluded that, after interviews with the 'highest echelons of British security and naval security', there was 'not one shred of evidence' that British intelligence was involved in what it admitted was the bizarre death of Miss Murrell. Assistant Chief Constable Peter Smith had interviewed 'very respectable people in very high positions' whom he had no reason to disbelieve when they told him that Miss Murrell was not being watched by their organisations. While the author has no reason to believe these 'very respectable people', he does accept that there is no evidence of an assassination by the security services or their surrogates.[13]

Although the murder remains a mystery, Miss Murrell's death does highlight the extent to which MI5 and other government departments rely on the co-operation of private companies for deniable operations. Partially revealed was the existence of a network of individuals who carry out 'dirty jobs' felt to be too sensitive for the official agencies and which need to be kept at 'arm's length' from operations that would prove to be politically embarrassing if they were to go wrong. In conversation with numerous operational Special Branch and MI5 officers, Gary Murray found that it was common practice to use private companies for covert government operations.

These companies were often in receipt of official information from Special Branch files. Some were nationally known security companies, used, occasionally, for 'cover' by MI5 which, at other times, created its own 'front' companies for similar exercises.[14]

Retired MI5 officers moved easily into the private sector, where the relationship with their former employers was never clear. Some certainly continued to operate under a 'civilian wrapper'. One legitimate operator was Jeremy Wetherell, who had worked for MI5 in F Branch and for the K5 section, which operated closely with MI6. He found employment in commercial security as a senior kidnap negotiations adviser. Wetherell had ties to Zeus Security and was editor of a *Handbook of Security* before setting up Lynx Security Services, which provided specialist security services for commerce and government. During 1984, Argen International Security Consultants, run by John Fairer-Smith, a former member of the Rhodesian Special Branch and associate of South African security services, contracted out to two 'independent consultants' the task of tracking down the fugitive Nigerian politician Umaru Dikko. Fairer-Smith was told that Dikko was being sought concerning a debt. The two former MI5 men found Dikko in June 1984 just before he was kidnapped by political opponents. Dikko was an irritant to Anglo-Nigerian relations and it was almost certain that Special Branch and MI5 were informed of the search for him by their erstwhile colleagues.[15]

Gary Murray had been surprised to discover that the IPI included officials from the armed forces, Special Branch, the Foreign Office and the intelligence world. Members attended training sessions with the Army and Air Force Special Investigation and Counter Intelligence branches. Murray attended a seminar at the Air Force security school at RAF Newton, where 'we were given lessons in interviewing, interrogation and surveillance'. He himself received firearms training at the Royal Military Police School at Chichester. Murray was also approached by an official of the Ministry of Defence and recruited by MI5 officers as a freelance operative. He was paid a monthly retainer and expenses but decided after a while that the work he was asked to do was 'a total waste of taxpayers' money'. He found his various operational controllers to be 'most unprofessional'; he was required to take part in illegal acts including providing bugging equipment, and received what he believed to be 'a request to act as an assassin'. In return information on a particular individual could be requested from his MI5 contact. The Home Office refused to confirm or deny Murray's allegations – 'no further investigations are warranted'.[16]

In February 1987, there were further revelations about the links between the official and private security worlds when forty-five-year-old David Coghlan was imprisoned and his assistant, former British Telecom engineer David Richards, was given a suspended sentence for their role in the telephone tapping of Seychelles political exile Gérard Horeau. A political enemy of Seychelles President Albert René, Horeau had been assassinated by a professional hit-man in North London on 29 November 1985, a murder in which the private eyes played no part.

René had hired a private detective, Ian Withers, to bug Horeau, the thirty-four-year-old head of the Seychellois National Movement. Since 1980, the maverick René, who had himself seized power in a coup in 1977, had been paying Withers to monitor his exiled political opponents in London in order to foil any attempted coups. Withers claimed that he then received 'authorisation' from the Foreign Office to carry out the operation. Despite René being a 'left-wing dictator', Britain has been careful in its relations with the former colony. René allowed the United States to continue to use a tracking station which is linked to GCHQ in Cheltenham, for which the Foreign Office has responsibility. Withers kept in contact with the head of the East African department of the Foreign Office, Nigel Wenban-Smith. In the manner of other officially sanctioned private operations, Withers then subcontracted out to a second private detective, fifty-six-year-old William Underwood, who in turn passed the assignment on to Coghlan.[17]

Underwood had received £200,000 to undertake the operation, which involved buying a house for £60,000 from which to conduct the surveillance and tapping of Horeau's telephone, that of a friend of Horeau and a nearby public telephone-box. Transcripts were supplied to René and reports based on them went to Wenban-Smith at the Foreign Office, who most probably passed them on to MI6. Anti-Terrorist Squad officers later raided Withers's offices, but he had left for the Seychelles two days earlier.

Coghlan was a former electrical engineer and regular Army sergeant whose skills in electronics were noted and used by the Intelligence Corps and 'certain departments' of the SAS. A supreme technician, as was the buggist in Francis Ford Coppola's film *The Conversation*, Coghlan was 'not really interested in what people are saying, just the quality of the recording'; he could supply better sound quality than government specialists. This made him particularly attractive to the security services, who used him as a 'cut-out' who could be denied should the operation go wrong. Coghlan was happy to keep in with them even though pay for 'official jobs', compared to that from foreign embassies and private firms, was 'lousy'. In 1981, he had been employed by MI5 to bug a flat in Helensburgh, Scotland, which was used by NATO officers and a suspect who was of interest to the security service. In 1982, Coghlan used a 'spike-mike' to pick up discussions at the offices of the Militant Tendency in Liverpool. The trust in which he was held by the Security Service was reflected in the fact that he supplied telephone monitoring equipment for Mrs Thatcher's private use. Special Branch had known about the bugging of Horeau but took no action until his murder, when Coghlan and his assistant were quickly dumped by their friends in the official agencies.[18]

Gary Murray also maintained a close relationship with the Secret Intelligent Service, in particular with a serving MI6 officer who had joined a private detective agency with which Murray was associated. The officer 'carried out private investigations of a covert nature'. Occasionally, Murray would act as a go-between, passing on 'very sensitive assignments through an internationally known security company based in London'. There was nothing unusual in the fact that MI6, which is supposedly restricted to the collection of intelligence outside of the United Kingdom, should be involved in domestic operations. A former RAF intelligence officer, Lee Tracey, was an MI6 contract employee for more than twenty years, including periods when he worked under journalistic cover on the *Daily Mirror* as a photographer. Tracey, who played key behind-the-scene roles in both the Profumo affair and the Lord Lambton scandal, would report regularly to his long-term case officer at MI6's headquarters, then at Queen Anne's Gate. When he left at the end of the sixties, Tracey became a manufacturer of bugs and other snooping equipment, while still keeping a close relationship with 'The Firm'. Tracey, who claims to have undertaken over five hundred 'black-bag' jobs for the intelligence services, told the BBC's *Panorama* programme that while 'the job of doing the routine tapping is the job of MI5 . . . on a boring long-term basis . . . the kind of jobs I would do means that I would have to gain entry by my wits, preferably invited in. The common movie idea of burglary is very seldom used, but is used, obviously has to be used, because there are occasions when that's the only way.'[19]

Tracey's operation was small-scale compared to Diversified Corporate Services (DCS), which had been set up in 1970 as a 'front' company by two former MI6 officers. DCS, which employed a number of experienced intelligence personnel, undertook covert bugging operations for MI6, domestically and abroad, which needed an arm's-length approach for freelance activity. Its head, a former aide-de-camp to Templer in Malaya, Colonel Alan Pemberton, was an Establishment figure with excellent banking connections and links to Buckingham Palace. DCS's star allegedly fell when it undertook a debugging operation on behalf of Prime Minister Harold Wilson without informing its 'friends'. DCS was tied, through directors, to another important company employing intelligence personnel, Control Risks.[20]

Although SAS members are sometimes secretly seconded to foreign governments for covert operations, there are occasions when even SAS men are too close to the government. The British government uses a series of private security and secret service 'front' companies to conduct security and training operations abroad. The companies are also reportedly involved in carrying out MI6 deniable operations. They offer 'plausible deniability' in areas which would prove politically embarrassing if conducted openly, or when diplomatic considerations do not permit formal intervention. These companies are controlled by a tightly knit group of individuals with similar backgrounds, who draw on a small pool of talent comprising former experienced SAS officers and foot soldiers.

London, where there is a level of secrecy which allows the business to flourish, is now the centre for personnel and arms for the special forces trade. There are two levels – almost a class system – in the mercenary world. There is the covert international world of special forces personnel, known as the 'Circuit', which employs 'the lads', mostly former members of the SAS. The smaller companies undertake the dirty work no one else wants to do. Special Branch keeps tabs on their activities but does not directly interfere, while MI5 monitors meetings with foreign contacts and 'friends'. According to one former SAS soldier: 'Nothing can really damage the circuit. You see, we're protected. As long as we don't step over the line then the authorites will cover for us. Of course, there is always the understanding that if we are caught, we're on our own. They don't want to know about it. Its total deniability.'[21]

At the top of the tree are the well-connected companies with friends and relations in the MoD, the Foreign Office, the security services, the City and the Conservative Party. They still operate largely on the principle of the 'old boy network', doing deals over lunch at London clubs. Insiders have admitted that the companies clear everything with the Foreign Office before accepting a contract.

There have always been such companies, David Stirling's Watchguard being the most famous. There was, however, a major expansion in the early seventies as the Heath government appeared to 'privatise' some of the more 'comic-book' operations of the intelligence services. The British government was no longer able to satisfy directly the demand for the training of special forces personnel in its former colonies and mercenaries for the many insurgency campaigns in the Third World. Terrorism was on the increase in Europe from Middle Eastern groups and there was plenty of work available for security protection. Kidnapping also provided an opportunity for the insurance companies in the City.

Control Risks was formed in 1973 as a subsidiary of Hogg Robinson, one of London's major insurance brokers, to advise Lloyd's insurance syndicates on risks and premiums in kidnap and ransom insurance. With the endorsement of the underwriting syndicate Cassidy-Davies, the company grew steadily in numbers and income until by the mid-eighties it employed over sixty full-time staff and had a turnover in excess of £3 million. Control Risks is now greatly expanded with offices in London, Washington and Melbourne. Its board of directors includes a sprinkling of former intelligence officers, top security and police officers from both sides of the Atlantic, all with experience of counter-terrorism operations and assessment. The company now advises over eighty-three of the world's top corporations on terrorism, kidnapping and security with the sophistication and secrecy of a minor intelligence agency. Officially, Control Risks deals only with the private sector, though rumours are persistent that its remit goes beyond assessment work. The company has built up a widely respected computer-based information service called CRIS, a data-bank on international terrorism. This is professional and detailed enough for MI6 to be a regular user of its files and the monthly, updated country risk analysis.[22]

Out of Control Risks grew the company KMS, a nondescript title standing for Keeni Meeni Services – an in-joke, being slang picked up by soldiers during the campaign against the Mau Mau in Kenya, meaning 'under the counter' operations. Formed in 1974, KMS (later revamped as Saracen) was designed to scoop up government contracts for security work, mainly abroad. KMS boasts that it has trained and equipped 'full-size Special Forces Regiments'. Military men have admitted that 'KMS doesn't do anything important that friends in Whitehall don't know about'. All important contracts are 'cleared' by the government.[23]

In 1977, KMS left its parent company under the directorship of David Walker, a former SAS major and leading light at Control Risks. He and his partner Colonel Jim Johnson OBE, a wealthy insurance broker with the Blackwell Green Insurance company and a Lloyd's 'name', turned KMS into the most prominent and important of the security companies. Until media exposure, in March 1987, of its links with the Iran–Contra affair made the connection controversial, the company's true ownership in Jersey was hidden behind nominees from Morgan Grenfell, a bank which has traditionally been close to MI6. In the sixties and seventies, a number of former MI6 officers found employment with the bank. KMS is now nominally controlled by a Jersey firm of accountants though there remains some mystery about the true ownership of a company which is alleged to have excellent contacts with the intelligence services. KMS links to the secret state are believed to be made through a former Rhodesian intelligence and 21 SAS officer who later joined MI6.[24]

David Walker (Cambridge and Sandhurst) is a former Tory councillor in Surrey who put himself forward as a 'man of action'. Jim Johnson is a former ADC to the Queen, who along with David Stirling helped organise the MI6-backed mercenary operation in the Yemen in the sixties. Both men are believed to be millionaires, Johnson allegedly being paid in gold bullion for his work in the Yemen. When Mrs Thatcher was in power, Walker was said to be 'on first name terms with the Prime Minister' and had access to Number 10.[25]

While budgets did increase for the security services in the Thatcher years there were financial constraints, with money being saved by using what were, in essence, privatised companies. Security companies prospered on lucrative foreign contracts and were able to expand their operations. Groups such as Defence Systems Ltd, run by former SAS Major Alastair Morrison, consolidated their operations, buying up some of the smaller ex-SAS security companies such as Intersec (formerly Laing Walker) and Falconstar, run by Jeremy Trevaskis, an SAS captain and son of former High Commissioner in Aden Sir Kenneth Trevaskis. DSL has had contracts in Angola guarding oil and diamond installations; in Indonesia training counter-terrorism teams; and in the Philippines, Uganda and Mozambique training special forces in the latter country against the South African-backed MNR terrorists. A subsidiary of KMS with a higher profile was Saladin Security, which supplied VIP personal protection to a number of Middle Eastern sheikhs and kings. The protection teams of former SAS men held Saudi diplomatic passports entitling them to carry weapons.[26]

KMS's most lucrative contract, thought to have been worth twelve million pounds per year, which was controlled by Lieutenant-Colonel Keith Farnes, involved training the Sultan of Oman's Special Forces at a base known as the Goat Farm. KMS is said to virtually run the internal security services, which have strong links with MI6. In 1970, MI6 organised the coup which led to the overthrow of the current Sultan's father. MI6 runs the Oman Research Department, which acts as an area base. KMS personnel were also employed in northern

Afghanistan, training the Mujaheddin and special forces at training camps in Pakistan. The most controversial contract was in Sri Lanka, helping to put down the revolt by Tamil guerrillas. Diplomatic relations with India prevented direct involvement by the Conservative government, which was against increased Indian influence in Sri Lanka, which it was thought might lead to Soviet interference. Requests from the Sri Lankan government for military aid were therefore directed to KMS. From 1984, former SAS major Brian Baty, who served in Northern Ireland, ran the KMS contract in Sri Lanka, employing a contingent of SAS personnel for guerrilla training and equipping the Sri Lankan Special Task Force. This all went embarrassingly wrong when the latter through no fault of KMS, who were no longer involved, began to engage in torture and assassination. In May 1987, about sixty mercenaries were sent back to England.

However, it was KMS's connections with the Iran–Contra scandal which caused the biggest upset and led to a loosening of ties with the government. Ministry of Defence disquiet over the adverse publicity forced Walker and Johnson to give up day-to-day control to Farnes and Baty, both formerly of 22 SAS. In the autumn of 1984, Lieutenant-Colonel William Mott, Vietnam veteran and deputy defence attaché at the American embassy in London, had approached a number of British security companies about supplying arms and men for the Contras in Nicaragua. Since there is an agreement between the American and British intelligence services about recruiting each other's citizens, it is almost inevitable that the approach was made with the agreement of the Secret Intelligence Service. Later, in October 1985, sanction was sought by CIA chief William Casey, while on a trip to Britain to debrief KGB defector Oleg Gordievsky.

In December 1984, Lieutenant-Colonel Oliver North, at the request of Navy Secretary John Lehman, had met with David Walker. The KMS man expressed interest in 'certain special operations expertise aimed particularly at destroying helicopters' belonging to the Sandinistas in Nicaragua. In the following spring, Walker organised the destruction of the El Chipote arms depot in the centre of Managua. A year later, KMS helicopter pilots flew with the Contras in Honduras and a number of six-man teams were sent out by KMS to train and support the American-backed insurgents. The trainers apparently found the Contras 'irritatingly stupid'.

In the same period, North also allegedly arranged for KMS to train Iranian military personnel and Afghan guerrillas. Meetings continued with North throughout the spring of 1986, including several secret visits to the United States and the Virginia-based company, Stanford Technology, which was later to be linked to the Iran–Contra scandal. Walker's involvement was one of the issues which remained firmly behind closed doors when Congressional committees began to probe the Iran–Contra affair. There is an agreement between the United States and Britain which prohibits discussion of intelligence matters involving Britain's Security Services. United States intelligence sources also alleged that details of KMS activities were kept to a minimum during the hearings because of 'the risk of compromising other operations'.[27]

While the operations of the larger security companies have a certain unofficial legitimacy, on the fringes of the circuit some of the 'lads' are prepared to undertake the real dirty jobs. 'They'll do anything,' suggests one member, 'if the price is right.' This includes 'contract killings'. Such activities are hard, if not impossible, to prove and are generally confined to unfounded rumour and the realm of 'faction'. Short-time SAS member Sir Ranulph Fiennes, in his 1991 book, *The Feather Men*, makes an implausible case for the existence of a twenty-year fraternity of ex-SAS men acting as a shadowy vigilante group against a group of Middle Eastern assassins, known as 'The Clinic'. According to Fiennes, the Feather Men were set up by David Stirling, backed by a well-known City industrialist, Tommy Macpherson. Not surprisingly, the SAS reacted with undisguised fury at this tale of scurrilous goings-on. However, there may be a grain of truth in Fiennes's pot-boiler. In the last few years, separate intelligence sources have alleged that there exists a secret assassination unit known as Group 13. Made up of experienced former SAS members, over the last twenty years Group 13 is said to have carried out a number of contract killings on behalf of the British government, through contacts in MI6 which has a 'General Support Branch' to handle dirty operations. One of the members was a former SAS officer who was involved in the 1970 coup in Oman and later served with distinction in Northern Ireland. The same sources believe that Group 13 has operated in Britain.[28]

18

Honourable Correspondents

> When I came back I was rejected by my wife, my family and my business associates . . . My life was totally changed by what I had become involved in.
>
> Greville Wynne

There is a British tradition of using 'honourable correspondents', private agents prepared to take part in 'the Great Game' of gathering intelligence for MI6. 'There is a category of people', according to Richard Norton-Taylor, 'who are particularly attractive to intelligence agencies. They may be informers, arms dealers, businessmen, even journalists. Their common value is their special access to groups or targets which the agencies have in their sights but cannot reach on their own. And if anything goes wrong, the agencies can always resort to the well-worn defence of "plausible deniability".' These honourable correspondents or 'approved unofficial agents' are not always highly regarded by intelligence practitioners.[1]

The double spy and traitor Kim Philby wrote how, in the late forties as MI6 station chief in Istanbul, he was 'cast back on the meagre sources of intelligence available'. Following standard procedure, he began to sound out the local British community, but 'it was rough going'. 'There are of course British residents abroad, businessmen, journalists and so on, who are prepared to stick their necks out . . . But these are usually the lesser fry and their potentialities are limited. The big men, with their big potentialities, are usually unhelpful. They have too much to lose; they have duties to themselves, to their families; they even have duties to their damned shareholders. They would usually agree to pass on anything that "came their way" – invariably valueless gossip.' Another MI6 traitor, George Blake, whose task it was to recruit businessmen, agreed with Philby's assessment. 'Most of the people I approached agreed to co-operate, but always made one proviso; that they should not be asked to do anything that might harm their commercial interests . . . I found, in practice, that this proviso enabled them to keep up the pretence of co-operating with us, while, in fact, doing very little.' During the Cold War, without any reliable intelligence sources inside the Soviet Union, MI6 increasingly relied on correspondents for a supply of 'gossip', however unreliable it might turn out to be.[2]

In the late fifties, MI6 began 'to exploit the rich field of opportunities provided by the thaw in relations between East and West' by recruiting on a massive scale anyone who might prove useful on their travels to the Soviet bloc. Despite the official policy that MI6 did not operate on home territory, the London-based Controller of Production Research was transformed into 'an agent-running organisation' enlisting hundreds of businessmen, journalists and academics to gather intelligence on the Soviet Union and or help with introductions to Soviet officials who might be 'turned'. The head of the operation was Dickie Franks, a hard-line future chief of the service; his deputy was George Blake, who betrayed to the KGB every name that crossed his desk. One of those names may have been that of the publisher and corrupt businessman Robert Maxwell.[3]

Before his death, Maxwell was accused by the American investigative journalist Seymour Hersh of acting for the Israeli secret service, Mossad. Another author, Yoel Cohen, in his book *Nuclear Ambiguity* dismissed the idea that Maxwell may have orchestrated the discrediting and exposure of Mordechai Vanunu, the man who revealed the existence of Israel's nuclear programme. Cohen suggested that Maxwell was too public a figure to be employed by a secret service. There was, however, nothing particularly implausible in the claim; Mossad has many low-level agents who assist the service. According to former Mossad agent Victor Ostrovsky, the agency has 'thousands of Sayanims [assistants] around the world; in London alone, there are about two thousand who are active'.[4]

While the newspapers had a field day over allegations of Maxwell's apparent links to Mossad, little was made of the much stronger evidence tying him to MI6. There can be little doubt that Maxwell's career owed a great deal to the sponsorship of MI6. In the early fifties, his scientific publishing company, Pergamon Press, evolved out of a project set up by MI6 to secure the release and publication of scientific papers and journals from post-war Germany and later the Soviet Union. On each step of the way, Maxwell, a Russian-speaking former interrogation officer for Army Intelligence, received the support and backing of MI6 'assets'. Deals were arranged through Count van den Heuval, a serving MI6 officer who recruited businessmen to the service and acted as 'fixer' for the banker Sir Charles Hambro. A former head of the Special Operations Executive, Hambro was transferred to MI6 after the war and was responsible, through his bank, for backing Maxwell's enterprises with substantial loans.

Maxwell's constant travelling to the Soviet bloc raised suspicions in the Security Service that he was acting as a Soviet agent of influence. These fears were partially dispelled in 1954 when his secretary, Anne Dove, formerly in SOE, was asked by MI5 to vouch for Maxwell's loyalty. This she did, though MI5 continued to view him with great suspicion. (It may not be a coincidence that former MI5 officer Sir John Cuckney has been asked to help trace the whereabouts of the *Mirror* pension fund plundered by Maxwell. Cuckney has clearance to see the files of MI6 and GCHQ.) Like his enemies in the City, the service was less concerned with allegations of corruption (such practices are fairly common among London's unregulated financial institutions) than with the fact that Maxwell was a foreigner and a Jew.[5]

It was a commonly held view in the City that Maxwell was

some kind of KGB agent. In addition, his biographer Tom Bower goes so far as to claim that Maxwell signed an undertaking in Berlin just after the war to help Soviet intelligence, and that when he was approached in 1968 to help, he agreed to assist. Unfortunately, everyone involved with this alleged incident is said to be dead, though, according to Bower, 'the existence of a document *seems* certain'.[6]

Following the publisher's death, much was made of a top secret document signed by the then KGB chief Vladimir Kryuchkov, who was imprisoned for plotting against Gorbachev in March 1992. The memorandum documented KGB fears about exposure of Soviet links with Maxwell. Conclusions were drawn that this proved Maxwell had been recruited by the KGB. Defector Oleg Gordievsky told the *Sunday Express* that Maxwell was 'a Soviet agent. Absolutely'. However, an alternative reading suggested that the KGB were concerned not about alleged intelligence links but about Maxwell's connections to the highest echelons of the Politburo. Gordievsky later informed the *Sunday Times* that other Soviet officers thought that Maxwell was a British spy, though he had personally tried to persuade them otherwise.[7]

Other former KGB officers, better placed than Gordievsky, believed that Maxwell had worked for MI6 since the end of the Second World War. Kim Philby had told his Soviet colleagues that former Military Intelligence officers kept up their contacts with the security services. The 'brilliant and level-headed' Mikhail Lyubimov, stationed in London between 1961 and 1965 and head of the KGB's British desk in the seventies, was regarded by colleagues as 'the Centre's leading British expert'. He confirmed that Maxwell was not 'a KGB agent'. The British businessman was treated with 'caution' by the KGB, which suspected him of being a 'plant'. Lyubimov's fears were entirely justified. At the height of the Cold War, Maxwell negotiated a deal with the Soviet authorities which gave him sole copyright on publishing Soviet scientific papers and journals in the West. When he returned from Moscow with the agreements, MI6's Dickie Franks approached him for assistance and information. 'Maxwell gave him the benefit of his observations.' To little effect, the KGB frequently warned the Politburo not to deal with Maxwell, because of his suspected MI6 links. The agency was so convinced of this that it compiled a huge dossier on him.[8]

The KGB believed that one of Maxwell's tasks was to re-establish contacts with the Soviet leader Leonid Brezhnev when relations with the West deteriorated following the Soviet invasion of Czechoslovakia in 1968 and the expulsion in 1971 of 105 Soviet diplomats from Britain. Maxwell was alleged to have 'played on Brezhnev's ambitions and vanity'. This was regarded as 'a very high calibre operation on the part of the British Government, aimed at establishing a bridge between Brezhnev and the British Government'. The KGB were sure that MI6 briefed Maxwell before he met the Soviet leader and that the content of the talks was reported back to London. 'Through him', Lyubimov adds, 'Britain also got access to members of the central committee's International Department, which usually didn't talk to foreigners at all.' This was an extremely important contact for MI6 because it was the International Department and not the KGB which was responsible for funding Soviet covert operations in the West. The KBG were not happy at the way Maxwell was treated. 'He dealt with the top nomenklatura, which was out of bounds for us. We believed that the British were creating their own Dr Hammer [an American industrialist prominent in East–West trade], an unofficial bridge between London and Moscow.'[9]

This goes some way towards explaining why, according to Joint Intelligence Committee administrative officer Robin Robison, Maxwell was not seen as a risk to British national security and was therefore not classed as an 'intelligence target'. Monitoring by the security services, and GCHQ in particular, instead centred on his many businesses abroad. During 1989, Robison saw material relating to Maxwell. Faxes and transcripts of telephone calls were intercepted by GCHQ and distributed via the Cabinet Office to Cabinet Ministers and the Bank of England. The package included 'faxes intercepted in Israel and the Mediterranean, probably from his yacht, the *Lady Ghislaine*'. Communications from Maxwell's yacht were intercepted by GCHQ with the help of British submarines after a tip-off from the CIA in the late eighties that *Ghislaine* might have been used for drug-smuggling. A full intelligence report on Maxwell was apparently prepared by the JIC at the time of his death on 5 November 1991. The government denied reports of the existence of intelligence material on Maxwell, but Robison believed that 'Most, if not all, of the material of any relevance relating to this story was shredded and burnt a long time ago. Mr Major can only rely on the civil servants who were probably not in the PM's office at the time.'[10]

Not all correspondents are high-flyers like Maxwell, though a few still suffer battered reputations or strange deaths. Neville Beale, who worked abroad for many years in the oil business, soon realised that several people he met on his travels were engaged in intelligence activities. He had his own experience of the secret world when, in 1973, he was approached by the Ministry of Defence and interviewed at the old War Office building in Whitehall by a 'military-looking gentleman and a woman in sensible shoes and thick stockings'. After he had signed the Official Secrets Act – a normal procedure on these occasions – they explained that they wanted to use his flat as a 'safe house' while he was abroad. Budgets were tight and safe houses were regarded as a 'very expensive' option. Vetted by Special Branch, Beale was told that MI5 could clear the matter with his employers. According to Blake, 'It was a strict rule that no employees of British firms were to be recruited as agents, or used in any way, without prior consent of the chairman, or managing director of the company.' Unsurprisingly, many senior figures in British commerce had served in intelligence during the war, which made such approaches all the easier. Nigel West has noted, for example, Lord Keith

(Rolls Royce), Sir Brian Mountain (Eagle Star), Sir Rupert Speir (Matthew Hall & Co) and Sir John Cuckney (Westland Helicopters). However, in this case Beale's boss was not so enamoured of the approach and turned down the request for 'unofficial assistance'. 'Embassy people involved in espionage are protected by diplomatic immunity. Businessmen are not.'[11]

George Blake was frequently reminded that 'large concerns like Shell or ICI were as much identified with the British government as any Embassy. If one of their employees was caught spying, the political and economic consequences could be both expensive and embarrassing. We should think hard before using them.' Michael Glenny, regarded as the foremost translator of Russian literature into English, was approached in the sixties by MI6 to spy on the Soviet Union. Glenny was a salesman for the pottery firm Wedgwood, travelling around Eastern Europe with his china samples. He politely declined the offer, 'because I had seen the damaging effect it had had on other people's lives'.[12]

Few were more damaged than Jeremy Wolfenden, who in 1962 was the Moscow correspondent of the *Daily Telegraph*. A homosexual and fluent Russian speaker who had undertaken his National Service in Naval Intelligence, Wolfenden naturally attracted the attention of Soviet Intelligence. Compromised in a KGB 'honeytrap' operation, Wolfenden was advised by an MI6 officer to 'co-operate with the Russians'. As Phillip Knightley notes in his account of Wolfenden's case, he was then 'well and truly hooked by both services'. At the time, MI6 had lost all its assets in Moscow following the arrest of the GRU traitor Oleg Penkovsky and his unofficial MI6 contact, British businessman Greville Wynne. The stress of trying to co-operate with both services led to depression and alcoholism. Hoping to disentangle himself from this desperate situation, Wolfenden married and arranged a permanent transfer to the *Telegraph*'s Washington bureau. Unfortunately, his MI6 control followed with a request to renew the intelligence game. The pressures of the task became too much for Wolfenden to bear and on 28 December 1965 he was found dead in his bathroom. He had cracked his head on the washbasin and suffered a cerebral haemorrhage, after fainting through excessive drinking and lack of food. Friends claimed that he had lost the will to live.[13]

Journalism has been a natural recruiting ground for the security services. John le Carré, who worked for MI6 between 1960 and 1964, has made the astonishing statement that 'the British Secret Service controlled large sections of the press, just as they may do today'. In 1975, following Senate hearings on the CIA which had revealed the extent of agency recruitment of both American and British journalists, sources let it be known that half the foreign staff of a British daily were on the MI6 payroll. In the mid-eighties, the present author was given, by a senior *Observer* journalist, a list of five foreign affairs journalists on a Sunday newspaper who had acted as correspondents for the intelligence services. No doubt the practice continues to this day.[14]

In many instances, the use of honourable correspondents became counter-productive. The KGB and other intelligence agencies, particularly those in the Middle East, assumed that all British journalists and businessmen were potential spies. A quick assessment of their biography would often convince a hostile counter-espionage officer that a suspect had the right connections and background for an MI6 contact. In the fifties, the news agency Reuters was widely assumed, and correctly so, to be a routine cover for British intelligence (though this is no longer the case). When one of its journalists, Jonathan Wright, went missing in the Lebanon in September 1984, Reuters' managing director felt obliged to issue a statement declaring that the agency 'had no association with any government and did not represent the interest of any one country'. The fact that the thirty-year-old Wright graduated from Oxford, spoke fluent Arabic and was due to become Reuters' bureau chief in Oman (site of MI6's regional headquarters) was enough to make his captors put a question mark against his name. Fortunately, he was released twenty-three days later. Others accused have not been so lucky.[15]

When, in 1986, British businessman Roger Cooper appeared on Iranian television admitting that he had worked for the 'British Intelligence Service' (BIS), his close friend, the BBC's Foreign Affairs editor, John Simpson, was reassured by the statement. Simpson later said that he thought Cooper, who had been through 'quite intensive interrogation', was sending a signal to his friends that he was innocent of the charge of spying. 'There is no such thing as the British Intelligence Service.' In fact, just as MI5 and MI6 used to refer to the KGB as the 'Russian Intelligence Service', it is still common for MI6 to be assigned the tag BIS.[16]

In 1956, as a student at Oxford, Cooper had 'mingled with insurgent Hungarians, earning his first, brief, imprisonment' in Hungary. During his National Service he was employed in Army Intelligence and friends regarded the 'adventurer' as 'in the tradition of John Buchan'. Cooper has conceded that he had a spy's profile. 'You know the elements: Old Persian Hand – very suspicious for a start; different, unconventional jobs – journalism, studying Persian, teaching private classes in English. And then as I got more into Iran, I went into business and started a printing and publishing firm.' In Tehran, Cooper organised 'a monthly Spy Lunch' at the Park Hotel where foreign correspondents and diplomats would gather to exchange views. 'It was a good way for people to get to know one another.' Although he made these observations on his return to Britain after five years' imprisonment, Cooper appears never to have categorically denied that he did work for MI6.[17]

Douglas Brand, who was imprisoned for life by Iraq for spying, after attempting to escape the country during the run-up to the Gulf War, was another with a profile which fitted Middle Eastern expectations of a British intelligence agent. A 'Walter Mitty figure' who was 'always talking about past exploits', Brand had served in the Special Boat Squadron and received the Military Cross after serving in Aden in 1964. During 1972–73 he served in Northern Ireland, attached to the Commandant General's news team and undertook some work for the propaganda unit, Information Policy. Later, he became an underwater and explosives expert. In 1986, Brand was jailed for six months for a plot to market 26 million forged dollars while working for a Mayfair arms dealer. In January 1989, aged fifty-one, he was employed on contract by Baghdad to clear mines from the Shatt-al-Arab waterway, laid during the Iran–Iraq war.[18]

Brand was also in Iraq to research an in-depth article comparing Iraq and Iran post-war, for a monthly magazine published in Washington, *Defence and Foreign Affairs*. Its owner, Australian journalist Gregory Copley, was a rather mysterious figure who, in 1987, unexpectedly saved the Ailsa shipyard in Troon, Scotland, from closure. The yard subsequently won several contracts from the MoD and others to build small high-speed armed patrol boats. Copley, who knew Mrs Thatcher on first-name terms, was also a special partner in an American consultancy firm headed by the former director of the CIA, William Colby. The magazine later came to prominence when it predicted the Iraqi invasion of Kuwait several weeks before this happened. Brand was charged with espionage by the Iraqis when they found the notes for the proposed article.[19]

Probably the most famous example, in recent years, of someone becoming tainted through association with the intelligence world, with damaging consequences both for himself and for his own mission, has been that of Terry Waite. During interrogation, Roger Cooper was told by his Iranian captors that the Archbishop of Canterbury's envoy in negotiations with the hostage-takers in the Lebanon was a CIA agent. Cooper 'pooh-poohed the idea'. He told his interrogator that 'somebody like that wouldn't get involved with the CIA . . . you call a lot of people CIA agents.' The Iranians said that they had proof. 'Waite, who had only just been arrested, had a bug . . . it wasn't a bug that transmitted but allowed a satellite to say where he was at any given moment.' Tehran Radio later put out reports that Waite had a secret transmitter hidden on his body which had been discovered by his captors, Islamic Jihad. None was ever found, though it seems Lieutenant-Colonel Oliver North did offer Waite a tracking device on earlier visits to Beirut. The US ambassador for refugees, Eugene Douglas, who travelled with Waite in the Middle East, believes that the envoy did accept, on his first trip to the region, a device 'for his own safety'.[20]

Waite first met North through contacts in the American Episcopalian Church, who heard in May 1985 of the Englishman's desire to help the Western hostages in the Lebanon. The CIA, which at the time had 'lots of lines in the water', was supportive of 'anyone who might open a line to the captors'. The CIA especially wanted Waite to help free William Buckley, the CIA station chief who had been seized by Hezbollah in March 1984. There was also a report that North wanted to use Waite as 'bait' in an attempt to pinpoint the whereabouts of Colonel Gaddafi in a plot to kill the Libyan leader.[21]

North set great store by Waite's information, but the churchman had exaggerated his role and abilities. He inflated the significance of his contacts and appeared to lie on other occasions, embroidering the role of the Church. Although North told the Operations Sub-Group, headed by Admiral John Poindexter, that Waite was 'the only Westerner ever to meet directly with the Lebanese kidnappers', it was untrue. Waite achieved only one 'face to face meeting' and that was on his visit to Beirut in November 1985. This had been arranged by a CIA asset code-named 'Spiro'. A London-born Jew, Ian Spiro, following the loss of a substantial fortune he made during the seventies property boom, had moved to Beirut in 1978 where he made a new life for himself. He engaged in a wide range of dubious business activities including arms smuggling. He also developed close links with leaders of Lebanon's Shia Muslim community, which brought him to the attention of MI6 and the CIA for whom he began to work. In the summer of 1985, CIA Director William Casey suggested to North that Spiro's Shia contacts would be invaluable for Waite's mission. Spiro was then asked by MI6 to meet Waite at his office in Lambeth Palace.

While the headlines praised Waite for his role in the release of a number of American hostages, in truth he played little or no part in the process. They were freed because of the sale by the United States of 1,000 TOW anti-tank missiles to Iran. A friend of Waite's thought it possible that Terry knew that North was involved in something but chose to turn a blind eye. Bizarrely, Waite claims that he never asked North what he was up to. As the *Observer* remarked, 'at best, Waite was a dupe, at worst a willing accomplice'. While Waite was praised by North, few diplomats had any real sympathy for him, and his collusion with the covert operator cast a dark shadow over his role as a negotiator.[22]

Much of this was known to British Intelligence, which had knowledge of the Iran–Contra scandal at a very early stage. GCHQ had been supplying Whitehall with communications picked up by its Cyprus station, but these were not detailed enough to provide a clear picture of what was really happening. On 8 December 1985, Robert MacFarlane, President Reagan's former National Security adviser, flew to London with Oliver North for a meeting with the arms dealer Manucher Ghorbanifar; two Israeli arms dealers, Adolph Schwimmer and Ya'acov Nimrodi; a Mossad veteran living in London, the British-born David Kimche, previously deputy director of Mossad and currently director-general of the Israeli Foreign Ministry; and Richard Secord, a retired US air force general who was responsible for arranging the transport of arms to Israel. MI5 bugged the secret meeting at a London hotel. Intelligence reports were not made available as per normal to the United States, but were passed by the Joint Intelligence Committee to the Prime Minister Margaret Thatcher, her deputy William Whitelaw, Foreign Secretary Geoffrey Howe, and Defence Secretary Michael Heseltine.[23]

On 20 February 1986, Sir Antony Acland, Permanent Secretary at the Foreign Office, and Sir Percy Cradock, chair of the JIC, flew to Washington for talks with Admiral Poindexter, MacFarlane's successor on the National Security Council. Without disclosing their own intelligence, Acland and Craddock informed the Admiral that 'there were on the diplomatic circuit rumours that there was some kind of deal between the Americans and the Iranians over the hostages'. Acland went on to confirm 'the firm view of the British Government that there should be no deals'. Poindexter gave Acland 'no indication of any kind that there was a deal'. Although London was angered at being misled, the British government refused to push the issue, mainly because of Mrs Thatcher's high regard for President Reagan.[24]

How MI5 discovered the existence of the December meeting in London has not been revealed but MI6 did have two 'assets' – one being Spiro – who were involved in the Iran–Contra deal and may have been privy to such knowledge. In May 1988, 'an arrogant wheeler-dealer in the cloak and dagger world of arms trading', Michael Aspin, was sentenced to six years' imprisonment for attempting to defraud the Iranian government of twenty-one million pounds by offering to sell it five thousand non-existent TOW missiles. As part of his defence Aspin claimed that he had been working for Oliver North in the British end of the Iran–Contra operation to free US hostages. Aspin and his co-defendants claimed that 'they had become fall-guys for top politicians and intelligence services on both sides of the Atlantic'. During his trial, Michael had been backed up by his brother, Leslie. Now dead, Leslie Aspin had been a low-level MI6 agent in the seventies providing information on IRA arms deals and later on mercenary recruitment operations. He was also a CIA 'contact agent' and claimed that William Casey had telephoned him in 1984 to request his help. At a secret meeting in London, North, who had placed five million dollars in a Paris account code-named Devon Island for the contract, had given the 'green light' for the TOW deal. This might have been dismissed, as the judge did at his trial, as 'lies, sham and pure fantasy', if Senator John Kerry's inquiry into the collapse of the Bank of Credit and Commerce International had not discovered from BCCI sources that there was indeed a top-secret account of that name in the Paris branch of the bank. Kerry tried to gain access to the account but was blocked by the British authorities.

In November 1986, North's 'arms for hostages' deal was exposed in a Beirut magazine, *Al Shiraa*. On 25 November, President Reagan was forced to act and sacked North. In December, reports surfaced that Waite had met North half a dozen times (in fact, at least twenty) and had used United States facilities, including travelling with a team of CIA agents in his attempt to free hostages held in Beirut. Waite asserted that his mission was 'independent of any government'.

On 23 December 1986, the British ambassador in Beirut, John Gray, flew to London to warn Waite that it was not safe to return to the Lebanon. MI6 intelligence identified Waite as a terrorist target, saying he would be kidnapped if he went back. These warnings appeared merely to put steel in his determination to vindicate his role and abilities. 'The simple truth is', said a former State Department official who was involved in the hunt for the hostages, 'Waite . . . totally trusted his own ability to move mountains. He was wrong.' At the beginning of 1987, Archbishop Robert Runcie warned his envoy not to go back to Beirut; however, he did not apply more pressure because Waite would have gone 'independently'.[25]

Waite returned to Beirut for his fifth and last visit on 20 January 1987. Secret tape-recordings made by Amal intelligence of scrambled telephone conversations reveal that Waite was still in contact with American intelligence sources and a CIA case officer, Eve K. Worse; the Hotel Riviera was under surveillance by the Hezbollah while Waite met with CIA representatives. He left the hotel with his Druze bodyguards for a rendezvous with Islamic Jihad. At the house of a middleman, Waite asked his bodyguards to leave, at which point he disappeared, not to be seen again for four and a half years. The CIA was so concerned about Waite's capture that it paid out millions of dollars to 'potential sources' for 'hard evidence' of his whereabouts, intelligence which was shared with MI6.[26]

A recipient of the CIA's largesse was Ian Spiro. When North's activities became the focus of media attention, MI6 and the CIA officially cut all links to Spiro. He was, according to one American intelligence agent, 'the kind of operative who is as disposable as toilet tissue . . . You use them and then chuck them away when they're of no more use'. However, sources suggest that Spiro remained in contact with the intelligence agencies and worked behind the scenes trying to discover Waite's whereabouts. In 1990, following a failed business deal to sell medical equipment to Iran, he was forced to abandon his clandestine activities and move to California.

The forty-six-year-old Spiro was found dead in his car in the California desert in November 1992. He had died from cyanide posioning, possibly self-administered. At his home, a hundred miles away in Rancho Santa Fe, north of San Diego, his wife and three children had earlier been discovered murdered, the result of a professional kill with shots to the back of the head. In the days leading up to his death, Spiro had been a 'frightened man'. He told his brother-in-law that 'something has come back to haunt me'. Initial reports suggested that Spiro had killed his family and committed suicide because of financial problems. However, later evidence showed that he retained a high credit-worthiness rating and was paying his bills. When the FBI became involved speculation turned to his involvement in the Iran–Contra scandal. In spite of being a known embrodier of the truth, he had been one of the few Westerners to know personally the leaders of the kidnap gangs. When his cover was blown by the release of Waite, Spiro offered his story to British newspapers and may have tried to blackmail the kidnappers. He said that he intended revealing details of British government secret deals to secure the release of hostages and its fore-knowledge of the Lockerbie bombing. According to one American official, MI6 shredders in Century House had been at work emptying Spiro's personal file.

By coincidence, one of the released Beirut hostages, Irishman Brian Keenan, had in October 1992 revealed a strange story connected to Lockerbie. Following his release in the summer of 1990 into the custody of the Syrians, Keenan was held a virtual hostage in their intelligence headquarters outside Damascus. 'Syrian intelligence was able to tell me that the British Government knew all about me. They certainly knew who was holding me . . . They said the British knew all along about Lockerbie. They said that the British had all sorts of advance information prior to the event.' Keenan knew little about it but thought: 'That's extremely interesting.' When he arrived in Dublin, he was interviewed by a woman MI6 officer, who was the worse for drink, and a young man carrying a side-arm. 'They were extremely concerned about my two days' debriefing by the Syrians. They would never tell me why.'[27]

The 'arms for hostages' project, besides being illegal and of dubious moral value, was in the end a failure in that it backfired, increasing the number of hostages taken as the arms shipments inflated the value of Western hostages, making kidnapping a highly profitable business. Large sums of money had been paid by Abu Nidal to take possession of two British hostages, Philip Padfield and Leigh Douglas. In response to the American bombing raid on Libya on 15 April 1985, the Arab Commando Cell – a Nidal front – killed Padfield and Douglas. Mrs Thatcher had given the go-ahead for the United States bombers to use British bases despite a report which originated with MI6 that the hostages would be killed in retaliation for the raid.

While Waite naïvely claimed that he was innocent of charges of collusion, American security officials confirmed that he had 'provided ecclesiastical cover' for the 'arms for hostages' deal. He had played a 'supportive and secondary role' maintaining contact with the hostage-takers and had been unashamedly used as the 'front man' to keep North's organisation out of the limelight.[28]

By the autumn of 1987, kidnap groups in the Lebanon were claiming that Waite was an American intelligence operative. Though this was an exaggeration, he had been completely compromised by his clandestine associations. His case was a warning to those 'honourable correspondents' who become entangled with intelligence agencies and covert operations. One Western intelligence source said, on Waite's release, that he 'was a very stupid man. But then nobody should spend five years in chains for being stupid.'[29]

19

Abu Nidal, Black Networks and BCCI

The Bank of Crooks and Criminals International.

Robert Gates, October 1988

On 2 July 1991, a Price Waterhouse auditors' report, code-named 'Sandstorm', prepared by a small, secret group of experts, was delivered to the Bank of England; the report related how the world's biggest banking fraud had been perpetrated. Three days later, the Bank of Credit and Commerce International (BCCI) was closed down. BCCI had manufactured billions out of nothing in order to conceal gaping 'black holes' in its balance sheet. The biggest victim of this massive fraud was the tiny Gulf emirate of Abu Dhabi and its ruler, seventy-five-year-old Sheikh Zayed. Within the Arab world, 'BCCI has been looked upon as one of Sheikh Zayed's personal assets since its founding in 1972'. The *Financial Times* estimated that Abu Dhabi's exposure to the bank amounted to $9.4 billion.[1]

BCCI operated out of London, a financial centre which might be said to resemble an offshore tax haven, in that regulation is weak while confidentiality is guaranteed. The even more shady BCCI (Overseas) was located in the Cayman Islands, still a British colony. A 1990 Bank of England report on BCCI concluded that its money-laundering activities were no worse than those of many other banks and thus not sufficient to warrant pushing the bank out of Britain altogether; a neat illustration that London can be the ideal place from which to run all manner of dodgy enterprises. BCCI's closure finally came two years after the world's leading economies, Group Seven, signed a declaration setting up an International Finance Action Group (IFAG), intended to track down the estimated $120 billion circulating in the world in the money-laundering networks. Clearly the IFAG has not been a success.[2]

BCCI was first registered in Luxembourg in 1972, its largest shareholder being an obscure Bromley solicitor, Geoffrey Wallis, who acted as nominee for persons never identified. Wallis, who was not involved in the subsequent fraud, was a close friend and legal adviser to BCCI's charismatic president, Agha Hasan Abedi, a man who 'thrived on conspiracy'. The bank operated on the frontier between Islam and the West and thus held many attractions for the intelligence services of a number of countries.[3]

An early leading light in the bank's hierarchy was Turkish-born Sheikh Kamal Adham, former head of Saudi intelligence (the bank loaned him $313 million in 1989). Adham, according to a former senior CIA counter-terrorism officer, Vincent Cannistraro, was 'both a wheeler-dealer with a tremendous number of contacts in the Middle East and was also the focal point of contact with all foreign intelligence agencies'. Adham had close ties to the CIA, which had trained him; one of his business partners was Raymond Close, a CIA station chief in Saudi Arabia in the seventies. Former bank officials claimed it was the CIA that cemented the partnership between Adham and Abedi, but the latter's exact relationship with the CIA, despite public denouncements as an agent, remains unclear. MI6, too, was close to Adham; Saudi intelligence employed a number of former MI5 and MI6 officers. In addition to running the country's security services, Adham also represented some of the world's largest arms companies in their dealings in the Middle East.[4]

The Foreign Office and MI6 viewed Sheikh Zayed as 'a reliable and stabilising force' in the Gulf and 'a potential valuable customer for arms'. On 6 August 1966, Zayed, backed by a group of British officers and organised by MI6, staged a successful peaceful coup against his elder brother,

Sheikh Shakbut. Zayed then began to assert command over the seven emirates of the region and, in 1971, formed the United Arab Emirates. From the start, he encouraged foreign links, particularly with Britain, and the British authorities had no wish to upset this relationship, particularly during the Gulf War. Zayed had met with Sheikh Kamal Adham in early 1991 – this relationship was one reason why, intelligence sources suggested, the Bank of England did not react earlier to alleged misdeeds at BCCI.[5]

BCCI with its 'bank within a bank' had many similarities to other CIA-tied bankrupt financial institutions, notably Nugan Hand in Australia, Mercantile and Trust in the Bahamas and the Castle Bank which channelled funds to the CIA's anti-Castro Cuban operations. These types of bank acted as a magnet to 'funny money' and are always an attraction to intelligence services, which need covert funds for clandestine operations. BCCI was particularly attractive to the CIA because of its extensive network of branches in over sixty countries of the Third World, South America and the Middle East. The CIA relied on the Saudi government to fund, through secret BCCI accounts, anti-communist groups such as Unita in Angola and the Contras in Nicaragua. The bank was also used to back CIA operations to aid anti-Soviet guerrillas in Afghanistan and to support the funding of Panama's President, General Noriega.[6]

Time magazine alleged that BCCI ran a 'black network', operating a lucrative trade in financing the purchase of arms, drugs and gold. It also claimed that the bank had ties to Western and Middle Eastern intelligence agencies, including accounts for the intelligence services of Libya, Iran and Syria. There were further allegations that the black unit funded a joint effort by Argentina, Libya and Pakistan to acquire a nuclear weapon, known inaccurately as the 'Islam bomb'. Gold supplied by BCCI was used to purchase key ingredients and components. Thus, the bank would have proved an enticing target for MI5 and MI6 in their counter-espionage role of penetrating rival services and in monitoring the proliferation of nuclear weapons.[7]

The CIA is an extremely large and at times cumbersome organisation in which, because of its security-derived compartmentalisation, internal departments are able to adopt many contradictory positions. While it appears that the covert action people were using BCCI for their own purposes, other departments in counter-espionage and counter-terrorism began, in 1983, targeting and compiling intelligence reports on the bank. The first CIA report on the bank's drug connections was prepared in 1984, followed shortly thereafter by an investigation of its terrorist links, principally those with the Abu Nidal group. This coincided with concern within the bank that the BCCI London headquarters was being bugged; executives then employed Pakistan's security service to sweep the Leadenhall Street premises for eavesdropping devices.

In 1985, concerned about the escalating terrorist threat and, in particular, the activities of the Abu Nidal network, counter-terrorist experts in the CIA and the US State Department proposed shaming European governments that were regarded as soft on terrorism. They were particularly annoyed with the Greeks for allowing a number of assassinations to take place and for the lax security at their airports. There was anger that the Abu Nidal terrorist network, Fatah Revolutionary Council, was allowed to operate in Athens, occupying a flat overlooking the airport. The Greek government reacted by claiming that Athens was being 'targeted' unfairly by the Americans.[8]

Relations between the United States and the UK on the one hand and the socialist government of Greece on the other were at an extremely low ebb during the early and mid-eighties. Athens was regarded as 'a hotbed of Libyan political infighting', the scene of a series of attacks and murders whose victims were opponents of the regime of Colonel Gaddafi. There was also a series of assassinations of foreign diplomats, initially suspected to be the work of Middle Eastern groups.

In November 1983, two American employees of the US–Greek military assistance group were shot at, and on 28 March 1984 Kenneth Whitty, first secretary at the British embassy and deputy director of the local British Council, was killed.

There was general unease about Premier Andreas Papandreou's planned trip to Libya for talks on trade, including the sale of arms, and the training of Libyan officers by the Greek armed forces. In a terse response, the Reagan administration rejected Greek requests for second-hand interceptor aircraft and, in a calculated snub, instead sold them to Turkey. Further tension was created when Papandreou expressed his determination to bring the KYP, the Greek Central Intelligence Service, once a hotbed of political intrigue and subversion, under his direct control. The KYP was closely tied to the CIA, having been established in 1952 with American guidance and technical aid. Papandreou aimed to demilitarise the KYP into a 'self-contained civilian service'.[9]

One particular incident had incensed both the Americans and the British. In April 1984, an Iraqi-born Jordanian, Fuad Hussein Shara, suspected of being a member of Abu Ibrahim's Baghdad-based May 15 terrorist group, was arrested at the specific request of the CIA and MI6, who believed him to be part of a terrorist network. Shara, first suspected of involvement in the series of assassination attempts in Athens, was alleged to have planted a booby-trapped suitcase on a London-bound airliner, rigged to blow up when it reached a set altitude. An Englishwoman known as 'Cotling', a partner of Shara in the legitimate trade of religious artefacts from the Middle East, was believed to have innocently carried the suitcase on board the plane from Israel to London. In the event, the suspected bomb never detonated. When she returned to Athens, Cotling was followed to the flat of the Jordanian, which Greek security men were keeping under intense surveillance. They were surprised to witness two men breaking into the flat and removing items from a briefcase. The two, who bungled the burglary, were a senior CIA operative, the deputy station chief code-named 'Huey', and an unnamed MI6 officer.[10]

For not pre-notifying the Greek authorities of this serious breach of sovereignty, the CIA officer was forced to leave the country. The Greek Prime Minister attacked Britain for 'proving staunch unquestioning support' of the United States. The charges might have been more severe if the MI6 officer had not been wise enough to leave the country immediately he was discovered. Shara was released from custody when Greek police said they had insufficient evidence – a photograph of the suspected suitcase – to charge and convict him. The CIA and MI6 regarded the release as an 'outrage'. A month after the explusion, American officials began briefing journalists that Greece was 'soft' on terrorism.[11]

The Foreign Office had been particularly enraged when British citizens became the target of a number of terrorist attacks claimed by a previously unknown group, the Revolutionary Organisation of Socialist Muslims, which turned out to be an Abu Nidal front group. Incidents included:

- the killing of Kenneth Whitty in Athens;
- the assassination of Percy Norris, Deputy High Commissioner in Bombay on 27 November 1984;
- the bombing of the British Airways Madrid offices on 1 July 1985;
- the bombing of a hotel near Athens, injuring thirteen people, including six Britons. The hotel was alleged to be 'a spy centre used against the Arabs and Islam';
- a bomb in Rome on 18 September 1985 at a café, described as a 'den of the American/British intelligence services', injured forty people.

These were crude attempts to put pressure on the British government to release four of Abu Nidal's being men held in prison in Britain. Three terrorists had been responsible for shooting and seriously wounding Shlomo Argov, the Israeli ambassador to Britain, outside the Dorchester Hotel in June

1982. A fourth had been involved in smuggling arms into the country; Abu Nidal made several attempts to persuade the British authorities to deal with him and, in one instance, offered to trade information he had gleaned in Libya on the IRA. The government refused these offers. Rebuffed, Abu Nidal began his bombing campaign, accusing MI6 of leading a Europe-wide intelligence effort against him. (Later MI6 had little need for Abu Nidal's information, having apparently recruited a certain 'Abd El Hamid', his liaison officer with the IRA. Hamid was executed by Abu Nidal's men as an informer in April 1987 after the discovery of an alleged 'British spy ring'.)[12]

While elements of the CIA were deeply implicated in BCCI's 'Black Network', other sections wanted to expose the Abu Nidal networks and the banks that operated in conjunction with them in those countries 'soft' on terrorism. This was rejected by higher authorities but counter-terrorism specialists did leak material to their counterparts in London, including information about three front companies used by the Abu Nidal network which had laundered money through BCCI. It was felt that it was better to monitor this network than to bust the ring.[13]

During 1984, four men had been netted in a US Customs sting. They were eventually jailed in 1988 for their part in a plot to supply £5.5 million worth of automatic weapons to Samir Najmeddin, commercial manager of the Abu Nidal organisation, Fatah Revolutionary Council, through his SAS Trading and Investment company in Poland. Letters of credit were opened in October 1983 from Najmeddin's account at the Hyde Park BCCI branch. US Customs learned of the Najmeddin connection through letters found in the office of David Mitchell, a Geneva-based accountant. Mitchell claimed that, in 1982, he had given British diplomatic staff documentary evidence that he had been asked by BCCI to participate in an arms deal. The British consulate in Geneva told him: 'You're mixing with some very dangerous people.' Diplomatic pressure ensured that information on these links was not published at the time and the Najmeddin deal went ahead without the Geneva connection. However, Mitchell's testimony indicated that British intelligence knew about Nidal and BCCI.[14]

The BCCI accounts under suspicion included those of Najmeddin, who, posing in London as an Iraqi businessman, had supplied arms to Iraq and to Argentina during the Falklands War. British intelligence surveillance of the Abu Nidal financial structure can be traced back to the activities of an expatriate Indian, Ben Banerjee, who had a licence to deal in arms in the United Kingdom. Banerjee was known to the security services through acting as an intermediary for arms manufacturers. At one point, he arranged the shipment of TOW anti-tank missiles to Iran and was on the fringes of the Irangate scandal. In 1981, Banerjee arranged for Najmeddin to open an account at the BCCI Sloane Street branch through the Syrian-born manager, Ghassem Qassem. Forty-eight million dollars were transferred from the Midland Bank, where it had been for the previous three years. The accounts would be used to finance arms deals with British and other European companies in which BCCI made commissions from the profits. The arms, placed with Royal Ordnance and granted an export licence by the Department of Trade and Industry (DTI), ended up in Syria.[15]

Najmeddin became a valued customer of the bank, and staff 'were employed for whole days simply dealing with Najmeddin's telexes'. Given GCHQ's knowledge about the monitoring of telexes, it is probable that the security services also had access to this information. It is known that during 1984 Najmeddin had a series of meetings with members of Iran's Military Procurement Offices in London, situated next door to the DTI. Until their closure in September 1987, the offices were subject to a major MI5 intelligence operation. With the help of GCHQ, MI5 was able to 'routinely listen to all telephone calls, intercept all telexes and facsimile messages and, using other systems, observe and listen to conversations between arms dealers and the Iranians'.[16]

Abu Nidal, who used the name 'Shakir Farhan' for company registration purposes, had direct access to a further $30 million in BCCI accounts. MI5 officers had allowed him to come and go in London because they wanted to monitor his activities. On one occasion in 1983, 'Shakir Farhan' was questioned by police and then taken by police car to Heathrow Airport. On his last visit to the UK in January 1985, his suitcase was stolen from the lobby of his hotel in mysterious circumstances. Although he reported the matter to the police, the known terrorist was not hindered from leaving the country.

BCCI manager Ghassem Qassem had met Abu Nidal and had worked with Najmeddin for four years but was unaware of their true identities and activities. Najmeddin's cover was eventually blown in the French magazine *L'Express*, which openly accused him, on the basis of a leaked FBI report, of being Abu Nidal's financier. Najmeddin successfully sued when the magazine could not produce the secret report in court. However, he had begun to feel unsafe dealing with BCCI in London. In 1986, the Abu Nidal accounts were closed and transferred to Switzerland and Poland. In the same year, Sheikh Adham withdrew investments from BCCI, a move that was noted by the security services and passed on to the Bank of England. That year, the CIA produced a report outlining many of the later revelations; this was sent to the National Security Council but was not however, forwarded to the Federal Reserve and the regulators.[17]

In mid-1987, Ghassem Qassem was approached by two MI5 officers at the Flemings Hotel in Mayfair and asked to provide information about the Abu Nidal accounts. Qassem then put MI5 'fully in the picture as to the movement of funds'. He was told that MI5 had been monitoring the bank since 1983. Although they had direct evidence of wrongdoing, it would appear that the security services wished the bank to remain open to enable them to monitor the rich harvest of terrorist links which had been uncovered. Former Labour Home Secretary Merlyn Rees has said that it was 'normal practice' for the security services to pass to the Prime Minister information linking terrorists and banks.[18]

In February 1988, MI6 produced a detailed 55-page report for the French DST outlining the financial assistance given to Abu Nidal's Fatah Revolutionary Council by Gulf states. In October, Robert Gates, later to be CIA chief, told US Customs that BCCI was the 'Bank of Crooks and Criminals International', though he refused to enlighten them on what information he had to justify such a comment. A few weeks later, US Customs officials were told by their British counterparts about secret payments made by the CIA through two accounts in BCCI to their agents in London.[19]

The British Customs' discovery evolved out of Operation Seachase, which led to the arrest and conviction of BCCI officials in 1988 for laundering drug money. Further investigation revealed that the CIA had paid nearly 500 British 'monitors' payments stretching over ten years. According to the *Guardian*, regular sums went to 124 people employed in government or engaged in politics; 53 in commerce, industry and banking; 75 in academic institutions; 24 scientists; 124 in communications; and 90 in the media. About 20 of these had received honours, including people in senior positions who had been long-term CIA contacts. Information supplied to the CIA by these 'monitors' included details of British arms sales and overseas contracts – often before they were concluded. The Customs discovery would have been acutely embarrassing for the government and for the CIA and MI6, who have a mutual agreement that no agents are recruited nor operations run on one's soil without the prior agreement of the other. The CIA appears to have been unhelpful to its British counterparts, refusing to wash any more dirty linen. While, for years, Customs officials passed on details of BCCI accounts being used to launder drug money, the priorities of the security services ensured that the information was not acted upon.[20]

Behind its wall of secrecy, the Bank of England was recognised as one of the best-informed institutions in the world. On this occasion it appeared to lack intelligence on which to act or else was involved in a massive cover-up. It was not until March 1990, two months after Qassem was moved from his post at BCCI and the MI5 operation closed, that the Under-Secretary at the MoD, who is legal adviser to MI5 and MI6, told the Bank of England the full extent of BCCI's involvement in terrorist funding and the identity of certain account holders. He revealed that MI5 had secretly monitored the bank for some time to trace the financing of terrorist groups and illegal arms deals in an operation regarded as a great success for the security services. However, the operation appeared to bear all the hallmarks of Security Service failure in counter-terrorism. MI5 had not taken heed of senior police criticisms, operating instead in a manner totally out of keeping with the business in hand. 'We have always been worried', said a senior policeman, 'that, while espionage can proceed at a stately, methodical pace, with each move debated and planned, you have to move very fast in anti-terrorist operations.'[21]

The Bank of England – nine years after the Abu Nidal accounts had been opened – set up an investigation, Project Q (Qassem). This included a Price Waterhouse partner, two senior BCCI officials and Roger Pierce, a Scotland Yard Special Branch officer. The Q team sent a progress report to John Bartlett, head of the Bank of England's supervisory section, in August 1990. In January 1991, he received the interim Q report identifying the core eleven customers and forty-two accounts, many of which were linked to Abu Nidal or his associates. One account dealt with howitzer shells destined for Iraq via Turkey and Jordan. In February, the Q team referred two accounts to the Special Branch under the Prevention of Terrorism Act. MI6 officers admit that the intelligence which they supplied to the Bank of England did not constitute evidence for convictions, but they expressed astonishment that the Bank did not move against BCCI earlier.[22]

New York District Attorney Robert Morgenthau, who was leading the initial United States investigation into BCCI, privately vented his frustration at the lack of co-operation by the intelligence services. According to Channel 4 News both MI6 and the CIA tried to dissuade key people from testifying against BCCI. Morgenthau said on camera: 'I am aware of those stories and am not happy about talking about that.' The authorities continually dragged their feet in pushing the investigation, according to former Senate investigator Jack Blum, because 'The various governments which had supervisory authority [over BCCI] were told by their various intelligence services that various things had been done by the bank for the services and to please be nice to them. In effect, the bank had bought the loyalty or support of various intelligence services by helping.'[23]

Morgenthau scored a major coup in July 1992 when Kamal Adham, the former Saudi intelligence man, agreed to pay a $105 million fine and tell all he knew about BCCI's 'black network' in return for a reduced sentence. Adham, who is believed to have been at the heart of the network, is 'expected to provide a rich vein of information into the inner workings of BCCI'. Only time will tell. In May 1992, Adham flew into Britain in his private jet under the protection of MI6 without hindrance from Customs or Immigration officials. When New Scotland Yard detectives arranged to raid his Grosvenor Square flat during his unofficial visit, Adham slipped out of the country, tipped off by his MI6 minders.[24]

In October 1992, Senator John Kerry's Senate sub-committee on terrorism, narcotics and international operations published its 800-page report on BCCI. It concluded that British regulators moved against BCCI only when forced to do so by United States investigators. The inquiry had been frustrated, Kerry said at a press conference, in its attempt to uncover the bank's assistance to terrorists, the building of a

Pakistani nuclear bomb and finance for Iranian arms deals by MI5, which had sealed documents which could shed light on these matters and the use of the bank by foreign intelligence agencies in the United Kingdom. The report of Lord Justice Bingham, who in August 1992 was named as the next Master of the Rolls, was a much more sedate affair. Bingham gently slapped the wrists of the Bank of England for failing to recognise some of the pieces of the jigsaw which it had been given. Details of the security service's interest in monitoring BCCI were shunted off into an appendix which was not published for 'security reasons'. All that was revealed was that 'a possible connection' between BCCI and terrorist accounts was mentioned to the Bank 'in a very general way' in April 1987. The Bank only learned in December 1988 that the Abu Nidal organisation held accounts in BCCI by way of an article in *Private Eye*.[25]

Bingham also failed to uncover what Nick Kochan, co-author of a book on the fraud, identifies as a series of BCCI-linked networks within the British Establishment. 'Evidence is now available of the multitude of leading British politicians who enjoyed BCCI's excellent hospitality, had accounts with its branches, and even (reputedly) collected envelopes containing fresh pound notes (for charity of course) on their visits to the Bank headquarters. With this network in place, it begins to be clear why the BCCI was able to keep its UK banking licence for so long.'[26]

20

Banks, High-tech and the man who never was

> Agents should be willing to die for their country but not for a company.
>
> Robert Gates, CIA Director

Much has been made, in recent years, of intelligence agencies seeking a new direction following the end of the Cold War, primarily through the acquisition of economic intelligence. The role of the economy in British intelligence affairs is, however, not new. There is a loose and, as yet, undeveloped theory that while in the past the domestic service, MI5, represented the interests of manufacturing industry and was responsible for protecting it from subversion and trade unionism, its sister service, the foreign-intelligence-gathering and covert action agency, MI6, has represented the interests of finance capital, namely the City of London.

MI6 officers have shared the same backgrounds as their counterparts in the City – families, universities and clubs. Their outlooks and interests are similar – as is their aim, which is, first and foremost, to protect Britain's overseas investment, which increasingly, as manufacturing goes into sharp decline, is one of the few wealth-generating sectors of the economy. It was the Head of the Civil Service, Sir William Armstrong, who shocked members of Edward Heath's government with his observation that the business of the Civil Service was 'the orderly management of decline'. He might well also have been talking about the Secret Intelligence Service.[1]

These differing perspectives have been partly responsible for the poor relations between the two intelligence agencies. They reflect the subtle but all-important class divisions which divide British society at all levels. MI5 has always tended to be on a slightly lower rung of the social ladder than MI6. Early on in his career, Anthony Cavendish, who served in both services, was privy to the internal intelligence war: 'those of us who worked with MI6 officers knew that that organisation was the tops and they – not us [MI5] – were the real professionals.' A year later, when he joined MI6, 'I said apropos dictating a letter, "How rude can we be to MI5?"' Peter Wright, from a lower-middle-class background, found this easy superiority exuded by MI6 officers galling. 'They invariably planned operations which, frankly, stood little chance of success . . . There was, too, a senseless bravado about the way they behaved . . . operating in the modern world with 1930s' attitudes and 1930s' personnel.'[2]

While retired MI5 officers have found employment as security consultants in industrial and commercial companies, merchant banking and other City institutions appear to be a natural home for former MI6 officers. Insider contacts, developed over many years whilst serving abroad, mixing with diplomats, politicians and potential leaders of countries, are seen as a valuable commodity. MI6 has been much more successful at penetrating to the heart of Britain's City-dominated economy and, hence, to the centres of power.

The Bank of England has had a good share of former intelligence personnel among its ranks. The assistant to the Bank's governor in the sixties was a Special Operations Executive veteran, Jaspar Rootham. Sir Robert Clark, chairman of Mirror Group Newspapers, worked for the SOE during the Second World War and afterwards joined the prestigious law firm Slaughter and May, where his old boss in SOE, Hilary Scott, was a senior partner. Later, as chairman of the merchant bankers Hill Samuel, he also became a director of the Bank of England. According to *Private Eye*, Hill Samuel had been known as the 'spy bank' because of its close ties with the intelligence world.[3]

In the post-war period, Hambro's Bank was closely connected with the Security Services. Its chair, and yet another director of the Bank of England, Sir Charles Hambro, had been head of SOE and was employed by MI6 for a time. The managing director, Henry Sporborg, a former partner in City solicitors Slaughter and May, had been SOE vice-chief, organising operations in Scandinavia where Hambro's traditionally had strong links. Peter Follis, who ran training schools for both SOE and MI6 during and after the war, was the bank's representative in New York, while MI6 officer John McCaffery, who had worked with Allen Dulles in Switzerland and Italy on the terms of the German surrender, served as the bank's representative in Italy. Kleinwort Benson was another bank associated with MI6 through Sir Rex Benson, cousin and colleague of its chief, Sir Stuart Menzies, and George Kennedy Young, former deputy chief of the service and director of the bank. Young's friend, former MI6 officer Anthony Cavendish, joined Brandt's Bank as its international director, later recruiting three of his former colleagues to the bank. Cavendish introduced the merchant bank's chairman, Lord Aldington, to the new MI6 chief, Maurice Oldfield, who became a frequent lunch guest at the bank. Another bank which is alleged to have recruited a number of former MI6 officers over the years has been Morgan Grenfell. In the seventies, Cavendish knew that there 'were half-a-dozen ex-MI6 men working in the City of London'.[4]

In the majority of cases, these ties may be completely innocent, but as Cavendish's memoirs illustrate, a former intelligence officer never completely cuts his links with his old service. There is always the odd favour to be done and the occasional piece of intelligence which can be passed on. Sometimes MI6 will use a bank to infiltrate an agent into a country where it lacks proper representation or needs an agent under 'deep cover' outside of the local embassy and its station officers. MI6 also needs banks and other financial institutions for 'funny money', to pay agents and fund covert operations.[5]

During the fifties, James Rusbridger was a managing director of a City firm of international commodity brokers whose dealings in Cuban sugar attracted the attentions of the CIA. The agency wanted him, at great expense, to help drive down sugar prices to weaken Castro's economy. In 1962, the thirty-four-year-old Rusbridger was approached by MI6. 'This charming man from "the Foreign Office" came to see me, seeking information that he could easily have got from *Whitaker's Almanack.*' He was introduced to 'some people' at the Naval and Military Club in Piccadilly, where retired military men mixed with spooks. 'They asked me if I would take various things into Eastern Europe, mostly money, and bring out documents for them.' Checking out the scheme with a brother who worked in Naval Intelligence, Rusbridger 'bought it' and spent the next few years delivering gold to agents. 'The upshot was I became an MI6 bagman, driving openly through Prague, Warsaw and Gdansk in my E-type Jaguar.' He retired as a commodity broker in 1974 and now lives in Cornwall, where he writes well-researched and often critical books about the intelligence services.[6]

In 1992, the *Independent on Sunday* reported that there were rumours in the City that sixty-seven-year-old Ephraim Margulies, known as 'Marg', the former chairman of S. W. Berisford, the commodity trading and sugar group, had been MI6's paymaster in Eastern Europe. A passionate supporter of Israel, Margulies lives with his wife and eleven children in the ultra-orthodox Hasidic Jewish community in Stamford Hill. An Eastern European *émigré* descended from a long line of rabbis and merchants, Margulies came to Britain in 1938 from that part of Poland now in the western Ukraine. After a wartime spent on a minesweeper in the Channel, he began in business selling groceries in London's East End. The seventies commodity boom turned his sleepy Berisford group into one of the best commodity performers in the UK market with a sprawling network of two hundred companies. In the eighties, the company's back was broken in a disastrous move into the property market at the height of the property boom.[7]

Another with an alleged MI6 pedigree is Peter Middleton, former chief executive of Thomas Cook, who, in September 1992, took up the £250,000 a year post of chief executive of Lloyd's of London. Middleton (not to be confused with Sir Peter Middleton, former Permanent Secretary at the Treasury) was attached to the Foreign Office for sixteen years, serving in Indonesia and Tanzania, and ending up with a prestigious posting to the Paris embassy. Described by colleagues as a 'teetotal aesthete', Middleton was a Roman Catholic monk before he joined the 'Foreign Office' in 1969. After leaving the service, he spent a short period with the Midland Bank's international division. During the eighties, the Midland Bank had a reputation as something of a 'spook's bank'.[8]

Fifty-four-year-old Dennis Skinner was the Midland Bank's representative in Moscow between 1978 and 1983. On the morning of 17 June 1983, he was found dead on the pavement beneath the open window of his fifth-floor flat on Leninsky Prospekt. Two days earlier, a clearly distressed Skinner had handed a note to a friend in the same block of flats, the manager of Rank-Xerox in Moscow, William Crane. Skinner claimed that he knew of 'a spy in the British Embassy' and that he feared being 'snatched' or arrested by the KGB. 'Please go to the Embassy for guards to be there, in case I try to make a run for it . . . Please do this for me – or I am a dead man.' In the event, Skinner went to that evening's reception without hindrance and talked to the British Minister, David Ratford. He alleged that he knew the identity of the spy and that the KGB were on his trail. Over the next two days, Skinner had two further interviews with embassy diplomats, including John Burnett, the MoD security officer, before returning to his flat on the night of 16 June. Just three hours before his death, Skinner telephoned the embassy saying he was convinced that he was about to be arrested by the KGB.[9]

After his alleged suicide, Foreign Office officials in London attempted to blacken Skinner's character, briefing BBC and *Daily Telegraph* journalists that he was disturbed, a loner who had developed some kind of 'persecution complex' as the day approached for his departure. He was said to be suffering from 'Moscow blues' and his death was blamed on a mixture of vodka and paranoia. However, as the post-mortem showed, there was no trace of alcohol or drugs in his blood. In fact, he had given up drinking and smoking some time before. Skinner was looking forward to a vacation with his wife and children, back home in London. He had a valid exit visa and a British Airways ticket for 20 June. While the circumstances of his death remain a mystery to this day, it appears that Skinner had found himself caught up in a web of espionage.[10]

In 1964, Skinner had been employed by the British computer manufacturing firm ICL. An excellent Russian speaker, in 1968 he was posted to Moscow, where his Soviet hosts gave him a secretary, Lyudmilla. The couple fell in love and, following his divorce from his English wife, married in 1973. Skinner knew that his wife had been 'planted' on him by the KGB, a then common event in the Soviet Union. She told him about her KGB connections in 1970 when he was himself approached and asked to 'co-operate'. Skinner told the British authorities and was interviewed by MI6 officers who asked him to continue the meetings. He continued to meet 'Alec', Alexander Barabeichik, a Radio Moscow employee, and another man known as 'Boris', twice a week. Each side knew that Skinner was in contact with the other's intelligence service, though 'to call him a double agent would be to glamorise his role'. The KGB told Lyudmilla that they were wary of her husband since he openly used what he knew to be bugged telephones. It seems that Skinner was caught in the middle of the secret war between East and West, though it would appear MI6 was happy with the situation because in 1974 he received an MBE on the recommendation of the Foreign Office.

The coroner at his inquest was Mary McHugh, a 'legend' among her colleagues and a woman of 'fierce independence, determination and obstinacy'. For reasons of national security, she had been willing to hold the inquest in private, but was rebuffed by the authorities, 'who denied any connection between the death and matters of security'. They were to rue that decision, as McHugh then openly 'pursued the truth to the embarrassment of the Home and Foreign Offices'. The coroner claimed that Skinner's 'contacts' were a 'cover' and that he was a 'very patriotic man'.[11]

KGB interest in Skinner had begun when the Soviets thought he might be able to supply computers, despite the West's ban on high-technology sales to the Soviet bloc. Skinner told the Soviets that he knew a way around the problem of obtaining an export licence. MI6 appears to have used these contacts to monitor the transfer of technology to the Soviet Union. Skinner also mixed with the highest circles of Soviet commercial and political life and was a frequent visitor to the Kremlin, with access to ministers and other top officials. This made him a prize catch for MI6, which was desperate to infiltrate the Soviet Union's closed society. Skinner's debriefings by MI6 were undertaken when he made trips home to London; the Moscow embassy was under such extensive surveillance by the KGB that any contact with the few resident MI6 officers would have been easy to spot. Skinner continued to meet with 'Alec' even though he described the KGB man as a 'sadist'.

Back in London in 1975, even though he had no banking experience, Skinner was head-hunted by Midland Bank. At the same time, his wife Lyudmilla was debriefed by MI6, required to sign the Official Secrets Act and given a contact telephone number. For a year, Skinner received what he described as 'some very highly specialized training'. From 1978 to 1983, he was the bank's Moscow representative, effectively under MI6 control. Midland's then chief executive, Geoffrey Taylor, later said that he was not privy to information on Skinner, who was 'clearly a no go area'. When senior executives searched Skinner's desk the day after his death they found it to be empty except for a single note which referred to his recruitment to the bank by former Head of the Civil Service, Lord (William) Armstrong, the bank's chairman from 1975 to 1980. Similarly, ICL files contained no personal records on an employee dubbed 'the man who never was'.[12]

Skinner's return to Moscow was made, according to his wife, 'under very controlled conditions'. She refused to disclose what those conditions were, merely stating that 'there were some pretty obvious conclusions to make about the second trip'. Skinner took with him a coded message which he was to send to the bank's head office if he was in any danger. Such a message was activated a few days before he died when the bank immediately sent a message asking for his return. After his death, Midland representives spent fourteen hours closeted in the embassy with Sir Iain Sutherland, the ambassador, in a 'safe' room known as 'the tank', which was shielded from KGB bugging.[13]

During his time in Moscow, Skinner was being put under pressure by Lyudmilla's former controller, 'Alec', who was using 'cruel threats'. Skinner was worried that allegations of illegal currency dealings, owning pornography and visa offences would be used against him. Further, it appears that Skinner had a girlfriend and he feared that the KGB might use this as blackmail or might frame him in an attempt to lure his wife back to the Soviet Union. (In 1981, Lyudmilla and the two children had entered Britain, saying that they had no intention of returning to Moscow.)

When the inquest into his death was finally convened after delays and allegations from the coroner, Dr Mary McHugh, that 'British Intelligence was connected with his death', the jury concluded that Skinner had been unlawfully killed. This was immediately assumed to be the work of the KGB, though American sources suggested he 'died at the hands of a British secret service hitman'. Coroner McHugh had attempted to get to the bottom of the affair but the 'Establishment closed ranks and not long after, McHugh's twenty years of service came to an end'.[14]

Who pushed Dennis Skinner out of the window in Moscow is not known. And precisely what murky enterprise the Midland Bank representative and former computer specialist with Britain's ICL was involved in and which marked him out as a threat has never been revealed, but it may have been connected with Western concern over the transfer of high technology to the Soviet Union.

A favourite conspiracy theory propagated by Western intelligence services in the early eighties was that of the 'global plan' plotted by the Central Committee of the USSR to steal, through an international maze of phoney companies, post office box addresses and mysterious middlemen, the West's technological secrets. This 'multi-billion dollar business' which involved 'twenty thousand agents' controlled by specialists expert in the theft of Western technology in Department T of the KGB, was judged by counter-intelligence authorities to be 'the central security issue of the coming decade', threatening 'the very foundations of Western security'. Whether there was any justification for these claims – though the parlous state of the current economy of the Commonwealth of Independent States (CIS) suggests that there was no need to worry – the primary concern of the Americans, who were the primary architects of the conspiracy, was more to do with commercial gain than technological loss. American security concerns, while containing an element of realism and truth, were shot through with hypocrisy. United States companies were afraid of losing their monopoly in supplying computers to Western Europe and fearful that other countries might muscle in on their trade with Eastern Europe. CIA director William Casey claimed that the Japanese companies NEC, Hitachi and Fujitsu were a threat to US national security. An IBM representative remarked 'we have a mission to sell high technology to the Eastern Bloc'.[15]

Following his election in 1980, one of President Reagan's

first actions was to direct the CIA to investigate technology transfers to the Eastern bloc. As a result of the CIA report, a specialist team was set up, the Technology Transfer Assessment Centre (TTAC), whose members in co-operation with Customs and Commerce officials organised Operation Exodus to enforce US restrictions on the sale of 'sensitive' high technology to the Soviet bloc by other Western governments.[16]

Under the guise of implementing these restrictions, the CIA began to collect commercial information in Britain which was of great value to US corporations. An intelligence source told Kevin Cahill, a journalist specialising in computer matters, that the US authorities 'had a complete list of every computer in the UK', including British-built ICL machines as well as American computers. It had been compiled between late 1981 and early 1982 by a CIA team working in Europe which at times included over two hundred agents, many working under commercial cover in American multinational companies as dealers and salesmen. Very few of the companies listed were engaged in any kind of illegal activity, but the excess of zeal under Operation Exodus guidelines started a witch hunt as intelligence officers spent months checking export licences for high-technology sales to Eastern Europe.[17]

The security justification for the operation was based on the debriefings of the French double agent 'Farewell', real name Vladimir Ipolitovitch Vetrov, who had revealed details of the KGB's Directorate T, the scientific and technical branch of the élite First Chief Directorate, whose overseas arm, 'Line-X', targeted specific items of interest in the electronics field. Vetrov hand-delivered the first of over four thousand documents to the Direction de la Surveillance du Territoire (DST), the French counter-intelligence agency, in the spring of 1981. Then, in October 1982, the flow suddenly stopped. After a drunken argument with his mistress, Vetrov on leaving her apartment had, in a panic, shot dead a policeman who approached his car. During his imprisonment, in December 1984, KGB interrogaters extracted a confession to espionage and he was executed by firing squad on 23 January 1985. The DST's dossier on the case, exposing the Line-X operation to illicitly transfer high technology to the Eastern bloc, was circulated to Western intelligence agencies. Additional intelligence on the internal workings of Line-X was gathered following the defection of the thirty-six-year-old KGB officer Vladimir Kuzichkin, who walked into the British embassy in Tehran in June 1982. With his aid GCHQ had apparently been able to break a number of Line-X communication codes.[18]

In 1982, the United States used the information on the TTAC list and the defection of Vetrov and Kuzichkin to organise the first high-level ministerial meeting in twenty years of the American-dominated extra-legal, non-treaty-based Co-ordinating Committee for Multilateral Export Controls. COCOM, which had been set up in 1949, shortly after the founding of NATO, drew up lists of technology which was banned from export to the Soviet bloc. Its secretariat operates out of an anonymous building behind the American embassy in Paris in the rue de la Boétie. The building at the end of an alleyway shows only a dentist's nameplate.

Following the meeting, Britain agreed to set up a top secret working party code-named SXWP with representatives of the JIC, MI5, MI6 and Customs and Excise. The working party examined specific means of stopping the illegal transfer and sanctioned the setting up of Project Arrow. Although officially a Customs and Excise operation, Arrow was a joint effort with the security services and included key MI6 and MI5 officers Robert Tresillian and Peter Hervine. The Security Service was instructed to make additional telephone taps of Eastern bloc embassies in London and keep surveillance on commercial operations, noting callers and businessmen attending receptions. The project was co-ordinated with the CIA, which has its largest overseas station in London. CIA operatives worked very closely with their British counterparts and officials in the Special Branch and Customs, while two CIA officers were seconded to an office in the 'Ministry of Defence' to report on opposition to the American policy. UK Customs officials were also sent to the United States to be trained in operations relating to Project Arrow.[19]

One of the first consequences of the new policy was the spreading of disinformation about Soviet intelligence efforts, including a smear planted in an American magazine, *Parade*, which was picked up by the *Daily Telegraph*. On 20 November 1982, the UK membership of the International Institute for Applied Systems Analysis in Vienna came up for renewal. The Americans claimed, according to the *Parade* story, that Soviet staff were using the Institute's computer to break into a Ministry of Defence super-computer at Reading and were using the information for Soviet nuclear weapon design. This was later shown to be completely false, but the story was picked up by the international media and was followed by the announcement that the Americans and, later, the British were pulling out of the only international computer institute of any note.[20]

The first public surfacing of the new hard-line approach came on Christmas Eve 1983, when a letter sent by IBM, the world's biggest producer of business computers, to thirty-two British firms involved in buying and selling computers, was leaked to a computer magazine. IBM disclosed that 'transactions within the United Kingdom involving "Advanced Systems" are also subject to the obtaining of US export licence approval'. In effect, American agreements would be enforced to override British sovereignty and European Community rules. United States officials later stipulated that the policy required US agreement to the movement of computers within the United Kingdom, including second-hand machines.[21]

The issue was taken up by *Computer News* journalist Kevin Cahill, who passed on details to the Liberal Democrat leader-to-be, Paddy Ashdown, MP. This was an interesting choice. Ashdown had been a member of the Special Boat Squadron, serving in Borneo during the early sixties campaign to stop communist guerrillas from Indonesia entering Sarawak territory. He subsequently spent two and a half years learning Chinese, then had a term in Northern Ireland, and was subsequently asked to join MI6. 'The halcyon days of my life', as he has described them, were spent after he was posted to Geneva, where he monitored the activities of Soviet bloc intelligence officers and liaised with Swiss intelligence on aspects of the Gladio stay-behind networks. His official work as First Secretary on the British Mission to the United Nations included working with the Conference on Security and Co-operation in Europe and the UN Conference on Trade and Development. Colleagues say that Ashdown left the service in disgust because he had no wish to take part in an operation to sabotage the UNCTAD trade agreement on higher levels for Third World commodity prices.[22]

Ashdown began a vigorous campaign to highlight the American threat to economic sovereignty. He complained to the Prime Minister and the Minister at the Department of Trade and Industry, Norman Tebbit – the man whose job it was to protect British companies – about the outrageous activities of the United States with the 'unwarranted encroachments on UK jurisdiction' which were 'contrary to internal law'. He did not get very far on a subject which the British found difficult to handle, as they were committed to Project Arrow. Tebbit's personal political adviser was Michael Dobbs (author of the political thriller *House of Cards*), a specialist in arms control and a personal friend of the man behind Exodus, the virulent anti-communist US Under-Secretary of Defence, Richard Perle.[23]

It is difficult to judge whether Arrow achieved any real success. A number of British businessmen were imprisoned and heavily fined for competing with US firms in supplying Soviet bloc countries, but in nearly all instances they were selling old and outdated technology. In 1985, a number of British businessmen in the computer field were expelled from Moscow in a tit-for-tat expulsion for alleged espionage. In one unfortunate incident, British Customs officials in the high-technology team arrested one of MI6's best sources in the Eastern bloc. In the end, CIA tactics became too much even for the Thatcher government, which in mid-1986 made a formal, though secret, protest to the United States government. It was admitted that CIA actions had damaged a Leeds-based computer company, Systime, which had been forced to shed over a thousand jobs. The company's main competitor in the United States had employed private detectives who told the company DEC that Systime was supplying computers to Libya, Iran and Pakistan. They also erroneously claimed that computers on the COCOM list were finding their way via Systime to the Soviet bloc. In a further US investigation, CIA officers operating under cover as Customs officials at the US embassy in London burgled Systime's offices.[24]

The Farewell operation had the effect of rehabilitating the French intelligence community in the eyes of Western intelligence, which had never been convinced of its effectiveness or ability to keep secrets. However, it was later suggested that the French counter-intelligence agency DST had, in fact, effectively terminated Farewell when its deputy director laid out details of the operation in an official publication in December 1983 – two months after his arrest but before his apparent confession to espionage. The traditional poor relations between French and British intelligence were not, however, to be repaired so easily.[25]

John Simpson has written that in the light of the changing relationship between what we used to call East and West and the increasing role of economic intelligence, 'James Bond will have to turn chartered accountant'. This has already happened. MI6 officers have been planted abroad under cover of such employment. Not only do they have to be qualified in these occupations, they have, on completing a day's work under deep cover, to carry out intelligence-gathering tasks at night and weekends.[26]

Forty-two-year-old Niall Campbell, an ICI economic forecaster, was murdered in France while on business trip to Paris in December 1983. Campbell died from drowning, but not before his killers had beaten him and fed him with a massive overdose of sleeping pills. His body was found two hundred yards from the L'Isle Longue nuclear submarine base at Brest, close to the site of the construction of France's first nuclear-powered aircraft carrier. The action service of the Direction Générale de la Surveillance Extérieure (DGSE) often carried out security checks of this sensitive installation, including feigned 'attacks', attempts to break into the base to test security. Ten months previously, Bernard Nut, an undercover agent of the DST, who had succeeded in penetrating the KGB's Directorate S, which infiltrates Soviet agents into the West, was found shot on an Alpine snowbank. Nut had uncovered a major espionage operation directed against the French naval base at Toulon, where the nuclear hunter-killer submarine *Rubis* was stationed. Understandably, the French were security conscious about any suspicious activity around their sensitive naval bases.[27]

Campbell was found 360 miles from his Paris hotel, which he had left to go shopping before taking that evening's flight back home. Although his family and the authorities discounted that his death was linked to espionage – police claimed he was the victim of a Paris drugs gang – the coroner said that the 'whole inquiry in my opinion still has a very big question mark hanging over it'. There were reports that before leaving England Campbell had been contacted by an MI6 officer, who asked him to 'collaborate' in some way. Three days before Campbell's body was discovered, a twenty-seven-year-old British accountant with the London-based Transport Development Group, Robert Graham, was reported missing from his hotel in Paris, where he had been attending business meetings. Graham's decomposing body was later fished out of the Seine.[28]

Two years later, a possible explanation for the deaths of Campbell and Graham was revealed by Roger Wybot, former director and founder of the DST, who was reported as saying that the exposure of the *Rainbow Warrior* affair had been MI6's way of 'getting even' with the French for drowning British agents Niall Campbell and John Graham. On the evening of 10 July 1985, French secret service personnel had placed a bomb on the hull of the Greenpeace ship *Rainbow Warrior* in Auckland harbour, New Zealand. Within minutes of the explosion the boat had sunk and a crew member, Fernando Pereira was dead. The British government remained predictably silent about this proven case of state terrorism, but it appears that MI6 did take some action behind the scenes.[29]

In late May 1985, a DGSE officer, Gerald Andries, using the pseudonym Eric Andreine, booked into a London hotel on a mission to buy a French-made Zodiac rubber dinghy as part of Operation Satanic. He purchased the boat from a marine centre in North London and in the process proceeded to break every rule of security. Everyone who met him noticed something odd about the Frenchman. He did not speak English, knew little about the boat and the required engine size, and purchased it with a roll of new £50 notes. The dinghy was later shipped off for New Zealand by cross-Channel ferry. While at the hotel Andries made a telephone call through the switchboard to an ex-directory number in Paris which turned out to be that of the DGSE. However, Andries had little reason to worry about blowing his cover.[30]

The French were worried from the beginning that the British would blow the operation to the New Zealand authorities. To put them off the scent a decision was taken by the DGSE to tell their counterparts in MI6 that they were planning a covert operation in their Pacific colony of New Caledonia, where the native population wanted independence against the wishes of the white settlers. New Zealand, where two agents would be placed under deep cover, would be used as a staging post in an operation to stop gun-running to pro-independence groups in the region. MI5 noted the arrival in London of a bogus married couple – 'Alain Turenge' and 'Sophie' – on their way to New

Zealand. 'Turenge', Major Alain Mafart, was well known to the British, having taken part in manoeuvres with the Special Boat Squadron. The cover story was apparently accepted by MI6 who, in the initial stages at least, went along with French explanations.

The French operation appears to have been brought up at a weekly meeting of the Joint Intelligence Committee in May 1985, which would have been attended by a representative of the New Zealand Security Intelligence Service (NZSIS). (Despite reports from the Reagan administration that it had cut off the flow of intelligence to New Zealand because of the latter's anti-nuclear policy, secret documents show that the US, and presumably the UK, still supplied 'intelligence concerning Soviet and Chinese shipping in the Pacific'.) The information passed on was far from specific and was not given to the New Zealand police, because the story about an operation in New Caledonia was believed.[31]

'After the bombing the French were stunned by how quickly the New Zealand police managed to trace back the mystery buyer of the Zodiac. Historical rivalries rumbled to the surface.' The *Daily Mail* soon revealed the DGSE goings-on in London. This was seen as a 'provocation' by the former DGSE head, Alexandre De Marenches, who though an Anglophile – his wife is Lady Whitchell – appeared to blame the British, suggesting that the salesman for the Zodiac boat was an MI6 agent (in fact untrue). The DGSE later launched their own internal inquiry and accused MI6 of going along with the French plan with the intention of exposing it later to damage France's standing in the Pacific. In August 1985, this disinformation was passed on to the state-owned radio station France-Inter which proceeded to spread the falsehood. The head of the action service, Colonel Jean-Claude Lascere, also fed a story to right-wing journalists that the bombing culprits were, in fact, the British, who were angry about sales of Exocet missiles to Argentina during the Falkands War.[32]

The publicity gave rise to security fears that, since the

Rainbow Warrior was a British registered ship, the Department of Trade might launch its own inquiry. The British government remained silent throughout. Discreet lobbying ended with the Foreign Secretary Geoffrey Howe assuring Parliament that neither the French nor the New Zealand authorities believed that MI6 had been involved in the bombing. A few weeks later, the proposed DTI inquiry was quietly dropped.[33]

The feud between the French and British continued with the capture of the boat *Eksund* in the Bay of Biscay in November 1987 and the arrest of its crew for transporting weapons and explosives from Libya to the IRA. With relations between the DGSE and MI6 at an all-time low, the French used the incident to upstage the rival service and gain valuable publicity for themselves. MI6 was acutely embarrassed because, in spite of the massive monitoring of Libya, it had failed to detect this major shipment of arms. Salt was rubbed in the wound when the DGSE informed British intelligence that this was the fifth such shipment from Libya to Ireland between 1985 and 1987. Revealing the details of what was meant to be a joint operation, the DGSE then proceeded to 'blow' MI6's Swedish network, including the identity of the Stockholm chief of station, Margaret Bradfield.[34]

The continuing *Rainbow Warrior* affair, which was just a glimpse of 'part of a larger, longer strategy in which successful operations had not been uncovered', was the last episode of a long-running saga of national and inter-service rivalry. In the late eighties, the Foreign Office's belief that the United States will eventually withdraw its forces from Western Europe led to closer co-operation between MI6 and the French DGSE. However, in view of past hostility between the two services, one wonders how long this happy state of affairs will last.[35]

21

Economic Intelligence

> Commercial traffic is now in the intelligence domain, and it can be used . . . for just plain information [or] for a great deal of political manipulation.
>
> Professor John Erickson, director of Defence Studies at Edinburgh University.

'The battle lines have been drawn for a struggle to control information in Britain,' said a 1979 draft Conservative Party policy document. 'Government administration, corporations, police and security forces, and foreign corporations and Governments all seek to preserve their own privacy while finding out as much as possible about everyone else.' It concluded that 'information is the commanding height of tomorrow's economy'. It might have added that, while information is the currency of intelligence agencies, 'economic intelligence' is the commanding height of tomorrow's CIA, KGB and MI6 operations. Following the end of the Cold War, these agencies have been searching for a new direction in order to preserve their budgets and personnel. They believe this has been found in the gathering of commercial secrets.[1]

Within Europe, Britain's security services remain concerned about the activities of the former KGB and its continuing interest in high-tech intelligence. On 10 April 1992, the Belgian security services rolled up a twenty-five-year-old KGB network Operation Gladio (not to be confused with the post Second World War Gladio network) which uncovered evidence that the network was still being run by the new Russian Foreign Intelligence Service, whose head since October 1991 has been Yevgeny Primakov . The operation began earlier in the year following the defection of the first secretary at the Brussels embassy, Vladimir Komopliev. During debriefings by the CIA, Komopliev disclosed the existence of the espionage network whose task was to supply Moscow with high technology for military purposes. A French intelligence source said that 'there is evidence that there were also operatives in Britain . . . The relevant warnings have been given and we understand that action has been taken.'[2]

However, Gladio had uncovered what was essentially an old network, evidence of what had been rather than an example of current activities. Today, with the former Soviet economy in collapse, the new-look Foreign Intelligence Service is less interested in recruiting agents in the defence and security agencies than in, say, the Bank of England or the Treasury. In May 1990, the then director, Vladimir Kryuchkov, declared that the KGB had 'an important service specialising in economic analysis' which would help Soviet firms 'acquire the necessary experience' to compete in international markets. 'You want agents of influence who will assist your economic interests,' John Simpson correctly asserts. 'It is a matter of urgency to receive advance warning of changes in international finance, rather than (as in the old days) of possible pre-emptive nuclear strikes. It would be useful for the Russians to know who, at the level of G-7, the IMF or the World Bank, are their real friends and who is holding up their chances of greater aid, and what can be done about it. From now on, Karla's spymasters at Moscow Centre will need degrees in international finance.'[3]

The CIA has been travelling down the same road. On 19 September 1989, before the World Affairs Council, CIA director William Webster said that economic competition was now the main target of CIA activities. The CIA was concerned about the 'national security implications of a competitor's ability to create, capture or control markets of the future'. He went on to say that the CIA is 'anxious to stay ahead of the curve so it has established a new directorate to identify changing requirements for intelligence in a changing world. Throughout the next decade we will continue to see an increased emphasis on economic competitiveness as an intelligence issue.' He revealed that policy-makers in the United States were already 'relying on CIA intelligence to illuminate the playing field, and to understand the rules other nations are playing by'. The agency had been busy recruiting economists, commodity specialists, financial analysts, perhaps in recognition that it had a notoriously poor record on assessing the size of the Soviet economy, consistently overestimating its size and strength.[4]

Webster's speech was delivered just days before the CIA and FBI, after a number of months of surveillance, uncovered a French intelligence network which had been stealing commercial secrets from American computer companies. He used the opportunity to call for a counter-economic intelligence unit. Webster's successor, Robert Gates, informed the Senate: 'We know foreign intelligence services plant moles in our high-tech companies. We know that they rifle the briefcases of our businessmen. We know they collect information on what we're doing.' Gates said that he knew of two countries which had run economic intelligence operations against American targets. CIA sources let it be known that he was referring to Japan and France. Increasingly, the CIA was targeting competitors, seen to be the European Community and the countries of the Pacific rim.[5]

'When it comes to economic and technological competition,' boasted the former director of France's DGSE, Pierre Marion, 'we are competitors.' He went on to say that the service 'performs well in industrial espionage'. In 1982, the FBI caught a DGSE agent who had infiltrated a major US computer company. Previously purloined material had been passed on in sanitised form to French competitors. Marion openly admitted the service's involvement in economic spying and stated that those used by the DGSE included Air France, whose first-class seats had been bugged by the DGSE since 1981 to capture the conversations of American businessmen, Thomson, Renault and the Ministry of Industry. The service had helped Dassault sell Mirage jets to India in 1982 by supplying complete files on rival aircraft firms. A DGSE man was expelled from Delhi after giving details of a rival British bid to French arms salesmen. At the end of 1989, the FBI and CIA dismantled another officially sanctioned French DGSE industrial espionage network which had penetrated the American computer firms IBM and Texas Instruments. It would appear that a high-level deal was made between the Americans and the French to avoid an embarrassing trial. The agents were returned to France and fired from their posts, but were eventually re-employed on other projects.[6]

In the last few years, the DGSE has expanded its economic intelligence-gathering operations even further, including spying on former friends. Its budget has been increased by 10 per cent, while an extra thousand staff have been taken on to increase the quality of its analysis and human intelligence. The French have realised, admitted one CIA source, that 'the cheapest and best way to keep their companies in the game is to steal information from the competition'.[7]

On the back of anti-Japanese feeling and resentment fuelled by the slowing of the American economy, the CIA appears to have replaced the 'red threat' with the 'yellow peril'. A CIA-sponsored report caused a storm when it was leaked in 1991. It described the Japanese as 'creatures of an ageless, amoral, manipulative and controlling culture' who were intent on 'world economic dominance'. Some senior American officials now see a non-democratic, racist Japan as the main threat to national security. This may not be as unreal as it sounds. It was a Japanese author, Shintaro Ishihara, who during the Gulf War pointed out that the United States was totally dependent on Japanese microchips and super-conductors for its high-technology weapons. Japan has no secret service to speak of, but this is often not necessary since large Japanese companies have their own intelligence set-ups with sophisticated technical means to bug or use counter-measures against their national and international rivals. According to American intelligence analysts, most Japanese intelligence gathering is aimed 'not at hardware secrets but at marketing data, prices or bid details'.[8]

Former CIA director Admiral Stansfield Turner admitted that 'as we increase emphasis on securing economic intelligence, we will have to spy on the more developed countries – our allies and friends with whom we compete economically.' Chair of the Senate Intelligence Committee David Boren agreed that 'more and more, the aim of espionage is to steal private commercial secrets'. He called for 'new and different assets' to be developed to keep the nation economically competitive. The director of the eavesdropping United States National Security Agency, Vice-Admiral William Studeman, admitted that his British colleagues had asked him 'lots of questions' about the prospects of the NSA spying on its 'friends'. He claimed to be unhappy with the new policy because 'if other countries decide the CIA is using NSA telephone taps for "offensive" economic aims, the NSA listening-posts around the world will be made unwelcome'. Studeman was probably more unhappy at the unwelcome publicity and public acknowledgement of a practice which had been going on for years. In December 1990, a CIA official admitted that the CIA had been 'involved in Gatt and every trade negotiation. We take tasks from US negotiators to find out about the [other countries'] positions. We usually have someone who's right there, or within cable reach. We review other countries' proposals against econometric models. We tell our negotiators, "Here's what the other side left out or is holding back".'[9]

A drive to gather economic intelligence on Britain's potential enemies and commercial rivals was made in the aftermath of a top-secret review in the spring of 1984 by the Permanent Secretary at the Treasury, Sir Peter Middleton. Economic intelligence gathering had been given a major impetus by the election of the City-led Heath administration in 1970. Priority was given to penetrating the EEC and Japan, and their diplomatic messages, particularly those with economic content, were subsequently routinely intercepted. Following the 1973 oil crisis, MI6 was tasked to penetrate the oil companies and the oil-producing countries of the Middle East with attention paid to international negotiations and investment of revenues.[10]

Later in the seventies, the Treasury downgraded the importance of such intelligence and the staff devoted to it were cut. Following the Middleton review the cuts were restored and extra resources employed by the Joint Intelligence Committee (Economic Assessments), which co-ordinates the work. The JIC (EA) includes representatives from the security services, the Foreign Office, the Ministry of Defence and the Department of Trade and Industry. In recent years, this sub-section of the JIC has monitored bank deals, transactions and loans – including those of the Bank of Credit and Commerce International before it crashed, aspects of the Maxwell empire, as well as reports on Tiny Rowland, chief executive of Lonhro. Former JIC clerk Robin Robison sifted 'an avalanche of data: commercial espionage designed to cheat on our allies; information obtained clandestinely from foreign car companies, electronics companies, steel producers, from engineering companies, finance houses, oil companies, mining and chemicals'.[11]

Under the new secrecy laws, protecting the 'economic well-being' of the country from outside threats is given a priority by ministers. However, ministers are often unaware of the true nature of this activity, which is directed by anonymous officials in the Cabinet Office and Treasury. The Overseas Economic Intelligence Committee of the Cabinet Office directs the security services in the gathering of commercial and economic intelligence. The committee is chaired by a Treasury deputy secretary who, with the chair of the JIC and the Co-ordinator of Intelligence and Security, makes up the ruling intelligence 'triumvirate'. Security-cleared 'indoctrinated' officials specialising in economic intelligence, with authority to see signals and secret material from MI6 and GCHQ, are located in most government departments, including the DTI, the Treasury and the MoD. The 'output' is widely distributed throughout Whitehall and also to the Bank of England. Sanitised intelligence is fed to 'certain industrial confidants' of the DTI, key British companies whose commercial activities are said to be identical with the 'national interest'. These have included major companies such as ICI, BP, Lonhro and Rio Tinto Zinc.[12]

Reflecting the growing emphasis on economic intelligence, the Bank of England has developed a close relationship with the JIC. Two Bank representatives, Ian Wilson-White and Peter Shore, are involved with the JIC economic sub-committee. The Bank receives weekly assessment reports from the JIC, and classified material protected by code-words is forwarded to the Bank's headquarters in Threadneedle Street where a middle-ranking official, Alan Whitehead, acts as a gatekeeper for sensitive information. According to a former MI6 officer: 'The Bank is a standard customer of MI5 and MI6, routinely receiving reports even on significant shareholdings.' The confidential information is passed on to interested parties within the Bank.[13]

GCHQ receiving stations have been specially built to eavesdrop on commercial satellites, and its listening post at its London station, 9 Palmer Street, known as UKC1000, targets International Leased Carrier communications. GCHQ intercepts commercial telexes (which are contractually binding), faxes and international telephone calls made by banks and large companies, especially those dealing with vital commodities such as oil. Telexes are routed to Palmer Street with the help of British Telecom's international telex network, and computers are programmed to look out for key words such as 'gold'. GCHQ will pass on intelligence, including 'a rich harvest of Third World traffic', which may prove useful to British competitors – BP, ICI and the 'big four' high street banks – from the monitored communications. It also intercepts the private communications of British private companies including Rolls-Royce, GEC and Marconi as part of its help to the British economy. GCHQ blithely ignores restrictions on its activities in this area. The 1985 Interception of Communications Act, while allowing the tapping of communications which 'safeguard the economic well-being of the United Kingdom', explicity restricts this right to 'the acts or intentions of persons outside the British Islands'.[14]

Elizabeth Finch, a former GCHQ official who worked at Palmer Street, told BBC Radio 4 she had regularly listened to 'random pick-ups' of commercial communications before she left the agency in the early seventies, thus confirming that such operations had been going on for many years. At the time, commercial traffic accounted for about 10 per cent of all GCHQ interceptions. Ms Finch said such traffic, in the form of telexes, was welcomed by staff because it was not coded and was therefore easy to understand. To get round the necessity for a warrant, the fourth floor of Palmer Street, which houses GCHQ computers, is staffed by a handful of BT workers, which satisfies the requirement that the telex traffic has never left BT hands.[15]

GCHQ is able to achieve impressive results in sweeping up commercial traffic because it lays down rules covering the encoding systems private industry may use. Computer firms have promised GCHQ that any systems they sell to private firms will be inferior to those provided to the agency, thus making it easier for GCHQ to decode commercial data. However, new applications of chaos theory to cryptography may prove a boon to private companies which seek to secure their messages from government surveillance. Information encoded by 'semi-chaotic systems', smaller than a lap-top computer, generates a higher rate of random values than the most powerful digital computers. Producing as many as a billion random numbers per second, such systems would be unbreakable. In the past, GCHQ and its partner in the United

States, the NSA, have managed to control the release of new technology, but appear powerless to stop these new advances. Currently, some of the most advanced electronic machinery, such as a voice recognition, is held not by GCHQ, but by security departments of banks, such as Hambro's which need increasingly sophisticated means to combat fraud.[16]

Unlike in the banking sector, according to David Benn, whose company, Lorraine Electronics, specialises in surveillance and bugging equipment, fraud is no longer the primary security concern of companies, 'It's the misappropriation of information because most businesses are information-based.' Information is now the key commodity, and it may be that in a period of increasing financial constraint, government agencies could come to rely on private companies for access to intelligence as the emphasis changes from military to economic and industrial targets. Consequently, the differences between the official and the private agencies, and legitimate intelligence gathering and spying, will be further blurred.[17]

In the past decade a number of high-powered international organisations, some employing former intelligence officers, have sprung up; these are, in all but name, full-blown intelligence agencies. As in their national equivalents, 90 per cent of the intelligence gathered comes from open sources such as commercial data-banks. They have developed highly sophisticated computer systems to assess the raw data which may, at the top of the range, provide country-by-country risk analysis for large multinational companies. The first such system was developed by the International Reporting Information Systems (IRIS), which established itself in Washington in the early eighties, with a cast of international statesmen on its letterhead and a sprinkling of former intelligence operatives on its staff. However, burdened with overly optimistic expectations, IRIS collapsed in 1983. Others have been more successful. In the spring of 1992, the Stanford Research Institute introduced the Business Intelligence programme, an 'integrated intelligence system that scans hundreds of publications and information sources', monitoring 'the business environment, industries, markets and technology, reporting on changes requiring response in corporate policy and management or operating strategies'.[18]

The American financial investigators Kroll Associates, founded in 1970 by Jules Kroll, a former assistant to the late Robert Kennedy, has thirty employees, including a number of former British and American intelligence personnel. It worked, until recently, out of the Security Service's former offices in Curzon Street. Experienced MI6 officer Michael Oatley joined Kroll after retiring from MI6 in early 1991. Oatley served in Hong Kong under cover of the Trade Commission, in Northern Ireland he negotiated with the IRA and he was then posted as counsellor to the British embassy in Harare. In the aftermath of the Gulf War, Kroll was asked by the Kuwaiti government to track down the assets of Saddam Hussein and the illegal secreting abroad of billions of roubles by the former organs of the Soviet Communist Party, following the failed August coup against Mikhail Gorbachev. Kroll investigators concentrate on company records and available information, though the network of contacts made available by their former intelligence officers will always prove invaluable. Wary of too high a public profile, Kroll decided in late 1992 to move out of Leconfield House to more conservative premises in Savile Row.[19]

One consequence of the City's 'Big Bang' and the boom in company take-overs in the mid-eighties was an explosion in the use of covert methods and dirty tricks against opponents. It was also a boom time for firms specialising in industrial espionage. Gary Murray, a private investigator who was involved in this field, has highlighted the lack of regulation in the industry. 'Nearly all the people in this profession will insist that they are solely in the counter-espionage business.' However, he estimates that '25 per cent are in what I would call aggressive industrial espionage'. According to David Benn, the industry has an annual turnover of £1.25 billion. Hugo

Cornwall, author of *The Industrial Espionage Handbook*, believes that private industrial espionage may involve as many as 100,000 people, some of whom will be engaged in activities which border on illegality. There are industrial intelligence agents and professional information intermediaries whose methodology is little different from that practised by national intelligence officers. Like their official counterparts, they will often be employed through cut-outs so as to guarantee deniability for covert operations. There are private investigators who may be involved in 'lifestyle checks' on executives, sometimes studying what people and companies throw in their dustbins – known as 'garbology'. There are those engaged in bugging and debugging operations, though increasingly it is the simple theft of computer disks which is sanctioned, as it is much more cost-effective than transcribing the results of endless and largely uninformative telephone taps.[20]

It may be left to the EC to regulate the huge growth in industrial espionage, but while Britain continues to engage in operations against its partners the situation would appear rather hypocritical. Robin Robison, an administrative officer for the Joint Intelligence Committee, says that 'as a matter of routine, Britain spies on its European partners, France and Germany, to get the bottom line on deals to do with the European Community'. The official Whitehall view is that the links between Britain and her partners are now so close that covert operations are not required or undertaken. This is nonsense. Peter Wright admitted in *Spycatcher* that 'for three years, between 1960 and 1963, MI5 and GCHQ read the French high-grade cipher coming in and out of the French Embassy in London'. The intelligence community had been under pressure to provide information 'about French intentions with regard to the pending British application to the European Economic Community'. Although President de Gaulle had already decided to veto the application, the intelligence from Operation Stockade was regarded by senior civil servants as 'simply priceless'. In the early sixties, a number of senior

National Union of Students officials joined the 'Foreign Office' and later transferred to the EC to take up administrative posts; they were known as the 'Century House Old Boys'. The *Observer* noted in 1985 that there were 'at least five MI6 officers in highly-paid jobs at EC headquarters'. It would appear that penetration of the Community has paid dividends. In December 1991, 'a flicker of speculation crossed [the] mind' of the BBC's chief overseas reporter, John Simpson, at John Major's considerable success in 'anticipating the ultimate positions of France and Germany at the Maastricht Summit'.[21]

With the collapse of communism in the Eastern bloc, MI6 was given a new priority to monitor events in Europe as the pace of events overturned traditional assumptions. The service was asked to provide regular reports on the upheavals in Eastern Europe and in Germany. Foreign Office officials, concerned that Mrs Thatcher's known antipathy to the EC and greater integration would leave Britain on the sidelines and without an integrated intelligence effort, sought agreements with the French to co-operate more closely on intelligence matters. Putting aside traditional rivalries, MI6 began sharing analysis with its French counterparts. Initially, this appeared to be a case of ganging up on Germany. Britain's policy objective, going back over a century, has been to remain outside formal alliances and prevent any one state from attaining a hegemony in Europe.

Although former Chancellor of the Exchequer, Nigel Lawson, has admitted that the Germans were Britain's natural allies on so many issues within the EC, Mrs Thatcher had, he has written, 'a pathological hostility to Germany and the Germans'. Mrs Thatcher was known to dislike Chancellor Kohl, apparently since the two were in opposition during the seventies when she discovered that the 'German leader had escaped to eat cream cake in an Austrian konditorei after cutting short earnest discussions with her on the future of conservatism'. Her views were shaped into policy by her private secretary and 'court favourite', Charles Powell, who had been recruited in 1984 from the Foreign Office 'to help her neutralise what she saw as the defeatist designs of his masters in their dealings with Europe'. Mrs Thatcher and Powell shared the same prejudices and willingness to operate outside of Foreign Office channels. He had disliked his appointment as UK Counsellor to the EC and appeared to be anti-German. A memorandum written by Powell on German reunification caused a row when it was leaked in 1990, because of its 'offensive odour'.[22]

Before the fall of the Berlin Wall, the British decided to divert extra resources, including personnel, to upgrade the JIC (Germany). The JIC(G), situated in Bonn, was asked to provide, through its liaison with the German counter-espionage agency BfV and the external BND, more frequent reports about intelligence and political implications of developments in East Germany. Following German unification, in March 1990, department heads within the BfV began restructuring counter-intelligence. This included treating previously 'friendly' Allied services as 'foreign' services and proposing the mounting of operations against the United States, France and Britain. It was reasoned, correctly, that the intelligence services of these countries would increase their operations on German soil to determine the country's new direction and to keep its perceived economic dominance under surveillance. The Allies were not pleased when, at the end of 1991, electronic installations in West Germany, formerly under American, French and British control, were taken over by German agencies. The Germans followed this up with a change of regulations which meant the Allied liaison officiers were no longer permitted to walk freely through German intelligence organisations, but instead had to be accompanied by an escort.[23]

While Britain has traditionally been wary of German dominance of the EC, there has also been concern on the part of the security services about the security of intelligence in the newly united country. The Allies had a shock when, in October 1990, Kalus Kuron, a top official in the BfV, gave himself up to the authorities, admitting that he had spied for East Germany for twenty-eight years. Kuron had betrayed his entire knowledge to the East; the worth of the material can be gauged from the huge sums paid to him by the East German secret service – the highest paid to any agent abroad. Other arrests appeared to suggest that remnants of the informer networks formed before unification by the former East German security service, the Stasi, were still active. The KGB had sought to use them to refocus its intelligence-gathering activities in the united Germany on economic targets to help Russia's ailing industries.[24]

When Mrs Thatcher was ousted from office and was replaced by the Hurd/Major axis, which has developed a friendly relationship with Chancellor Kohl, there began a drive for greater foreign policy co-ordination within the EC, which was allied to the need to save money as suddenly a great many new states were born in Eastern Europe. Co-operation was also sought with the Germans and, in a surprising move, Britain and Germany proposed that EC countries share embassy facilities in the former Soviet republics. (Fourteen new joint missions, some shared with the French, have been opened in the last eighteen months.) Discussions took place at the beginning of 1992 for a joint Anglo-German representation which would provide better co-ordination for EC diplomats and would counter American dominance in the region. The EC has also launched a recruitment drive for specialists to support the External Relations Directorate of the Community. While member states support the idea of 'diplomacy union', there are concerns about the highly sensitive area of intelligence gathering and the deployment of spooks in embassies. However, Treasury cuts announced in the Autumn of 1992 have clearly enhanced the prospect of some degree of co-operation.

The Ministry of Defence will have substantial cuts in its budget over the next three years, while the cut of 10 per cent in the diplomatic service budget by 1994 could involve the closing of 'all posts in black Africa, except Pretoria and Lagos, and all but three embassies each in the Middle East and Latin America'. The staff of our major embassies in Washington, Bonn and Paris, which have essential security and intelligence liaison roles, have already been cut by 10 per cent. Only the prosperous Far East would remain inviolate. The effect on MI6, which relies on the embassies for 'light cover', would be dramatic. Further, Foreign Secretary Douglas Hurd has begun to argue that the need for covert intelligence gathering abroad has diminished since the end of the Cold War and that it is now important to strengthen diplomatic representation, especially in the republics of the former Soviet Union. He has been reported as saying that one way of making up diplomatic budgets is to raid MI6 funds. The shortfall in the budget will be made up out of the MoD's already depleted funds. Besides cost, there are many advantages to sharing facilities with the Germans. 'The Germans are going to have assets in Central Europe that we don't have', suggests academic Kenneth Robertson, 'and that's going to tilt the balance and incline us more towards them.'[25]

In February 1993, it was reported that John Major had ordered an informal 'total' review of Britain's overseas commitments, including those of MI6. This initiated fierce defensive lobbying within Whitehall as the Prime Minister pushed for more aggressive commerce, and arms sales-led intelligence gathering.

22

Arms, MI6 and the Death Merchants

Britain and Iraq – THE BIG PRIZE

Foreign Office advisory paper, 1990

According to Joint Intelligence Committee administrative officer Robin Robison, Mrs Thatcher, the only Prime Minister to sit in on JIC meetings, was fascinated by the intelligence world and the international arms trade.

Arms sales are given a high priority in British intelligence 'targeting'. Britain is the third largest arms exporter, with a trade worth £3 billion a year. The industry represents 11 per cent of all manufacturing production and soaks up nearly half of all government expenditure on research and development; there are over 600,000 defence-related posts and any failure in this sector would have an immediate impact on the economy. The 1992 Central Statistical Office figures show Britain running a visible trade surplus in only one area – oil-exporting countries, which buy large quantities of arms from the UK defence industry. The arms industry thus enjoys a privileged position within the whole economy, and because of this arms deals are one of the sensitive areas on which Whitehall refuses to open up. Defence Minister Alan Clark told the Commons that it had been 'the practice of successive administrations not to provide information about arms exports as it relates to specific countries'.[1]

Intelligence in this field is gathered from intercepted telexes and telephone calls, MI6 agents abroad, military attachés and informants among the arms dealers, most of whom have some relationship with the security services. It is also true that all military export companies, by necessity, liaise with the intelligence services, most notably MI6. Robison claims that GCHQ-generated 'sigint' (signals intelligence) about arms deals goes to a wide range of customers, including the Bank of England, the DTI, the Foreign Office, the MoD and the Export Credit Guarantee Department (ECGD), which helps to finance arms deals. A Quaker, Robison is worried about the lack of parliamentary scrutiny of these operations, and the purpose to which this sensitive information has been put. 'They say it was to keep an eye on illegal arms sales but the only reason I could think of was it was being used to facilitate arms deals.' Anything of value concerning a potential arms deal, especially contracts being negotiated by other countries, is passed immediately to an authorised official of the MoD's Defence Export Sales Organisation (DESO) in Soho Square. The DESO then forwards this intelligence in sanitised form to major British arms manufacturers, for use in undercutting foreign bids. The manufacturers are then dependent on government together with non-government financial institutions to finance the deals.[2]

The Midland Bank's reputation as a spook's bank has been particularly strong in the field of defence sales. From 1978 to 1988, a non-executive director was the former 'tough no-nonsense' MI5 officer Sir John Cuckney. For much of the same period he was chair of the government-owned defence sales organisation International Military Sales (IMS). In 1986 the IMS formed its own finance organisation, IMS Export Finance House, which enables companies to obtain insurance for arms deals which the government ECGD would not cover. Like the bank's murdered Moscow representative, Dennis Skinner, Cuckney had been recruited by the bank's chair, Lord (William) Armstrong, who naturally had close ties to the security services.

In 1982, the bank created the Midland International Trade Services (MITS) division, which later suffered a series of problems and losses of up to £100 million which were put down to 'funny practices'. From 1984, MITS operated a secretive defence sales unit, the Defence Equipment Finance Department (DEFD) which employed 'exotic consultants'. One of the more interesting figures linked to the bank was the 'urbane, extremely polished and charming' Stefan Kock, who until the summer of 1990 was consultant to the Midland's secret arms-financing department. Of Central European origin, Kock was a former member of the Rhodesian SAS and security adviser to Sir Edgar Whitehead, Prime Minister of Rhodesia – a post closely tied to MI5. An internal newsletter of the explosives manufacturer Astra Holdings said that he 'served in both the Air Force and Army, including service in military intelligence and special forces. Following his military career Kock carried out special assignments for the Foreign Office' – presumably for MI6. In January 1990, he was arrested in Scotland for brandishing and firing a semi-automatic pistol during a roadside argument and fined £650. Police said the case was 'very delicate' because of Kock's intelligence connections and the intervention of 'big names' on his behalf.[3]

The DEFD aimed to exploit the growth of arms sales under the Thatcher government, building links with domestic manufacturers including Plessey, GEC and Astra Holdings. The Midland became the 'most enthusiastic of all banks in its pursuit of defence export financing' and played a key role in financing the more sensitive Middle East contracts in the eighties. US journalist Kenneth Timmerman, in his book *The Death Lobby*, claimed that the Midland was involved in the flourishing trade with Iraq and had 'financed some of Saddam's earliest weapon purchases in the West'. In late 1988, Christopher Cowley, a metallurgist with Gerald Bull's Space Research Corporation, was in Baghdad where he met a representative from the DEFD. He told Cowley that he was involved in setting up a loan for arms 'worth something like a quarter of a billion dollars' which would be covered by the ECGD. Approval for the deal was made, the representative said, 'through our government connections' – International Military

Sales and the Joint Intelligence Committee. He went on to say that 'our people have military or intelligence backgrounds . . . we're pretty hush-hush. Many people in the bank don't know about us and that includes senior executives.'

In 1989, the Midland played a key role in setting up trade credits for Iraq of £340 million; in the following year a syndicate headed by Midland set up a further £250 million. The bank later denied that it had knowingly financed arms sales to Iraq. However, former bank officials acknowledge that they did help defence firms which gained contracts in Iraq, but only on projects supported by the government. These were what they termed 'non-offensive' items, an elastic phrase open to all kinds of definition. Mrs Thatcher's visit to Malaysia in 1988, which resulted in a £1 billion defence contract, was preceded by a delegation from the Midland led by Stefan Kock, who was hoping for 'a big slice of the action', MoD officials and a group from the SAS. Contracts included setting up a special forces base. Mrs Thatcher referred in speeches to the proposals being headed by the Midland; Kock later played down claims that he had close links to the Prime Minister.[4]

Mrs Thatcher was an enthusiastic promoter of Britain's arms industry and successfully lobbied to secure the country's biggest post-war arms deal with Saudi Arabia. In April 1985, Britain had been able to use intelligence gathered by MI6 through its intelligence network in Saudi Arabia to thwart French and American ambitions to supply their advanced aircraft to the Saudis. Marketing men, with the full backing of the Prime Minister, went to work aggressively selling the merits of Britain's aircraft to the Saudis. The Prime Minister was able to persuade King Fahd to buy the Tornado, the ground attack version of the European fighter. The deal agreed in September 1985 was worth $10 billion and the final package, signed in 1988 and known as Al-Yamamah – to be paid for in oil – was worth nearly $30 billion.[5]

During the late eighties these massive arms deals provided the background to what Gerald James, managing director of explosives manufacturer Astra Holdings, saw as a mysterious world of 'people who knew people', with intelligence links, with access to Whitehall and even Downing Street, and who now moved into the arms world.

Stefan Kock was closely tied to what has become known as the 'Savoy Mafia', alleged by James to be an influential group of people who conducted arms deals from the Savoy suite of Lotus cars director Alan Curtis. Curtis used the Savoy Hotel as his informal London business base where, he admitted, guests included civil servants and politicians in discussions on 'overseas marketing, technology transfers and the automotive business'.[6] It is highly likely that the hotel room where the 'Savoy Mafia' met was bugged by the security services.

James was introduced by Curtis to Syrian businessman Wafic Said, who was described as 'the British Aerospace agent in Saudi Arabia responsible for winning the Tornado and Al-Yamamah deals and a close friend of Mark Thatcher'. 'Contact man' Curtis helped secure a job for Mrs Thatcher's son in the United States in 1984. Curtis was also a friend of Denis Thatcher, and worked closely with Mark's best man and business associate Steve Tipping. Curtis was said by James to have 'extraordinary pulling power' in the British defence industries. 'He had an entrée to Downing Street where he seemed to visit regularly.'[7]

Between March and May 1989, the Lonrho-owned newspaper the *Observer* published a series of articles alleging that large bribes had been paid to middlemen following the multi-billion-pound Tornado deal with Saudi Arabia. Mrs Thatcher had pressed the Attorney-General, later Lord Havers, to prosecute Lonrho, but he informed her that if the case was to succeed she would have to submit to cross-examination in court. In the same period, an anonymous 'classification restricted' document dated 2 May 1989 had been sent to Labour MP Jeff Rooker, a member of the Commons Public Accounts Committee, this referred to 'Newspaper articles on BAe and HMG bribes to obtain Tornado etc, business'. The memorandum which referred to the Saudi Arabian and Malaysian deals was passed on to the 'appropriate authorities' and to Mrs Thatcher. After the Committee was refused details of the secret Saudi agreement, a report was ordered in 1989 from the Comptroller and Auditor General, Sir John Bourn.[8]

There have been reports that, in 1990, Mrs Thatcher personally ordered GCHQ to intercept the international telecommunications links of Lonrho, after the government's law officers advised her against having the company prosecuted because of the *Observer* article. Mrs Thatcher had apparently been 'stung' by comments made about her conduct by Lonrho's chief executive, 'Tiny' Rowland. She had been 'infuriated' about accusations of impropriety involving herself and her son, Mark. According to Robin Robison, transcripts of the GCHQ intercepts were passed via the Joint Intelligence Office to the Prime Minister's Office.[9]

The report by Bourn, a former under-secretary of state for defence procurement at the MoD, though not directly involved in the Al-Yamamah deal, was suppressed for fear of embarrassing the Saudi royal family and the risk of losing a second £10 billion contract. The Committee's chair, Labour MP Robert Sheldon, was allowed to see the report in secret by Sir Michael Quinlan, Permanent Secretary at the MoD. Sheldon assured the Committee that the correct procedures had been carried out by the MoD during the contract. He insisted on confidentiality because 'many jobs are at stake'.[10]

The risk of mass unemployment in the armaments industry has provided a useful cover for dubious arms exports and led Mrs Thatcher to seek co-operation with a number of pariah states, including Chile. The foundations had been laid in the wake of the invasion of the Falkland Islands by Argentina on 2 April 1982. Within a week of the invasion, a series of 'understandings' had been agreed between Britain and Chile. The secret deals with the military dictator General Pinochet provided arrangements for the British to use Chilean bases while, in return, Britain would use its diplomatic muscle within the

United Nations to persuade governments to 'lay off' Chile on human rights issues. This, Britain attempted to do by declaring Chile to be a 'moderate and stabilising force' while Britain abstained on votes in the UN which criticised Chile's violation of human rights.[11].

RAF spy planes were allowed to use bases in southern Chile for secret reconnaissance overflights, while SAS special forces were given a base in order to conduct sabotage missions in Argentina, destroying Exocet-carrying Super Etendard aircraft on the ground. The agreement allowed for a complete exchange of intelligence, with members of MI6 and signals intelligence using the intelligence centre at the Punta Arenas base to monitor and break the radio codes of the Argentinian military and navy. The intelligence exchange was considered ultra-sensitive within Whitehall and the MoD, with material restricted to a very small group of civil servants.[12]

British restrictions on arms sales to Chile were also relaxed. This coincided with a big effort by the MoD's arms sales subsidiary, the Defence Sales Organisation, to sell arms to the country. From 1984 onwards, a whole range of previously restricted high-technology offensive weapons were offered to the Chilean government, while the close co-operation on intelligence matters developed during the Falklands War was encouraged. Deprived of the Buenos Aires base, its only station in South America following the cuts of the late sixties, MI6 opened an office in Santiago (there is some speculation that another was opened in Uruguay).

Relations between Britain and Chile remained close until 31 March 1990, when a twenty-eight-year-old British defence journalist, Jonathan Moyle, was found dead in his room at the Hotel Carrera in Santiago. For the past three years, a wreath of red roses has been laid at the Cenotaph with the message: 'Jonathan Moyle, murdered for, covered up and betrayed by his country'.[13]

Moyle was found, naked and hanging from a clothes rail with a shirt wrapped around his neck, in a cramped wardrobe eight inches shorter in height than his body. The door was shut from the outside. His head was covered with a pillow case and his legs showed signs of being bound. A chambermaid claimed there were pinpricks on his feet. He was also wearing 'a nappy' made from a towel and polythene bag over two pairs of underpants, apparently designed to prevent bodily fluids escaping and drawing attention to the odour. There was blood at the foot of the bed and on bedsheets which later disappeared. Moyle appeared to have been asphyxiated before being hung in the closet. The autopsy revealed that sedatives, Bromacepam and Diazepam, the residue of a sleeping draught, were present in his stomach. Two files and a briefcase were missing. The official view was that he had committed suicide.

A 'brilliant and opinionated' right-wing defence specialist, between 1980 and 1985 Moyle had read international politics and strategic studies at Aberystwyth University on an RAF bursary. Recruited by Special Branch, Moyle is report to have helped break a heroin drugs ring operating at the university. He may also have been investigating links between the IRA and Welsh nationalist students and has been credited with stopping a long-running feud between Iraqi and Iranian students on campus. In 1983, he received a first-class degree, then wrote an MA thesis on 'Air Attack on Britain' which allegedly included fourteen months' research at the MoD. The Ministry later said that it 'has no record of Jonathan Moyle ever having worked for the MoD' and denied that the thesis was classified. An RAF helicopter pilot, Moyle graduated from RAF Cranwell but was grounded for being 'reckless'. He left to become a journalist and in 1988 was made editor of *Defence Helicopter World*.[14]

Moyle arrived in Santiago on 24 March 1990, the week before his death, to attend FIDAE, an international aerospace fair organised by the Chilean air force. He was investigating reports that Chile's biggest arms manufacturer, Carlos Cardeon, had agreed to supply fifty low-cost attack helicopters to Iraq. Moyle's notes of his trip contained several references to

Helios, an advanced guidance system used in conjunction with the TOW anti-tank missile and which could be fitted to the helicopters. Britain prohibited the export of Helios, which went on the market in 1986, to Chile and Iraq. He is also believed to have stumbled on a deal which included the supply of special oscilloscopes required to test equipment for Baghdad's nuclear development programme. Cardeon had made his fortune selling arms to Iraq, and by 1989, 95 per cent of his business was with Saddam Hussein. He operated in the 'murky netherworld of arms deals' known as the 'grey market', involving deals that were 'not public, and not officially approved by governments, but having tacit or sometimes secret government backing'.[15]

Moyle had also been investigating another Cardeon project, one of NATO's most advanced naval mines, Stonefish. Marconi had opened discussions with Cardeon about Stonefish, with the approval of the British authorities. This was outside Moyle's area of specialisation, but he apparently met with a British Naval Intelligence officer whilst staying in Santiago. Naval Intelligence conducted an internal inquiry into Stonefish and an officer visited Moyle's father after his son's death. 'It was obvious to me that they wanted to know how much Jonathan had found out about a Chilean Stonefish.' Shortly after his death, the naval and military attachés and the first secretary at the British embassy left their posts. Key witnesses made themselves unavailable.[16]

The British government's silence on the Moyle murder was prompted by a wish not to embarrass the Chilean government, with which there were continuing good relations. On 31 May 1990, at a British embassy reception for the Archbishop of Canterbury, a long-term British resident put forward the view that Moyle had accidentally strangled himself, masturbating while engaged in a bizarre sexual practice which went wrong. On the same day, MI6 officials offered a similar version of his death in a briefing to journalists in London. Chilean investigators believed that the smear was designed 'to distract us from the direction our investigation is taking'. A British official in Santiago later apologised to Moyle's father for the sexual smear.[17]

A second investigation, by the Chilean élite criminal investigation unit, SO-7, proved that Moyle had not committed suicide but had been murdered. He had been the subject of a forcibly administered injection. The investigation concluded that 'merchants of death' from 'a foreign intelligence agency may have been involved in the murder'. It was probably undertaken by 'very professional assassins'. They may have thought that Moyle was 'a member of the British Secret Service'. Moyle once told one of his close friends that 'he'd been asked to spy'. Sources close to the investigation believed that 'he was a victim in the battle between the British and Iraqi secret services'. A senior investigator claimed that 'Jonathan was involved in all sorts of things . . . but things went badly wrong here'. A defector from the Iraqi secret police, the Mukharabat, claimed that he had seen Moyle's name on intelligence files in Baghdad. Moyle's father, who has sustained a one-man campaign against an official wall of silence, claimed at one point to be 'within an ace' of identifying the two assassins of his son.[18]

The former Iraqi Mukhabarat officer also claimed that Moyle had been threatened by a representative of Cardeon and warned not to continue to investigate the facts concerning the sale of helicopters to Iraq. Moyle is said to have interviewed Cardeon and his chief of public relations on the night before his death, though both men denied that the meetings took place. Exposure of a possible deal involving Helios would have posed a threat to Cardeon's lucrative trade with Iraq and his relationship with the new Chilean President, Patricio Aylwin, to whose election campaign Cardeon had contributed £1 million. This would have proved doubly embarrassing for President Aylwin, as he had made a conscious effort to rehabilitate his country with the West following the fall of the Pinochet regime. The British embassy did not want to damage the delicate and politically sensitive relations which had developed between the two countries and gave the Chilean investigation little co-operation. Instead, it attempted to discredit Mr Moyle senior's search for the truth and appeared to want 'to cover up everything that might cause embarrassment to the British authorities'.

In November 1992, despite the British embassy's refusal to put pressure on the government of Chile to re-investigate Moyle's death, a Chilean court sanctioned fresh moves in the case. Speculation mounted that the British government's embarrassment centred on its involvement in a secret international arms network in which British companies had supplied weapons to Iran and then Iraq, in contravention of its own embargo on arms sales to these countries. The activities of the company at the centre of the network, Allivane, were well known to MI6, according to investigators into the Italian end of the arms pipeline; as were the dealings of the Coventry-based tool-making firm, Matrix Churchill, which had taken part in negotiations with Carlos Cardeon to supply Baghdad with machine tools for the manufacture of proximity fuses. In mid-1988, company executives, who were also acting as informants for the security services, met with Cardeon in Baghdad. The following year, an inter-departmental committee approved the granting of licences for machines destined for Iraq, for which there was only one purpose and that was to make bombs. On 29 July 1990, just four days before Saddam Hussein's invasion of Kuwait, Britain's Department of Trade and Industry had given the green light to the contract between Cardeon and Iraq.[19]

A year later, in May 1991, the former Chilean dictator General Pinochet, who remained commander-in-chief of the Army, slipped into Britain for a one-day visit to a research centre where an Anglo-Chilean arms project was being developed. An offshoot of Royal Ordnance, now owned by British Aerospace, had joined with the Chilean government armourers, FAMAE, to provide the South Americans with the technology to produce their own missiles. Pinochet was also due to meet with senior MI6 officials to discuss future intelligence sharing (in 1990 Pinochet integrated the Central National de Informaciones intelligence service into the Army). American sources claimed that Pinochet was so incensed by the official snub to his visit that he broke off the ten-year relationship with MI6. This, however, was highly unlikely, given the importance of the intelligence link, and the claim appears to have been no more than mischief making on the part of the Americans.[20]

23

Iraqgate

There seems to be considerable merit in keeping as quiet as possible about this politically sensitive issue.

W. R. Morgan, DTI official, July 1988

As we have seen in chapter 5, only one terrorist survived the Iranian embassy siege in April 1980. Nineteen-year-old 'Ali' apparently 'sang like a bird during his subsequent interrogation'. He revealed that an Iraqi Mukhabarat officer, Sami Muhammed Ali, code-named 'the Fox', had been the mastermind behind the operation. Despite this information, no sanctions were placed against Iraq and no diplomats were expelled. Two years later, the Mukhabarat sent one of its officers to activate a cell of 'sleepers' led by the nephew of Abu Nidal. The cell was tasked with the assassination of the Israeli Ambassador in London, Shlomo Argov (see chapter 19). For these actions and others, Iraq was placed on the United States State Department's list of governments which sponsored terrorism. However, policy was changing within the Reagan administration.[1]

At a secret meeting in 1983 between Secretary of State, George Shultz, and the Iraq Foreign minister, Tarek Aziz, Iraq was advised that improved relations with the West depended on their distancing Baghdad from the Nidal organisation. Before the year was out, Saddam Hussein had expelled Nidal's supporters and the State Department had taken Iraq off its blacklist. It was about this time, with the war between Iraq and Iran in full flow, that the CIA began delivering to Baghdad, via Jordan's King Hussein, raw intelligence data on co-ordinates of Iranian troop positions taken from satellite photographs. The policy aim appears to have been 'to keep Iraq in the war and to bleed Iran'. By 1985, CIA director William Casey had opened a CIA station in Baghdad to manage the intelligence traffic. This was seen as 'bait on the hook' to draw Iraq away from the Soviet Union into a more 'responsible' relationship with the West. So began the secret policy tilt towards Iraq by the United States and Britain.[2]

British and Iraqi intelligence began to develop a close relationship. The Iranian Military Procurement Offices in London were subject to a major MI5/GCHQ surveillance operation and the intelligence gathered on Iran's war effort was passed on to Saddam's chief of intelligence, Barzan Ibrahim al-Tikriti. MI6 also put Barzan in contact with former members of the SAS to help train Iraqi special forces at 'probably the most sensitive military installation in the country'. However, Foreign Secretary Geoffrey Howe told Parliament that official policy remained that Britain 'was strictly impartial in the conflict'.[3]

In 1985, the British government introduced an embargo on the export of lethal weapons which would 'significantly enhance the capability of either side to prolong or exacerbate the conflict', to Iraq and Iran, after which date ministers insisted that Britain played no part in arms sales to Iraq. When a ceasefire was signed, the policy remained that 'direct and significant assistance to either country in the conduct of offensive operations in breach of the ceasefire' was banned. Exports of high-technology and sensitive military weapons to Iraq came under COCOM restrictions and were subject to scrutiny by a Whitehall committee, the Security Export Controls Working Party, chaired by a senior MoD civil servant. To police the embargo, the Foreign Office also set up a special Inter-Departmental Committee, however, this proved to be largely ineffective as economic necessities and political priorities changed. Later, the Foreign Office blandly asserted that it was unaware of the scale of Iraq's defence procurement operation.[4]

'It seemed, and was the received wisdom from the Foreign Office at the time,' explained Department of Trade minister Alan Clark, 'that the threat in the area was Muslim fundamentalism.' Saddam Hussein was an anti-communist and was seen as a counter to a radical Islamic Iran, which threatened to sweep across the Middle East and undermine the oil kingdoms in the region. Despite evidence of Mukharabat involvement in terrorism, relations between Britain and Iraq improved as the Foreign Office was prepared to turn a blind eye to Iraq's terrorist activities against British citizens. There was a requirement to expand trade in the Middle East and retain some political influence in a region where Britain's diplomatic relations with Iran, Syria and Libya were in ruins. Human Rights issues were raised but quickly forgotten as 'pragmatism and economic interest blinkered us to reality.' In 1986 Alan Clark visited Baghdad to promote British business interests. An outspoken right-winger, 'brimming with self-confidence bordering on the arrogant', Clark made it clear that he was not going to allow the government's free trade philosophy to be overridden by requests for further restrictions on the export of equipment to Iraq.[5]

During 1987, with the Iran – Iraq war still in progress, Clark signed an agreement to lend Iraq £200 million to buy British goods, including computers, for the Iraqi armed forces. At the end of the war in 1988, British companies with the enthusiastic backing of the government, which secretly altered the guidelines without reference to Parliament, saw an opportunity to boost their trade in the Middle East. Much of the trade was underwritten by the government's Export Credit Guarantee Department (ECGD) with substantial backing from the banks and with few strings attached. 'Whitehall cosmetics' were 'lavishly applied to keep the records deliberately ambiguous'. Leaked minutes of a 1988 DTI meeting with engineering companies show that Clark, who found the guidelines 'tiresome and intrusive', had given advice on how to meet the stiff export regulations for the sale of equipment to Iraq. With 'stretching and bending' it was possible to get a result. Clark told the directors that the 'intended use of the machines should be couched in such a manner as to emphasise the peaceful aspect to which they will be put. Applications should stress the record of 'general engineering' usage of machine tools.' The advice to omit the potential military use from the application was, Clark later admitted in Court, 'our old friend economical . . . with the actuality'. John Nosworthy, director-general of the Machine Tools Trade Association (MTTA), recalled that 'the government gave considerable encouragement to us for export to that area when Saddam Hussein was in favour.' Clark promised the MTTA that he would support its companies 'up to Cabinet level', where he forged a 'sympathetic and unlikely friendship with Mrs Thatcher'.[6]

Britain's policy towards Iraq was mainly dictated by the prospect of favours from a key regional power with the potential to be the world's second-biggest oil producer. In the aftermath of the Iraq–Iran war, imports of Iraqi oil expanded at an enormous rate – from nothing in 1987 to 8.2 million barrels in 1990. The price at which Baghdad sold the crude to Britain was lower than that from any other Middle East source. There was, however, an additional price to be paid. According to Congressman Henry Gonzalez, who has investigated the trade with Iraq, 'Saddam Hussein wanted cash, credit and military technology. Oil made it all possible.' The Ohio branch of machine tool company Matrix Churchill outlined the policy in a November 1988 memo; 'Our company is dealing with Iraq in many multi-million dollar projects. We would like to barter some of these projects for Iraqi crude oil.'[7]

It would appear that British intelligence, which monitors the international arms trade, used the opportunity to extend its intelligence gathering, deciding to allow companies to break the government's official embargo on arms sales to Iraq in order, as one commentator put it, 'to peer into the pool of intrigue'. Although the CIA had a presence in Baghdad, it was not engaged in intelligence gathering and the agency had to rely, increasingly, on MI6 for that task. In January 1988, Alan Clark admitted that British policy on Iraq was dependent on Washington and that intelligence was being shared between MI6 and the CIA which, in some instances, went straight to the White House. Thus, it would appear that the government's wish to promote trade, the Foreign Office diplomatic efforts and the interests of MI6, all conveniently coincided in what the *Daily Telegraph* deemed to be 'a bizarre tale of spying, murder and political intrigue'.[8]

However, it would be wrong to assume that British policy had put the 'short-term interests of intelligence gathering and arms sales before the long-term good of stability in the region'. Evidence coming from both sides of the Atlantic suggests that there was a co-ordinated effort, very early on, closely monitored by the intelligence agencies, to build up Iraq's military arsenal as part of a Middle East strategy to counter Iranian Shi'ite fundamentalism. A declassified National Security directive signed in October 1989 by President Bush considered it a top priority to give money and technology to Iraq because Saddam was seen as the 'West's policeman in the region'. With the knowledge of the CIA and MI6, Iraq funded its weapon procurement network prinicipally through the Atlanta branch of the Italian-government-owned Banca Nazionale del Lavoro (BNL). Between 1985 and 1989, BNL made $5 billion worth of illegal loans – the biggest fraud in American history. Although the US Justice Department later suggested that the Atlanta branch had acted 'independently', its manager, Christopher Drogoul, said that the orchestration of the loans had been far wider and involved 'former US intelligence agents'.[9]

According to Congressman Gonzalez, there was routine liaison between the CIA, MI6 and Mossad on intelligence about BNL. As early as June 1989, if not before, MI6 was aware that loans had been made by BNL to Matrix Churchill. MI6 was also aware that BNL received the bulk of its funds from the Bank of Credit and Commerce International which supplied money at the unheard of interest rate of 0.5 per cent.

BCCI had a 'special relationship' with Iraq, a fact known to the Bank of England. Kickbacks from some of the arms deals are said to have been salted away in secret Iraqi BCCI accounts in the Cayman Islands. According to *Independent* sources, MI6 used BCCI to fund arms sales to Iraq.[10]

On 4 August 1989, FBI agents raided the Atlanta offices of BNL and discovered evidence of large loans made to companies, including Matrix Churchill. A September US Federal Reserve report indicated that the loans to Matrix were intended to fund the purchase of missile casings. (Matrix's former managing-director, Paul Henderson, was later granted immunity from prosecution by US authorities in relation to the BNL scandal.) A month later, the CIA sent a report on the Matrix Churchill network to the National Security Council and forwarded a report to MI6, identifying the company as 'the UK's leading producer of computer controlled machine tools that can be used for the production of sophisticated armaments'. According to Gonzalez, the CIA was monitoring Iraqi contacts with the Matrix Churchill network and 'had legal authority to intercept these communications abroad', indicating that the CIA was operating on British soil. The CIA report to MI6 warned that 'Baghdad has created a complex procurement network of holding companies to acquire technology for its chemical, biological, nuclear and ballistic missile development programs'.[11]

Iraq made London the centre of its arms procurement programme through a front company, Technology and Development Group, based in Chiswick. The TDG, owned by the Al-Arabi Trading Company in Baghdad, operated through more than fifty undercover companies and agents in Europe. Al-Arabi was, in turn, controlled by the Iraq Ministry of Industry and Military Industrialisation (MIMI) whose head was Hussein Kamil, brother-in-law of Saddam Hussein and chief of Iraq's top-secret intelligence agency, the Secret Security Organisation (SSO). TDG directors Fadel Jawad Kadham and Dr Safa al-Habobi were identified by the security services as senior officials in Saddam's administration and members of Iraqi military intelligence. Given this knowledge, it would be remarkable if the TDG had not been put under intensive electronic surveillance by the Security Service.[12]

In 1987, the TDG helped organise the buy-out of the machine-tool firm Matrix Churchill, in a DTI sanctioned deal partly financed by BNL. The Iraqis were introduced to Matrix's parent company, Tube Investments (TI), by an Essex businessman known to MI6, Roy Ricks, who owned a consulting firm, Meed International. Ricks later developed links with Sir Brian Tovey, former director of GCHQ, who introduced him to the 'In and Out club'. A non-executive director of TI was former MI5 officer, Sir John Cuckney. Although Cuckney has said that there was nothing unusual about the sale of Matrix to an Iraqi company, former managing director Paul Henderson now believes that it had greater significance. 'There is no doubt in my mind that the business was sold to the Iraqis so that we could monitor them.' Executives of the company, who were later charged by Customs and Excise for violating export controls when exporting machine tools to Iraq, met regularly with officers from the security services. They were asked to sign the Official Secrets Act as part of a deal to exchange confidential information. TDG ownership gave Henderson and others an entrée into Iraqi business, political and intelligence circles. MI6 was, at the time, 'obsessed' with obtaining intelligence about Iraqi threats from nuclear weapons, long-range missiles, and biological and chemical warfare.[13]

'I helped the intelligence services willingly,' says Henderson, 'because I believe in my country.' Henderson had first been contacted in 1970 and then recruited as an unpaid informant in 1973 when four MI5 officers visited Matrix to lecture executives intending to visit the Soviet bloc on security measures. A few days later, a woman officer invited him to become an agent. The company's senior executives had already turned down the request but MI5 went ahead anyway. She became the first of four controllers. Henderson proved to be useful catch. The company traded regularly behind the Iron Curtain and, in 1986, Henderson became Chair of the Anglo-Soviet Working Group on the development of the machine-tool trade. He was approached again in 1989 when MI6 sought more intelligence on Iraq. An MI6 field officer, 'John Balsom', described as a Middle East expert, met Henderson over twenty times, occasionally at the Coventry offices where he clocked in as an official from the DTI. Balson provided Henderson with a contact in the Foreign Office to facilitate the obtaining of export licences. The MI6 officer later described Henderson as 'a very brave man' for his intelligence gathering activities.[14]

Against its own guidelines, MI5 had been running sexual 'honeytrap' operations against Soviet officials who visited Britain and may have hoped to use the same form of entrapment against members of the Iraq procurement network. The export manager for Matrix, fifty-one-year-old Mark Gutteridge, was recruited to supply information to MI5, K3(a) Section, in December 1986 and did so until October 1987. He met his 'handler', 'Michael Ford', on more than thirty occasions. A huge overweight man, Ford told Gutteridge, who was known as source 528, that MI5 was interested in political, military and economic information and material on particular personalities. The intelligence was passed on to MI6, and a new handler 'Ian Eascott', which distributed it to interested parties in Whitehall. Gutteridge was told on one occasion that his information would end up on the desk of the Prime Minister.[15]

Matrix Churchill directors were informed by the security services that they were fully aware that the machines being sold to Iraq had a dual purpose and could be used to manufacture armaments. One officer told them 'it gave him no cause for concern'. The contract for machines to produce mortar shells was known to the Foreign Office. 'Everybody knew the equipment could be used for making shells,' said Mark Higson, a former Foreign Office official involved in vetting export licence applications to Iraq. 'The idea that they were non-lethal was spurious.' In 1988, MI6 persuaded the DTI to abandon its plan to ask Matrix executives detailed questions about the uses to which their equipment was likely to be put by Iraq. The service also argued that without the Iraq deals the company would be forced to close, which would shut down its 'pipeline' of intelligence.[16]

British intelligence appears to have had little intelligence of its own on Iraq's massive procurement of weapons of mass destruction. Its own access, the Service admits, was 'abysmal' and it had to rely on the information supplied by Gutteridge, Henderson and other travelling businessmen. When it did acquire reliable intelligence, it appears that it chose simply to ignore the evidence. MI6 had known since 1977 that Iraq was setting up a chemical weapons programme when ICI, which had been approached by the Iraqis to build a modern pesticide plant, informed the authorities. Unfortunately, such information appears to have been 'put in the drawer somewhere'. On other occasions, the Foreign Office chose to ignore intelligence on the arms network. During 1989, the Defence Intelligence Staff became aware of the nature of the Matrix Churchill contracts, including computer numerical controlled (CNC) lathes which 'may be intended for use in munitions production'. In a memo to colleagues, a DIS officer, P. R. Jeffries, noted that the Matrix shipment represented 'a significant enhancement of capability contrary to ministerial guidelines'. The response of officials was to ask: 'Can interpretations for Iraq be relaxed further?' Without informing Parliament, ministers at an Inter-Department Committee meeting agreed to more flexibility in the issuing of export licences. When Alan Clark heard that the DIS was investigating the Iraqi procurement network he told colleagues that he 'would make sure it was stopped. It's outrageous the DIS should spend its time trying to damage our trade surplus.'[17]

In the summer of 1989, David Gore-Booth, Assistant Under-Secretary in charge of Middle East affairs in the Foreign Office spoke to Saddam Hussein about cementing 'a working relationship between our countries'. In July, British metal-working machines and technical expertise were exported to Iraq under a DTI approved licence as part of Saddam's scheme to provide its Scud missile with a longer range. Iraq had turned to Britain after the USSR had refused to supply the long-range version of the missile. Deeply interested in these developments, MI6 regularly debriefed the machine-tool makers on their return from Baghdad for their reports on Project 1728. The service was interested in the Saad 16 research plant, the centre of Saddam's missile programme, on which it held only morsels of intelligence. Designed by Dr Gerald Bull, Project Bird was a long-range ballistic missile made from a cluster of eight Scuds and capable of putting an intelligence-gathering satellite into orbit.

In February 1990, West German intelligence intercepted documents which were being sent from Bull's Geneva office to Baghdad. A few days later, GCHQ eavesdropped on telephone conversations about 'Bird' from its Cyprus base. In the following month, a well-informed article in the *Independent* chronicled the problems facing the Iraqis and their inability to test the missile booster. It said that two British aerodynamic experts were helping to correct the supersonic airflow problems in their wind-tunnels. An MI6 officer lunching with a journalist from the paper asked if the article's author would provide 'the names of the two consultants who went to Iraq.'[18]

MI6 was also interested in the mysterious explosion on 17 August 1989 at Al-Hilah, site of the top-secret Al-Qaqaa establishment, which killed hundreds of people. Once again, MI6 had little reliable intelligence on what it believed to be part of Iraq's nuclear programme. In 1987, when Saddam Hussein directed the Iraqi effort to produce nuclear weapons, MI6 began collecting intelligence on what was known as Project K1000, assessing that if Iraq succeeded then it would be used against Iran to bring the war to a swift conclusion. The Joint Intelligence Committee instructed MI6 to co-operate with the CIA and Mossad in order to try and stop Saddam from achieving his nuclear ambition. MI6 knew that TDG's Safa al-Habobi had made inquiries about importing gas centrifuge technology which is used to enrich uranium. The security services again stressed to Whitehall officials that it was important to allow Matrix executives continuing access to the Iraqi procurement network in order to maintain them as an intelligence source on nuclear matters.[19]

Al-Qaqaa, where a number of British lathes went into operation, was the place that London-based journalist, Farzad Bazoft, was arrested. Thirty-one-year-old Bazoft was executed on 15 March 1990 by the Iraqis for spying. In his 1991 book *Instant Empire, Financial Times* journalist and Middle East specialist Simon Henderson alleged that Bazoft had been 'trained in the arts of espionage' and that his six press trips to Iraq, during which he had no problems, were 'convenient cover rather than his main line of business'. Bazoft was used when British businessmen, aware of the risks involved and consquences of getting caught, spurned requests from MI6 for help. 'Into this problem,' writes Simon Henderson, 'walked an opportunity: a naive, Iraqi-born journalist, working regularly, but not on the staff, for a British Sunday newspaper, the *Observer*. He was Farzad Bazoft – already on the books of British intelligence.'[20]

Bazoft was allegedly 'tasked' by MI6 to investigate the August explosion. Posing as an Indian doctor, Bazoft was to collect soil samples from the area of the blast in the expectation that this might include particles from the explosives used in the non-nuclear section of an Iraqi bomb. According to Henderson, Bazoft delivered the samples to his MI6 contact at the British embassy, 'Michael', who then forwarded them to London through the diplomatic bag. As soon as Bazoft was arrested by the Iraqi authorities on 15 September 1989, 'Michael' quietly slipped out of the country. Typically, Bazoft was 'left out to dry' by MI6 after his arrest.[21]

Immediately after his death, Saudi sources leaked several damaging stories about Bazoft to British newspapers in a disinformation campaign which *Private Eye* suggested was the work of British intelligence, which was anxious not to upset the Iraq government. The Saudi Arabian security services are known to employ a bank of former MI6 and MI5 personnel. For the small group of people who write on intelligence matters, accusations that Bazoft worked for British intelligence were no surprise; he fitted the profile of a small-time agent, having been in contact with Special Branch during his time in London. It would appear that he was used by the security services and played a small part in the surveillance of the Iraq war machine, ending up as just another victim of the intelligence game. The Iraqis despatched his corpse to the British embassy – 'We sent him home in a box.'[22]

Even though Bazoft's death drew a 'crescendo of publicity' about the nature of the Iraqi regime, Whitehall continued to approve the export of arms-related equipment to Baghdad. Trade Secretary Nicholas Ridley, informed the Overseas Policy and Defence Committee in June 1990 that Britain's exposure through government loans in Iraq was £1 billion. He wrote that failure to relax the guidelines still further would have implications for Britain's Public Sector Borrowing Requirement. In the same month, Matrix Churchill offices in Coventry were raided by Customs and Excise officers investigating the illegal sale of arms-related equipment to Iraq.[23]

MI6 and MI5 immediately dropped Henderson and Gutteridge. They had both assumed that the security services would protect them but they failed to oblige. Henderson's MI6 controller had warned the businessman that if he became 'involved in any illegal activity, that was entirely his own responsibility, and we could not, nor would we, help him any way'. However, as the court case in the autumn of 1992 revealed, Matrix's dealings with Iraq were well known by Whitehall and ministers, during which period the security services had allowed them to continue. The subsequent prosecutions showed that there was little love lost between the nominally independent Customs and Excise and the security services. The interests of the security services did not always coincide with the law. One intelligence officer said in court that it was not for them to consider what was legal. Gutteridge was particularly bitter. He had supplied MI5 with a considerable amount of intelligence: 'Who on earth would want to help them now?' An MI6 officer admitted that the case 'shows again the dangers of us concentrating our anti-proliferation efforts on British businessmen who often end up getting into trouble'.[24]

In a desperate effort at damage limitation, three Cabinet Ministers, Kenneth Clarke, Michael Heseltine and Malcolm Rifkind, plus Foreign Office minister Tristan Garel-Jones signed certificates claiming 'Public Interest Immunity' (PII), which suppressed documentary evidence of Whitehall knowledge of arms sales to Iraq. The prosecution claimed that the withheld documents contained 'nothing of assistance to the defence'. In the event they proved to be crucial. Fortunately, but reluctantly, the judge released the five hundred pages of Whitehall letters and minutes which contained details of security services involvement. Henderson's solicitor said that reading them was like 'treading in a field of diamonds'. The Judge was forced to abandon the trial after four weeks when Alan Clark gave damaging testimony which revealed that ministers had colluded in breaching the guidelines on arms sales.[25]

In the subsequent furore following the collapse of the trial, fifty-eight-year-old Lord Justice Scott, one of the youngest judges to be appointed to the High Court, was asked by the Prime Minister to head an inquiry into the Matrix Churchill affair. Colleagues said that he 'would get to the bottom of it. He's not going to be anybody's little dog.' During the *Spycatcher* saga, Scott had said that 'the ability of the press freely to report allegations of scandals in government is one of the bulwarks of our democratic society', which was an encouraging sign that he might fulfil his promise of being 'robustly independent'. However, a similar inquiry into the Supergun Affair failed to uncover the truth.[26]

24

Murder, Intrigue and the Supergun

I cannot make any response which illuminates the activities of the security services.

Alan Clark, Minister for Defence Procurement, 27 February 1992.

The supergun saga began to unfold when, on 10 April 1990, Customs officers raided the port of Middlesborough and confiscated eight large cylindrical wooden crates containing steel tubes destined for Iraq. The tubes had been built by two British companies, Sheffield Forgemasters and Walter Sommers, which claimed they were for a petrochemical project. Customs had missed another shipment, when, in February 1989, a special Iraqi air force Ilyushin-76 cargo plane took off from Manchester airport loaded with steel segments specially commissioned from the two companies for use on a 350mm gun.

Although the Export Licensing Unit at the Department of Trade and Industry (DTI) had expressed no reservations about the £350,000 order, Dr Rex Bayliss, managing director of Walter Sommers, had doubts about the project from the start. Conservative MP Sir Hal Miller, a business partner of Bayliss's successor, Peter Mitchell, arranged to put Bayliss in touch with an official in the 'spooks department'. Officially described as a 'material scientist', Bill Weir was a senior intelligence officer with the Defence Intelligence Staff (DIS). In June 1988, Bayliss spoke twice to Weir, describing the tubes as looking like 'a giant pea-shooter'. The intelligence officer concluded that they were 'pressure vessels of some kind, the function of which was unclear'. Sir Hal, in turn, alerted the DTI, the MoD and 'another agency' (MI6) in the summer of 1988, again in 1989 and yet again in 1990. He made strenuous efforts to co-operate with the authorities and outlined, in a letter, the willingness of Walter Sommers to 'withdraw from the contract, to meet the contract and *enable it to be traced* [emphasis added]. The company is a Ministry of Defence contractor. They are not stupid.' This account agrees with the statement of a former Iraq desk officer at the Foreign Office, Mark Higson, that 'we knew all about the Iraqi "Big Gun" a long time before the story broke'. However, the Trade Secretary, Nicholas Ridley, was to claim in April 1990 that the government had only 'recently become aware in general terms of the project'.[1]

The supergun project was hardly a secret; it was common gossip among European arms dealers and in political circles, though those heavily engaged in clandestine arms deals are known as 'the dogs that do not bark'. In April 1989, the Baghdad military arms fair was attended by virtually all the major British arms suppliers, including British Aerospace, Thorn EMI, Rolls-Royce and GEC-Marconi, and representatives of the Defence Sales Division of the Midland Bank. Also present were the British embassy military attaché and David Hastie, a former British Aerospace employee on secondment to the MoD but released from departmental duties for the fair. A number of contractors have said that a prototype of the supergun, known as 'Baby Babylon', was on display along with scale models of the launchers. All that Ridley would acknowledge in his statement to the Commons was that his department had known that Dr Gerald Bull's Space Research Corporation (SRC) had been involved in ordering large metal tubes from two British engineering companies in the summer of 1988.[2]

Ministers were probably unaware that MI6 had a great deal of information on Dr Bull. In 1980, MI6 had opened an extensive file on Bull, shortly after his imprisonment for six months for exporting howitzer technology to South Africa.

Bull bitterly resented the sentence, claiming that the CIA had sanctioned the deal. According to author William Lowther, military work that SRC did for China in the eighties was undertaken with the 'blessing' of intelligence services who wished to see continuing *détente*. According to his project manager, Christopher Cowley, Bull kept in regular touch with 'security' contacts in the MoD's subsidiary, International Military Services, Rothschild Bank and Midland Bank's defence sales offshoot (Gerald James of the propellant manufacturer Astra Holdings alleged that the Midland Bank was behind the financing of the supergun order, though the bank denied this.) Colleagues knew that Bull talked at length with British embassy officials in Baghdad and had briefed MI6 officers in September 1988. Cowley was 'in the room when Bull briefed MI6. He told them everything.' In effect, Bull was treated as an agent. 'He was visiting Iraq and seeing MI6 regularly. Thus the British had a man inside Saddam's most secret weapons research establishments.' Jersey arms consultant Robert Turp, who had briefly worked for MI6 after the Second World War when military attaché in Paris, was told by Dr Bull that MI6 knew all along about Project Babylon.[3]

The MI6 handler of Matrix Churchill's Paul Henderson repeatedly asked him what he knew about Babylon. In return, Henderson was able to supply MI6 with the blueprints of SRC's 'Iraqi Long-Range Projectile' project. He also briefed his handler on plans to make parts for a 1/200 km range gun. Acçording to an MI6 officer this information went a 'high ministerial level'. In September 1989, Henderson had a day-long session in London of intensive questioning by a panel of six officers, mostly scientists attached to MI6 and, presumably, the Defence Intelligence Staff, which probed his knowledge of the project. By the following month, MI6 was referring in reports to Project Babylon, expressing concern about Iraq acquiring technology for a gun with an 'extremely long range'. Reports would eventually be forwarded to the secret Iraq Gun

Committee, a body whose existence was not revealed to the Commons Committee which investigated the supergun.

William Lowther discovered that one of Dr Bull's go-betweens throughout the China contract was a London businessman, George Wong, who, in September 1988, was told in detail about Babylon. The Belgravia 'independent wheeler-dealer with links to European financiers doing business in the Far East', who worked for the Rothschild bank and for a time in the Foreign Office, is alleged to have forwarded details of the dealings to Downing Street. In the autumn of 1989, GCHQ had eavesdropped on a telephone conversation between a London businessman and a Belgian arms dealer in which they allegedly discussed the financing of the supergun and the commissions to be paid to those involved. Joint Intelligence Committee clerk Robin Robison claimed that he passed on the computer print-out details to an assessment officer in the Cabinet Office. The intercept may have been discussed at the weekly JIC meeting and passed on to the Prime Minister's office and other relevant ministers in the weekly summary of GCHQ intelligence known as the 'Red Book'. In addition, all communications leaving Iraq were monitored by GCHQ's intercept station at RAF Episkopi, Cyprus. Testimony from witnesses revealed that many of the details of the project were discussed in uncoded long-distance telephone conversations between the Middle East and Europe.[4]

Project Babylon was co-ordinated on Bull's behalf by Liverpool-born metallurgist Christopher Cowley, who insists that the object of the supergun was to put satellites into orbit. The fixed-site nature of the gun and the fact that the firing would produce seismic patterns which would pinpoint its position made it an unlikely offensive weapon. Not only that, it could not be aimed and could only be fired once. Whether true or not, an MI6 officer operating from the old Admiralty House did brief selected journalists that Babylon was not a supergun but a satellite launcher.

The proposed satellites needed carbon-fibre casings and thus, in September 1989, SRC, backed by Iraqi money, attempted to buy the Lear Fan carbon-fibre plant in Belfast with the blessing of the Northern Ireland Office. Using MI6 intelligence the Foreign Office eventually blocked the deal after pressure from Israel and the United States. CIA officers had met with their counterparts in London to discuss the possible use of the factory to help build Iraqi missiles. British intelligence had initially wanted the sale to go through because it wanted to monitor the project, but the United States, as a member of the Missile Technology Control Regime, was committed to the prevention of the proliferation of missile technology and forced MI6 to act. Problems arose when MI6 identified some of those involved in the deal as Iraqi military intelligence officers, including Dr Fadel Jawad Kadham, a senior member of Saddam's government. MI6 already had an 'asset' in the SRC Composites management who 'had co-operated with Intelligence for years and had fallen into place at SRC by chance. He had been hired because of his legitimate expertise and background. And London was certain that he would act as an inside source.

A SRC executive, Stuart Blackledge, did provide MI6 with intelligence. Arrested by Customs on 31 January 1991, at the height of the Gulf War, Blackledge received a suspended sentence for evading export controls. He agreed to a plea bargain after being prevented from calling government witnesses when ministers signed Public Interest Immunity certificates. 'SRC Composites' technical director was James Brooks, who had previously been project manager at Shorts for the Blowpipe shoulder-fired surface-to-air missile programme. (MI6 had covertly supplied Blowpipe to the Afghan rebels.)[5]

Western tolerance of Dr Bull ended when he moved from creating the supergun for projecting satellites to the design of a high-altitude gun, SRC Project 839. Sheffield Forgemasters later built the cradle for the barrel, which was intercepted in Greece on its way to Iraq. The senior intelligence officer, Bill Weir, who been told about the project by Walter Sommers, later popped up in Iraq as a member of the United Nations team which dismantled the supergun. He claimed that the supergun, which had been moved from its original siting to a mountainside location, had been test-fired four times, allegedly in the direction of Israel, in March 1990. Although only one of the five guns was ever assembled, Iraq had needed just eight more pipes to complete the 1,000mm gun. Whether Allied surveillance satellites spotted the gun is not known. Washington had apparently known full well what Bull was up to but regarded the supergun as unworkable. 'Militarily speaking it was a dinosaur, and its importance to Saddam was psychological. The US took the view that a happy Saddam was a safer Saddam.' However, the Israeli government took the opposite view. Arms consultant Turp, who offered to talk to the Commons Committee investigating the affair but was not called, discussed the supergun with Bull and was in no doubt that 'his systems would indeed have worked'.[6]

The Cabinet Office had known about Bull's arrangement with Iraq since May 1988, when the Belgian government had informed Downing Street of the details, while MI6 had probably known all along about the existence of the supergun. They chose not only to cover up this knowledge but to attack those who were privy to information which might prove embarrassing to the government. The former chair of Astra Holdings, Gerald James, criticised the government and the security services for their 'apparent and deliberate effort to fudge and confuse the issue by attacking manufacturers and industrialists when they were meeting requirements initiated by government'. He maintained that his firm was hijacked and exploited by covert forces who wanted to use the company as a conduit for sanction-busting arms deals.[7]

A company that was achieving rapid growth in an area of intense international competition, when Astra was placed on the stock market in 1986 it seemed in a position to challenge the big boys. Astra was encouraged to acquire a Grantham-based ammunition manufacturer, British Manufacturing and

Research Company (BMARC), by Sir Peter Levene, who was in charge of military procurement at the MoD, and certain Conservative politicians. Astra was assured that ministers were acting on clear signals from Downing Street for greater competition. The idea was to create a challenger to British Aerospace (BAe) in the munitions market. However, unknown to Astra, government policy had changed and the MoD had already signed a deal with BAe which guaranteed the company 80 per cent of the market. Industry sources alleged that the agreement, Explosives, Propellants and Related Products (EPREP), was concluded over the heads of senior civil servants. Three months after agreement was reached in May 1988, MoD officials were still denying to Astra that EPREP had been signed.[8]

Without the MoD deal Astra looked like heading for trouble; however, influential people close to the centres of power persuaded the company to expand further. The next target for acquisition was Belgian propellant manufacturer Poudreries Réunies de Belgique (PRB). One man to encourage the deal with PRB was Sir John Cuckney, who played an influential role in Astra's affairs as chair of one of its largest shareholders, 3i. Another Midland man involved was the mysterious Stefan Kock, who was introduced to Astra by a Guernsey-based tax exile involved in the Middle East arms market. Kock boasted of playing a key role in Astra's expansion but denied reports that the Midland had been instrumental in getting him his post as non-executive director. According to the *Independent*, Hervé de Carmoy, former head of Midland's international arm, was partly responsible for selling PRB to Astra when he was chief executive of its former owners, Société Générale de Belgique. The bank's defence expert, Campbell Dunford, who had served a spell with the Moscow Narody Bank, a posting which appears to have included clearance by MI6, agreed that Astra was pressed 'very hard indeed' by Kock and the government to take over PRB. Astra paid £22 million to buy PRB even though it was technically bankrupt. One reason for the pressure to buy PRB appears to have been fears that Gerald Bull, with Iraqi finance, was preparing to purchase the company. This became clear to Bull when Belgian bankers 'went quiet on the deal'. He concluded that 'they accepted the Astra bid over his own for political rather than business reasons. Bull recognised the deal had gone against him because of his ties to Iraq.'[9]

When Astra required additional finance for the PRB deal, its management was introduced to the 'Savoy Mafia', the influential group of people who allegedly conducted arms deals from the Savoy suite of Lotus cars director Alan Curtis. The first meeting between James and Curtis, to discuss finance, was arranged by Richard Unwin, whose BMARC company had been taken over by Astra in May 1986. In July 1988, Unwin introduced James to Mark and Denis Thatcher. James was also introduced by Curtis to Syrian businessman Wafic Said, the BAe agent in Saudi Arabia said to be responsible for winning the Al-Yamamah deal. One of Said's biggest British investments was in Aitken International, an investment company whose deputy chair was Conservative MP Jonathan Aitken. In 1988, James was introduced by Aitken, who was a consultant to BMARC, to members of the Saudi royal family. Aitken is now minister for defence procurement.[10]

Unknown to Astra, in November 1988 Gerald Bull's SRC had contracted PRB to supply over 200 tonnes of propellant for Project Babylon. Jordan was listed as the end-customer, to foil any Western suspicions, though the use of Jordan as a conduit for arms intended for Iraq was so well known the two countries were known as 'Jorq'. Within days of taking over PRB in September 1989, Astra's chief executive, Christopher Gumbley, was approached at the Royal Naval Equipment Exhibition by the MoD's deputy head of armed sales, Roger Harding. He was asked to scrutinise all PRB contracts 'against the background of the known involvement of continental European munitions firms in the export of armaments to Iran and Iraq'. Astra soon discovered the contract with SRC and, in October, both Gumbley and James informed British intelligence of their suspicions that the propellant was for a large gun, while PRB director John Pike handed over documents to the security services showing the role played by Bull. James and his directors found members of the intelligence community to be 'extremely well-informed' about the project and thought it inconceivable that the information passed to Harding had not been referred upwards, including to the Prime Minister's office. During September, without consulting the chairman, non-executive director Stefan Kock telephoned MI6 about the propellant's existence. He later told MPs that he made the call after visiting propellant plants in Belgium belonging to PRB. He forwarded a further full report on 11 October 1989.[11]

Both Gumbley and James subsequently received visits from Harding's colleagues Bob Primrose and Roger Holdness, the latter allegedly working for MI6. MPs were denied the opportunity to question Harding and Primrose; ministers considered it 'inappropiate and unproductive'. Primrose, fully aware that this was a military contract, advised Gumbley to proceed with a £3 million sample delivery to Iraq, via Jordan, of propellants from the £35 million SRC contract. Later in October, Gumbley passed details to the MoD in the form of a memorandum which specifically referred to Project Babylon, while the managing director of Astra subsidiary BMARC met clandestinely in St James's Park with 'a man from Foreign Office technical intelligence' (a department of MI6). The following month, Astra provided further documentary evidence confirming 'the gun connection'.[12]

The Foreign Office secretly put pressure on the Belgian government to control PRB operations, but even when it became clear that the propellant was reaching Iraq, ministers appear to have been kept in the dark. Civil servants from the MoD told the Commons committee investigating the supergun that in December 1989 a decision was taken by Roger

Harding not to inform ministers. Harding denied this and was later reported to be angry at being made the 'scapegoat'. Defence Minister Alan Clark said that it was, in fact, the Foreign Office which had taken the decision, and later admitted that he was 'not entirely happy' that the matter was dealt with solely by officials.[13]

In mysterious circumstances on 5 December 1989 an explosion at the PRB factory destroyed the presses containing the propellant. Insurance assessors told James that they believed it was sabotage. Astra then lobbied, without success, Alan Clark at the MoD and the Prime Minister's office to gather support for a new arms order to fill the void made by the loss of the £35 million contract.[14]

Astra executives believed they had been duped by PRB. The company almost collapsed after acquiring PRB, when it was discovered that millions of pounds were missing from the Belgian firm. Astra managing director Christoper Gumbley was told by Gerald Bull that Société Générale had defrauded Astra on the sale of PRB. The Belgians later set up an investigation into PRB's trading activities, under former Prime Minister André Cools.[15]

The failure of the PRB acquisition, which at one stage threatened to force Astra into liquidation, led Astra shareholders, encouraged by Kock, to call for the dismissal of the management. Kock then attempted to restructure the board. Supported by 3i, he 'pressed the button' on three Astra directors. Gumbley was fired and James was removed from the board. According to the *Independent*, the boardroom upheavals began in May 1990 when Gumbley returned from Thailand after discovering that PRB had paid out hundreds of millions of pounds in secret commission payments. Gumbley proposed exposing an arms ring which 'reputedly spreads from Whitehall to Washington via Belgium and other loosely regulated countries to some of the world's most pernicious regimes, including Saddam Hussein's Iraq'.[16]

On 22 March 1989, Bull was killed outside of his Brussels

flat by an assassin who fired two shots into his neck and three into his body from a Colt pistol fitted with a silencer – a murder which Western intelligence agencies believe was instigated by Mossad with the knowledge of the United States. Just a few hours before the assassination, Gumbley had met with Bull and had been warned that his removal from Astra had been engineered. Bull also told him about the large kickbacks involved in Middle East arms deals including the Al-Yamamah project. James later claimed that investigations by Sir John Bourn, the Comptroller and Auditor General, into the Saudi Arabian Tornado jet contract were being 'muzzled' because of large commissions paid to British officials to secure arms contracts. Bull also provided another explanation for the extraordinary events which surrounded the acquisition of PRB and the eventual demise of Astra, which was forced to call in the receiver in February 1992. Gumbley was shown surveillance reports on members of PRB's staff. He was told that MI6 had used the company, which was close to the MoD, for covert operations.[17]

British Customs officials refused to enlighten the Commons inquiry into the supergun as to why it took them six months after the various tip-offs before they seized the last eight sections of the Babylon barrels at Teesport on 9 April 1990. They refused to answer questions about their co-operation with other Whitehall departments, while committee members were met with blank faces when they asked about the exchange of information with the intelligence agencies. The Customs raid, code-named 'Big Bertha' after the giant German gun which had shelled Paris during the First World War, was the result of information passed on by Mossad intelligence sources to MI6. According to this account, the Iranian intelligence service, SAVAM, had received information on the supergun project from a Muslim employee of Walter Sommers but, distrusting the British, had passed the information via a cut-out to Israel, which then passed it on. The impetus for the operation appears to have come from the Americans, who had become increasingly alarmed by Saddam's interest in weapons of mass destruction, particularly in the nuclear field.

During 1989 US Customs officials began to suspect that Matrix Churchill was trying to obtain nuclear switches for the Iraqis and so set up an undercover operation to entrap the buyers. In March 1990, a consignment of what were believed to be nuclear triggers – krytons – was seized at Heathrow Airport in a joint US – UK Customs operation. Simon Henderson suggests that Farzad Bazoft's mission in Iraq was tied to this 'sting within a sting' which had been going well until the explosion at Al-Qaqaa, where the journalist was arrested. If this is true, then Bazoft's death was doubly tragic in that it would appear that the capacitors had nothing to do with the construction of a nuclear bomb.[18]

On 28 March 1990, forty capacitors in crates marked for 'air conditioning parts', were seized *en route* to Iraq in the cargo shed at Heathrow Airport as part of Operation Argus. They had been imported by the small company Euromac, run by a British citizen who was an Iraqi national, Ali Daghir, and Kassim Abbas, who was working for the former head of Iraqi intelligence, Barzan Ibrahim al-Tikriti. The capacitors, which came to be known as 'krytons', had been ordered from CSI Technologies, the president of which, Jery Kowalsky, believed that they could only be used as parts of a detonator for a nuclear warhead. Kowalsky was recruited as an *agent provocateur* for US Customs and, at a bugged meeting with Iraqi engineers at the Cavendish Hotel in London, a sting was put into place. The ultra-high-speed, high-voltage switches ordered from CSI were exchanged for tiny energy-stores common in electrical goods such as food mixers. In sentencing Daghir in June 1991 to five years' imprisonment, the judge told him: 'To take part in a plot to get components which were intended for use in a nuclear weapon into the hands of scientists in Iraq was a serious offence which could have had terrible consequences, not only in the Middle East but perhaps for the world.' But the plot was not all that it seemed.[19]

The original intention had been to quickly deport Daghir and avoid an embarrassing trial, but this plan fell apart when it became clear that he was a British citizen. (An Iraqi Airways employee, Omar Latif, involved in the plot was expelled after the Home Office accused him of heading Iraqi intelligence in London.) A specialist witness for the defence said that the components were consistent with capacitors used in laser technology. Euromac had links to Gerald Bull's SRC company and it would appear that the capacitors were for use in studying the 'sabot separation' process after the launch of a rocket or supergun shell. Later, Mr Daghir's constituency MP, Ian Taylor, was denied access by Peter Lilley, Trade and Industry Secretary, to a United Nations report of its investigation into Iraq's nuclear programme. Lilley insisted that the report, which is believed to show that the capacitors were not key components of a nuclear bomb, was confidential. Secret documents seized by the International Atomic Energy Agency from an Iraqi Atomic Agency Commission building in Baghdad, show that Saddam had no need of imported capacitors as they were manufacturing their own versions. Daghir, who was denied transfer to an open prison because of the 'political implications' of his case, was, in May 1992, freed on bail pending an appeal. Daghir has become convinced that he was a 'soft target in an orchestrated sinister geo-political plot'. The seizure of the 'krytons' was the belated signal to stem the tide of weapons of mass destruction which were flowing into Iraq, and became a key element in the psychological warfare which was waged in the run-up to the Gulf War.[20]

As Astra was being dismembered, employees suffered harassment from the authorities, which James was convinced was linked to the company's knowledge of the supergun. In April 1990, Christopher Gumbley received a letter from 10 Downing Street warning him not to ask too many questions. When MoD police arrested him on charges of bribing an MoD official on the night before the seizure of the supergun parts on Teesside, they told him that he 'had caused a lot of trouble'. During his trial it was revealed that the order to arrest him had come 'from very senior levels of the Ministry of Defence procurement executive' and that 'a Government minister' was involved in the decision. Sentenced in March 1991 to nine months' imprisonment, Gumbley maintained that he been set up by the government because he had tipped off the authorities that PRB was supplying the Iraqis with propellant.[21]

In November 1990, the prosecution of Dr Christopher Cowley, project manager with SRC and Peter Mitchell, managing director of Walter Sommers, for illegal arms procurement was abandoned, to the amazement of defence lawyers, who recognised a *prima facie* case. Accusations then began to be aired. Customs officials let it be known that they felt let down by the MoD in their attempt to secure convictions, asserting that they had been 'stabbed in the back' by Whitehall mandarins. They also claimed that they had reported 'straight to Downing Street' throughout their investigation but, to their intense frustration, it was Number 10 which forced the dropping of charges. It was known that Cowley and Mitchell would have claimed that the government knew and approved of Project Babylon. Sir Hal Miller had taken detailed notes of conversations with the DTI and MI6, including the contents of a letter to Mrs Thatcher, and had threatened to provide this information at the trial. While Sir Hal said that he had seen written records of his conversations, the government insisted that they did not exist. Miller was later subjected to an officially inspired smear campaign; he said that he had never before come across 'so much lying in high places'.[22]

Attorney-General Sir Patrick Mayhew later told the Commons inquiry into the affair that it was extremely important that the evidence leading to the decision to drop the prosecution should not be 'paraded in public'. According to one source, an additional reason for the dropping of charges was acute pressure applied on Whitehall. American and British intelligence agencies wished for the co-operation of those arrested, to help them in gathering intelligence on Saddam Hussein's weapons programme following Iraq's seizure of Kuwait in August 1990.[23]

On 18 July 1991, as sixty-three-year-old André Cools, the man investigating the circumstances surrounding the sale of PRB, opened his car door, a 'professional, cold-blooded and audacious' assassin fired five 7.65 bullets through his throat and left ear. Cools had just received, from a 'British source', Bank of Credit and Commerce International bank statements and documents which showed that civil servants had been given 'sweeteners' to secure the use of Belgian air force freighters to ship cargoes of the supergun propellant to Iraq.[24]

The long-awaited investigation by the eleven-man all-party but Tory-dominated Trade and Industry Select Committee, which was published in March 1992, just before Parliament was dissolved, was something of a disappointment. The chair, Kenneth Warren, played a key role on the Committee and his casting vote was often crucial. Warren, like Stefan Kock a member of the Special Forces Club, was formerly director of a finance company, Gulf Guarantee Bank, whose board included two Iraqis. He was also the onetime director of US defence contractor Loral International, a large manufacturer of super-sophisticated electronic military equipment, whose products figured on the Allied side during the Gulf War.

Behind-the-scenes pressure was put on key witnesses who were making damaging allegations. Back-bench Tory MP Gerald Howarth talked to Gerald James before he appeared before the Committee. According to James, Howarth said that 'he'd been speaking to Warren about me. The gist of what he said was that Warren wanted everything to be "low key". He told me not to go "over the top".' Howarth told him that 'he was working for Mrs Thatcher's private office', which James took to be a form of intimidation. When asked about the telephone call, Howarth claimed that James had become 'paranoid'. The two had been members, in the early seventies, of the ultra-right-wing Monday Club, while Howarth had been a consultant to Astra Holdings and was a director of Richard Unwin International, an Astra subsidiary. Warren had also met with Dr Christopher Cowley the night before he gave evidence to the Committee. Warren said there was nothing 'sinister' about the meeting.[25]

The Committee's conclusions were typically muted, brushing aside the idea of a conspiracy or cover-up and instead settled for a case of bureaucratic mishandling. It accepted the view of MoD officials who blamed the failure to recognise the supergun on 'compartmentalisation'. This was compounded by the failure of MI6 to pass on details on the supergun project until two months after it had officially learned of its existence. The Foreign Office claimed that it had been 'duped by Saddam'. The Committee decided that 'knowledge within government of the project was like a number of people all holding pieces of jigsaw without realising that they were the same pieces of the same jigsaw'. However, it did acknowledge that its evidence was far from complete. The inquiry had been 'obstructed' by Customs, and members of the Committee felt it was 'particularly strange' that senior Customs officials consulted the Attorney-General, Sir Patrick Mayhew, and the Leader of the House of Commons, John MacGregor, before giving evidence. Labour members of the Committee branded it a 'blatant political fix'.[26]

The Committee did not have access to intelligence sources, with several ministerial witnesses making it clear that such access 'could not be permitted'. The Committee did, however, reach a conclusion which put oversight of the intelligence services back on the agenda: 'We believe the long-range gun affair raises serious and important questions about the accountability of the intelligence services, both to ministers and to Parliament.' Warren said it was important that accountability 'should be measured and trusted' by Parliament. Prime Minister John Major appeared to take note, within the space of a few months informing the House of Commons that legislation would be brought forward to legitimise MI6 by officially acknowledging its existence for the first time. The government would also institute a form of parliamentary oversight.[27]

25

MI6 and The Secret State

It is the secret seething hinterland of the British state, which for the past 20 years has come to pose the greatest threat to the quality of British democracy.

Hugo Young

The real, hidden, permanent government resides largely within the Cabinet Office and the committees servicing it. According to Peter Hennessy, this is the engine room of British central government, where political and bureaucratic power meet. The central figure, Cabinet Secretary Sir Robin Butler, works out of an office the size of a squash court within Number 70, Whitehall. The modern world appears to intrude little on the grand splendour of this room with its pink-domed ceiling, designed by William Kent in 1736, primarily because Sir Robin dislikes computers. His predecessor, Sir Robert Armstrong, had a certain reputation for deviousness which culminated in his humiliation in an Australian court during the *Spycatcher* case. Butler is no liberal – he supported Mrs Thatcher over the banning of trade unionism at GCHQ, though he has voted Labour in the past. He is regarded as 'cool and uncomplicated', his manner of 'cultivated detachment' marking him out as a typical mandarin.[1]

The Cabinet Secretary's power within the secret state is derived from chairing or supervising the 'myriad of half-committees' making up the intelligence empire, which help to obscure the way in which intelligence policy is formulated. As George Simmel once said, 'The purpose of secrecy is, above all, protection.' Key decisions are made on these committees, by unelected officials who escape any form of democratic control or constitutional legality. What accountability there is tends to be 'a charade, a piece of theatricals which enables officials not to take things seriously' and where, admits one former Permanent Secretary, 'Economy with the truth is the essence of a reply to a parliamentary question'. The prejudice against accountability is, according to Anthony Verrier, 'almost entirely based on this residual belief, a lingering illusion, that the ethos, the sacred flame, whatever one likes to call it, of a British empire which, in reality, came to an honourable end decades ago, can be sustained, kept alight by the British public remaining ignorant of matters which are often common knowledge elsewhere.' The arrangement of the supervising intelligence apparatus mirrors this residual belief.[2]

The authority to direct and supervise the work of MI6 rests with the Permanent Secretaries' Committee on the Intelligence Services (PSCIS); this includes senior civil servants from the Cabinet Office, the Foreign and Home Offices, the Ministry of Defence, the Department of Trade and Industry and the Chief of the Defence Staff. However, the power is only advisory and, needless to say, the service remains 'self-regulating'. The Committee approves the budget and overall intelligence-gathering priorities; it can also after consultation with senior ministers give the go-ahead to the Joint Intelligence Committee to recommend major covert action operations. The Prime Minister, who has overall responsibility for the intelligence services, or the Foreign Secretary, whose department has nominal control of MI6, will inform the Cabinet Secretary of the requirements in verbal form; nothing is written down.[3]

Also sitting on the monthly meetings of the PSCIS is the Co-ordinator of Intelligence and Security, a post with responsibility to the Cabinet Secretary for checking MI6's budget. The Co-ordinator, who reports to the Prime Minister, also examines the long-term plans and priorities of MI6 and reports to the PSCIS, for which an annual review of the functioning of British intelligence is prepared. The Co-ordinator also maintains five-year forecasts of the intelligence agencies and their assets. Sir Christopher Curwen retired from the Co-ordinator's post in the autumn of 1991 when he was put on the Security Commission. Normally, the Co-ordinator's job would have gone to the retiring MI6 chief; however, Sir Colin McColl had been asked to remain in post by the Prime Minister. Instead the post passed to sixty-one-year-old former diplomat Gerald Warner, a member of the Police Complaints Authority, though it is thought he was, in fact, a deputy chief of MI6. A career officer with a great deal of experience in the Far East, before returning to London in 1977, Warner served in Peking, Rangoon and finally as counsellor in Kuala Lumpur, where MI6 has always had a strong presence.[4]

Another part of the Cabinet Office machine is the Joint Intelligence Committee (JIC) which, although it officially does not exist, is at the heart of the secret state. The JIC 'retains a degree of independence which may be disliked by prime ministers . . . but which reflects the relentless determination of Whitehall to resist encroachments on its roles by politicians'. The JIC is responsible for collating and analysing intelligence from MI6 and other agencies and acts as 'the central filter between expert assessors and ministers'. The secure, debugged JIC room is connected by a single door to Number 10, illustrating its importance and closeness to the centre of power. The chair of the JIC always has the right of personal access to the Prime Minister, though he reported to the Cabinet Secretary. Until Sir Percy Cradock (officially described as the Prime Minister's foreign policy adviser) retired in the spring of 1992, to be replaced by the former British ambassador in Moscow, Sir Roderic Braithwaite, he chaired the weekly Wednesday meetings of the JIC. His deputy, General Sir Derek Boorman, head of the Defence Intelligence Staff, was, on retirement, appointed a member of the Security Commission. Other JIC members include a deputy secretary from the Foreign Office, the director-general of MI5, the chief of MI6, the head of GCHQ, the deputy secretary of policy and programmes at the MoD, a deputy secretary from the Northern Ireland Office and a representative of the Treasury. Other senior officials are called in on an *ad hoc* basis.[5]

Also sitting on the JIC is the head of the Assessment Staff in the Cabinet Office, which is responsible for daily reports and long-term analyses and estimates for policy making. The Joint Intelligence Organisation receives all raw intelligence, channelled by the sackful from the different agencies, including MI6 'CX'. Once categorised, the Assessment Staff decide where the 'wizard' material contained in the 'red books' should be routed; direct to the JIC or to one of its sub-committees which look at day-to-day intelligence. The sub-groups, known as Current Intelligence Groups, focus on specific areas such as Eastern Europe, Latin America, the Middle East, Northern Ireland and Terrorism. In some ways, the JIC also operates as another intelligence agency in that there are representatives of the Committee in Washington, Ottawa and Canberra. A JIC (G) based in Bonn and chaired by an MI6 officer monitors developments in Central and Eastern Europe while a JIC (C) on Cyprus is concerned with events in the Middle East.[6]

The first half of the JIC meeting is attended by the liaison officers of the Canadian, New Zealand and Australian intelligence services and the London station officer of the CIA. This collaboration is formalised under a secret intelligence agreement, the UK – USA Treaty (known in Whitehall as 'you-koo-sah'), which was signed in 1946. The liaison officers withdraw for 'domestic' business. The Americans are said to rate highly JIC input which produces a synthesised product – in contrast to their own set-up, where intelligence agencies compete. On Thursday morning, the results of the deliberations are considered by the JIC 'A' Committee, which deals at Permanent Under-Secretary and Chiefs of Staff levels with major issues, and the 'B' Committee, which deals with minor items. The final reports are distributed to interested parties in the evening, in 150 copies of the red book. Unexpurgated reports are sent to ministers, including the Chancellor, Home, Foreign and Defence Secretaries and the Secretary of State for

Scotland. However, in an illustration of the powers of the secret state, some specially classified files are withheld from Cabinet ministers. The books, once returned to the JIC, are shredded and then burned.[7]

A copy of the red book is also forwarded to Buckingham Palace. One of the most interesting relationships in the intelligence community is that between the JIC, MI6 and the monarchy. We have already seen the role MI5 plays in monitoring the friends of members of the Royal Family (chapter 2), but the nature of the connection to MI6 is much more mysterious. There is an intriguing fragment in the book, *Colonel Z: The Secret Life of a Master of Spies* which suggests of a formal link. We are told that, on being appointed, the chief of MI6, 'C', accepts from the Queen a small plaque, the 'Ivory', 'as a token of office and as a pass giving access in times of trouble'. Is this, perhaps, one reason why the British state has gone to such lengths to deny the existence of the service? Does MI6, in fact, have a secret constitution? Is MI6 Her Majesty's Secret Service? This appears to be another of those archaic aspects of the unwritten British constitution about which the public is told nothing. Another – the royal prerogative, which is exercised not through Parliament but through ministers – still retains its uses. The monarch's Privy Council was responsible for the 'order in Council' which banned trade unions at GCHQ.[8]

Every day, at nine o'clock, the Queen begins work on the government boxes. She receives all Cabinet papers as well as unamended JIC weekly reports, on which she will make concise comments; she is better informed than most ministers. The Queen's private secretary, Sir Robert Fellowes, is in daily contact with the Cabinet Secretary and the principal private secretary to the Prime Minister. These three, who advise the Crown on political matters, are known as the 'golden trio'. Fellowes is also in regular contact with MI6 chief Sir Colin McColl. Reports between the two are still sent in green ink, a tradition started by the first chief, Sir Mansfield Cummings –

a practice which, in Celtic mythology, is a harbinger of bad luck. 'Highly sensitive' data from MI6 – presumably about friends of members of her family – is sent to the Queen direct. 'MI6 does not spy on members of the Royal Family,' according to a senior intelligence officer, 'but risk assessments are carried out when they travel abroad and discreet surveillance is kept to see they come to no harm.' Station officers keep in close liaison with local security officials. According to the *Sunday Express*, details about the close friendship between the Duchess of York and American oil executive Steve Wyatt, following an unexpected trip to Morocco in the Wyatt family jet, were given to the Queen in early 1990.[9]

It is likely that the intelligence reports the Queen values most are those concerning the Commonwealth. The Queen takes seriously her role as head of the Commonwealth and, although she has no real formal powers, she is, unlike in the domestic arena, able to exercise a degree of influence. Her stewardship, which gives her a sense of purpose, has, it could be argued, been crucial in holding the Commonwealth together over the past forty years. The Queen often displays a remarkable knowledge of a particular country's affairs or an individual statesman, some of which is, no doubt, derived from secret intelligence. MI6 took over responsibility for security work and intelligence gathering in Africa from MI5 in the early sixties, though it was not until later in that decade that the service was fully integrated into the work of the British embassies. In 1979, Queen Elizabeth played a key role at the Lusaka summit, which she attended against the wishes of the Prime Minister, thus helping to smooth the way for the Lancaster House talks on Rhodesia/Zimbabwe. It is known that the Queen was concerned about the effect on the Commonwealth of Mrs Thatcher's support of South Africa. MI6 was particularly active in South Africa throughout the eighties; the National Intelligence Service, formerly BOSS, and Military intelligence complained that MI6 and other Western Agencies were 'constantly trying to collect information'. The

South African security services were on the watch, especially during the war in Namibia, for agents operating under cover of scientific or anthropological research.[10]

In October 1983, Foreign Secretary Geoffrey Howe was angered when MI6 failed to alert him to the American invasion of Grenada, an operation which embarrassed the Queen. Howe was said to be convinced that MI6 must have been forewarned by the CIA about American intentions and blamed the chief, Sir Colin Figures, for the intelligence failure. Figures pointed out to the Foreign Secretary that his liaison officer in Washington had been in no better position than other senior diplomats in the embassy, who also had no inkling of what was to take place. There was an MI6 presence on the island. A Sandhurst graduate, whom sources identified as the station officer, claimed that 'he watched the shooting of Maurice Bishop through an eighty-power telescope, and although he did not see the aftermath, estimated that at least fifty people died'. An SAS unit, which had been dispatched to rescue the Queen's representative on Grenada, Governor-General Sir Paul Scoon, stood down when the Americans decided to invade. Mrs Thatcher took no steps to sack Figures. On his sixtieth birthday in 1985, he left to be replaced by Sir Christopher Curwen, who had the active support of the director-general of MI5, Sir Antony Duff. Figures then became Cabinet Office Co-ordinator of Intelligence and Security, giving him more time to pursue his hobbies of gardening and beachcombing.[11]

According to a former assessor, Robin Robison, those working for the Joint Intelligence Committee 'believed passionately in what they were doing'. Some intelligence officers and senior civil servants were not 'bad people at all' but they 'had been in it too long, steeped in blood too much. It was easier for them to go on than turn back, people with high mortgages and so on.' There was a feeling, Robison found, that it was 'really rather pleasant to be privy to what was going on. A rather silly feeling of power, seeing minutes no one else ever sees, seeing JIC minutes which very, very few people ever hear about. It's the seduction of power.' As Sissela Bok notes: 'The separation between insider and outsider is inherent in secrecy; and to think something is secret is already to envisage potential conflict between what insiders conceal and outsiders want to inspect or lay bare.' There was a degree of over-classification, according to Robison. 'They didn't want a leak to come out because it would be politically embarrassing. It was being used to cover up mistakes' which had little to do with 'national security'.[12]

The biggest failure the JIC suffered was in its handling of intelligence in the run-up to the Argentine invasion of the Falkland Islands in April 1982. This was an intelligence failure not by the person-on-the-ground but at the level of assessment and by a government which gave scant attention to the Falklands. The government had previously overlooked the advice of its diplomats that a refusal to negotiate meaningfully with the Argentine government would lead to an escalation of the dispute.

When it came to the Falklands, normal advice and intelligence were ignored by the assessors. Nick Barker, former captain of the British Antartic Survey ship *Endurance*, says that he gave repeated warnings in November 1981 and January 1982. 'I saw signs and signals of war but my warnings were ignored and a thousand lives lost. It seemed that my alarm signals stayed at the bottom of some civil servant's in-tray.' The chief of station in Buenos Aires and the defence attaché from the Defence Intelligence Staff operated on limited resources; they had no reliable sources inside the junta headed by General Galtieri, but MI6 did receive reports from low-level agents within the Argentine regime. Open information from press conferences provided hard intelligence that the Argentine navy was referring to a possible invasion. The MI6 officer 'gave London ample warning about a possible attack on the islands' and the building of an 'invasion atmosphere'.[13]

It appears that key members of the assessment staff within the Cabinet Office were on extended leave at the time, and so important intelligence which should have been passed on to the Current Intelligence Group on Latin America was not acted upon. Between July 1981 and March 1982, the CIG (LA), which fed information into the JIC, met eighteen times but did not discuss the Falklands once. Members of the CIG thought the threat assessment was the same as it had been for several years, while the JIC was wedded to a mid-1981 assessment of the situation. One well-placed official told Peter Hennessy that they were 'imprisoned in the continuum of the past'. It was thought that the junta would not launch an all-out assault. For the Whitehall intelligence community, which was concentrating on the all-important Soviet threat, the Falklands were a backwater.[14]

By the end of February 1982, MI6 'reported the first clear indication of a firm Argentinian intention to invade', though no date was fixed. The report went via the JIC to the Chiefs of Staff, who focused on the word 'intention' and thus thought the threat could, if necessary, be countered by the dispatch of a nuclear submarine. According to the then Armed Forces Minister, Jerry Wiggin, 'at a ministerial level we were certainly not being briefed and I don't think the Foreign Office ministers were either'. Three weeks passed between the MI6 reports and the Cabinet receiving an assessment. The Buenos Aires MI6 station did receive notice of the 26 March decision to invade, but it is believed that the source was not regarded as totally reliable. Because of tensions within the embassy and with Whitehall, it took five days for this information to be passed to London. The JIC then failed to pass on vital information to the Prime Minister on the final decision by the Argentine junta to invade the islands.[15]

The report of the Privy Counsellors, chaired by Lord Franks, is a sober document which did not attach any blame to the Thatcher government and stated that 'the invasion of the Falkland Islands on April 12 could not have been foreseen'. Franks, a member of the 'great and the good' who are wheeled out on such occasions, was not out to rock the boat. In 1954 he said, 'We assume that our future will be one of a piece with our past and that we shall continue as a great power. What is noteworthy is the way we take this for granted.' The loss of Suez did not batter such illusions. Wiggin regarded the way Whitehall handled the aftermath as a 'whitewash' and a 'farce'. Such committees are at the mercy of the Prime Minister and the civil servants who control the flow of information and access to officials. 'I think we have a very interesting way of covering things up. The Franks inquiry did its best but it was couched in very bureaucratic terms. The hard truth is that in a system as complicated and as well established as ours, getting things right doesn't always apply.' Warnings of the invasion were, he suggested, 'covered up' by civil servants who went unpunished. Franks remarked on Barker's evidence that 'the Ministry of Defence and Foreign Office saw his reports and took them into account along with other intelligence information. None of his reports warned of an imminent invasion.' Barker brushed off the statement, which he thought 'reflected Whitehall characteristics of arrogance, obsession with secrecy and refusal to admit mistakes'.[16]

In the wake of the Franks inquiry, the heads of the intelligence services were given the opportunity to have their views considered by the various groups which feed the JIC and through it ministers on the Overseas and Defence Committee. A new system was put in place to ensure that reports are not pigeon-holed once the JIC has considered them. The process of assessment and analysis was also streamlined but, still, mistakes are made, as illustrated by the invasion of Kuwait. 'The British system of intelligence assessments,' according to one insider, 'although it has great strength, lives with risk. The bulk of it is done in the Cabinet Office by diplomats and someone plucked off the bridge of a destroyer. There are few professional intelligence estimators and there is little back-up. Its key strength is that the Cabinet Office intelligence community is small. But it can seem very seat-of-the-pants and amateur. There are no panaceas.'[17]

MI6 did achieve one major success during the Falklands War by thwarting Argentine attempts to buy more Exocet missiles on the European arms market. Anthony Divall, a Hamburg-based businessman, was asked days after the Argentine air force had sunk HMS *Sheffield* with Exocet missiles, to pose as an arms dealer to penetrate the Argentinian military procurement mission in Paris. Divall had worked for MI6 since leaving the Royal Marines in 1945 and continued to do so until December 1987, during which time he had been used on a number of operations in the murky world of arms dealing. Most famously, he was involved in the capture of the gun-running ship *Claudia* off the Irish coast in 1973. He had helped plant direction-finding devices on the ship when it left Libya.

Backed by a £16 million draft handled by Williams and Glyn's bank, Divall fooled the Argentinians into believing he could deliver thirty Exocet missiles for £1 million each from Libya and Iraq, thereby discouraging the mission's director, Captain Alfredo Corti, from using the services of genuine arms dealers. The successful operation, which deprived Argentina of whatever chance it had of gaining more missiles, cost only £35,000. When the war was over, Divall was instructed to leak the Exocet scam to a 'quality British newspaper'. The story duly appeared in the *Sunday Times* in October 1982, without mention of Divall's name. Unfortunately for Divall, in December 1984 his clandestine activities aroused the suspicions of the West German police, and MI6 had to persuade them to drop arms-dealing charges against him. The service then unceremoniously cut its ties with Divall. 'Back in London, the Firm [MI6] was terrified my unlawful spying activities might surface in a grubby Hamburg court room and that Whitehall could be embarrassed.' Divall subsequently attempted to sue the agency for £200,000 expenses after his last case officer, 'Tony Bridger', told him that 'the Firm wanted to cut me off for good. I was left without a lifeline – no pension, no security and still without my expenses being paid.' In

March 1988, Divall went public, disclosing the full extent of his and MI6's role in the operation.[18]

The Falklands War saw a revival of the 'special relationship' between Britain and the United States, particularly within the intelligence community, where relations had been damaged over Iran. The Shah of Iran believed that Britain was behind most of the troubles inside his country, and in the late sixties, in an attempt to placate the naturally paranoid autocratic ruler, the Foreign Office decided to withdraw the MI6 station. The service was left to rely on SAVAK, Iran's security service for intelligence, with only a minimal presence within the British embassy in Tehran. The Foreign Office vetoed all political action which might hinder economic relations with one of Britain's major markets for its arms industry. This led to difficult relations with the United States, particularly after Ayatollah Khomeini seized power. Much to the dismay of Howard Bane, the CIA officer responsible for co-ordinating intelligence on the disastrous Desert One hostage rescue attempt, when six United States embassy staff managed to escape being taken for hostages and sought sanctuary at the British embassy, they were turned away. At the same time, the Foreign Office withdrew MI6's very experienced man on the spot and replaced him with a junior official. The CIA was not happy.[19]

The CIA had provided help in 1980 for an MI6-backed covert operation in South Yemen in which 'several small teams were being trained to blow up bridges'. CIA director Stansfield Turner, who had a dislike of all covert action programmes which involved loss of life, described the scheme as 'hare-brained'. He also thought MI6 was 'leaky' and that too much sensitive information was being shared with the British, who 'had a virtual intelligence stranglehold on the United States'. Intelligence sharing fell to an all-time low. Reagan's nominee as director, William Casey, had different ideas; he was an Anglophile who had served in London during the war. He made sure that the intelligence channel was reopened and was instrumental in ensuring that 'a batch of secrets' was delivered to MI6 during the Falklands period. The CIA had good human sources which were tied to the junta; the National Security Agency (America's equivalent of GCHQ) had listening posts in Chile, as well as satellites, which enabled the British to read many Argentine codes and provided a steady flow of intelligence. There was covert use of SR-71 Blackbird spyplanes to photograph Argentinian positions, although poor weather made these worthless. A small group of Anglophile American officials also helped organise a top-secret operation to supply Britain with vital weapons during the conflict. In a clandestine operation which came right out of a spy thriller, Stinger missiles were delivered in darkness to waiting British diplomats in a Washington car park, breaching a ban on transferring high-tech weapons to another country.[20]

There is always a price to be paid for such co-operation and, in return, MI6 was expected to support the anti-communist crusade launched by William Casey. President Reagan found an enthusiastic supporter in Mrs Thatcher's administration, which increased MI6's budget and removed the constraints on foreign operations. Aggressive covert action was back in vogue, and during the mid-eighties MI6 officers found themselves working alongside the CIA on the agencies' major operations; in a few cases, MI6 even took the lead role as congressional inquiries began to focus on the CIA's involvement in some of the more unsavoury operations.

Britain has useful connections to former imperial countries, and MI6 has traditionally strong links to India and Pakistan – ties which proved useful in attempts to bring down the Soviet-backed regime in Afghanistan. For nearly a decade, MI6 helped the CIA fight a covert war against Kabul from bases inside Pakistan, in what became the largest covert operation since the Second World War. Ahmed Rashid, who covered the war for the *Independent*, found that the intelligence agencies often used Western journalists, medical aid workers, refugee experts, academics and freebooters to gather information. In 1983,

Radio Kabul made great propaganda from the disovery of the body of a man identified as 'Stuart Bodman'. With a false passport and operating under cover as a journalist, Bodman was connected to a British company, Gulf Features Services, which had been formed to 'report and record news intelligence and information'. According to the *Observer*, Bodman had been working for the Americans with the knowledge of MI6. He was part of a five-man team, including former SAS men, who had been sent to Afghanistan to retrieve Soviet weapons. Equipment was appearing in Afghanistan that was only rumoured to exist in Warsaw Pact countries. Most of the material collected by these 'freelance' mercenaries found its way to the military testing laboratories of the United States, Britain and France.[21]

The CIA had its biggest station in Islamabad, where the MI6 chief of station between 1984 and 1988, Anthony Hawkes, liaised with Pakistan Inter-Service Intelligence, generally regarded as the best intelligence agency in the Third World. MI6 was apparently cautious in its assessment of the fall of the communist regime in Afghanistan, and, although it worked in close co-operation with the CIA, it pursued an independent strategy by promoting the ex-king Zahir Shah; British intelligence has always had a soft spot for former kings. Afghan mujaheddin were trained, sometimes by the British private security company KMS, in Saudi Arabia and Oman, where there were secret CIA and MI6 bases. During 1986, as a favour to the CIA, MI6 ran a covert operation to supply the guerrilla commander Abdul Haq, of the fundamentalist Hezbe Islami, with British Blowpipe missiles. However, the Afghans found the missiles, which had been paid for by the Americans, to be poor weapons against Soviet helicopter gunships and aircraft.[22]

In the House of Commons, former Tory MP Enoch Powell attacked Mrs Thatcher's slavish devotion to President Reagan over matters such as Afghanistan. 'How long will the UK continue to be dragged at the coat tail of the disastrous misconceptions of American policy?' he railed, but to little effect. MI6 was allowed to become embroiled in some particularly despicable operations. The United States had supplied money, weapons and surveillance intelligence to Pol Pot as part of the anti-communist campaign in Cambodia. In 1985, when the Irangate scandal threatened to expose CIA covert support for a number of unsanctioned operations, Britain was asked to supply SAS specialists to train Cambodian guerrillas. According to one official, 'MI6 don't like it. But they emphasise that it was ministerial orders coming from the top.' A request was made to the Special Forces secretariat in the MoD to supply suitable personnel for an operation whose costs were to be born by the MoD and the Foreign Office, and channelled secretly through MI6. The operation began when signal and sabotage specialists were sent to two camps in Thailand, near the Cambodian border, and a secret camp in Malaysia to train guerrillas in mine-laying techniques and the handling of sophisticated weapons. At one point there were up to 250 special forces personnel on the border. The training continued until 1989, when the full scale of the operation was exposed in a television documentary by John Pilger, *Cambodia: Year Ten*. In 1992, Rae McGrath of the Mines Advisory Group published an account entitled 'Land Mines in Cambodia: The Coward's War' in *Asia Watch*, in which he found that Cambodia has 'the highest percentage of physically disabled inhabitants of any country in the world'. He revealed that surgeons perform between 300 and 700 amputations a month because of injuries from mines.[23]

Mrs Thatcher had told Parliament that there 'is no British Government involvement of any kind in training, equipping or co-operating with the Khmer Rouge forces or those allied to them'. However, in June 1991, Armed Forces Minister Archie Hamilton was forced to admit that the government had 'provided training to the armed forces of the Cambodian non-communist resistance'. Officials maintained that it was designed to assist the forces of Prince Sihanouk and strengthen his position in relation to the Khmer Rouge. The following month in London, Cambodia's defence minister, General Tea Banh, acknowledged that the Khmer Rouge had indirectly benefited from British training. He said that the Khmer Rouge had infiltrated the two non-communist factions of the coalition formed to combat the Vietnamese who had overthrown Pol Pot in 1978. It was known that the three guerrilla groups 'share everything'.[24]

John Pilger maintains – to much personal abuse – that the SAS did train the Khmer Rouge directly; something which caused a 'mini-rebellion' among the SAS personnel and which was regarded with 'mounting tension' by officials in the MoD. In the wake of publicity, support for Pol Pot's men became 'very much more covert', with MI6 becoming more directly involved with help from the American embassy. MI6 employed, on contract, former full-time SAS soldiers in teams of one officer and six soldiers. Some came from 'R' squadron – officially described as 'Territorials' – containing some of the regiment's more experienced soldiers, who are considered the most reliable for deniable operations. According to one senior SAS officer, they first went to Thailand in 1984, attached to the Thai army. 'We trained the Khmer Rouge in a lot of technical stuff – a lot about mines. The very latest mines were used that came originally from Royal Ordnance in Britain, which we got by way of Egypt, with markings changed.' Until November 1989 and his withdrawal from the post, the teams were answerable to the MI6 station chief in Bangkok, a former SAS officer who had served in the Gulf. In 1991, the Cambodian government had to employ another British firm, Hazardous Areas Life Support, to begin clearing the mines from the countryside.[25]

In May 1992, on the anniversary of the Falklands War, in an echo of Dean Acheson's statement, made thirty years previously, that Britain had lost an empire but had failed to find a new role, American military historian and strategist Professor Edward Luttwak mocked Britain's victory and reasoned that

'Argentinian air power could finally have achieved Britain's inordinately delayed liberation from the iron grip of its own myths'. Central to these myths has been the relationship between the 'Cousins' (CIA) and the 'Friends' (MI6) developed during the Second World War which, as Kim Philby remarked, 'doomed the British Services, in the long run, to junior status'. In 1978, Chapman Pincher wrote that 'Britain is totally dependent on the USA for intelligence . . . dependence is so great and co-operation so close . . . that the security and intelligence chiefs would go to any length to protect their linkup'. During the Thatcher years there was no threat and the link apparently thrived.[26]

Senior diplomats in the Washington embassy play down talk of a special relationship because 'it implies a crawling obsequiousness or that the Americans owe us something'. It is known as the 'natural relationship'. The fact is 'they have other special relationships. But with us there is a quality of naturalness they have with nobody else.' Some analysts were claiming, during the Gulf War, that Anglo-American co-operation had returned to the levels of the Cold War and even the Second World War. While this was an exaggeration, since the war was an American show – sometimes events unfolded too fast for Whitehall assessments to be fully evaluated and passed on to the Cousins – British diplomats said that there was an 'undoubted closeness'. 'You can talk to any American. They are completely open with us. There is a different set of rules for the Brits.' The special intelligence link was said to have worked 'like clockwork'.[27]

The special intelligence link could not, however, hide the poor record of the British intelligence community – caught napping over the fall of the Shah, the Falklands, the Iraq supergun and finally the invasion of Kuwait.

26

The Defence Intelligence Staff

The Cinderella of the secret services.

The Times, 2 April 1984

The Secret Intelligence Service receives the majority of its specific directives from the Ministry of Defence, with whose intelligence service, the 'stolid and unglamorous' Defence Intelligence Staff (DIS), it works in close co-operation. Established in 1964, as a central unified intelligence organisation, the DIS is 'an often forgotten and frequently underestimated branch of the intelligence community', which provides a round-the-clock regime of intelligence gathering and objective all-source assessments of defence intelligence matters.[1]

The DIS was created by a fusion of the Naval, Military and Air intelligence organisations, MoD security departments and the Joint Intelligence Bureau, which provided analysis based on military considerations and political, economic and psychological factors connected with the national interest. The creation of the DIS met with fierce criticism from those who held the old agencies in high regard, but it has been claimed that its increased efficiency achieved savings of 30 per cent in manpower and a better product for the Chiefs of Staff. It was also intended to meet, more effectively, the need for a second Whitehall centre of world-wide intelligence to set alongside the political assessment fed into the Joint Intelligence Committee. In particular, it was meant to provide practical assessments of 'what may be on the other side of the hill' ranged against NATO and to take the long view on the Soviet economy, technology and weaponry. Its primary task during the Cold War was to provide a warning of preparations for war by a potential enemy, in particular, detailing the threat posed by the military might of the Soviet Union and the forces of the Warsaw Pact. The agency has not had a perfect record and has occasionally delivered 'bad' intelligence. David Owen recalls that before leaving the MoD on the evening of 21 August 1968, he read highly classified reports on Czechoslovakia which 'said there would be no invasion. I was then woken up to be told that the Russians were invading.'[2]

With the end of the Cold War, the role of the DIS has been thrown into some confusion. However, the service's brief is world-wide and it also studies defence industries, economic aspects of defence, scientific and technical developments, nuclear proliferation, chemical and biological weapons, and arms traffic and control. The DIS, which has nearly ninety individual departments, relies on overt, official and covert sources of information – the 150 defence attachés stationed abroad in sixty-five missions are supplied by the DIS and are *de facto* intelligence officers. Naval and air force units concentrate on signals, electronic and photographic surveillance from their remaining foreign bases and specially equipped vessels and aircraft. Undeveloped film is processed at the Joint Air Reconnaissance Intelligence Centre at Huntingdon, which played an important role during the Gulf War. The intelligence is assessed alongside material drawn from the 'corporate memory', its huge computerised database. DIS 'product', which is tailored to meet customers' specific needs – including those of the MoD, Defence Export Services Organisation, NATO, the United States and 'certain government departments' i.e. the Joint Intelligence Committee, GCHQ and MI6 – is handled by a central secretariat which acts as the 'front office' for the DIS. The DIS also has a responsibility for the internal defence of the British state, including involvement in Northern Ireland, requiring it to keep in close liaison with MI5, which has its own office within the MoD. Its reports and assessments on IRA strength and capabilities appear to have been both realistic and accurate.[3]

According to Louis Le Bailly, who served for three years as Director-General of Intelligence of the DIS, the principal task of the DGI is 'To tell those who won't listen all the things they don't want to know.' The staff have to 'collate and analyse the several million separate items of intelligence received each year and then distil these into a coherent picture of the enemy's intentions . . . then the DGI has to feed this picture into current discussions on national strategy or Service discussions on tactics and weapon procurement.' Below the DGI, Chief Air Marshal Sir John Walker, three director-generals cover the former Warsaw Pact, Rest of the World, and Scientific and Technical Subjects, with a fourth directorate looking after the Management and Support of Intelligence. The latter provides military support to other intelligence agencies – including several major eavesdropping posts for GCHQ and the MI6 training school at Gosport, which is disguised as an Army training camp.[4]

The DIS Scientific and Technical officers are posted to the agency from MoD research establishments, while the Intelligence officers are normally retired service officers embarking on a second career. A number of Research and Linguist officers are recruited from university as long-term professional intelligence officers, but not nearly enough to satisfy the demand for analysts and a high quality of assessment. Although the primary aim of its officers is, according to one analyst, 'to try and get into the cranium of the man in Moscow', a competence in the Russian language 'has never been seen as a significant professional requirement'. Government cut-backs in education have meant that there are relatively few linguists specialising in the languages useful to the intelligence services. Much of the analysis is undertaken by military men 'on temporary desk-work ("Driving a desk" as they self-derisively call it)', so the creation of graduate-level civilian experts has not been fully undertaken. The prospects for research officers are not good and the pay has been depressed, thus restricting the recruitment of the best graduates.[5]

Intelligence analysts distinguish between 'hardware', which

means equipment, troops, order-of-battle, and 'software', which covers 'not only political intentions, but combat readiness, training, morale, non-military distractions'. Hardware changes slowly, while software is much more unpredictable, particularly now when the future of the former countries of the Soviet Union looks so uncertain and the status of their armed forces is difficult to verify. According to Peter Hennessy, 'The mercurial nature of "software" factors pushes intelligence analysts towards the view that "hardware" is what really matters – what kind of advanced weaponry a future set of "nasties" in the Kremlin would have at their disposal.' Here the horizon is the turn of the century and beyond. The DIS appears in the past to have over-compensated for previous failures by over-inflating the potential of the 'hardware' and presenting the politicians with 'worst case scenarios'.[6]

In 1989, Sir Reginald Hibbert, a former member of the Special Operations Executive and the Foreign Office diplomat where he had extensive contact with the intelligence agencies, attacked the over-reliance on 'hardware' analysis in a lecture on 'Intelligence and Policy'. He believed that 'through being a bit more occupied with weapons counts than with the study of human beings and human institutions, British official thinking about the Soviet Union and Eastern Europe had been taken more by surprise by perestroika than it needed to have been'. He went on to say that any real improvement in the quality of assessment 'probably depends on opening it to a wider circle of informed criticism and checking the trend of the past few decades towards secrecy, exclusiveness and narrowness'. Michael Herman, former MI6 officer and a research fellow of Nuffield College, Oxford, believes that while the intelligence community has 'admirable national arrangements for the production of interdepartmentally-agreed assessments' the system lacked 'the orchestration of the long-range official research on which these assessments ultimately depend'. Herman posits that 'the work has depended too long on luck, improvisation and the fortunate availability of one or two exceptional people who cannot go on for ever'. He possibly had in mind the leading Kremlinologist, Malcolm Mackintosh, who worked for MI6 on a study group on the Soviet Union in the fifties and then ran the Soviet desk in the Cabinet Office, a post he held until his retirement in 1987.[7]

The DIS failure to conduct a systematic assessment of open Soviet military sources has drawn some criticism. A *Times* editorial on 11 December 1991 concluded that there were better ways of gathering intelligence than by the use of secret intelligence agencies. It asserted that attention to the specialised and general media would produce more reliable results than the efforts of this 'useless profession'. It is a view shared by those who exercise oversight of the intelligence agencies in the United States. Senator Joe Bidden, who has seen many intelligence reports, and John Rich, a deputy staff director of the Senate Foreign Relations Committee, wrote a paper for the *Georgetown Law Journal* in which they suggested that a good journalist's analysis of events abroad was often better than a highly classified CIA report. Michael Herman believes that with proper funding more attention to open sources would reap benefits for the intelligence community.[8]

However, Herman recognises that while 'the unglamorous activity of culling books and newspapers for useful information is an essential element of the intelligence business' it has been usual practice for the DIS to regard such sources as 'an occasional bonus rather than part of the mainstream, especially in time of limited resources'. There has been a general fear throughout the intelligence services that 'overt material may be a vehicle for deception'. Paradoxically, covert sources were to be trusted more than open ones; a view articulated by Sir Peter Tennant in a reply to the *Times* editorial. Tennant, who helped set up the 'shadow' Ministry of Information at the beginning of the Second World War, wrote that the use of covert means was sometimes necessary to discern the truth because the KGB and its allies so often planted misinformation in the press. In his book *The Soviet Military*, Air Commodore

E. Williams dismissed the idea of wholesale disinformation as it presupposed 'a double bluff of a magnitude beyond even the capabilities of the Soviet propaganda machine'. In published Soviet military debates of the technical problems of non-nuclear operations, he discovered that the charge of disinformation was unfounded: 'On the whole, the debates were remarkable for the frankness with which problems and failures were discussed, and they were marked by a distinct lack of ideological claptrap'. Herman believed that assessing published Soviet sources provided a 'distinctive flavour of seeking to view the Soviet armed forces through indigenous eyes, without the distorting mirror of Western cultural and professional preconceptions'.[9]

There are, inevitably, areas on which there is little published material and the intelligence services do have to resort to covert intelligence gathering. However, when the gathering of intelligence in closed societies such as the former Soviet Union and Iraq proves difficult, there has been a temptation to manipulate the evidence to suit preconceived ideas or political initiatives. Such a case occurred in the summer of 1984 when Mrs Thatcher set up an ultra-secret ministerial committee, without a Cabinet name or number, to consider proposals to start production of nerve gas. In the spring of that year, the Joint Intelligence Committee had prepared a report on the chemical warfare capability of the Soviet Union. The JIC report claimed that the Soviets had stockpiled some 300,000 tonnes of modern chemical agents. Members of the committee and the military Chiefs of Staff, who prepared the options for a British response, were given background intelligence drawn up by MoD staff – 'to the surprise of the service chiefs the DIS briefing was short on hard facts and information about Soviet intentions . . . it emerged that there was very little information available'. According to Dr Julian Robinson of Sussex University, an authority on chemical and biological warfare, all that the JIC had done was to take an average of wildly differing estimates from the United States.[10]

As the Directorate of Scientific and Technical Intelligence assessment had shown, there was no means of predicting the size with any degree of accuracy. A 1983 United States Special National Intelligence Estimate, which undermined the JIC claim that the Soviet stockpile was 'massive and growing', produced a figure of between 50,000 and 100,000 tonnes, only slightly larger than America's own stockpile. However, a political decision had been taken and 'questions designed to highlight the Joint Intelligence Committee's assessment of the Soviet "threat" were planted in Parliament, while some of the contents of the JIC report were subsequently leaked by senior military officers to the *Sunday Times* at the end of August [1984]'. Disinformation included the spurious claim that one task of the Soviet special forces, the Spetsnaz, would be 'to release chemical weapons deep behind the enemy front line, in Washington and London, to create the maximum possible disruption'. These were the opening shots in a campaign by the protagonists of chemical weaponry, including the Chiefs of Staff who were said, according to a senior MoD official, to be 'all for it'. Using the dubious JIC figures, the British government put considerable pressure on the Reagan administration, which in 1985 persuaded Congress to authorise the resumption of chemical weapons production.[11]

To bolster their case, the Chiefs of Staff went outside the intelligence community to an Army expert on Soviet strategy, Brigadier John Hemsley. He produced a classified report, while a second unclassified report supporting the view of the Chiefs was published as a book by the Royal United Services Institute in 1987. The publication angered the DIS, which responded by sending the Special Branch to interview Hemsley about possible breaches of the Official Secrets Act; but there turned out to be none. The case illustrated a point made by former DGI Vice-Admiral Sir Louis Le Bailly that 'at one time or another' DIS customers are 'unwilling to face the facts as served up. The pressures to trim assessments, either for reasons of prejudice ("We know better"), or lack of understanding or, more often, plain wishful thinking are powerful and persistent'.[12]

While the DIS appears to have had no accurate intelligence on Soviet chemical stockpiles, it later gained access to a Russian scientist who worked on a secret biological weapons programme. Dr Vladimir Pasechnik, former head of a 'civilian' research institute, was kept under wraps by MI6 but his intelligence proved invaluable in persuading Russian leaders to reveal details of their biological stockpiles and it helped form the basis of a US intelligence report to Congress in March 1992. Pasechnik's institute is now the subject of intensive surveillance by MI6 and the CIA.

The failure to exploit open sources is mirrored by the dismissal of the views and assessments of outside bodies which sometimes have proved to be more accurate than government departments. This concerned the House of Commons Foreign Affairs Committee which, following a review of the Soviet invasion of Afghanistan, investigated evidence that knowledge of the invasion had been foreshadowed in the Soviet press. The Committee persuaded the Foreign Office to agree to close co-operation between academic bodies and government departments, including the MoD. However, it appears that 'nothing much happened as a result' – a view confirmed by former MoD civil servant Clive Ponting, who revealed that studies published by the respected London-based International Institute for Strategic Studies (IISS) were usually greeted with 'amused contempt'. The view of the Permanent Secretaries was that such bodies did not know enough to join in the 'advanced' level of debate inside the MoD. This is, however, a circular argument, since Whitehall is not prepared to release information to outsiders even when it is, in fact, unclassified. The decision-making process is deliberately shrouded in mystery, and the Official Secrets Act, which Ponting described as 'the cement that holds the closed world of Whitehall together', is routinely used to hide mistakes, failures and inefficiency.[13]

This was starkly illustrated by the 1991 edition of *The*

Military Balance, published by the IISS, which concluded that key assumptions about the Soviet Union made by the military planners during the eighties were wrong. 'Developments which began in 1988 in Soviet defence policy to reduce the size of the armed forces . . . have led to the collapse of the Warsaw Pact as a military alliance.' It also said that the Soviet Union's Gross National Product was only a third of that of the United States and not a half as assumed. Other sources confirmed that the rate of growth of Warsaw Pact forces had been wildly overestimated, while the command structure differed from the assumptions made. In truth, the DIS analysts pay little heed to revisionist studies of the Cold War which suggest that the 'whole huge and costly enterprise of the British defence programme was based on a misconception'. The whole basis of their work centred on the notion of a 'forward' USSR policy which planned that any future war would start in someone else's territory and not on Soviet soil. The Western response would, therefore, be required to meet this 'forward' policy. Such thought patterns would appear to have little relevance in the new world, but whether any changes have been made in DIS philosophy is not known. The MoD, despite recent cuts, does not seem to have altered its basic orientation towards the former Soviet bloc.[14]

In 1983, the case of Lance Corporal Philip Aldridge, a young Intelligence Corps NCO on temporary secondment to the DIS in the busy aftermath of the Falklands War, who was employed destroying secret documents, revealed that security procedures were lax. Aldridge, who was hoping to sell a JIC weekly assessment to the Russians, was unmasked by MI5. In the mood of general economy in Whitehall, Defence Secretary Michael Heseltine introduced a review and implementation of the management information system known as 'minis'. The DIS, whose employees numbered a thousand, suffered a series of cuts of up to 35 per cent.[15]

The DIS was reorganised again in 1988, when the economic section was disbanded, and there have been further changes under the Options for Change review following the end of the Cold War, which took away its primary target. The DIS's intelligence product, portrayed by the service as a 'force multiplier' which enables ministers to deploy foreign and defence capabilities to maximum effect in times of uncertainty, has not proved to be entirely reliable. The service was as surprised as the man in the street by the pace and direction of change in the Soviet bloc, while ministers have yet to come to grips with the new direction. There is some uncertainty about the DIS's own future; however, alterations to the old War Office, which is currently being gutted, continue in preparation for the service's new headquarters. The cost, originally estimated at £9 million, has shot up to more than £40 million, mainly as a result of the problems in installing a large mainframe computer, which requires a carefully controlled environment, into a hundred-year-old building. This takes place despite persistent rumours that, as part of the general review of intelligence by Whitehall, MI6 is tipped to absorb some DIS and Treasury intelligence sections. Increasingly, the DIS has been overseeing the centralisation of the information needed to verify arms control treaties and the collection of details of the stockpiles of conventional weapons in the former Warsaw Pact. It also plays a leading role in assessing the current arms race in the Middle East and Asia.[16]

Perhaps more than with any other agency, the 'cobwebs of secrecy' which shield the Defence Intelligence Staff need to be blown away. Certainly, its poor performance during the Gulf War begs a number of questions about the role, direction and worth of the service and, a point frequently overlooked, its accountability. An over-reliance on electronic and signals intelligence failed to provide information on the Iraqi invasion of Kuwait, while its assessment of the Iraqi 'order of battle' was remarkably inaccurate. This is precisely the sort of intelligence the DIS was set up to provide, and here it failed.

27

Desert Storm

No worries . . . there is no serious threat.

British embassy diplomat, Kuwait, 31 July 1990

Former MI6 chief Sir Dick White, who died in February 1993, had said in the wake of Saddam Hussein's invasion of Kuwait on 2 August 1990 that 'It is very common practice to say that those who have to produce intelligence, don't produce it when it's needed most.' MI6 apologists, stung by the criticism of the service for failing to predict the invasion, pointed out to Phillip Knightley that 'in a closed society such as Iraq, intelligence is not easy to gather . . . the Service, no doubt, knew quite accurately the strength of Saddam Hussein's forces – it was what he intended to do with them that was difficult to tell.' However, the picture was more complicated than these off-the-cuff remarks suggested; there were significant 'intelligence gaps'.[1]

In January 1992, the International Institute for Strategic Studies published *The Gulf Conflict: A Political and Strategic Analysis*, which identified three key failures of Allied intelligence: failure to predict the invasion of Kuwait, overestimation of the strength of Iraqi forces in the Kuwait theatre of operations (KTO); and ignorance of the extent of Iraq's nuclear programme. The CIA had provided the White House with clear satellite intelligence showing that Saddam Hussein's forces were massing in sufficient strength to invade Kuwait, but President Bush appears to have overruled the warnings. Even the US analysts were caught napping when the tanks did finally roll over the border, and the American intelligence does not appear to have been passed on to the 'friends' at Century House.[2]

MI6, with its 'camel corps' of Arabian scholars, has always prided itself on its special knowledge of the Middle East and its strong links with many of the intelligence services of the region. However, MI6's intelligence gathering was deficient on this occasion and, at the same time, Foreign Office was not in an ideal position to assess what little intelligence was forwarded. At the start of the conflict, the British ambassador in Baghdad, Harold Walker, was on holiday in England, while the senior official on the Middle East desk was abroad elsewhere. Some of the agent handling was incompetent and contributed to a general failure in intelligence gathering. A senior MI6 office ran a source in Oman who provided top-class intelligence, but the agent became disillusioned with his case officer and transferred his loyalties to the Defence Intelligence Staff. According to the *Guardian*, one MI6 officer stationed in the Middle East did correctly predict the invasion but his dispatch was rubbished by his ambassador, who was later rewarded with a knighthood. Another report filed to London stated that an invasion would not happen, though it is said that this was because field reports are expected to be negative or positive in their assessment, never inbetween. Several days before Iraqi troops crossed the border, business executives based in Kuwait were told by embassy diplomats that there was 'no real serious threat'. MI6 had concluded that a full-scale invasion was 'very remote'. The Foreign Office had 'no hard evidence' that Saddam was going to invade and appears to have accepted his word that he 'wasn't going to'. George Carver, former deputy for National Intelligence at the CIA, thought that this was an analytical error of 'mirror imaging' on the part of the Foreign Office and MI6, both of which had assumed that Saddam would see the world in essentially the same way as they did.[3]

The Foreign Office made its assessment of Saddam's likely intentions in the knowledge that the government wanted to see increased trade with Iraq. It was prepared to forgive the Iraqi leader almost anything in the hope of restoring friendly relations, following the execution of the journalist Farzad Bazoft. Unlike with the Soviet threat, the Joint Intelligence Committee was willing to soft-pedal its assessment and, in this instance, did not present ministers with a 'worst-case scenario'. There were parallels with the Falklands; sources told Richard Norton-Taylor that Whitehall's judgement was 'distorted by wishful thinking: the JIC persuaded itself, and then ministers, to believe what it wanted to believe – namely that Saddam was bluffing and would stop short of an invasion of Kuwait.' Former Foreign Secretary David Owen thought he detected 'some evidence that [the] refusal to think ill of military dictators was still dominant in the British and American intelligence communities in the summer of 1990 when Iraq invaded Kuwait'.[4]

Once the invasion took place, MI6 opened new channels to friendly intelligence services in the region in an attempt to assess the Iraqi leader's next move; the general consensus was that he had no intention of invading Saudi Arabia. However, US intelligence agencies prepared a comprehensive satellite analysis which convinced the Saudis that Iraq was indeed poised to move south. So began Operation Desert Shield, the protection of Saudi Arabia, during which a great deal of time and effort were spent trying to obtain information on Saddam Hussein and his inner circle. Intelligence officers began drawing up lists of potential targets connected with his ruling clan. Britain, because of its long involvement with Iraq and its training of the Iraqi military, had a small number of agents who unfortunately, depending on which accounts one reads, yielded little or no intelligence; they proved to be inadequate and an unreliable source for the planning of successful covert operations.[5]

MI6 did achieve one major intelligence coup during Desert Storm, the removal of Iraqi forces from Kuwait, when the chair of the KGB, Vladimir Kryuchkov, offered to hand over intelligence about Iraq's military capabilities. Offers of co-operation had been made in the past but had always been rebuffed by the CIA, so this time the Soviets chose London rather than Washington as the channel for intelligence liaison.

However, this intelligence bonus did not appear to help the Defence Intelligence Staff in their assessment of the Iraqi military strength in Kuwait. The detailed information derived from surveillance by satellites, aircraft and listening to Iraqi broadcasts appears to have mesmerised the analysts. The estimates were wildly inaccurate.[6]

Iraq's order of battle (ORBAT) was assessed from the whole range of electronic intelligence gathering by the massive technological resources of the Coalition forces. The programme of 'ferret' satellites which was at the centre of the intelligence effort was run by the US National Reconnaissance Office, an organisation which until late 1992 did not officially exist. The prime reason it was not acknowledged, according to former CIA director William E. Colby, was the 'diplomatic objection that other nations would create difficulties if they were compelled to admit that many of their tightly protected secrets were in fact not secret at all'. Since its inception in 1960, the NRO has cost the American taxpayer over $100 billion. Other countries, including a consortium of France, Italy and Spain with Helios, Israel, India and Germany, are exploring similar options in setting up their own military satellite programme. Britain's electronic spy satellite, Zircon, is believed to have been put into orbit in 1989 in a position which enabled it to survey the Persian Gulf.[7]

American giant 'electronic vacuum cleaners' – the signals intelligence ('SIGINT') satellites Magnum and Vortex – monitored Iraqi radio signals and telephone conversations, while photographic (PHOTINT) satellites code-named Kennan and Crystal and a short-wave radar satellite, Lacrosse, which can see through cloud cover and smoke, crossed the Gulf once a day. The photo-reconnaissance Keyhole satellite series, KH-11, are capable of a resolution in good conditions of six inches, and in average conditions of between one and three feet wide. This array of surveillance equipment could easily discern troop movements, marshalling of troops and vehicles, roads and aircraft. Although the photographic satellites normally operate only during daylight, new advanced versions use night-vision sensors and provide colour images which can detect the use of camouflage. The various satellites were linked to a batch of British and Allied signal listening ground stations. However, the cover provided by these satellites is not perfect and for twenty-one hours of the day Iraq was out of range of each individual satellite. Additional intelligence came from the many American reconnaissance aircraft, including the SR-71 'Blackbird' spy planes which flew from the British base at Alconbury, Cambridgeshire, to the Middle East, carrying electronic intelligence (ELINT), side-looking radar and infra-red cameras.[8]

The Nuringa satellite station in Australia, staffed by American and Australian signals personnel, was part of a string of monitoring posts which tracked Scud missiles as they were fired from Iraq, providing early warning of an attack on Israel. However, the tracking was not able to pinpoint the firing sites as the Scud launchers were mobile and able to be moved quickly. Photographic interpreters (PIs), or imagery analysts, were especially active in trying to pinpoint the site of the Scud launchers, which General Schwarzkopf, commander of the coalition forces, admitted was like 'seeking a needle in a haystack'. The PIs, 'chosen for their intelligence, analytical minds and ability to communicate their findings' had little success in spotting the Scud sites.[9]

Similarly, there was little success with monitoring COMINT – communication signals of both voice and data. Landline communications cannot be intercepted and Saddam Hussein was very adept at using a 'hard wired' fibre optics system, buried underground, to exchange messages with his commanders. Because of this problem, the goal became to 'force him on the air where communications became more revealed'. Saddam himself had been a target for elimination, but the massive electronic intelligence effort failed to discover his exact whereabouts.[10]

Inside the American embassy in Grosvenor Square, London,

is the Special US Liaison Office which is the link between the code-breakers of the National Security Agency (NSA) and its British counterpart, GCHQ. Military analysts working at the two agencies were able, using their Cray supercomputers, to break most of the Iraqi military codes routinely collected from the thousands of intercepted and deciphered messages from the Middle East, code-named 'Umbra', which passed through Grosvenor Square each day. As part of the UK–USA pact, which covers the collaboration between Britain, the United States, Canada and Australia in monitoring the world's communications, GCHQ has responsibility for Europe, Africa and the Middle East. GCHQ has a string of eavesdropping stations in the Middle East providing ELINT and SIGINT, including one in Kuwait which helped to provide intelligence about Iraq's military capabilities. During the Gulf War, bases in Turkey, including the American Diogenes station at Sinop, manned by GCHQ technicians, were switched from monitoring Soviet missile tests to watching Iraqi targets. A GCHQ base at Abut, Oman, which uses NSA-financed surveillance equipment, scooped up intelligence on Iraqi air power which it then sent to an American base at Bad Aibling in West Germany. From there it was passed on to Fort Meade, Maryland. Another vital link was the British radio base run by the Army's No.9 Signals Regiment at Ayios Nikolaos, Cyprus, six hundred miles from Baghdad. This became the main Western listening post for monitoring Iraqi military forces' and diplomatic signals.[11]

There were, however, not enough Arabic speakers to translate the mountain of intercepts harvested from the listening posts. 'You can tap everything. The difficulty is differentiating between signal and noise or the important and the trivial.' Nor were there enough analysts to make the data intelligible to the commanders in the field. There were further problems in disseminating satellite intelligence to personnel in 'real time', i.e. as it happened. 'Constant Source' was the code-name of a development from the US Defense Department programme,

Tactical Employment of National Capabilities, under which information from spy satellites was channelled to personnel on the ground. However, a lack of suitable equipment capable of transmitting the data to dispersed sites away from the command centre at Riyadh meant that much of the intelligence gathering was wasted. The dissemination was also hampered by the sheer volume of material which swamped headquarters and left military managers responsible for air strikes in Kuwait 'overwhelmed with data'. There are occasions when there is just too much intelligence, which can paralyse operations and decisions.[12]

Allied intelligence believed that there were 540,000 Iraqi troops in the Kuwait theatre of operations (KTO). The British figure was even higher at 590,000, and at one point went up to 623,000 before being revised down to 'over half a million'. The DIS had estimated that there were thirty-six to thirty-eight Iraqi divisions in the KTO with a 'paper strength' of 15,000. However, there was no reliable 'HUMINT' – human intelligence – as to the exact strength of the divisions. They were assumed to be at full strength, whereas in reality some were as low as 50 per cent. There were, at most, 300,000 soldiers, and even this may be an overly optimistic estimate as it is known that several of Saddam's best divisions were withdrawn before the Allied thrust into Southern Iraq and Kuwait was launched. There were reports that photo interpreters repeatedly lost track of Iraqi units and, on one occasion, the entire 80,000-strong Republican Guard was lost. No intelligence analysis can be expected to be perfect, but there was embarrassment all round when a Florida newspaper, the *St Petersburg Times*, checked the Pentagon's figure by buying satellite photographs of Kuwait from a Soviet commercial agency. Experts who viewed them discovered no sign of a massive Iraqi military build-up. There had either been a major intelligence failure or the figures had been massaged in the run-up to Desert Storm.[13]

Estimates made by the intelligence services before the Gulf

War about Iraq's nuclear bomb programme assumed that the country was ten years away from producing a viable weapon. More by default than design, this appears to have been a reasonably accurate assessment. It would seem that Iraq managed to hide what it had or had not achieved from the prying eyes of the world's most sophisticated intelligence services. The various agencies did not have reliable intelligence and, in the propaganda battle, resorted to guesswork in order to satisfy political requirements. At the beginning of the conflict, the CIA announced that Saddam was at least two years away from producing a bomb, but when it became necessary to bolster support for the war, the world was informed that Iraq had the capability to build a crude nuclear weapon 'within six months'. The *Sunday Times* went further, citing a figure of 'two months' from an American Defence Intelligence Agency (DIA) report. Intelligence sources conceded that the DIA report had been designed to frighten the politicians into action.[14]

Much of the later information on Saddam's nuclear ambitions was provided by Iraqi scientists who defected to the Coalition between May and December 1991. They alerted military debriefers to Iraq's investment in electromagnetic enrichment, using machines know as calutrons. They also pinpointed the location of a secret cache of documents which proved Iraq was engaged in designing nuclear warheads. During 1992, MI6 and CIA officers set up a base at Amman, Jordan, to attract more defectors, whose information was subsequently fed to the United Nations Special Commission; this later helped investigate and destroy Iraq's secret stockpiles of weapons of mass destruction. Iraqi claims that the UN special teams visiting Baghdad were a tool of the CIA, while inaccurate, were not entirely wide of the mark. The Commission does work hand-in-glove with Western intelligence agencies; although the Special Commission is based at UN headquarters in New York, it takes its direction from Washington and, according to the *Independent* sources, 'has close links with US intelligence, the CIA and the National Security Agency'. A British member of the team, Bill Weir, who worked for the DIS, was closely involved in the destruction of the supergun.[15]

These intelligence ties became apparent during a well-publicised incident, when members of a Commission team were blockaded in a car park in Baghdad with the cache of documents which they had successfully removed from a government building. Deputy team leader Robert Gallucci, a former State Department arms control expert, used the UN satellite telephone to transmit details of the seized documents directly to the State Department's operations room. After leaving Baghdad, the documents did not immediately show up at International Atomic Energy Authority (IAEA) headquarters in Vienna but they were copied, translated and analysed by American officials before being passed on several weeks later. For these underhand actions, the UN Secretary General felt it necessary to rebuke Dr David Kay, the team leader.[16]

Dr Kay was not a nuclear engineer or physicist but was due to join the Uranium Institute in London, which trades in uranium and spent nuclear fuel. He played a very high-profile role within the Special Commission which uncovered Iraq's Petrochemical Three (PC-3) nuclear bomb programme. In October 1991, he suggested that Iraq was only two months away from developing a nuclear weapon. This, however, was clearly untrue. In May 1992, the IAEA was reported as suggesting that when the Gulf War began, Iraq was at least three years away from producing a single small bomb of uncertain reliability. This was later amended to at least 1995 or 1996. Even this turned out to be optimistic, based as it was on the unlikely prospect of the programme progressing without technical problems or hindrance.[17]

MI6 and the DIS lacked any intelligence on whether Iraq had a working centrifuge for producing weapons-grade uranium, although they were well aware that Saddam had made efforts to obtain the necessary technology. UN inspectors discovered that Matrix Churchill machine tools were used to make components for gas centrifuges and calutrons. Despite MI6 having intelligence assets within Matrix, secret briefing notes reveal that intelligence assurances had been made to officials that the company was not involved in supplying Iraq with nuclear technology. They were surprised by the discovery that Iraq had been trying to use unreliable techniques, developed during the Second World War, to produce enriched uranium. However, at the time of the Gulf War, Iraq did not have an enrichment factory in operation and the UN inspectors failed to find a single working centrifuge or calutron. Frank Barnaby, former director of the Stockholm International Peace Research Institute, found that the intelligence estimates were 'more propaganda than based on what is technically feasible'. He said that it would take at least five years and possibly twice as long for Iraq to produce weapons suitable for military requirements.[18]

Intelligence on chemical weapons appears to have been just as vague. In February 1991, British defence sources claimed that Iraq had moved chemical weapons forward to the front line and had distributed them to artillery and multiple-rocket launcher units which had the authority to use them 'at will'. A senior Cabinet source told the *Sunday Express* that the intelligence had been derived from satellite observation. During the war, journalists who met Army field intelligence officers were given bogus details of the stock held by the Iraqis in front-line positions. There never was any evidence for the intelligence estimates and, despite the consistent publicity given to this threat, no large stocks of chemical weapons were discovered in Kuwait. Likewise, the UN inspectors concluded that, although Iraq had been experimenting, it did not have actual biological, as against chemical, warfare weapons. The chemical stockpile threat was one of many disinformation projects swallowed wholesale by the media during Desert Storm.[19]

Military 'minders' attached to the British Joint Information Bureau controlled the 'pool' reporting and the flow of information during the war. Few journalists were willing to leave the pool and jeopardise their lifeline to the MoD and the Foreign Office and were thus easy prey to the manipulation of the psychological-warfare warriors. Following government cut-backs and the closure of the psy-ops training course at the Army Intelligence Centre at Ashford, Kent, the MoD lacked the necessary experienced and qualified operators and was forced to recall out of retirement a number of old hands from the propaganda war in Northern Ireland. Observers were surprised to see Colonel David McDine, who, in 1975, had retired after suffering a heart-attack, make an appearance on television during the Gulf War. He had been in overall charge of Information Policy, a special unit which dealt in black propaganda. Its commander, Colonel Jeremy Railton, who had retired to Wiltshire to run a pig farm, also turned up in the Gulf.[20]

Despite the sophistication of the commentators and the audience, the 'spectacle' of massive media coverage and continuous analysis of the campaign enabled the flow of disinformation to proceed largely undetected. It seemed to confirm James Angleton's dictum that 'disinformation might be the chief job of an intelligence agency'. Those brave enough to stand firm and present a more balanced view of the war were discredited with smears. Here are some of the many and varied disinformation projects, ranging from the tragic to the laughable, run during Desert Storm by Allied Intelligence and press 'minders':[21]

- The first had shades of some of the funnier efforts of Information Policy. It was alleged that computer viruses ('Trojan horses') had been planted in radar equipment, jet fighters and guns sold to Iraq by France. The Paris daily, *Libération*, and the *Sunday Telegraph* reported that 'if hostilities break out, radar screens could be blanked out, planes become uncontrollable and Exocet missiles set to crash before hitting their target'.[22]
- At the beginning of January 1991, the BBC reported that 'a steady stream' of Iraqi soldiers had surrendered while Iraqi helicopter pilots had defected to Saudi Arabia. Journalists

were told that the helicopters had been escorted by a United States fighter to a base inside Saudi, where the crews were being interrogated. On another occasion, fifty tank crews were reported to have defected to Egyptian forces. All three claims turned out to be untrue. In the initial stages, defections amounted to a 'trickle', but the stories – embellished with convincing details – made the headlines.[23]

- Special forces were depicted in the press and in subsequent accounts as the 'true unsung heroes of the war'. In January 1991, the *Sunday Times* reported that the SAS had stolen a surface-to-air missile in Kuwait and had delivered it to Saudi Arabia for dismantling. Later it was 'reliably' reported by American sources that as many as one-third of the Scud launchers destroyed by fighter aircraft had been identified and targeted by SAS men. According to the *Sunday Telegraph*, after the conflict Prime Minister John Major told an Anglo-Israeli dinner: 'I'll tell you who destroyed the Scuds; it was the SAS. They were fabulous.' The *Daily Telegraph* reported in January 1991 that 'initial allied sorties took out the bulk of static launch sites . . . later attacks found eleven mobile launchers. Six were destroyed although bad weather prevented the rest being hit.' During the campaign intelligence officers told journalists, off the record, that *only* two hundred Scud batteries had been destroyed. All these claims turned out to be untrue. Intelligence analysts who later reviewed their assessments concluded that the Allies had failed to destroy a single Scud launcher. Film released during the war showing the destruction of launchers is thought to have depicted the bombing of a fuel tanker convoy. Over-optimistic claims by pilots and SAS personnel hid a major intelligence and military failure.[24]
- Diplomats who were 'eager to release their information' claimed, and it was prominently reported in the newspapers, that Saddam Hussein's wife had fled Iraq to seek refuge in, first, the military-ruled Islamic state of Mauritania, and, second, a few days later, in Zambia.[25]
- United States intelligence 'conclusively' identified the powdered milk factory which was bombed by the Allies as a 'biological weapons plant'. Film evidence at the time

contradicted this statement, but the BBC's defence correspondent, Christopher Lee, was privately told by government sources 'not to believe the Iraqi propaganda machine'.[26]

- Many of the atrocities which received widespread publicity in the run-up to the military engagement and the 'hearts and minds' campaign proved, on closer examination, to be either exaggerated or false. The charge that the Iraqi occupiers of Kuwait took babies from incubators and left them to die was later shown to have been fabricated.[27]
- The bombing of the Amiriya concrete shelter in Baghdad, which led to the death of hundreds of civilians, appears to have been a monumental intelligence blunder. It was neither a 'military command' nor a 'leadership' bunker as first identified by intelligence analysts, nor a 'military personnel bunker' as believed by military sources. To try to deflect revulsion at the bombing, senior officials contrived a story in which Saddam had somehow 'set up' the situation. This was led by Defence Secretary Tom King, who said; 'I suspect a trap.' The *Express* headlined a story 'Saddam allowed families to be slaughtered for a sick propaganda stunt', and cited numerous intelligence sources to back up the claim.[28]

Although a former senior official of the CIA, Ray Cline, had stated at the beginning of the campaign that it would be an 'intelligence war' and that intelligence would win it, this was only partially true. Indeed, the intelligence effort was both massive and impressive but, in reality, it was the overwhelming military might of the Coalition forces which secured the quick and, for the Allies, painless victory. The intelligence component had produced a vast overestimation of Iraqi strength and capability which fed Coalition fears about the potential loss of life. This led Coalition commanders, much to the chagrin of their political masters, to wait until their forces were overwhelmingly superior in strength, quality and preparedness before delivering the final blow. However, intelligence did play an important role in Desert Storm, and important questions were raised about the supremacy of electronic and signals intelligence over the spy on the ground.

Most commentators argued against the over-reliance on electronic means and canvassed the need, which appeared to have the backing of the intelligence services, for more human intelligence sources. Some of these arguments were spurious, since it was the intelligence agencies themselves which had, in many cases, fought for increased electronic intelligence gathering at the expense of the intelligence officer. Although capital costs are initially high, over time technical means of intelligence gathering tend to be cost-effective. Recruiting, training and managing officers in the field is an expensive business and is not always successful. The main problem during the war had been, not the intelligence which was generated, but the lack of experienced analysts with language skills and appropriate training. If there is to be an expansion in the recruitment or transfer of human resources, then it should be in the number of people who have the mundane and often tedious job of analysing intelligence. This is despite the fact that the war demonstrated that analysing intelligence is not a science but an experimental process which relies to a great extent on guesswork. In November 1991, the *Wall Street Journal*, in noting that the 'most important person in the intelligence business is no longer going to be the spymaster but the analyst', concluded that the new model would be 'less James Bond than Sherlock Holmes'.

Covert action – a highly dubious activity – still has its supporters and it is an area in which the MI6 officer does not appear to be in danger of replacement. The prime targets of MI6 special action programmes are Iraq and the Yemen, which supported Saddam Hussein during the Gulf War. Britain has cut aid to the Yemen, which was the target of joint MI6/CIA operations in the early eighties, and has allowed Saudi Arabia to carry on its border dispute with the country, aware that there are lucrative Saudi arms and oil contracts at risk. During the Gulf War, aid was given to the Joint Action Committee, an alliance of seventeen Kurdish, Sunni, Shi'ite and other Iraqi dissident groups formed in Beirut in a bid to bring down Saddam Hussein. Small, discreet delegations from the JAC visited Foreign Office officials for talks. London became the focus of attention for the competing anti-Saddam groups partly because of its traditional tie with the Middle East but mainly because of their distrust of the United States. MI6 worked closely wth the French in supporting these groups, but the operation failed because of the wide political differences between the disparate groups. Western Intelligence reports told of cracks appearing in the edifice of Saddam Hussein's dictatorial regime, with reports of anti-war protests in major cities, however, no evidence was ever produced for fear of 'compromising intelligence sources'.[29]

At the end of Desert Storm, British Prime Minister John Major inititated a plan, Operation Haven, to provide 'safe havens' for the Kurdish people in northern Iraq and the Shi'as around Basra. A defence debriefing team based at the Intelligence Centre, Ashford, was dispatched to the north with the title 'Kurdish Liaison Team'. British Intelligence officers with the KLT interviewed many of the educated and influential Kurds in the camps, from whom they gained 'important information', which presumably went towards building up a picture of Iraq and providing intelligence for the Kurdish guerrillas being backed by MI6. However, many of the intelligence officers involved felt 'bitterness and guilt' at unknowingly being part of an operation which was seen as a betrayal of the pledges made to the Kurds.[30]

In the spring of 1991, following the failure of the uprising of the Kurds and the Shi'as, who were 'hung out to dry after receiving US encouragement', Britain was at the forefront of calls for more aggressive covert action to remove Saddam. President Bush authorised a major covert action programme costing more than $40 million, with much of the cash coming from Saudi Arabia. The programme was designed to assist at least three Iraqi opposition groups with funding and training for their guerrilla forces. Kurds and Shi'as were secretly flown to Saudi Arabia for training in tactics, communications and weapons, which had been purchased from the former Soviet Union. The President ruled out the assassination of Saddam as an option, though it depends on how the word – derived from the habit of assassins on the Iraqi–Turkish border smoking hashish before killing – is defined. Clearly, the heavy bombing of shelters in Baghdad was designed specifically to kill the Iraqi leader. A former MI6 officer with long experience in the Middle East told the *Guardian* that 'No non-Iraqi is going to get near him in a clandestine way'. Saddam uses elaborate security measures learned from the experience of the PLO leader, Yasser Arafat, to protect him. He is always on the move. MI6 and the CIA would not rule out the use of an Iraqi who could manage to get himself into Saddam's immediate circle.[31]

Part of the aim of the covert operation was to tighten the psychological pressure on Saddam Hussein through increased surveillance and anti-Saddam propaganda. This included reactivating the CIA-sponsored Voice of Free Iraq, an anti-government radio station modelled on Iraqi national radio, which sought to help opposition groups and called for a populist overthrow of Saddam. The CIA launched Operation Maseraagh ('laundry'), which flooded Iraq with forged dinars to undermine the economy. Britain's Foreign Office helped by refusing to release as a 'humanitarian commodity' millions of banknotes printed by currency printers De La Rue.[32]

At the begining of 1992, CIA director Robert Gates travelled round the Middle East states to drum up support for renewed covert action. A potential coup plot by defecting senior officers in the Iraqi army was said to have been shelved in March 1992 because of lack of support from the Allies. It was also reported that the coup was a disinformation ploy by the Americans, to create paranoia within Saddam's circle. At the same time, Syria, Saudi Arabia and Iran set up new discussions in the Syrian capital Damascus to unite the fractious groupings on a common platform. However, the move was not welcomed by other Middle East countries which no longer saw Iraq as a threat; they were much more concerned about Iran. In June 1992, the Iraqi National Congress (INC), which is based in London, was formed at a little-noticed conference in Vienna from the most pro-Western and liberal-minded of the anti-Saddam groups. In July, INC representatives toured Europe and the United States seeking support, during which time talks took place with Lady Chalker, Minister for Overseas Development. Guaranteed Western support, for the first time Islamic groups endorsed the concept of democracy and joined the INC. Despite the hard work put into creating a united opposition, the chances that the INC will provide an effective base for sustained covert action must, given the history of the participants, be rather slim.[33]

At the end of 1991, an Israeli army border patrol in the Lebanon security zone arrested, but later released following the intervention of Mossad, a man who spoke fluent Arabic and who claimed to be Lebanese. He said he was undertaking 'research' – a favourite euphemism for intelligence or special operations – on behalf of a Beirut cultural institute. Further inquiries revealed that he was an MI6 officer, one of a number of extra spies sent into the field. MI6 has, once again, focused its attention on the Middle East, a traditional battlefield because of the risk of disruption to the world's oil supplies. There have been strong ties between MI6 and Mossad which have undergone occasional disruption. There was a four-month break in relations and exchange of intelligence between the two services after MI5 had uncovered the activities of Mossad agents in Britain, which led to their expulsion in June 1988. Relations resumed in December 1988. Following the arrest and detention of the British officer, a Mossad officer claimed that 'MI6 is the best intelligence service in the Middle East . . . They have a traditional heritage of espionage work in this part of the world. The Arabs think the British are more reliable than the Americans.' This view is endorsed by an MI6 officer: 'Quite simply, for our size we have the best sources in the business.'[34]

The Secret Intelligence Service

> There is no point in making denials of these services and they are now acknowledged; and that's an improvement – but it's a small one.
>
> Sir Dick White

Chief of MI6 since April 1989, Sir Colin McColl is the son of a Shropshire GP. Although an official secret, his address is listed in full in the Old Salopian Club list of old boys from Shrewsbury School, where he was a contemporary of Board of Trade president, Michael Heseltine, whose department is a major customer of MI6's economic 'product'. A friend at school, Colin Leach, now a Fellow of Pembroke College, Oxford, said that Sir Colin 'was not known for being intelligent, except in classics. He was an extremely jovial boy. At Oxford he frequently threw parties.'[1]

A good shot and high-spirited sportsman, McColl joined the service in 1950 and spent his first two postings in the Far East, where he was known as a keen amateur dramatist. A 'nice, witty man', during a posting to Laos, 'he broke the ice with the Royal Family with a display on the flute'. He is said to have an encyclopaedic knowledge of the Third World. He spent a period in Warsaw during the middle sixties and was posted to Geneva in 1973, where he remained for nearly four years prior to being replaced by Christopher Curwen. McColl is married to the daughter of a retired diplomat.[2]

Sir Colin was persuaded to stay on as chief for an extra two years following his sixtieth birthday in September 1992, to oversee the new legislation legitimising the service – a process known in Whitehall as 'avowal'. The decision to open up MI6, according to a letter from the service's 'welfare officer', was taken with the full agreement of MI6 staff. However, the letter added that 'the avowal of the Service does not mean that we can reveal anything about our previous association with the Service to outsiders.' Further evidence that the 'cobwebs of secrecy' had not been swept away was in evidence when the D-Notice Committee requested newspapers not to publish pictures of Sir Colin as a young man.[3]

Sir Colin will be in post to oversee MI6's transfer to new premises, a public event which is an indicator of the service's future significance. MI6 currently occupies a twenty-storey grubby concrete office block, Century House, 100 Westminster Bridge Road. A large-scale development in the style of Le Corbusier, designed in 1961, reminiscent of Eastern European buildings and with its first eight floors protected by anti-bomb netting, it is said to be a dreary place, unpopular with officers and in a poor state of repair. The best description of life inside is said to have been shown in the *Sandbagger* books, written in collaboration with a former MI6 officer, which were accurate down to the colour of the carpets and the painting in the chief's room. MI6 will be moving away from the centre of power and clubland to south of the River Thames at Vauxhall Cross. In 1981, Michael Heseltine described the site as 'as outstanding an opportunity as is offered anywhere in the Western world, straddling as it does a major approach to the capital'. The £240 million 'aggressive single-purpose fortress' opposite the Tate Gallery has been designed by post-modernist Terry Farrell, 'in many ways the quintessential British architect of the eighties'. The nine-storey 200-feet-high Aztec-like structure in green and cream has, said one critic, 'the sobriety of a Busby Berkeley set'. It is not due to be completed internally until the beginning of 1994.[4]

MI6 is estimated to have up to three thousand staff, two-thirds of them full-time officers. When elected to office in 1979, Mrs Thatcher issued a 'no cuts in intelligence' edict which has served MI6 well, though control of its budget is said to be notoriously tight. The service's financial resources are believed to be smaller than those of MI5. In 1985, MI6 was estimated to have a budget of £140 million; 1992's figure is thought to be twice that. The free-enterprise government has been reluctant to apply to the intelligence services the tests of effectiveness and efficiency which have been applied to other sectors of government. Secret sources make the claim that in recent years MI6 has been highly successful and an excellent value-for-money service which has saved the country more than its entire annual budget by the quality of its intelligence: however, there is at present no means of checking whether this is true. The only evidence the public has is where the system has gone wrong.[5]

The exact internal structure of MI6 is hard to ascertain, given that there have been so many changes in the world of intelligence gathering over the past few years. The service operates a number of regional 'desks', in the same manner as the Foreign Office, which are organised into six geographical areas under the supervision of controllers. They include Europe, Russia and republics of the former Soviet Union, the Middle East, Africa and the Far East, which is also responsible for the one station in South America. The Requirements and Production departments, which were previously separate, are now combined and cover sections for political affairs, air, naval, military, counter-intelligence, economic, financial, GCHQ and scientific under a single division. Counter-intelligence operates closely with MI5's K5 section, which is headed by a senior MI6 officer; there is also a security sub-section within Century House keeping the staff under a watchful eye.

Requirements and Production is 'the Service's shop front', responsible for discovering the 'needs' of its customers – mostly the Foreign Office, the MoD and the Joint Intelligence Committee – which are then furnished with the 'finished product'. Much of the intelligence is, in fact, not collected by MI6, and a great deal of the analysts' time is taken up with material from GCHQ, where during the Cold War electronic surveillance of the Soviet bloc assumed near-primacy. A

Directorate of Special Support is responsible for providing technical assistance to operations and is staffed by locksmiths and video and audio technicians. Although officially MI6 does not operate on the mainland it does have a London station involved in the monitoring of foreign embassies and targets in the capital, including the recruitment of agents within the country. The overall day-to-day responsibility for running the divisions and all routine administration is held by the director of MI6, deputy to the chief.[6]

Even before criticisms were raised about the performance of the intelligence services in the Gulf War and their over-reliance on electronic means, spies on the ground – HUMINT – had once again become fashionable. In the last few years, there has been an increasing demand for new stations abroad, necessitating a crash course in the languages of the former Soviet Union. There are, however, problems recruiting operatives of the right calibre who fit in with the high-tech world of modern intelligence gathering. Cuts in funding have hit university language departments and the numbers studying relevant languages such as Russian, Japanese and Chinese are low. In the seventies, changing attitudes to patriotism and what had been perceived as the glamorous image of spying created difficulties in recruiting suitable staff, and now that the Cold War is over and, along with it, the Soviet 'threat' that provided a tangible reason for working in intelligence, joining the service looks a lot less attractive. MI6 has trawled the universities and, in a worrying move, has turned to specialist regiments such as the SAS, whose gung-ho philosophy seems more suited to covert action than patient intelligence gathering. MI6 has also had to fill posts with diplomats on secondment from the Foreign Office. Other recruits have included Special Branch officers and former MI5 men who have worked abroad as security liaison officers – postings which hinder career prospects within the Security Service. The service is believed to be contemplating discreet advertising for recruits. In the early eighties, MI6 used the services of an outside talent scout,

Colonel 'Jim' Scobie of F. H. Scobie and Associates, St James's Square.[7]

In 1979, following the intervention of Prime Minister James Callaghan, recruitment to MI6 was formalised by the use of the Civil Service Commission and the university careers service. These days, not as many top-quality personnel are joining the intelligence services, though MI6 has managed to attract a steady flow of young recruits. 'The Firm', as MI6 is known to staff, or the 'Friends' as it is referred to by the rest of Whitehall, still has a much higher percentage of first-class degree holders than MI5. Even so, the service has been forced to take on candidates who fail the Foreign and Commonwealth Office examination but are thought to have 'the right aptitude'. Wartime involvement in intelligence work provided a network of 'talent-spotters' at Oxbridge and a number of other key universities such as Durham and Exeter. While the links with Oxbridge are no longer as strong, a number of academics still carry on with the tradition. Fewer public school- and more grammar school-style recruits are being brought into the service, though MI6 still relies to a great extent on recommendation and remains more class-based than MI5.[8]

Graduates who apply to join the Foreign Office are told of other appointments which 'occasionally arise in addition to those covered by the diplomatic service'. If they express interest they are steered towards the 'FCO Co-ordinating Staff', as MI6 is known. Suitable candidates are then put through the fast-stream Civil Service Selection Board. The main interview for the service at the spacious John Nash designed house, 3 Carlton Gardens, which overlooks St James's Park, is very general, with no mention of intelligence work. The interviewers are there to assess character and are looking for candidates who are 'good at getting on with people: life-and-soul-of-the-party types who could persuade the Turkish ambassador's secretary to go through her boss's waste-paper-basket, that kind of thing'. Anthony Sampson has described those inside the service as 'buccaneering and tricky people, with a good deal of aggression or acquisitiveness'. It would be interesting to know how MI6's first CND member, recruited in 1985, fits in with his/her colleagues.[9]

There are many women in MI6, though fewer than the 54 per cent said to be in MI5. It has been claimed that around 40 per cent of field officers are female. The Tel Aviv station was, for a long time, staffed by women officers, after relations between Britain and Israel became fraught. Until the recent exposure of Margaret Ramsay (referred to in the Preface), the most famous and senior female MI6 officer had been Daphne Park. Before becoming MI6 divisional head for Africa, Park had been chief of station at Léopoldville when the Congo's first Prime Minister, Patrice Lumumba, was assassinated. Retiring in 1979, she became principal of Somerville College, Oxford, taking with her Miss Fletcher, her assistant inside MI6. Highly regarded by Mrs Thatcher, she was made a governor of the BBC, where she played a key role in helping to suppress Duncan Campbell's controversial *Secret Society* series. In one of those strange examples of self-censorship at which the British excel, the BBC still refers to Baroness Park as an 'ex-Foreign Office diplomat'.

There have certainly been some very odd characters in the service who have made all sorts of strange claims about the ethos of the work. In the late fifties, the deputy chief, George Kennedy Young, had the extraordinary notion that during a period of 'moral stalemate' the spy 'finds himself the main guardian of intellectual integrity'. The spy was called on to 'remedy the situation created by the deficiencies of ministers, diplomats, generals and priests'. The creator of George Smiley, John le Carré, has written that 'Espionage is the secret theatre of our society. In the large back rooms we find out who we are – what we want, what are our ethical priorities, what freedoms we value and what other freedoms we will give up to protect them.' The experience of Anthony Cavendish was that 'working for a secret intelligence service almost always brings about a state of mind which permits anything if it is done for the benefit of the service and hence for the good of one's country'. 'Theft, deception, lies, mutilation and even murder are possibilities which are considered if and when necessary.' While mutilations and murder may now be a thing of the past, blackmail remains a favoured means of recruiting a source, and it is still true that the 'best of them are capable of . . . setting in motion dirty work without soiling their own hands'. It is still true that an MI6 officer 'lies from his first day in the service', for lying is part of his cover. Today, probably more than ever, 'idealism is a rare motive'.[10]

On entering the service, recruits are offered a grade higher than normal Foreign Office diplomats, along with overseas allowances and subsidised private schooling for the children. Officers retire at fifty-five, though many will be asked to undertake further small jobs when they finish work, such as mail drops, recruitment and liaison duties. Trainees learn to use the computer system, methods of intelligence gathering and the house style of report writing. Lack of numbers requires that trainees acquire a broad range of knowledge across the field of intelligence 'tradecraft'. They will be better trained than their colleagues in other agencies 'in languages . . . able to move from one area of the world to another with relative ease and with a great deal of background knowledge'. Foreign intelligence agencies admire the high quality of the work of MI6's experienced officers, but there are critics who prefer less literal and more academically inclined reports. According to a KGB assessment, the British 'appoint the best man obtainable to deal with a given subject, and will then be prepared to accept his finding with relatively little question'. While the method is 'rapid and more easily leads to a readable style of composition, and often allows brilliant work . . . its disadvantages are obvious in the lack of control and the tendency to rely upon individual reputations'.[11]

Trainee officers are put through a course of small-arms training – more extensive than in other intelligence services – at the 'nursery school' – le Carré's term – at Fort Monckton,

Gosport, before being assigned to an overseas post. They will have little choice of location. 'You're allowed to turn down one job,' according to an insider, 'but you're then obliged to take the next or get out.' Around fifteen years is spent in the field, where the normal diplomatic structure is followed and officers 'are kept strictly in their place where protocol is concerned: not more than half-a-dozen hold a cover rank as high as counsellor [including France, Italy and the United States]'.[12]

By the time officers achieve seniority in the service, their main task as part of the London staff at Century House will be to compile assessments, plan operations, liaise with foreign intelligence agencies and networks and, most importantly, support the four to six hundred officers who work in the field, though only half that number will be abroad at any one time. The operational base for overseas officers is known as the 'station' and is used for planning, intelligence gathering and communications. The station is usually staffed by two people, with its own communications with London separate from the rest of the embassy. Within the embassy, MI6 officers remain incognito to the junior members of the diplomatic staff, though the 'light' cover under which they operate does not fool rival services.[13]

During the forties and fifties, MI6 personnel were easily identified on the embassy roster as 'Passport Control' or 'Visa' officers. Others were spotted 'attached' to various thinly disguised organisations. The defections of Kim Philby and George Blake meant that the cover of as many as 90 per cent of overseas officers was blown. Officers were, from the mid-sixties, much more integrated into the embassy structure, though references in the Foreign Office Diplomatic List such as 'seconded Northern Ireland', later changed to 'seconded Home Civil Service', provided only transparent cover. As a result of the naming in the mid-eighties of a number of officers in radical magazines, the Diplomatic List was further refined until there appeared on the surface to be little difference between them and ordinary diplomats. However, there are only a limited number of positions that an officer can use in an embassy, and these are usually the same for each tour of duty; thus, despite the simplified biographical details, identification is relatively easy for a trained eye.

'When the diplomat clocks off at six and prepares for cocktails, the work of the MI6 officers begins,' according to one former officer. There still remains a good deal of compartmentalisation within the embassy, which means that, effectively, only the ambassador is informed of MI6 activities. Not all ambassadors are happy to have intelligence operations, particularly covert actions, undertaken in their area: nevertheless, even 'disapproved of' operations are carried out. Former CIA officer Miles Copeland wrote that the 'British station is almost identical with that of the CIA except perhaps that it is smaller, better covered and better integrated into the embassy to which it is assigned. Also it is poorer, its budget normally being about a third of the budget of its American counterpart. For this reason, it is in most parts of the world a primary duty of the British station chief to use his superior prestige and cunning to persuade his CIA colleague to join with him in joint Anglo-American operations for which he supplies the brains and the CIA colleague supplies the funds.'[14]

Likewise, given the financial restraints and pure operational practicalities, diplomats are increasingly encouraged to help the service and, while some are happy to oblige, the partnership is not always a happy one. Andrew Balfour, a vice-consul in Dubai responsible for issuing visas to Middle Eastern nationals, provided invaluable assistance to local MI6 officers who were attempting to recruit local agents. His relationship to the 'friends' was so close that before his posting to Dubai, while stationed in Damascus during 1986, Syrian intelligence forced his expulsion after naming him as a spy. In the field, it is said that more foreigners volunteer their services than MI6 has time to vet. Their recruitment is based on a 'hierarchy of loyalties' – 'whether it be political opposition to their own regime, professional failure in their ordinary job, the need to support a mistress or pure greed'. Balfour and his wife hosted dinners 'where certain targeted individuals would attend with the MI6 officer'. One of those invited to dinner was a former Iranian arms dealer, Mehrdad Ansari, whose name was fed to Balfour by the local station officer. Balfour cultivated the businessman until a new MI6 station officer arrived and expressed a very low interest in Mr Ansari.[15]

Balfour thought no more about Ansari until, to his astonishment, in August 1989, he was suspended from his post by the Foreign Office and then arrested by Special Branch officers under the Prevention of Terrorism Act. He was suspected of helping a 'suspected gunrunner and terrorist', and Balfour took this to be a reference to Ansari, who had been granted a long-term entry visa to Britain. Balfour was accused of 'receiving large sums of money from influential people in the Middle East' and taking bribes for issuing visas. On one occasion, the Iranian had asked Balfour where he could get some commercial printing done and was told about Balfour's brother-in-law who ran a printing business. However, the print job never went ahead and the approach was forgotten. In January 1990, Balfour was informed by the Attorney-General, Sir Patrick Mayhew, that he had no case to answer, but this did not stop the Foreign Office sacking him. His career in ruins, forty-one-year-old Balfour believes he was the victim of false corruption allegations made by MI6. Details of his arrest were subsequently fed by MI6 to the *Daily Mail*, which carried a front-page story, ensuring that he could not work for the Foreign Office again. His telephone has been tapped and he has been warned not to speak to the press.

Andrew Balfour laid the ground for a compensation hearing at an industrial tribunal; however, the Home and Foreign Secretaries successfully used ministerial certificates to ensure the non-disclosure of an immigration file on Ansari, on the basis that it contains information on 'the work of the security and intelligence services' and is, therefore, 'detrimental to the national interests of the United Kingdom and its allies'. All mentions of the security services were deleted from documents, while MI6 officers were refused permission to give evidence on Balfour's behalf. His wife Pat told the *Observer*: 'Ugly forces are at work when people like us – loyal, long-service, a happy family – can end up having to fight their way through a very murky pool in a world that for most people exists only on television.'[16]

The Balfour case illustrated that MI6 is still and is likely to remain a closed book. It does not open its files to anyone, not even to the Prime Minister. 'If any MI6 activity prompts an inquiry, it is merely expected to report honestly on what happened.' This suits the politicians who do not want to know what their spooks are up to. 'Why don't they want to know?' asked Melanie Phillips in the *Guardian*. 'Because they don't want to confront the difficult decisions, the illegal, improper or immoral activities that go on; they are happy to pretend it isn't happening as long as it's all tidied away and there are no embarrassing scandals.'[17]

There have been continual turf battles within the Civil Service about the exercise of control over the security services, with attempts to bring them under direct remit of the Cabinet Office. There has been tension between the Foreign Office, which wants to hold on to and extend its control of MI6, and the Cabinet Office, which pushes for a more centralising role. These moves have invariably failed as the permanent secretaries in the Home, Foreign and Defence ministries have vetoed the plans of the Cabinet Office. 'It is much better to have the power diffused in the hands of the Foreign Secretary and the Home Secretary, with the Prime Minister keeping an eye on it,' believes former Foreign Secretary David Owen. However, the aim of both lobbies has been to keep the politicians at arm's length, and in that they have succeeded. Power continues to remain in the hands of the officials who hide behind a maze of committees and liaison procedures.[18]

The Prime Minister has overall responsibility for the security services, while MI6 is departmentally responsible to the Foreign Secretary, who 'unless there is a need to know, steers clear of operations'. Only those intelligence cases which have a 'political content' – there are no definitions of this term – are referred to the Foreign Secretary. Foreign operations are planned by MI6's requirements division then, on completion, are submitted to the service's Foreign Office adviser, who consults with the relevant regional department. If the plan is accepted it is passed back for clearance by 'C', who will submit it via the adviser to the deputy under-secretary in the Permanent Under-Secretary's Department. This department deals with 'general co-ordination duties and responsibility for liaison with the Cabinet Office and other government departments'.[19]

The Permanent Under-Secretary's Department (PUSD), which also includes supervises the work of GCHQ, is responsible for all intelligence and strategic matters in the Foreign Office and is the direct link between MI6 and its Whitehall customers, ensuring that there is a constant flow of high-grade intelligence. The Prime Minister receives a daily box from 'C', which is distributed to the Cabinet Secretary and selected Cabinet ministers and senior advisers. MI6's chief has the right, if necessary, to forward raw intelligence directly to ministers; however, it is never a good policy to go behind the back of the PUSD. The current deputy under-secretary is the 'tall and rather solemn but shrewd' fifty-five-year-old Nigel Broomfield. He is a Russian speaker with experience of the former Soviet bloc, having served as Britain's last ambassador to East Germany. In giving the go-ahead for operations, he can consult yet higher authority in the shape of the Permanent Secretary or the Secretary of State. The results of these deliberations will be reported to the Joint Intelligence Committee.[20]

Once the go-ahead is given to an operation, MI6 is left to its own devices to get on with its primary role of intelligence gathering. However, the scope and overall direction of its activities and setting of 'targets' reflect the desires and intentions of the foreign policy makers. Normally, policy is generated by a small band of officials, members of the permanent government, principally in the Foreign Office. The process is protected from outside scrutiny by the umbrella of the Official Secrets Act and references to 'national security'. Governments and ministers can and do influence and, occasionally, change policy, but overall the direction has been set with little reference to Britain's democratic institutions and depends on a consensus which, in the main, survives changes of government. This is reflected in the permanent government's 'historic concentration on strategic rather than economic issues in the formulation of foreign policy'. While there were certainly occasions when the Thatcher government did impose its own political agenda, Britain today has a Foreign Secretary who is a product of the system and completely in tune with the ethos of the permanent government.[21]

Douglas Hurd is said to rule all sorts of roosts, most notably the Overseas Policy and Defence Committee, the key instrument of foreign policy planning. He also appears to dominate John Major in foreign affairs; the Prime Minister is said to be prepared to leave day-to-day delegation to his Foreign Secretary on many matters. In place of Mrs Thatcher's foreign policy adviser, Charles Powell, a former diplomat who stayed longer than expected at Number 10 and in the process 'went native', often formulating policy at variance with his former colleagues, Major appointed Stephen Wall, a career diplomat more acceptable to his fellow mandarins whose advice rarely deviated from the Foreign Office line. He controlled the flow of documents to the Prime Minister's desk. His place has been taken over by another Foreign Office nominee, Rod Lyne.[22]

Hurd is the most patrician of recent occupants of the post. All his past life appears to have been a preparation for his role as Foreign Secretary, including his days at Eton where his disciplinarian streak as a cane-wielding prefect earned him the sobriquet, 'Hitler Hurd'. Two other ministers at the Foreign Office are Old Etonians, all three, sneered the *Telegraph*, 'Honourables by dint of all being sons of peers'. Hurd has drawn criticism for his lack of passion or vision and for 'sounding like a sort of superior I Speak Your Weight machine'.[23]

Throughout his career, Hurd has been on the fringes of the intelligence empire. Joining the diplomatic service in 1952, he no doubt met MI6 officers during his postings abroad, and later, as private secretary to the Permanent Secretary at the Foreign Office, would have gained some knowledge of its workings and operations. In February 1978, while in opposition, he had secret meetings with leaders of Sinn Fein, and as Northern Ireland Secretary of State, 'the Siberia of British politics', he would have had day-to-day contact with members of the security forces and the intelligence community. Some of this knowledge provided background for his co-authored, safe and rather predictable thrillers. The novels show politics as a 'glamorous activity undertaken by the good for the benefit of the rest of us. There is a dislike of investigative journalists, and an admiration for the secretive and high-powered games that politicians play'. The security services, however, are not always portrayed in a good light. The 1985, *Palace of Enchantments* has a junior Foreign Office minister who 'normally paid little attention to the intelligence reports which crossed his tray. A quick glance, a quick tick, and into the out-tray. He found them pretentious.' Once Hurd became Foreign Secretary, he did his best to protect the security services, developing a rather romantic view of their activities.[24]

The Foreign Office and Joint Intelligence Committee have not laid out a public policy for the intelligence services in the nineties, but a sense of the new directions can be gained from studying the Foreign Secretary's more recent speeches. Hurd betrayed his roots as a member of the Round Table, the remnant of the Cecil Rhodes empire which had virtual control over British foreign policy for the first half of this century. In an interview with the *Independent* in September 1992, Hurd said that the United Nations had to gear itself up to take on an 'imperial role', usurping national sovereignty and taking over controlling power when governments such as those of Somalia and Cambodia collapsed. 'It is putting blue on the map. It is an imperial role, but it's more a mandate. It is becoming clear that we're at a new stage in the way the world's going to have to run its affairs.' The Cold War was 'dangerous, but predictable. Under its shadow, other conflicts were few and far between.' But now since the break-up of the former Soviet Union there have developed 'crisis areas'.[25]

Hurd is a Euro-enthusiast who believes that 'cohesion is needed in a fractious, fragmented and dangerous world'; collective efforts are essential to tackle the problems of an 'anxious and uncertain world'. He believes policy is required to work for a stronger Western Europe, to build peace and security in the whole of Europe and for a willingness to 'intervene in the affairs of particular European states to prevent anarchy and bloodshed'. Referring to organisations such as the United Nations, NATO, the EC and the Conference on Security and Co-operation in Europe (CSCE), Hurd has said that Britain would lead the way in helping to 'reshape the work of these institutions for the new world'. The United Nations is being encouraged to take on an intelligence-gathering role, so as to provide an early warning on potential conflicts and crisis areas. Confidential papers circulated in the spring of 1992 by the EC, Russia and the white Commonwealth countries proposed an independent means for gathering intelligence which would also cover international terrorism and drug-trafficking. This was coupled with a call for the creation of rapid-response contingents of special forces. The United States has opposed the proposals, which might bring the United Nations into conflict with the CIA, though MI6 might welcome a balance to the recognised power of the world's biggest intelligence agency.[26]

Since the fifties, representatives of the intelligence services of NATO have met regularly in Brussels to exchange information about counter-espionage, counter-subversion and counter-terrorism. A Special Committee within the Supreme Headquarters Allied Powers Europe (SHAPE) was established for this purpose. Exactly what was decided by these discussions and what, if any, operations – other than the setting up of the stay-behind anti-communist Gladio network – were planned, is not known, though the end of the Cold War must have had a dramatic impact. Britain has defended US interests in NATO, but the development of a 'European Defence Identity' has led to fears that France, in co-operation with Germany, will use the opportunity to exclude the Americans from Europe. During the Gulf War, France tried to get the previously moribund Western European Union to set up a special cell in the French Defence Ministry to co-ordinate intelligence on the war. WEU countries, including Britain, agreed in August 1990 to set up 'contact points' to co-ordinate the intelligence effort. However, Britain was concerned that this should not interfere with its own exchange of information with the United States.[27]

The reactivation of the WEU, which represents nine EC countries, is one reason which has led to the development of new ideas on NATO's tasks outside of its traditional theatres of operation. The Pentagon has suggested that this might include NATO becoming involved in defending oil supply lines and deterring mass 'militant' migration to the prosperous West. More likely is the role of dealing with a proliferation of nuclear weapons and the neutralisation of other weapons of mass destruction. In effect, NATO would function principally as an intelligence agency. At the end of 1989, Jamie O'Shea, the public relations officer to the General Secretary, said that he could imagine that NATO 'in twenty years would only exist as an organization to monitor disarmament'.[28]

The CSCE, which was set up in 1972 and includes thirty-four member nations, has set up its new secretariat in Prague, following an overhaul which is designed to make it more relevant to the security needs of its expanding membership. The CSCE-negotiated Open Skies Treaty, signed in Helsinki on 24 March 1992, legalises aerial surveillance over three continents. Spy flights carried out by specially equipped planes will begin in 1993. The intelligence gathered will be available to all treaty signatories, enabling those countries without their own satellites or access to Russian or US pictures to get their own. However, the material gained will be classified. 'It's sharing a military secret among the right people,' said an MoD source. Britain will be able to make twelve flights a year including three over Russia.[29]

In 1991, in a review of a Ted Allbeury novel, Hurd wrote that 'intelligence services will certainly persist, however the world evolves. One day, perhaps, there will be a new wave of writing, not quite in the style of John Buchan, but returning to some sense of the enthusiasm for what men and women attempt in a good cause.' The officers around Sir Colin McColl are said to be 'liberal, eager and good operators', however, the Chief is known as an old-style service officer saddled with the attitudes of the Cold War.[30]

29

'The Violent Peace'

The Cold War, despite its menace, was at least predictable.

Canadian Security Intelligence Service's first annual report, 1992.

MI6 has, until now, survived the post-Cold War period, without any cut in budget or staff, by restructuring its role to meet new demands. However, some of the new tasks which it has sought have little to do with most conceptions of intelligence work. According to the *Sunday Times*, MI6 'has also recently taken on additional work reporting on worldwide environmental pollution, including analysis of the destruction of the rainforest'. It would seem that MI6 officers do not have to go far to discover the culprits. In the same edition, the newspaper ran a headline – 'British aid used to destroy rainforest'. The article alleged that the Overseas Development Administration was paying £850,000 to establish a logging development in the Tapajos National Forest in Para, northern Brazil.[1]

Former senior MI6 officer, Nicholas Elliott, has said that MI6 has plenty of targets: terrorism, drugs, nuclear and arms proliferation and economic threats including, it has been reported, attempts to undermine the pound. In the mid-eighties, extra funds were made available to cover the cost of a new directorate to handle counter-terrorism. In 1987, the more enterprising members of MI6 set up, with the support of the Minister of State at the Foreign Office, David Mellor, a Counter-Narcotics Crime section, which also studies and investigates money laundering without which the drug cartels could not survive. MI6 now has a major international role in the field and liaises with the FBI, the US Drug Enforcement Agency and with British and American Customs officials. It also co-operates with international forums such as the Financial Action Task Force which is specifically designed to combat money laundering. In Colombia, MI6 officers have worked alongside a fifty-strong SAS team in helping to train government anti-narcotic special forces teams in a twelve million pound operation to stem the flow of cocaine to Britain. According to Tom Mangold: 'Their ability to cross borders, patch into the extensive and underemployed cold-war spy apparatus and bend the odd rule here and there is proving invaluable.' MI6 sections dealing with weapons of mass destruction have been expanded following the Supergun Affair. In other areas, special emphasis will be placed on the Middle East because of its instability and the extent of British interests, and on the former Soviet republics because of their volatility. Isolated flashpoints will be Hong Kong, China, South Africa, India and Pakistan.[2]

There is disagreement within the intelligence community about the role of MI6 in Eastern Europe. Some argue that the former Warsaw Pact countries should no longer be given the same priority – they previously took up around 50 per cent of the service's resources – and that officers engaged in intelligence gathering in the area could be switched to new roles closer to home. However, MI6 has pressed for more resources in the light of the developments in Central Europe, which is seen by the Foreign Office as a human buffer zone for the West. Instability in the former Soviet Union, the rise of extremist forces and rampant nationalism have produced new threats, including the fear of mass 'militant migration'. Poland, Czechoslovakia and Hungary, which make up the Visegrad group, named after the city where an alliance was made between the three countries in 1991, might become the dumping ground and the first point of call for many refugees. MI6 argues that, far from diminishing the need for surveillance, uncertainty has been created which demands the presence of more agents on the ground. The service argues that it can no longer rely on electronic eavesdropping, satellites and code-breaking to achieve its aims. It hopes to cut the electronic surveillance budget and increase the number of human intelligence gatherers. The Foreign Office and MI6 have reportedly withdrawn some staff from South America to beef up their presence in Europe.[3]

There have been rumours that MI6 has, once again, been sponsoring publications, just as it did in the early fifties at the height of the Cold War. This time, however, any propaganda activities in Eastern Europe are likely to be semi-overt or completely open.

During 1989, Foreign Office ministers considered whether to fund a 'multi-million'-pound (assessed as being as much as £25 million) initiative to encourage democratic changes in the former Warsaw Pact countries through parliamentary contacts, without 'being accused of interfering in their internal affairs or reverting to Cold War propaganda'. Minister William Waldegrave hoped to channel the money through research institutes and commissioned Dr Michael Pinto-Duschinski to study similar German foundations attached to political parties. The Foreign Office decided to set up a cross-party independent body, the Westminster Foundation for Democracy (WFD), to help the new democracies 'strengthen pluralist democracy'. However, by March 1992, the recession had meant that the money available was down to £1.2 million. Each project is approved by a board consisting of ex-Tory vice-chair Sir James Spicer, MP, Labour MP George Robertson, Liberal Democrat Sir Russell Johnson and, representing the Scottish Nationalists, Margaret Ewing. Serving on the board is Diana Warwick, former general secretary of the AUT. The Foreign Office is represented by the head of the Planning Staff, Robert Cooper, whose role is to avoid allocations to 'inappropriate organisations'. The WFD, whose brief now includes Africa, has so far funded a newspaper for opponents of Dr Hastings Banda in

Malawi and a bulletin in the Ukraine on how the country is viewed by the West.[4]

In August 1992, Leonid Shebarshin, former head of the KGB's intelligence section the First Directorate, in ranking the world's intelligence agencies in terms of performance failed to find a place for MI6. Inevitably, an MI6 source countered the claim by suggesting that MI6 'was probably the leading western intelligence agency in terms of its success against Soviet targets'. During the eighties, MI6, which continues to run a number of highly placed sources in Moscow and other capitals of the former Warsaw Pact, had a very good record in recruiting agents in the KGB.[5]

MI6's most successful mole – the jewel in its crown – Oleg Gordievsky, was reported to have been personally run by Sir Colin Figures, the chief of the service. Figures' greatest triumph was when he was able to tell his opposite number in MI5, Sir John Jones, that he had a spy in his ranks, a tip-off from Gordievsky which led to Michael Bettaney. The existence of a spy in the First Directorate of the KGB was a secret known to only a few officials. Before his escape from Moscow and defection to Britain in 1985, Gordievsky had operated as a secret agent for MI6 for eleven years. When, in 1974, he was promoted to First Secretary with a cover post of press attaché in Copenhagen, Gordievsky made contact with MI6 and began to supply the service with 'a goldstream of documents and observations from the heart of Soviet intelligence'. His information led to the arrest, in July 1986, and imprisonment for ten years of a husband and wife spy team, living in Hounslow, Reinhard and Sonja Schulze. An MI5 bugging operation revealed that they had been controlled by the East German intelligence service, HVA, and were responsible for the collection and collation of scientific, military and political data. Gordievsky acted as a consultant to the Cabinet Office 'Gorbachev Committee' which was set up to monitor the Soviet leader's chances of survival. It was co-ordinated by the Permanent Under-Secretary at the Foreign Office, Sir Patrick

Wright, the co-ordinator of Intelligence and Security, Sir Christopher Curwen, and the Chief of MI6, Sir Colin McColl. Gordievsky's information on old security scandals in Britain proved to be less impressive and is still the subject of controversy. Defectors' public utterances are usually tightly controlled and the Gordievsky memoirs were bound, according to Phillip Knightley, to 'show what an indispensable, brilliant and far-sighted service MI6 really is'.[6]

Following the end of the Cold War, MI6 discovered that there were far too many potential defectors and it had the luxury of repelling intelligence officers from Eastern Europe, who had only minor intelligence to offer. Appalled at the flood of Russian defectors, Leonid Shebarshin said that they were 'traitors motivated by money who would betray the West as well'. Thirty-three-year-old Mikhail Butkov, a senior KGB officer in Norway, who was operating under cover as a journalist, defected to Britain with his mistress in the summer of 1991. He was debriefed by MI6 and named a number of KGB agents active in Scandinavia. The subsequent expulsions from Norway and Denmark were closely monitored by intelligence officials from the Baltic states of the former Soviet Union. The Baltic states have now begun co-operating with their Scandinavian neighbours, with meetings often conducted in English. Before and during the Second World War, MI6 developed links with the Baltic states and has always had strong ties with Norway.[7]

Viktor Oshchenko, who served in London during the mid-seventies, had been based in Paris since October 1985. An economics counsellor in the Soviet embassy, who in his intelligence work specialised in science and technology, Oshchenko defected to MI6 in July 1992 when he was about to be exposed as a double agent. His defection led to the expulsion from France of four Russian embassy officials, following the break-up of a spy ring. In Britain, Oshchenko's debriefing led to the arrest of a former systems sales manager at GEC-Marconi, Michael Smith, who was charged with breaching the

Official Secrets Act. In an exclusive in the *Sunday Times*, it was alleged that the GEC-Marconi employee was 'a professional agent, highly trained in tradecraft', who had passed secret defence details to the Russians. A row was said to be going on inside MI5 because in 1976 the Security Service had identified the man, who had gained a high security clearance while working for EMI, as a likely KGB mole. MI5 had known that he was a member of the Communist Party, but had failed to deny him access to sensitive defence material. Oshchenko was believed to have been the British mole's case officer during the mid-seventies.[8]

Jamie Jameson, a former senior CIA officer and vice-president of the Jamestown Foundation, which looks after Soviet bloc defectors, made a frank admission in September 1991. He stated that while defectors from the KGB had been sources of 'interesting intelligence', they had not been as important contributors to the understanding of the Soviet Union as 'the scientists, diplomats and some of the financial people that have come out'. Most of the best defectors had been 'walk-ins', agents who 'recruited themselves, and who finally made contact and produced their information'. However, barring their information on spies in the West, 'their contribution of positive intelligence to our understanding of their own system has sometimes been overstated'.[9]

In 1982, Vladimir Kuzichkin, a senior KGB officer serving in Iran, had walked into the British embassy in Tehran demanding political asylum. During his debriefing by MI6, Kuzichkin named a number of KGB agents and supplied a list of several hundred members of the Tudeh, Iran's Communist Party. There followed a horrendous decision resulting in many deaths. In an attempt to heal relations with Iran, the list was handed over to the mullahs, who used it to purge the Tudeh Party and, in the process, executed hundreds of its members. Kuzichkin did, however, also supply MI6 with a unique understanding of the KGB. His memoir, *Inside the KGB*, is a devastating account of a bureaucratic, inefficient and bumbling institution which was much less effective than Western intelligence agencies had assumed. It would be interesting to know if the picture it painted has been taken seriously by MI6. The book appeared in 1990 when the first accounts of the changes inside the KGB began to be published in the Soviet Union by serving officers. However, by then the KGB was in even more disarray.

At a conference of former intelligence personnel and commentators held in Potsdam, under the auspices of the International Freedom Foundation, in November 1991, KGB officers admonished their Western counterparts for their simplistic view of what was happening to the KGB. The process of restructuring was far more complicated, they said, than delegates realised. 'I have a notion', said Major-General Oleg Kalugin, former head of the KGB Line KR which was responsible for foreign counter-intelligence, 'that they base their opinions on the KGB as it functioned during the Cold War and that they have not yet caught up with the realities of developments in the Soviet Union today. I am very sorry for them because events are changing the political landscape so dramatically that even junior officers, schooled under the old system, are today fleeing the KGB because they no longer see a future for themselves within this organization.'[10]

In September 1992, the head of the Russian Foreign Intelligence Service (FIS), which had taken over some of the functions of the old KGB, Yevgeny Primakov, revealed the depth of the problems facing his service in a country where attitudes have turned against intelligence because of past abuses by the KGB. Colonel Vladimir Rubanov, former chief of the Analysis Department of the Gorbachev-reformed KGB, told the Potsdam conference that 'Constitutional breakdown has led to confusion around the legality of security service activities thus exacerbating political and legal uncertainties in the operation of future security services'. According to Rubanov, many of the proposals on reform of the KGB were, in fact, 'borrowed from already known structures and practices from

Western intelligence and counter-intelligence services'. Unfortunately, this included MI5, whose director to be, Stella Rimington, visited Moscow in December 1991 to discuss suitable oversight measures. Kalugin and Rubanov derided Western intelligence assessments of FIS activity. The FIS had been hit hard by budget cuts, they said, and had been forced to close thirty stations world-wide. Primakov claimed that operations had ceased in most of Africa and the Far East. By the end of 1992, the number of overseas staff had been halved. The types of political operations abroad, such as the funding of political groups, had been forbidden, according to Primakov. The FIS was finding it increasingly hard to work abroad because it could not find cover for its operatives; businessmen and journalsists were being withdrawn. 'The Foreign Minister does not want to keep them,' reported Rubanov, 'nor do the media people of the trade organizations . . . Aeroflot never took spies seriously – so there is actually little room left for Primakov and his people.'[11]

When Kalugin made a private visit to London in October 1991, the local FIS chief of station expressed a desire to see him. When they did meet, the station chief told him, in desperation: 'Listen, I want some direction and I do not know what to do in London.' Kalugin did not wish to be compromised and refused to help, but the request confirmed his view that 'They do not do anything because they do not know what to do – that is the problem. They have lost their targets and their direction.' Operatives were reduced to reading local national newspapers for the intelligence reports, which they forwarded to Moscow. The main task of other agents appears to be to check out foreign companies undertaking business in Russia.[12]

In September 1992, Primakov went so far as to offer other countries a 'no-spy deal' if 'intelligence services say they will stop their activities' in Russia and provided 'there is a government guarantee'. The Bulgarian Deputy Foreign Minister, Nikolai Bogdanov, had already informed foreign countries in

May 1991 that, in future, embassies abroad would be staffed by only one intelligence operative, whose identity and duties – counter-terrorism and crime – would be declared to the host country. The FIS would, claimed Primakov, concentrate on acquiring economic and scientific intelligence and knowledge about critical technologies. These proposals were not welcomed by hard-liners in MI5 and MI6 who pointed to and leaked details on the activities in this area of Oleg Oshchenko. However, these operations had taken place during the Cold War and involved covert operations. Times have changed, and the idea of FIS intelligence officers poring over scientific journals in university and specialised libraries – a completely legal activity – is not one that should produce disquiet. Perhaps instead we should turn a blind eye to these spying efforts and see them as a form of economic assistance to a beleaguered nation.[13]

The FIS is co-operating with MI6 and sharing intelligence on such areas as drugs and terrorism. This begs the question whether this co-operation can be extended and, thus, whether an expansion of MI6 resources is at all warranted. Russia has nothing to hide, according to Rubanov. 'There are no secrets left any more. Probably in the narrow fields of science and research and in military technology, but for instance, in the field of politics and economics I can find hardly any. The greatest secret is our weakness.' Theodore Shackley, who spent twenty-eight years in the CIA, including a spell as Associate Deputy Director for Operations, believes that some of the changes now taking place are 'mind boggling'. In Eastern and Central Europe, Shackley believes that 'about eighty per cent of what policy makers will want to know will be available overtly. The prime sources are going to be newspapers and magazines, as well as scientific, academic and trade journals.' More information will come from the international organisations such as the International Monetary Fund, the World Bank and the United Nations, 'which will tell us more about their economies than we ever knew before'.

The development of electronic databases, where a great deal of the material is available commercially, will make many current intelligence operations redundant.[14]

MI6 has a long tradition of operating in Central Europe, and in the last couple of years has been helping to train officers from former Eastern bloc intelligence services, which, ironically, have introduced oversight systems much more comprehensive than those in place in Britain. MI6 now enjoys cordial links with services in Romania, Hungary and Czechoslovakia, where it trained President Havel's bodyguard. A group of Polish officers spent a time at MI6's training school at Fort Monckton and at Hereford, where they received weapons training from the SAS. MI6 had a good reputation, according to the Poles, because 'it is so secret'.[15]

The 'vassal relationship' between Czech intelligence and the KGB has formally ended and relations with Western agencies, including MI6, have blossomed. The Czechs have been searching for a new partner and MI6 has been seen as a favourite. In 1989, anti-drug and anti-terrorism offices were set up with central databases and a unit for international co-operation. Czechoslovakia and Poland have been targets of Mafia and Colombian cartel operations, with money poured into the countries for drug production as an entry point into Europe. In the summer of 1992, Foreign Secretary Douglas Hurd signed a memorandum of understanding with the Czech government to co-operate in combating terrorism (Czechoslovakia has halted production and export of the Semtex explosive), drug trafficking, organised crime and money laundering. Also agreed was a general exchange of information and assistance on specific investigations and inquiries. Another agreement was reached limiting the number of intelligence officers allowed to work in the other's country to six, while some Czech businessmen used as intelligence agents and members of the First Directorate of the StB have been withdrawn. MI6 has also been asked to provide help in rooting out communist spies. According to former Interior Minister Jan

Lagos, the federal intelligence agency FBIS had quickly established efficient methods with help from MI6 and the CIA.[16]

While acknowledging that some of the changes have been remarkable, Theodore Shackley also believes that there will have to be an intelligence-gathering effort as long as Russia maintains intercontinental ballistic missiles and large nuclear stockpiles. Following the attempted Soviet coup against President Gorbachev by hard-line Communists of the old regime, British Cabinet sources told the *Sunday Telegraph* that intelligence reports spoke of a total breakdown of security around nuclear weapons depots in the former Soviet republics. There were alarmist intelligence reports that there might be a nuclear civil war in republics outside of Moscow's control. This led to fears that nuclear weapons might also find their way to the Islamic countries bordering the former Soviet Union. A series of scare stories which were spread in the Middle East in October 1991 included the claim that Iran had succeeded in buying nuclear warheads from Kazakhstan. In March 1992, General Viktor Samoilov, who was in charge of disarmament questions at the Commonwealth of Independent States' general staff, claimed that three nuclear warheads had gone missing. This was confirmed by a top-secret report from the newly formed Russian FIS and by Western intelligence sources.[17]

The Russians were just as worried about these reports and, despite the fact that MI6 and other Western intelligence agencies were as active as ever in the former Soviet Union, the deputy head of the Russian KGB, Major-General Vladimir Podelyakin, offered the services of the KGB to fight against nuclear proliferation and to pool information on the rogue republics. While it was true that three nuclear artillery shells had indeed 'gone missing', they were later discovered in mine shafts used for bomb testing. In May 1992, Western intelligence sources confirmed all nuclear weapons were now in Russia and that it was unlikely that any had disappeared. There had been no loss of central control. A State Department official added that the official view was that Iran 'is at least ten years away – which is the official language for saying they are nowhere'.[18]

Parallel to these stories, the spectre of the nuclear terrorist was raised by the London-based Research Institute for the Study of Conflict and Terrorism. There were fears that weapons-grade plutonium would find its way on to the black market. A number of stories confirming this have appeared, but their level of truthfulness is open to question. In October 1989, a British subject suffering from radiation sickness, Derek Smith, was arrested in Athens carrying 5.5 pounds of uranium, said to be a sample of a larger order for Libya. In October 1992, German police seized a small quantity of weapons-grade uranium in Munich. In November, the *Sunday Express* had a major story on the seizure of plutonium in Bulgaria, a find, if confirmed by scientists, that would be the first known appearance in the West of smuggled raw material for a nuclear bomb from the former Soviet bloc. The press made a great deal of the international black market trade in a strange substance known as 'Red Mercury', which is supposed to be a potential source of cheap nuclear weapons. However, scientists dismissed the substance as 'a half-baked scam'. The CIA has set up dummy firms to entrap nuclear smugglers but has so far failed, according to one intelligence source, to come across a single genuine deal. 'There have been literally thousands of claims but when we track them back the cases have fallen apart.' What caught the attention of the intelligence services was that Libya, Iraq and Iran were apparently paying huge sums for this mystical substance. MI6 has been paying out large sums to penetrate the 'nuclear mafia' which is alleged to be selling plutonium to the Middle East, according to a former officer.[19]

The respected International Institute for Strategic Studies warned of the danger of 'white-coated mercenaries' – demobbed Soviet scientists selling their nuclear knowledge to the highest bidder. A story that Libya had tried to entice a nuclear scientist with a large salary to build a nuclear bomb was said by 'intelligence sources' to be 'the public tip of a secret iceberg'. MI6 and other intelligence agencies have been monitoring this 'back-channel' recruitment under the guise of academic or commercial technology by turning around the intelligence-gathering apparatus and assets previously used to keep surveillance of illegal technology shipments to the Eastern bloc. However, because of the intense security and compartmentalisation in the communist regime, few scientists had access to knowledge outside of their own narrow field of specialisation. In January 1992, the International Atomic Energy Agency in Vienna dismissed intelligence claims on the subject and said that there was no evidence of Soviet experts actually taking up employment in other countries.[20]

An MI6 source has said that the service was learning the lessons of Saddam Hussein's successful operation in securing nuclear technology and expertise under the noses of regulatory bodies such as the International Atomic Energy Authority. Much nuclear-significant technology was not subject to control until the introduction of the London Nuclear Suppliers' Group revised list was approved in January 1992. Iraq's nuclear programe had heightened concern about other nations nursing nuclear ambitions – Iran, Algeria, North Korea, Libya, Syria and Taiwan. There is a fear that the nuclear expertise of the 'threshold states' Israel, India, Pakistan, China, South Africa, Brazil and Argentina might be sold to other countries. Iraq had a design for a nuclear warhead which is believed to have come from abroad – Pakistan, India and China were the prime suspects. Sudan was identified as a clearing house for the international trade in nuclear material and technology. In February 1992, Pakistan, for the first time, admitted that it had the components and expertise to assemble at least one nuclear bomb, though it claimed that it had permanently frozen production of new weapons cores. The admission was designed to appease the Americans after a secret bilateral accord, reached in 1989, under which Pakistan agreed to limit its nuclear programme, collapsed when military hard-liners advocated the production of an 'Islamic bomb'. South Africa has announced that it has abandoned its own nuclear weapons programme, but while it has claimed that it had the technology to produce a nuclear bomb, it has never admitted building one. Despite close liaison, Western intelligence never did publicly establish whether South Africa (and Israel) had, in fact, succeeded in their ambitions.[21]

The use of the Scud missile during the Gulf War has added to concerns about proliferation of such weapons and the developments being made by a number of Middle Eastern and Asian countries which might lead to the use of nuclear warheads. Britain is a member of the informal Missile Technology Control regime, which was set up in 1987 to restrict the free-market sale of missile technology. In 1990, a Defence Intelligence Staff team along with MI6 set up a working party to monitor countries acquiring 'high-leverage low-cost tactical ballistic missiles'. In particular, it was concerned about the Condor-2, which was being developed jointly by Argentina, Iraq and Egypt. The Gulf War ended Iraq's involvement and Egypt was squeezed out of the programme by the Americans, but Argentina is still believed to be developing its own version, known as the Alacran.[22]

Western concerns about nuclear proliferation centre on the Islamic fundamentalist countries, a target which appears to be the new bogey stalking the intelligence world. The private view of the Ministry of Defence is said to be that control of nuclear proliferation is 'a lost cause'. However, this reflects the MoD's desire to protect its budget and the view of its military planners, who believe that they may be able to use, if necessary, small, low-yield nuclear weapons as a 'shot across the bows' in the Third World and the Middle East.[23]

A former CIA senior analyst on Middle Eastern affairs, Graham Fuller, has said that 'there is now a struggle for the soul of Central Asia'; a handy scenario to replace the Soviet threat. *The Times* listed some of the new security concerns which now exercise the minds of those in the intelligence community: Pakistan's acquisition of nuclear expertise, Algeria's building of a nuclear plant, arms buying by Iran in Russia and North Korea, the attempt by Iran to use Sudan in order to export militant Islam, the attempted supply of arms to Muslims in Bosnia. Added to which, there is the likelihood of regional conflict. In such circumstances, 'wild cards (national sentiment, fundamentalist religion) begin to litter the deck, and the need becomes urgent for a more widespread, diversified flow of intelligence of precisely the kind no single nation can afford. What is required is a better global division of intelligence between the Western countries.' There has been increased co-operation between European intelligence agencies and Egypt, which is regarded as the key to Middle East stability, even though there are serious flaws in its democracy. There is a view among the agencies, a dangerous throwback to the fifties, that an army coup would be preferable to the prospect of a radical Islamic state developing an arsenal of nuclear weapons.[24]

Western intelligence agencies have claimed that Saddam Hussein secretly sent 'ten tonnes of natural uranium' and a team of nuclear scientists to Algeria to circumvent United Nations scrutiny. GCHQ-intercepted telephone calls between Iraqi officials in Baghdad were said to describe the route of the nuclear consignment from Iraq to Jordan and then by ship to the port of Algiers. As long ago as 1988, there were reports that China, the world's most aggressive exporter of nuclear technology, was helping Algeria with its nuclear programme, while in January 1990 CIA satellite pictures revealed the existence of Algeria's Chinese-built nuclear reactor in a heavily guarded desert location at Oussera, one hundred miles south of Algiers. Algeria, which has not signed the non-proliferation treaty, has denied that the plant will be used to produce weapons-grade plutonium. Dismissing the denial, MI6 apparently fears that the two countries might form a 'nuclear axis' to build an 'Islamic bomb' of 'Nagasaki' proportions by 1995. A Joint Intelligence Committee report to the Cabinet concluded that the pact posed a threat to southern Europe, Israel and the Middle East.[25]

To counter the threat, MI6 has been devoting extra resources to monitoring political and scientific developments in Algeria. The Foreign Office had assumed that Algeria's professional middle class and relatively liberal society would be a brake on Islamic fundamentalism. However, the halting of the second run-off, following the success of the Islamic National Salvation Front in the first round of the elections in December 1991, was seen as only a temporary halt in the advance of the fundamentalists. Following the assassination of the movement's leader, Mohammed Boudiaf, intelligence assessors feared that Islamic-inspired unrest might spill over the borders. This has led to increased co-ordination between intelligence agencies to monitor the activities of Muslim terrorists in North Africa. Intelligence reports spoke of up to a thousand 'hard-core' terrorists who had fought in Afghanistan operating within Algeria. Financed by Iran, many of the 'Afghan veterans' of the 'Expiation and Sin' group had been trained in Pakistan under control of the CIA. Bitter at their failure to dislodge the communists from Kabul, they returned home to carry out terrorist attacks inside the country. This illustrated a familiar problem, what to do with well-trained guerrillas and terrorists when their services are no longer required.[26]

Another area of uncertainty is South East Asia, where oil wealth found beneath the South China Sea is fuelling an explosive arms race in which British arms sales people have been prominent. Every nation surrounding the waters, including Britain's closest ally in this area, Brunei, has announced a major weapons build-up fearing that post-Cold War withdrawal of American and Russian forces will bring to the boil long-suppressed territorial and maritime claims. Defence spending was, in 1992, the highest outside of the NATO area.[27]

Since the end of an east of Suez defence policy, MI6 has been rather thin on the ground in the Far East, and in its role as 'aggressive foreign intelligence collector' has relied on the close co-operation of the Australian Secret Intelligence Service (ASIS) in developing links with the security and intelligence agencies in the Pacific rim area. Operations are closely integrated throughout the Far East with swapping of intelligence and individuals. MI6 and ASIS officers are free to enter each other's premises and seek help and support from one another. An ASIS official works in Century House, specialising in Chinese 'counter-intelligence targeting' with others employed on operational duties and planning 'Special Operations'. MI6 intelligence liaison officers are involved in training ASIS officers, the exchange of sensitive technical equipment and the sharing of up to 50,000 secret intelligence reports per year.

Naturally, given the importance of Hong Kong as the major financial centre in the Pacific rim, the British government recognises that the need for intelligence on China will increase in the run-up to the transfer of sovereignty in 1997. At the beginning of 1991, the Foreign Office set up a special section to concentrate on events in southern China and Taiwan. Hong Kong is the key centre for 'China-watching', with an MI6 station under cover of the 'Study Group' inside the military headquarters of British Forces in the province. There is also believed to be a base in Singapore attached to the ANZUK (Australia – New Zealand – UK) 'Intelligence Group'. The political adviser from the Foreign Office chairs the super-secret Hong Kong Local Intelligence Committee, which comprises the director of the Special Branch, the MI5 security liaison officer, the head of the 'Study Group', the head of the GCHQ, and military intelligence representatives. The intelligence services are also interested in events across the Pearl River estuary in the Portuguese enclave of Macau, which reverts to Chinese rule in 1999. Intelligence sources report North Korean representatives transferring millions of dollars to banks in Macau for a spending spree on Western military equipment. Portugal is one of the few countries to have diplomatic relations with North Korea, whose last remaining ally is China.[28]

The size of the intelligence community in Hong Kong can be gauged by the 6,300 passports with right to abode in Britain status given to people described as working in 'military and civilian roles who were exposed to special consideration and special factors during the course of their duty'. This is a minimum figure, given that some Special Branch officers have had their request for passports turned down. The secretive Special Branch was set up by MI5, after Mao Tse-tung and the communists swept to power in China in 1949, to guard against subversives. It was run by expatriates with the assistance of security liaison officers from MI5 stationed in the colony. In turn, past senior officials such as Brian Slevin, Commissioner, and Christopher Dawson, Deputy Commissioner, have been recruited by MI5 for its China desk (probably now the preserve of MI6). Special Branch runs Chinese agents and keeps tabs on 'sensitive political and counter-terrorist matters' in the colony. It also monitors the Chinese hinterland. When the Chinese take over the province, Branch records will be transferred to London. These will be subject to Britain's Official Secrets Act, which was introduced in Hong Kong by order of the Privy Council in June 1992.[29]

Chinese defections, and in particular those of intelligence officers, are relatively rare in comparison to the number from the former Eastern bloc. Seven Chinese embassy staff are believed to have defected to Britain while serving in London since the Tiananmen Square massacre in 1989, but most were of a low rank. In March 1992, Feng Baosheng, First Secretary at the Chinese embassy in London, sought asylum. During 1991, Feng had contacted Chinese dissidents from the crushed pro-democracy movement, and when his political sympathies were discovered he and his wife were given two days to return to Beijing. Instead, he chose to defect, embarrassing China, which put out the false story that Feng had wanted to live with his mistress.[30]

The highest-ranking defector to the West has been the seventy-four-year-old Xu Jiatun. MI6 wanted to debrief Jiatun, who had served for seven years as China's *de facto* ambassador to Hong Kong and was a confidant of Deng Xiaoping, to gain information about Beijing's true intentions towards the territory. Xu was placed off limits by the Bush administration, which played down his defection in April 1990 as it did not wish to embarrass the Chinese leadership. He was a director of the New China News Agency (NCNA) in the colony between 1983 and 1990, where he was privy to all workings and policies of the Chinese government and its plans for Hong Kong. Deng Xiaoping had sent Xu to Hong Kong to prepare the territory for its return in 1997. A hard-line communist, Xu is said to have gradually become a liberal in favour of the free market. In 1989, he gave tacit support to officials who backed the pro-democracy movement in China. His defection led to a purge among the NCNA staff.[31]

Britain has promised the Chinese that it will close down its GCHQ composite signals station on the south coast of Hong Kong island in 1994. This was regarded as Britain's most important intelligence-gathering base in the area and was responsible for monitoring military, commercial and political life in China. During the 1989 pro-democracy demonstrations the base played a key role in building a picture of Chinese military intentions. Previously sited at Little Sai Wan, it was, in 1982, the subject of allegations by GCHQ employee Jock Kane, which were suppressed by the British government. He cited breaches of security, corruption and the operation of a call-girl ring. It was eventually closed when the Australians, with whom the site was shared, withdrew from the project and it was relocated to its present site near Stanley in 1984. The Chinese regarded the base as a hostile spy station and, under the agreement to transfer sovereignty in 1997, demanded the right to inspect the site. The Foreign Office refused the request and, in consultation with GCHQ and MI6, decided to close it down in the interests of a smooth transition.[32]

MI6 has been investigating the prospect of relocating its intelligence-gathering facility to a number of countries in the area. A British expert was sent to Manila in the Philippines, where MI6 does not have a station, to discuss the idea but decided against it because the country is regarded as too unstable. Singapore, with which the Foreign Office has excellent relations, site of the regional security headquarters in the fifties, is believed to have insisted on an exchange of information which would mean difficulties for MI6, with its agreements under the UK–USA treaty on intelligence. Northern Australia has also been considered, however, the Kowandi Radio Communications base south of the GCHQ base at Darwin which had been jointly operated by MI6 and ASIS for more than twenty years, was closed down in March 1993. The relay facility at Kowandi, which was the control centre for communications for MI6 and ASIS operations in South East Asia, has been superseded by new technology. The Whitehall favourite appears to be the oil-rich state of Brunei, where British influence, with the help of a Gurkha regiment, remains strong since independence in 1984.[33]

As can be seen, the intelligence community has not been slow in adapting itself to the post-Cold War world and has been very adept at finding new directions and targets to keep itself busy during the nineties. However, while some of the fears about Islamic fundamentalism may be genuine, even at the most extreme there is no comparison with the nuclear arsenal of the old Soviet Union and the balance of terror which existed during the Cold War. In May 1992, while acknowledging that the secret development of nuclear weapons was causing 'the greatest concern', Paul Wolfowitz, under-secretary for defence policy at the Pentagon, remarked that 'it is a measure of how much more peaceful the world has become since the end of the Cold War, that we can only cite Korea "as a source of potential danger".' It is perhaps time to stop thinking in old terms about 'threats' and instead look calmly at 'risks' – 'the new security challenge is to stop those risks becoming threats'. This means effective arms policing and the stiffening of international agreements. The intelligence services will continue to have a vital role, but it does not, or should not, involve the implementation of new covert action operations which appear to be on the minds of some practitioners in the intelligence community.[34]

Conservative United States military analysts see the Cold War being replaced by an era of North–South confrontation, countering future Third World threats to US political and economic interests. United Kingdom military strategists have begun to move in the same direction. This is known as 'keeping the violent peace'; the new target being 'that swirling pot of poison made up of zealots, crazies, drug-runners and terrorists'. There is a tendency to overplay the instability threat caused by the end of the Cold War. It is, of course, in the interests of the intelligence services to play on these fears, and they are very inventive at creating new bogeys – militant emigration, narco-terrorists, nuclear terrorists, eco-terrorists, Islamic fundamentalism, etc. The list appears to be endless and, just as we discovered at the end of the Cold War that many of the threats generated by the intelligence services in the previous four decades had been mostly exaggerated and, in many cases, just simply manufactured, we may find at the end of this decade that today's fears were similarly unwarranted.[35]

Conclusion

> In this crisis, I must hold my tongue or I must speak with freedom. Falsehood and delusion are allowed in no case whatever: but, as in the exercise of all the virtues, there is an economy of truth.
>
> Edmund Burke, *Letter on a Regicide Peace*, 1796

I understand that MI5 officers within Gower Street are 'very sensitive' and 'mystified' about the bad press which they have received over the past few years. There is a plaintive cry of 'why?' One answer was provided in the House of Lords in December 1992 by Lord Jenkins of Hillhead, who had twice been nominally in charge of MI5 as Home Secretary. He claimed that ministers spent more time dealing with 'internecine quarrels' within MI5 and MI6 than with any effective information which the security services provided. He advised new ministers: 'Never sign automatically anything coming up from the security services – and be very cautious about signing it. It is increasingly my conviction that the security services cause more trouble than they are worth.'[1]

If former ministers no longer trust the security services, it is not surprising that the public at large question their relevance. There are a number of reasons for this continuing bad press. Firstly, there has been the residual build-up of feeling after a long series of scandals which have gone unanswered. This book has listed just a few. Oversight of security services in other countries has come about only after inquiries into wrongdoing and security failures. Only after an intensive judicial inquiry into the numerous scandals which took place in the seventies and eighties will it be possible to conduct a serious debate and move on to the second stage, which is the development of proposals for oversight. It is not possible to make reforms unless one knows what worked and what did not work in the past. As long as the secret state and the service refuses to countenance such a move, distrust will remain. The cleaning of the stables needs to be carried out in the open.

Secondly, MI5's record over the years is poor. Between 1945 and 1971, not one Soviet spy was arrested in this country on the initiative of MI5. The identification of famous spies came about when defectors to the United States informed the CIA and the FBI about the lack of security in the British secret state. Despite an enormous number of man-hours spent on counter-espionage, the service failed to recruit KGB officers. In its defence, officers will claim that it succeeded in its primary role of defending the realm; however, MI5 is not allowed to publicise its successes during the Cold War, and we are asked to take this statement on trust. Outsiders such as Robert Cecil, former Foreign Office adviser to MI6, rush to MI5's defence, insisting that the KGB made a 'contribution to Britain's industrial decline' and that this was the 'enemy within'; without MI5's presence the situation would have been much worse, they say. While not dismissing the role that the KGB did play, the evidence, such as it is, does not justify the rhetoric. As more and more KGB files are opened and former officers tell their stories, historians, I am sure, will reveal that the 'threat' during the Cold War was exaggerated. Maybe this was a simple miscalculation, a human error. Unfortunately for MI5, Peter Wright's memoirs reveal that key officers within the service really did believe in the conspiracy view of history, in the 'Red' plot.[2]

All this might not have mattered overmuch had it been confined to George Smiley type intelligence games within the ranks of the Establishment – notwithstanding that it led to the destruction of a number of innocent lives – and had it not formed the basis for the assault on 'subversion'. Immense damage was done by F Branch, the scale of which is only now becoming clear. The public would be shocked if it knew the full extent and range of the surveillance and recruitment operations carried out in the seventies.

Although MI5 has made significant cuts in its counter-subversion work, F Branch still exists. Any reform must start with its abolition. Both the Australian and the Canadian security services, which were modelled on MI5, have abandoned the term 'subversive'. Australia's Security and Intelligence Organisation dropped the term as being too general and open to abuse. The definition of the word, reformers found, could be 'endless' and, in practice, open to continual abuse. 'Subversive' has been replaced with 'politically motivated violence'. The ASIO director-general said that the public did not expect the service to be involved in the monitoring of trade union activity; terrorism and espionage are the proper targets.[3]

There is no doubt that changes for the better have been made within MI5. Management was always poor and supervision fragmented with too many short-term appointments. During the eighties there were five director-generals within a decade, which, as Jonathan Aitken pointed out in Parliament, 'is an astonishing turnover in the world of counter-intelligence where a long perspective is often needed'. Similarly, within counter-espionage there were at least four different directors. Walker and Stella Rimington did impose reforms and refocused the service to meet new demands. However, it is my feeling that this was too little too late. The simple fact is, the Security Service is one agency too many. In the post-Cold War world there is little bureaucratic justification for both a Special Branch and a Security Service. In the United States, the Federal Bureau of Investigation covers both police and counter-espionage functions.[4]

The tide of history has been running against MI5. In the sixties, with the end of empire, MI5 closed its E Branch, which ran and liaised with security organisations in Africa and some parts of the Middle East. MI6 took over the role and also began to encroach upon the counter-espionage functions of K

Branch, putting its own officers into Gower Street. At the same time, Special Branch began to expand its surveillance of the 'far and wide left' and MI5 appeared to be in decline. However, it was saved by making an intervention into Northern Ireland and putting forward its own bid for counter-subversion work. All went well until the end of the Cold War, when, conscious that its reason for being had effectively disappeared, the service began to refocus its targeting. F and K Branches were decimated and counter-terrorism now came into vogue. While this reshuffle satisfied ministers, it had a hasty, ill-thought-out look about it, designed more by fear of redundancy and bureaucratic necessities than any reference to what a security strategy required. A better, rational and more common-sense solution would be to close the service down completely. In 1990, in one of those ritual responses which occur every few decades, Whitehall did consider plans to merge MI5 and MI6 in an effort to cut costs and share resources in recognition of their close co-operation, particularly in areas such as international terrorism. The move failed to materialise, principally because of a lack of will at the usual infighting.[5]

No doubt a fierce bureaucratic battle would begin if moves were made to abolish the Security Service. While the example of Gough Whitlam's similar move in Australia in the early seventies highlights the dangers (ministers and eventually the government fell following a series of intelligence-backed smear campaigns), a committed government that sought police support for an FBI-style force and cynically joined forces with MI6 would succeed against the inevitable political flak and smears directed against it. Most of MI5's functions could easily be carried out by existing departments: Protective Security could go to the Ministry of Defence; an opportunity would arise for politicians to close down F Branch and its surveillance of 'subversives'; S Branch's computer security work could be given to GCHQ; counter-espionage and world-wide counter-terrorism operations could be transferred to MI6, who are known to be keen to accept responsibility for these areas;

domestic counter-terrorism would be the province of a single specialised police-based unit. MI5 would wither on the vine.

The dangers of allowing the Security Service to assume overall control of the counter-terrorism effort became apparent in early 1993. MI5's massive over-reaction in monitoring alleged firebombers in North Wales and its intelligence failure in capturing mainland IRA bombers – most of those arrested having been captured through luck or police vigilance – only exacerbated inter-service rivalries. The turf-battle between the Security Service and police turned into what the *Guardian* describes as a 'covert war of secret briefings and counter briefings that is beginning to be-devil MI5'. Sources close to Stella Rimington indicate that some of the briefers may even be senior MI5 officers, eager to see the back of Mrs Rimington.

Something most certainly should be done about domestic operations. A number of cases during the autumn of 1992 gave a public glimpse of the dangerous spread of surveillance. During her industrial tribunal hearing into sex discrimination directed against her when she was Deputy Chief Constable of Merseyside, Alison Holford referred to her telephone calls being tapped, while a couple of 'freelance spooks' based in Belgium claimed that they had been approached by the security services to 'bug' Ms Holford. Lord Spens, who was cleared of involvement in the Guinness affair, attacked the security services and other agencies for having 'left no stone unturned in their effort to convict us. There have been telephone taps, harassment and overt threats to me and my colleagues.' Protesters against the building of a motorway across Twyford Down had been infiltrated on behalf of the Department of Transport and their telephones were tapped. Fifteen hundred pages of documents stolen from the Lothian and Borders police revealed an extensive telephone-tapping operation which included monitoring calls to the regional council, government offices and lawyers. What made the operation controversial was that it included the use of telephone metering by British Telecom; this requires no warrant from a Secretary of State.[6]

The greatest threat to civil liberties comes from the one agency over which there is no judicial oversight of any kind or any outside body monitoring its activities. GCHQ, headed by fifty-three-year-old John Adye, has some 11,000 civilian and military staff and a budget of over £800 million coming mainly from within MoD expenditure but supplemented by the United States National Security Agency, with which it retains close institutional and treaty ties. Officially, GCHQ is responsible to the Foreign Secretary; however, the annual reports on warrants issued for telephone tapping do not identify which, if any, are actually authorised by Douglas Hurd on behalf of the agency. GCHQ is nevertheless able to scoop up – through a network of computers, collectively known as 'The Dictionary', which searches for specified combinations of key words and names – thousands of telephone calls, telexes and faxes, seemingly without restraint.

As MI5 has moved out of the domestic arena under the weight of increasing criticism, GCHQ has expanded its monitoring of 'subversives' and 'internal' targets by setting up a special unit, K20. This move disturbed some members at Cheltenham. Dennis Mitchell, a cryptanalyst for thirty-two years, said in 1987 that some of GCHQ's activities 'would be considered unacceptable by the general public were it aware of them'. In an article in the *Guardian* he wrote that 'GCHQ is an industrial complex. Its product is intelligence. Intelligence imparts power; power which may be used to withstand a threat – or to apply one; to avert ill, to bestow a benefit – or to exploit it. Intelligence shared is power shared; intelligence withheld confers power over the unaware. GCHQ provides power to the British government; and governments with which it is allied. GCHQ staff have a moral responsibility, both corporate and individual, for the use to which that power is put.'[7]

Taking heed of Mitchell's concerns, in June 1992 an anonymous group of highly placed signals intelligence operatives issued a statement, published in the *Observer*, concerning what they considered to be 'gross malpractice and negligence within'. They had 'witnessed and participated in activities and practices that are certainly contrary to commonly accepted ethics, when not technically illegal'. According to investigations carried out by the *Guardian* and the television programme *World in Action*, GCHQ routinely spies on charities such as Christian Aid and Amnesty International; companies and trade unions; individuals, including a ninety-three-year-old active peace campaigner, Kathleen Tacchi-Morris, and the General Secretary of the Scottish Trade Union Congress, Campbell Christie, with no justification on the grounds of national security. These operations took place under procedures known as 'Mantis' for telephone taps and 'Mayfly' for telex taps and are often made 'on speculation' and without warrants.[8]

More than any other agency, GCHQ is in need of reform and 'avowal', the process of official and legal recognition. Following the banning of trade unions at Cheltenham in 1984, morale slumped and a flood of talent – scientists, engineers and, most crucially, highly prized linguists – left the agency, many to work in the private sector, where they are able to earn more and where their talents gain appreciation. However, GCHQ still appears to be a bloated agency, overstaffed – one report 'implied that twenty per cent of the workforce is idle for half of the day'. The agency is badly organised and inefficiently run, with some sections 'unmanageable', and, even after the changes made following the conviction of the traitor Geoffrey Prime, lax in its security. GCHQ is currently in the middle of a three-year inquiry into a 'redirection effort', which so far has suggested staff cuts of 10 per cent. This is, it would appear, an internal inquiry, when what is really required is an outside investigation into the whole range of its activities.[9]

The future of the Secret Intelligence Service (MI6) looks much more secure. Discreetly, MI6 has begun to open channels to the media, letting it be known that it welcomes its new 'legal' status. 'I would like to believe', said former chief Sir Dick White, 'they will not make such a mystery of everything and discuss events after they have taken place and are of no operational interest. A lot of sensible arrangements could easily be made that will make life easier for everybody.' There is talk of creating at some future date a front office to deal with press enquiries.[10]

However, the window dressing hides a number of fundamental questions which need attention. Although one might argue that in a democracy 'gentlemen should not read other people's mail', realistically governments of all political persuasions will continue to require information to be gathered. The question is, does this require a secret agency? The answer is probably no. Data collection will grow apace with commercial satellites providing more and more material at a cost-effective price. The beauty of this 'open skies' arrangement will be its availability for all countries and citizens. Information systems will expand and information as a commodity will become ever more important. The potential for private, commercial intelligence services is enormous and, as in so many areas, Japanese corporations are likely to show the way.

Too many people – especially those with power and influence – are in thrall to secret knowledge. They assure us that they are privy to what is really going on – a fact, as this book has illustrated, that is very rarely true. Better analysis of diplomatic reports, newspaper accounts and other open sources would have provided the necessary warnings about the Falklands, Iraq and other trouble spots. When the CIA was set up in the late forties, debate centred around the question of whether it should be an open agency or a secret one. The Paris head of station requested of headquarters that he be allowed to advertise his name and address in the French newspapers, as so many people with information were having difficulty finding him. Unfortunately, this was at a time when the Dulles brothers had wrested control of the agency from the Democrats and had begun their anti-communist drive. The shutters came down and an era of covert action began. There is now an opportunity to reverse the trend. A model might be the forerunner of the CIA, the Office of Strategic Studies' Research and Analysis branch, where academics, scientists, economists and specialists presented reports on countries and specific areas of interest. An analysis branch could operate as an open agency delivering reports on anything from oil to nuclear proliferation to government and to the commercial market. The Russian Foreign Intelligence Service demonstated the possibilities of such an approach when, in February 1993, it released an 118-page report on arms developments from Chile to Korea, described by analysts as 'the most comprehensive report on the spread of nuclear, chemical and biological weapons ever issued'.

This would leave aside the thorny problem of covert action – which may include anything from assassination to rigging elections. Although there are well-thought-out arguments (coming particularly from former practitioners) that covert action is unnecessary, it would not be realistic to believe that any government would be willing to dispose of this option, particularly if there appears to be a threat from a terrorist group. However, there is no reason why such operations should not be regulated by ministerial warrants in the manner of buggings, telephone tappings and mail openings. Major covert actions undertaken abroad should be subject to pre-sight by a Select Committee, as in the United States. MI6 should be reduced to a small, tightly controlled organisation, better reflecting Britain's standing in the world and the requirements of our foreign policy and economic position.

If the security services do have a genuine complaint, it is that ministers have refused to take their responsibilities seriously. They have insulated themselves from the actions of the various agencies for fear of being held to account in Parliament. This has resulted in a lack of clear direction and policy. These problems could be rectified by the election of a single minister responsible for the security services. The minister would be asked to set out general annual intelligence requirements and guidelines on security which would then be available for debate in Parliament. At the moment, Members of Parliament express little interest in intelligence matters, declaring that they receive few letters from the public on the subject. However, in the midst of a recession every MP should be interested in an industry which costs the British taxpayer over £1 billion per annum.

The public is entitled to reassurance that its spies are under the control of elected representatives, and the best means of ensuring this is by a Select Committee of the House of Commons. However, British officials have found this a difficult concept to accept. British participants to a Ditchley conference on 'The Oversight of and the Limits on Intelligence Work in a Democracy', held in October 1988, 'listened with varying degrees of surprise, delight and horror' as American speakers declared that the cons of oversight had 'not proved too onerous, nor had they outweighed the pros. No covert operation is believed to have been compromised.' 'Not for the first time,' wrote Simon Jenkins, former editor of *The Times*, 'they were hearing "travellers" tales from the wilder shores of participatory democracy and were alarmed.'[11]

Those who support the status quo, such as Michael Mates, a minister in the Northern Ireland Office, dismiss parliamentary oversight of the security services because 'all the ensuing partisan connotations would be the least satisfactory means of achieving' proper supervision. However, Mates believes that we have been 'excellently served' by our security services, that ministers carry out their duty and that some MPs are not to be trusted. The real fear of such critics is that reform would 'render the nation's guard dog toothless'. Mates worries that there is no longer a 'consensus' within the House of Commons on national security affairs. The 'dwindling band of former ministers' who do are being replaced by Labour MPs who do not share the 'world view of past Labour governments, let alone the present Conservative government. In such circumstances, the danger of deliberate leaks from a Select Committee would greatly increase.' This remains the view of the Secret State.[12]

David Holliday, who has served as a staff member of the US Senate Select Committee on Intelligence, and other US officials have said that this is largely a 'red herring'. Former CIA director William Colby believed that oversight in the United States had worked well and the intelligence committees have shown that 'they know the secrets and keep the secrets'. There will be leaks, suggests Holliday, because nothing is perfect, but that should not stop what is a sensible policy. 'What we have to do is work together as hard as we can to minimize much of that exercise from occurring. There are a number of ways we can do that, including classifying those things that need to be classified, and not the reams and tons of information that are classified primarily to protect the interest of the agency which is involved.'[13]

The primary role of oversight is control of the budget for the intelligence community, which gives the committee involved considerable power. The committee must also monitor the propriety and legality of the services' activities, but at the end of the day no such system can ensure complete compliance with statutes and the law. An agency that wants to bypass committee controls will always find a way. But there are also advantages for the security services in complying with oversight, in that the members of the committee can become advocates for the services, making the case for adequate funds and providing a buffer of trust between the agencies and MPs and the public. The American experience has shown that oversight lowers the 'absurdity factor' that accompanies a complete blanket ban on discussion of the security services, and it tends to raise morale inside the services. The CIA has become a better service, partly because of oversight.[14]

In his influential 1988 book, *The Rise and Fall of the Great Powers*, Professor Paul Kennedy pointed out that it was still the case that 'The divergence between Britain's shrunken economic state and its overextended strategical posture is probably more extensive than that affecting any of the larger powers, except Russia itself.' The special but completely unbalanced relationship between the CIA and MI6, and particularly between the National Security Agency and GCHQ under the 1946 UK–USA SIGINT agreement which provides a division of effort on intelligence gathering, has been used by the permanent government as a means of maintaining that posture and shoring up Britain's waning power. It has been a policy which has had little to do with reality. Edward Heath once remarked that shredding the 'special relationship' with the United States would be more difficult psychologically than the withdrawal from empire ever was. What partially lay behind the decision in the mid-eighties to ban trade unions from Cheltenham was 'the fear in GCHQ, and perhaps in the government as well, that the NSA would take its ball away and stop GCHQ playing a major part in the international game of intelligence'. The United States had already begun to shift its intelligence-gathering requirements away from Britain.[15]

A revealing April 1982 letter from the Civil Service Union's Composite Signals Organisation (the official cover-name for GCHQ) Committee noted that 'in the past Allied operational policy was based upon close ties with, and a begrudging reliance on, GCHQ. Time alone has severed many of the close personal ties as hot and cold war colleagues retired, died or otherwise moved on. The need for reliance weakened as the collaborating effort matured in terms of techniques and manpower.' The United States had begun to set up intelligence bases in West Germany, with whom the term 'special relationship' is perhaps more appropriate, carrying out tasks which had previously been the province of the British. GCHQ management realised that 'it is unlikely that the tasks would revert to UK resources. At best GCHQ would continue a hopeless parallel action which, without back-up, would not be cost effective. At worst there would be no work to do.' At that stage GCHQ's contribution rested on the effort provided by H Division (GCHQ's cryptanalysis section responsible for breaking complex codes) which management had estimated at 75 per cent of GCHQ's practical worth. Without it there would be no special relationship.[16]

As with the health of Britain's economy, GCHQ and MI6 (and even MI5) are going to find their futures, in the realm of economic intelligence and in other areas of intelligence gathering, more and more closely tied to the development of the European Community. The old certainties about sharing a common enemy – the KGB – have gone, and as the CIA begins to treat the EC as just another competing economic power which must be penetrated, then suspicions about where Britain's security services' true loyalties lie will no doubt surface. There will be suspicions from EC partners that MI6 and, more importantly, GCHQ, which relies heavily on the Americans for finance and shares all of its intelligence with the NSA, are just a Trojan horse for gaining intelligence-gathering access to the Community. Painful choices will have to be made, and are being made; old distrusts – principally of Germany – will have to be put aside.[17]

Although effective co-operation between the security services of the EC is at an early state, French DST officials say that talks have started with 'MI5 and other European services to form a European organization' to combat industrial espionage. (This has already led to counter-espionage services drawing up a document to protect the £6.4 billion Eureka European research programme.) The countries of the EC have realised that the gathering of economic intelligence is 'less a matter of [one country] versus the world than of Europe versus North America and the countries of the Pacific Rim'. The logic of the drive for economic intelligence is that old alliances, principally the Atlantic alliance, will have, at some stage, to be jettisoned. With the departure of Mrs Thatcher, the 'last great spokesman for the American connection', the security and intelligence link-up with the United States will increasingly come under scrutiny. John Ranelagh in his book, *Thatcher's People*, notes that 'Britain has started treating Europe as truly real: not as the place over the water, but as something that Britain is part of. Ambitious people no longer think of a non-European alternative: the functionaries, the higher civil servants, politicians generally, business, the City, are thinking in European terms.' Ranelagh might have added the 'spooks' to the list for, though in secret, it is they who are making the most of the 'organic' connection with Europe. However, for the time being the progressives are being held back by the natural conservatism and reaction of the British secret state.[18]

For the moment, the security services, MI5 in particular, survive not on the basis of rational debate or decision-making but because a small select band in Britain's secret state still lives in a world of illusions, hankering after the certainties of the Cold War. Perilously clinging on to power, members of the permanent government concentrate as much control as possible at the centre while paradoxically finding that power becomes ever more diffuse. Faced with loss of imperial pretension and international prestige they retreat from the new realities with anxiety, neurotically projecting new enemies on the landscape. The security services were tasked with protecting the permanent government during the long period of Britain's economic decline but, in the face of the modernising trends of the European Community, which threaten our rulers' age-old seats of power, and with the great communist monster dead, they scamper around desperately seeking a cause to follow – anti-terrorism today, economic threats tomorrow. It fails to convince. However flawed in its democratic processes and its treatment of asylum seekers, the EC does attempt to treat its own inhabitants as citizens with rights with regard to protection of data, access to information, and oversight of secret bodies. They are not seen as subjects who can be filed, surveilled, burgled and bugged with impunity.

Despite rearguard action, gradually and painfully, the silent conspiracy which has surrounded Britain's secret state is being broken up. By the end of the decade we may have a citizenry which is informed about and confident of its security services.

Postscript

In July 1993, the veils of secrecy surrounding Britain's secret state were briefly lifted when the Security Service's director-general, Stella Rimington, gave a press conference. The service also went public with a 36-page glossy brochure, accompanied by authorised photographs of Mrs Rimington, which outlined the service's activities.

The brochure produced few new facts. However it did confirm that, following the end of the Cold War, the majority of the service's work is devoted to counter-terrorism. T Branch now accounts for 70 per cent of the service's work, of which 44 per cent is concerned with Irish and domestic terrorism and 26 per cent targeted at international terrorism, mostly Middle Eastern groups. Twenty-five per cent of the total workload involves traditional counter-espionage activities, including a growing battle against the proliferation of chemical and nuclear weapons – evidence of which was seen during the Matrix Churchill trial. The remaining 5 per cent of work is concerned with monitoring political subversion.

Initially, the response to this measure of openness was encouraging for the service but it quickly became apparent that this was an end rather than the beginning of any avalanche of information. Observers felt that a well-orchestrated publicity campaign with photo-opportunities was not a substitute for genuine accountability and only a few months later the service was again the subject of criticism for displaying the same disregard for rules of evidence for which it had been known in the eighties.

In September 1993, charges under the Official Secrets Act

against Territorial Army intelligence officer, Carole Maychell, were dropped due to insufficient evidence. Despite the existence of procedures in Security Service manuals that 'ensure that methods of investigation are lawful, respect the rights of others and are proportionate to the threat' and that 'the reliability of information obtained and used is properly evaluated', Ms Maychell had been held in solitary confinement for four months and later, after protests, in a military hospital under the care of a psychiatrist. During this period, she had been subjected to four days of aggressive interrogation by MI5 officers. In a hang-over from the Cold War, the Security Service had made allegations, eventually shown to be unsupported, that she had been seen in what had been East Berlin. At the same time, stories – also untrue – were fed to the press that she had been recruited by the East Germans in a 'honey-trap' operation.

In the House of Lords, in December 1993, Lord Jenkins of Hillhead, the service's most trenchant and informed critic, continued to attack MI5. He told peers that as Home Secretary he had 'experienced what I can best describe as an inherent lack of frankness, an ingrowing monoculture and a confidence-destroying tendency of engaging in the most devastating internal feuds'. It was a 'distorting and Alice-Through-The-Looking-Glass world in which falsehood becomes truth, fact becomes fiction and fantasy becomes reality'. As a first step Lord Jenkins suggested that MI5's political surveillance and political intelligence roles should be abandoned.

The Security Service's response to Lord Jenkins was to point to the fact that only 5 per cent of its work now concerned the monitoring of political subversion. This is, however, highly misleading since in many cases targets which were in the domain of F Branch (counter-subversion) have simply been transferred to other areas. Radicals and left-wing groups previously targeted because of alleged pro-communist links are now investigated for pro-Irish and pro-Republican sympathies. In the process, old files, going back 25 years according to one source, have been reassessed as being of interest to T Branch. It also remains the case that the service refuses to destroy old files – such as those on Harriet Harman and Patricia Hewitt – even when the information collated can be shown to have been collected illegally. Likewise, the flow of intelligence from the still active counter-subversion work of the Special Branch and GCHQ has not diminished.

However it is counter-terrorism that is MI5's prime task and this has propelled the service into the political arena, dealing with civil servants and the police in a manner not previously envisaged. Although Mrs Rimington has been quoted as saying that relations with the Anti-Terrorist Squad are 'excellent', this opinion is not shared by all concerned. The police in particular have been infuriated by MI5's tactics: in the aftermath of the Harrods' bombing by the IRA in January 1993, much to the annoyance of the police, MI5 suppressed photographic evidence for 33 days, refusing to release video stills of the alleged culprits until another device exploded in North London a month later.

Evidence from recent court cases has added substance to critics' fears about MI5 taking on responsibility for anti-terrorism on the mainland. In a little publicised case in Leeds and in another at the Old Bailey, two sets of terrorists belonging to the Irish National Liberation Army (INLA) were convicted on the basis of information supplied by a long term MI5-controlled informer. Evidence produced at the trial strongly suggested, however, that the informer had gone beyond simply providing intelligence and that he had acted as an *agent provocateur*, something not allowed under the law and Home Office rules.

During the trial in March 1993 of Welsh nationalists, in which one young man was found guilty of sending incendiary devices to prominent Tory politicians while two others were found not guilty, M15 was criticised for its heavy-handed approach in a case which appeared flimsy at best. Up to 30 officers were involved in the surveillance and bugging operation which was met with accusations that it was a set-up and that MI5 officers had planted a 'package of bombs' after being frustrated that the three-month operation had failed to reveal any incriminating intelligence.

Lawyers and journalists began seriously to wonder whether the Security Service, in its desperate bid to become the lead agency in the fight against Irish terrorism, had manipulated terrorist cases in order to improve its credentials with politicians and the Home Office.

One month after the first ground-breaking press conference, in October 1993, the government released, as another sign of openness, a second glossy booklet, *Central Intelligence Machinery*. This detailed the structure of the Whitehall intelligence community, although once again it contained nothing that had not appeared in print before. At the news conference, more spymasters came in from the cold and journalists were introduced to Pauline Neville-Jones, a career diplomat and head of the Cabinet Office defence and overseas secretariat, who in the new year took over the chair of the Joint Intelligence Committee from Sir Roderick Braithwaite. In a surprise move, after only a month in the post, the high-flying Ms Neville-Jones moved on to a senior post in the Foreign Office to be replaced by Paul Lever, a long-serving diplomat. Lever will be responsible for introducing a new, efficient system for handling sensitive intelligence which has been instigated by the Cabinet Secretary, Sir Robin Butler, as a result of the ongoing Scott inquiry into the sale of arms-making equipment to Iraq. (The inquiry subjected the intelligence-gathering community to severe criticism as senior ministers dismissed most intelligence they received as 'worthless', admitting that the most important papers often did not reach them.)

It was a much more discreet affair in November 1993, when the Chief of the Secret Intelligence Service (MI6), Sir Colin McColl, and the Director of the Government Communications Headquarters (GCHQ), Sir John Adye, emerged from the shadows to introduce the new Intelligence Services Bill which puts the function and powers of MI6 and GCHQ – responsible for electronic intelligence-gathering – on a statutory footing, in a similar manner to the 1987 Security Service Act. Unlike Stella Rimington, neither Sir Colin nor Sir John were willing to be photographed and were determined to keep a 'low profile'. There would be no opening up of the files and secrecy would remain paramount.

During the first debate in the House of Lords on the Intelligence Services Bill, the Lord Chancellor, Lord Mackay, admitted that MI6 had a responsibility to protect the 'economic well-being' of the country. It helped to boost British firms by keeping 'a particular eye on Britain's access to key commodities, like oil or metals'. As well as this the service has opened a new department, Global Issues, which deals with the 'motherhood agenda' of drug trafficking, transnational crime and money-laundering. The sums involved in these criminal activities are vast and often relate to drug money used by ethnic groups to fund their paramilitary operations. The department gathers intelligence and is involved in 'disruptive actions'. A small sub-section also specialises in hacking into financial computer systems. On top of this, Global Issues is deeply concerned with operations in eastern Europe where MI6 has a good reputation. (The service won the contract to overhaul the intelligence services of Poland, Hungary and the Czech Republic, on the basis of its experience, when offers of money and technology from the CIA were spurned.)

There appears to have been little debate about the wisdom of allowing a largely unaccountable service into specialised areas, previously the provenance of the police and Customs and Excise. During the Lords debate on the Intelligence Services Bill, Lord Jenkins of Hillhead said it was wrong that they should 'invent new targets when old targets had disappeared' and questioned the desirability of MI6 becoming involved in combating international crime. That remained a matter for the police.

Only a few months later, in January 1994, a well-publicised, massive drugs bust which involved pure Colombian cocaine drilled into lead ingots, collapsed, much to the anger of Customs officials who were not informed of the full facts. A shipment was allowed to 'run', financed by CIA money, following a meeting in Caracas between CIA and MI6 agents. 'Operation Teesport', which made the headlines as an attempt by loyalist terrorists to buy a large shipment of arms from Eastern Europe, turned out, on closer investigation, to have been a 'sting' organised by MI6, which failed to 'entrap' any terrorists.

Although the new Bill puts on a statutory footing the requirement for ministerial authorisation for covert action, the minister involved has full discretionary power and is unhindered by any formal guidelines. The Bill gives *carte blanche* to MI6's overseas activities, allowing the service and its officers to engage in disruptive actions, which would be illegal if committed in Britain.

The Intelligence Services Bill introduces limited accountability through a six-strong committee of MPs and peers chosen by the Prime Minister after consultation with the leader of the opposition. The committee will be allowed to 'examine the expenditure, administration and policy' of MI6, GCHQ and MI5, but not operations. The committee's ability to discover a true picture is likely to be undermined by the draconian controls on the information available to it. Information can be withheld on the say-so of the Secretary of State, regardless of whether the information is sensitive or not. A committee report will be made to Parliament but only after it has been suitably 'sanitised' by the Prime Minister on grounds of 'security', thus effectively downgrading the link between the committee and Parliament.

During the budget debates, the Prime Minister informed the House of Commons that expenditure in 1994 on the three main security and intelligence services – MI5, MI6 and GCHQ – would amount to an estimated £900 million. In this first exposure of the budgets, previously hidden in various Whitehall departments, it was suggested that the Ministry of Defence would contribute £570 million to GCHQ, while the budgets of MI6 and MI5 would amount to £150 million and £200 million respectively. Simple estimates of how much it costs to run departments of their size indicates that these are low budgets. The Prime Minister failed to mention the vast sums spent on new building programmes for the services – in the Spring of 1994, MI5 began moving into its new premises on Millbank, near the Houses of Parliament, enabling the service to bring together its previously widely separated departments under one roof – including a contribution from the Foreign Office budget in 1993 of £45 million, while the cost of equipping the new Vauxhall Cross headquarters for MI6 will be met by the Department of the Environment.

The budgets are to be cut by 4 per cent each year for the next three years. There will be cuts in manpower, with MI6, currently estimated to have 2,000 personnel, reverting to the staffing levels – 1,800 – of the last year of the Labour government in 1979, down from 2,300 at the height of its power in the eighties. Sir Colin McColl acknowledged that the service, with 51 stations and 150 spies abroad, was having 'a difficult time'.

In March 1994, following Sir Colin's retirement, a new chief of the service was named. David Spedding, aged fifty-one, a Middle East specialist in charge of covert operations during the Gulf War, will be required to defend the service's interests while a secret review of the country's 'foreign intelligence requirements and capability' is undertaken by the former permanent secretary at the MoD, Sir Michael Quinlan.

Sir Percy Cradock, former chair of the Joint Intelligence Committee and foreign affairs adviser to Lady Thatcher when she was Prime Minister, justifies continuing to spend large amounts of taxpayer's money on the intelligence services because 'we are a permanent member of the Security Council, a great trading nation . . . we need to know where the water is going to be stormy'. In fact, both notions are in jeopardy.

The real reasons are self-serving and are to be found in the illusions of the past. Cradock went on to tell BBC's *Panorama* that 'we have inherited a great position. We have a powerful intelligence machinery and a close relationship with the United States. These are big assets, top cards, which we should play for all their worth.'

Cradock felt that the United States connection was a 'less unequal bit of the relationship than almost any other'. At about the same time, a British diplomat, Jonathan Clarke, who had recently resigned from the Washington embassy, went public suggesting that 'tagging behind [a] friendly superpower' is 'a path of self-delusion'. For Clarke there 'really is no "third way" for Britain as a bridge between the EC and the US'. Instead, he suggested we should start by encouraging the intelligence services to share more of their product with their European counterparts.

The Secret Intelligence Service did make one further foray into the public relations field in 1993. Although former deputy chief George Kennedy Young was given permission by Maurice Oldfield to respond to criticism of the service in the press, Baroness (Daphne) Park was the first MI6 officer to be allowed officially to talk about the service's work when she appeared on BBC's *Panorama* programme at the end of 1993. She said that one of MI6's favourite ploys was to set people against each other. 'They destroy each other. You don't destroy them.'

The feeling remains that while these moves on the part of the security services towards openness are in the right direction and an advance on previous procedures, they fail to measure up to the systems of parliamentary scrutiny in place in most western countries and even of those set up by the new democracies of eastern Europe. The British secret state still finds it difficult to tread the path of reform.

Stephen Dorril
18 March 1994

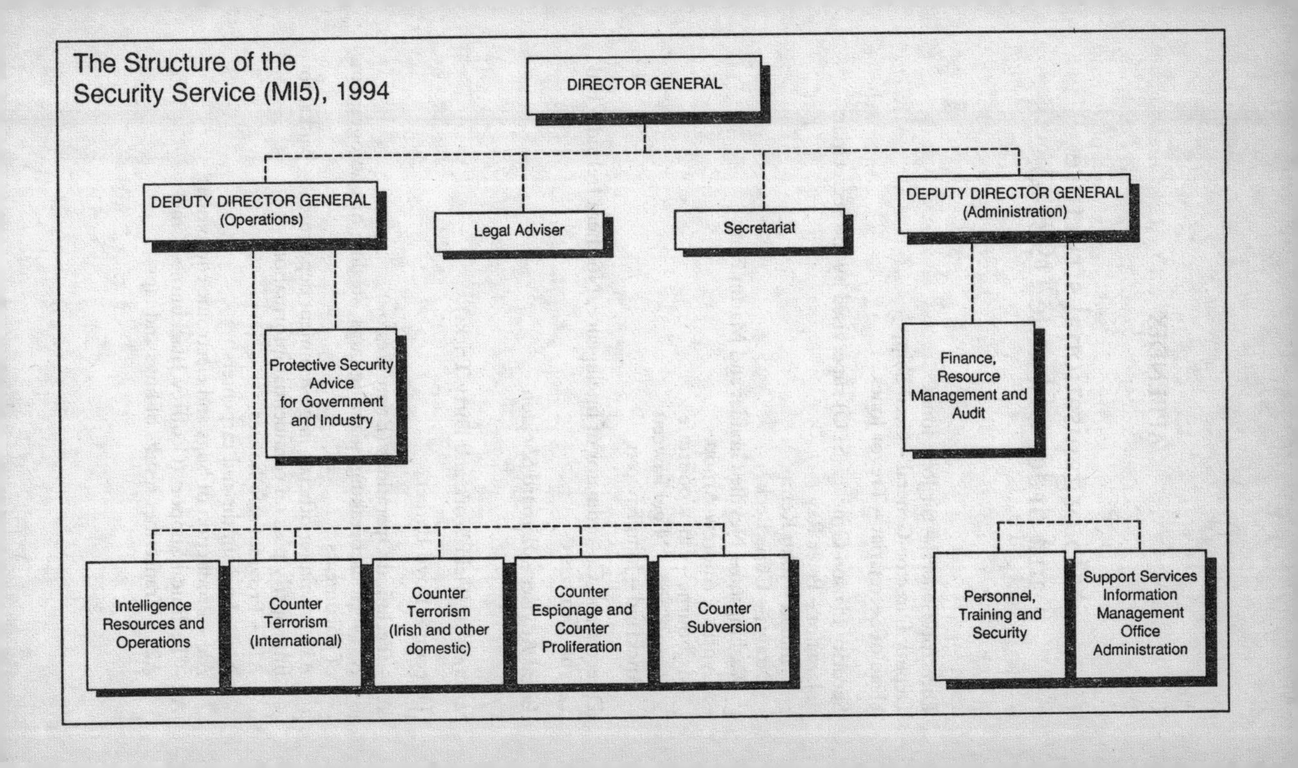
The Structure of the Security Service (MI5), 1994
DIRECTOR GENERAL
DEPUTY DIRECTOR GENERAL (Operations)
Legal Adviser
Secretariat
DEPUTY DIRECTOR GENERAL (Administration)
Protective Security Advice for Government and Industry
Finance, Resource Management and Audit
Intelligence Resources and Operations
Counter Terrorism (International)
Counter Terrorism (Irish and other domestic)
Counter Espionage and Counter Proliferation
Counter Subversion
Personnel, Training and Security
Support Services Information Management Office Administration

APPENDIX

MI5 organisational structure and order of battle, 1981–3

Director-General – Sir John Jones
Deputy Director-General – Cecil Shipp
Head of Secretariat – Trevor Jones

Security Liaison Officers (SLO) supervised by the Secretariat:
 Jamaica – Peter Ray
 Trinidad – John Kemp
 Ottawa – Chris Beck
 Washington – Neville Giraidet and Martin Flint
 Cyprus – Andrew Arnott
 Melbourne – Ian Woodruffe
 Hong Kong – Nigel Fawcett
 Auckland – John Fawcett

Director and Co-ordinator of Intelligence, Northern Ireland – Hal Doyne-Ditmass

Legal Adviser – Bernard Sheldon

A BRANCH (Field Work and Dirty Tricks)

Director – Royd Barker

A1 – Technical Operations (Brian Weston)
 A1a – Housebreaking, planting bugs, stealing or photographing of documents
 A1b – running officials in government departments, banks, to improperly pass on confidential information
 A1c – Provides safe-houses
 A1d – Locksmiths and carpenters
 Ale – Production of bugs and electronic equipment
A2 – Technical Support (Geoffrey Blackburne–Kane)
 A2a – Transcribes results of bugs and taps

A2b – Provides photograph service, also laboratory work and liaison with GCHQ
A3 – Liaison with Special Branch, now disbanded
A4 – The Watchers. Surveillance service for trailing suspects, based at Euston Tower building (Julia Faux)
A5 – Scientific Research and Development (John Birtell)

B BRANCH (Personnel)

Director – Robert Holden

B1 – Recruitment and security of MI5 including vetting of staff (Keith Thomas)
B2 – Personnel management and welfare (Martin McOnachie)
B3 – Management services, personal and physical security of MI5 officers and building (Michael Knight)
B4 – Finance (Stan Brashier)

C BRANCH (Protective Security)

Director – David Horsley

C1 – Security policy in government (Ian Hollands)
C2 – Vetting and security of government contractors (John Snelling)
C3 – Vetting of government department staff, police and armed forces (Sir Graham Lake, Bt)
C4 – Counter-sabotage. Runs exercises with the SAS and police, drawing up contingency plans to deal with possible terrorist attacks such as the occupation of a nuclear power station (Harold Magnay)

F BRANCH (Counter-Subversion)

Director – David Ransom

F1 – Investigated the Communist Party of Great Britain (Bill Ruckstan)
F2 – Trade Unions and production of Box 500 reports to government (Stella Rimington)

F2n – Trade Unions
F2r – The media, education, Members of Parliament
F3 – Terrorism, excluding Irish terrorism (Alan Fernyhough)
F5 – Irish terrorism (Loyalist) (Patrick Walker)

FX – Controls F4 and F6. Long-term infiltration of agents and informers (Tony Crassweller)
F4 – Trade Unions and CPGB (Simon France)
F6 – Trotskyist and radical organisations (Jim Clayphan)

F7 – Investigates Trotskyist, anarchist, feminist, pacifist, black power, nationalist and other radical groups, also fascists (Ray Whitby)

K BRANCH (Counter-Espionage)

Director – John Deverell

KX controls:
K1 – Government departments (David Bannerman)
K2 – Soviet Intelligence Service, illegals (Nigel Croom)
K3 – Soviet agent recruitment (Ian Chalmers, on secondment from MI6)

KY controls:
K4 – Order of battle, Soviet diplomats and nationals surveillance (Anne Orr-Ewing)
K5 – Soviet bloc and Chinese agent recruitment (John Grayburn)
K6 – Hostile intelligence services, Warsaw Pact (Duncun Waugh)
K7 – Counter-espionage within UK services, all allegations of penetration (Imbert Bourdillon)
K8 – Non-Soviet diplomats and nationals surveillance (Bill Patten)

S BRANCH (Back-up services)

Director – John Parker

S1 – Joint Computer Bureau. The JCB is linked to MI6.
S2 – Registry. Personal Files (PFs) are held on the first floor at Curzon Street (R3) and there is an alphabetical computer index (R2)
S3 – Training
S4 – Supplies and travel

Notes

Preface

1 *Sunday Express*, 1/12/91. *Daily Telegraph*, 19/8/92. *Observer*, 17/11/91. *Independent*, 28/1/91. *Sunday Times*, 1/12/91 and 19/7/92.
2 *Guardian*, 25/11/87.

1 MI5: The Thatcher Years

1 House of Commons (hereafter HOC), *Hansard*, 21/11/79 and 28/7/77.
2 *Benn Diaries*, vol. 4, 25/10/78, 1/11/78 and 30/11/78. *Private Eye*, 17/3/78.
3 *Sunday Times*, 3/3/85.
4 Cockerill, p. 185. *Observer*, 17/1/88. Pincher, *Too Secret*, p. 426. Leigh, pp. 253–4.
5 Pincher, *Dirty Tricks*, p. 40. *Lobster*, nos 17 and 18. Dorril/Ramsay, p. 330.
6 West, *Molehunt*, p. 82. HOC *Hansard*, Oral Statement, 26/3/81. Peter Wright evidence at *Spycatcher* trial, New South Wales Supreme Court, November/December 1986.
7 *Sunday Times*, 3/3/85.
8 Gordievsky in Andrew, *KGB*, pp. 436–7.
9 Leigh, p. 207.
10 Hennessy/Jeffries, pp. 234–5. Whitehead, p. 76.
11 Hennessy/Jeffries, p. 136. *State Research*, vol. 2, *The Hidden System*. HOC *Hansard*, Security Service Bill, col. 52, 16/1/89.
12 Wright, *Spycatcher*, pp. 360–1. *Independent*, 29/3/91.
13 See *Lobster*, no. 20.
14 Wright, *Spycatcher*, pp. 360–1. *Independent*, 29/3/91.
15 HOC *Hansard*, col. 612, 3/12/86.
16 *Observer*, 17/3/85.
17 HMSO, Cmnd. 8540, pp. 3–4.

18 HOC *Hansard*, Security Service Bill, cols 1159 and 1114, 15/12/88. Letter from Leon Brittan to John Prescott, 25/1/85.
19 Written parliamentary answer, 3/4/85. Hollingsworth/Norton-Taylor, p. 8.
20 *Observer*, 24/2/85.
21 *Guardian*, 17/4/84. Quoting Wright's new book *The Encyclopedia of Espionage*, *Independent*, 29/3/91.

2 Bettaney and Massiter

1 *Daily Telegraph*, 17/4/84.
2 Leigh, p. 207. Norton–Taylor, *In Defence of the Realm*, p. 9.
3 *Sunday Times*, 3/2/85. Summers/Dorril, pp. 115–16.
4 HOC *Hansard*, Security Service Bill, col. 64, 16/1/89.
5 *Guardian*, 10/5/85. *Sunday Times*, 22/4/84 and 3/2/85.
6 Franks Committee Report on the Reform of the Official Secrets Act, 1972, pp. 244–8, HOC *Hansard*, Security Service Bill, cols 188 and 198, 17/1/89.
7 *The Times*, 31/3/84.
8 *Sunday Times*, 4 and 25/3/84. *Guardian*, 26/3/84. *Observer*, 18/2/85, quoting letter from Bettaney to Labour MP Stuart Bell, 9/3/84.
9 HOC *Hansard*, col. 1140, 15/12/88. Bettaney, B67313, letter to Mark Brand, 2/12/87. Thanks to Harvey Lilley for supplying letter.
10 Wright, *Spycatcher*, p. 299.
11 *New Society*, 31/5/84. *Guardian*, 17/4/84.
12 *New Society*, 31/5/84.
13 Statement published in the *Daily Telegraph*, 17/4/84. *Guardian*, 5/11/91.
14 Andrew, pp. 488–507.
15 *Guardian*, 10/5/85. *Sunday Times*, 22/4/84 and 3/2/85.
16 *Observer*, 17/5/87.
17 *Guardian*, 19/4/84. *Observer*, 3 and 10/3/85.
18 *Observer*, 3/3/85. *City Limits*, 7/8/86.
19 *City Limits*, 7/8/86. *Daily Mail*, 23/4/83. Information from Piers Wooley, 10/6/87.
20 This raises the interesting notion that legitimate political groups, such as republicans, those who wish to abolish the House of Lords and the current constitutional reform group Charter 88, are regarded as potential subversives in MI5 files because they wish to reform the British state, albeit by parliamentary means.
21 *Guardian*, 1/3/85. Charles Elwell, *Tracts Beyond the Times*, Social Affairs Unit.

22 *Guardian*, 7/12/91.
23 Hollingsworth/Norton-Taylor, p. 132. *Guardian*, 15/12/90. *Observer*, 16 and 23/12/90.
24 *Guardian*, 1/3/85 and 22/2/85. *Observer*, 24/2/85. Affidavit of Catherine Ann Massiter, 12/7/85 and 4/11/86. Bettaney letter, op. cit.
25 *Private Eye*, 29/6/84. *Observer*, 1/7/84. *Guardian*, 27/7/84.
26 *Daily Express*, June 1982 (day unknown). *Phoenix*, 15/2/85 and 15/3/85. This was not a new idea. George Wigg had done much the same for the Labour government in the sixties. *Daily Telegraph*, 25/8/92; *Sunday Mirror*, 30/8/92; *Independent*, 26/8/92 and 5/12/92; *Daily Mirror* 16/11/92.
27 *Observer* and *Sunday Telegraph*, 24/2/85. *Intelligence Newsletter*, 15/1/92.
28 *Monochrome*, April 1985.

3 Antony Duff

1 *The Times*, 24/7/84.
2 *Guardian*, 22/5/91.
3 *Observer*, 10/3/85.
4 *Guardian*, 18/12/91 and 17/1/92. *Private Eye*, 22/3/85.
5 See William Blum, *The CIA: A Forgotten History*, London, Zed Press, 1986. Facts about the *Daily Mirror*/Windsor story can be found in *Free Press, Journal of the Campaign for Press and Broadcasting Freedom*, no. 64, June 1991, and *Guardian*, 22/5/91. Inland Revenue: *Guardian*, 3/8/92.
6 *Guardian*, 17/12/85, 17/12/88 and 18/12/91. *Observer*, 9 and 23/12/90. *Sunday Times*, 4/11/90. *Independent on Sunday*, 11/3/90.
7 Hart has friends in high places including the intelligence world. He was a friend of the late William Casey, director of the CIA, and Herb E. Meyer, who was until 1986 vice-chair of the CIA National Intelligence Committee, which collated intelligence assessments for the President. He was also in regular contact with Sir Percy Cradock, chair of the Joint Intelligence Committee, and was a friend of successive editors of *The Times* and an acquaintance of former SAS officer David Walker, who ran the security company KMS, whose activities surfaced during the Iran–Contra investigations.
8 HOC *Hansard*, Security Services Bill, col. 1139, 15/12/88. *The Times*, 10/5/85.
9 *The Times*, 6/6/83.
10 Ibid., 19/3/84. *Sunday Times*, 3/3/85.
11 *Private Eye*, 22/2/85.

12 *Observer*, 2/9/84, quoting Jeffrey Davidow, *A Peace in Southern Africa*, London, Bowker, 1980.
13 Wright, *Encyclopedia*, p. 93.
14 *The Times*, 4/6/84.
15 Ibid., 14/5/85. *Sunday Times*, 12/5/85. *Observer*, 17/3/85.
16 *Sunday Times*, 1/3/85. *Private Eye*, 17/5/85. Urban, p. 100.
17 *Guardian* and *The Times*, 27/4/85; *Sunday Express* 17/3/85.
18 *Independent* 2/5/90.
19 *The Times*, 14/5/85.
20 Wright, *Spycatcher*, pp. 30–1. *Sunday Times* and *Observer*, 15/1/89.
21 *Observer*, 2/10/88.
22 *Daily Telegraph*, 30/4/87. *Independent*, 1/5/87. *The Times*, 5/5/87. *Observer*, 10/5/87.
23 *The Times*, 6/5/87.
24 *Guardian*, 5/5/87.
25 HOC *Hansard*, Security Service Bill, cols 50 and 64, 16/1/89. *The Times* and *Guardian*, 10/5/85. BBC Radio 4, *My Country Right or Wrong*, 29/5/88.
26 *Guardian*, 21/11/85.
27 *Observer*, 17/1/88.

4 Patrick Walker

1 *Observer*, 17/1/88.
2 *Sunday Times*, 10/9/89.
3 *Observer*, 25/4/87.
4 *Now!*, 12/10/79.
5 On the anti-Oldfield smear campaign, see Cavendish's book, Deacon, '*C*', pp. 230, 242, and 246; Pincher, *Traitors*, p. 112, and Junor, p. 257. Urban, p. 110.
6 *Guardian*, 7/9/89.
7 HOC *Hansard*, col. 779, 23/1/89.
8 Ibid., col. 1130, 15/12/88.
9 Contribution made at the Anglo-American Ditchley Foundation at Ditchley Park, Oxfordshire.
10 *Independent*, 14/12/88.
11 *Lobster*, no. 15. See Norton-Taylor, chapters 7 and 8.
12 HOC *Hansard*, Security Service Bill, col. 108, 16/1/89.
13 Ibid., cols 1141 and 222, 15/12/88 and 17/1/89.
14 *The Times*, 18/1/89.
15 HOC *Hansard*, Security Service Bill, col. 1141, 15/12/88. *Independent*, 5/9/89.

16 *Guardian* and *The Times*, 15/9/88. *Observer* and *Sunday Times*, 18/9/88.
17 *Independent* and *Daily Telegraph*, 11/7/91.
18 Bridge quoted in the *Sunday Times*, 14/4/91. *Guardian*, 27/11/91.
19 *New Statesman and Society*, 9/2/90.
20 *The Times*, 5/3/90 and 10/9/90. HOC *Hansard*, col. 1177, 5/7/90.
21 *Guardian*, 14/2/90. *Private Eye*, February 1990.
22 *Guardian*, 5/3/90.
23 Ibid.
24 An appeal by Mr Colin Wallace to the Civil Service Appeal Board: Advice and Recommendations. David Calcutt, Queen's Counsel, 10/8/90. *Guardian*, 14/9/90. *Independent*, 14/9/90 and 4/4/91.
25 *The Times*, 23/2/85. *Sunday Times*, 12/12/76.
26 *Independent*, 21/3/91. *Guardian* 19/10/89.
27 *Daily Express*, 28/5/89. *Guardian*, and *Independent*, 5/6/89. *Private Eye*, 24/5/91.
28 *Sunday Times*, 1/12/91. *Guardian*, 28/6/89. *Daily Telegraph* and *Guardian*, 29/1/92.
29 *Observer*, 21/6/92.
30 *Guardian*, 4/10/91.
31 Muggeridge quoted in *Lobster*, no. 11.
32 *Monochrome*, April 1985.

5 Shoot-To-Kill

1 *Sunday Times*, 4/9/88.
2 Kitson, p. 52.
3 *Internal Security Defence Review*, vol. 1, no. 1, March 1983, p. 46.
4 *Sunday Telegraph* , 9/2/92.
5 M. R. D. Foote, 'Special Operations', in Elliott-Bateman, p. 19. Bethel, p. 302.
6 Bethel, pp. 302–3. *Lobster*, no. 10.
7 Farran, pp. 348–81. Clutterbuck, *Army Quarterly and Defence Journal*, no. 81, October 1960, p. 167. Bethel, pp. 302–3.
8 David A. Charteris, 'Special Operations in Counter-Insurgency: The Farran Case, Palestine 1947', *RUSI Journal*, June 1979. In mid-1988, the Israeli government instituted their own form of 'death squads' in the occupied territories against Palestinians. Undercover army personnel operated against the intifada dressed in work clothes and sometimes as old men and women while packing automatic machine pistols. *Guardian* 24/6/91.
9 Information on Kenya from Harry Hilton.

10 Cloake, p. 260, 'Intrepid trouble-shooter' Lt-Col Hugh Rose worked in intelligence in the late thirties, and at the end of the war commanded the Gurkhas in Malaya. In 1950, Rose came out of retirement to act as deputy director of operations against Coptic and Muslim guerrillas in Eritrea, where he introduced the 'Ferret Force' system later adopted by Templer in Malaya. In 1954, Rose was attached to the Joint Intelligence Committee, Far East, in Singapore. The Ferret Force was made up of former SOE Force 136 personnel and Gurkhas such as Lt-Col James Hislop, who led one of the units. Obituaries of Rose and Hislop; *Daily Telegraph*, 13/9/91 and 26/2/92.
11 Carver, p. 429. Seymour, p. 308, and Geraghty, pp. 193–4.
12 See Dillon, chapters 2 and 3, and Faligot, chapter 2.
13 Holroyd/Burbridge, p. 47. Adams/Morgan/Bambridge, p. 72. Urban, p. 39.
14 *Guardian*, 5/9/88.
15 Adams, *Secret Armies*, pp. 167–8, and Adams/Morgan/Bambridge, pp. 64–5.
16 Adams, *Secret Armies*, pp. 169–70. *Sunday Times* Insight Team, *Siege*, Hamlyn, 1980, pp. 126–7.
17 Mark Urban, 'Silent but Deadly', *GQ* magazine, April 1992.
18 Ibid. Murray, p. 255.
19 *Sunday Times*, 23/2/92. Urban, *Big Boys' Rules*, p. 139.
20 *Guardian*, 5/9/88. *Independent*, 6/9/88. Murray, p. 255. Urban in *GQ* magazine, April 1992.
21 Urban, *Big Boys' Rules*, pp. 162–4.
22 Ibid.
23 Ibid., pp. 167–8.

6 Stalker

1 *Independent*, 20/1/90. P. Taylor, pp. 32–3. Urban, *Big Boy's Rules*, p. 152. The inquest into the deaths of McKerr, Toman and Burns was finally convened in June 1992 but was quickly adjourned after suspicions that the jury had been packed by police from those not on the list. *Guardian*, 10/6/92.
2 *Guardian*, 30/1/88. P. Taylor, p. 12.
3 *Independent*, 8/2/88. Murray, p. 258. *Guardian*, 30/2/88.
4 Asher, p. 256. *Guardian*, 22/7/91.
5 Adams/Morgan/Bambridge, pp. 90–1 and 92. Murray, p. 271. In the late seventies, the RUC had set up the military-style counter-terrorist unit the Special Patrol Group, which received close quarter shooting and counter-insurgency training from the Operational Training Unit.

Some of its volunteers included 'Brits' who had served with the SAS. After two years' probation in the SPG they could then graduate to a new undercover unit which it was rumoured was being proposed for the province. The RUC had never liked the various intelligence agencies working on what it regarded as 'its patch' and pushed for its own 'active measures' unit. One model was the covert Bessbrook Support Unit, set up in 1979, which liaised with the SAS and the Irish Garda on cross-border operations against the IRA and was something of a forerunner of the later specialist units.

6 *Listener*, 31/10/85. *Sunday Times*, 11/8/85. The first recorded instance of the use of HQMSU personnel was in July 1982 when two members were flown by helicopter to North Yorkshire to advise police who had cornered the thirty-seven-year-old gunman Barrie Prudom in the town of Malton. Prudom, who had killed a policeman during a chase across the county, allegedly killed himself with his .22 Birretta prior to a hail of stun grenades and automatic fire raining down on his hiding place. Locals reported seeing plain-clothes policemen, with what looked like SAS badges, carrying machine guns.
7 Stalker, p. 98. *Guardian*, 30/1/88. Urban, p. 95.
8 P. Taylor, p. 60. Urban, pp. 105/6.
9 Stalker, pp. 33, 35, 59 and 60.
10 Ibid., pp. 27 and 30. P. Taylor, pp. 62–3 and 101. The withdrawal of co-operation may have been influenced by an earlier inquiry into leaks of secret information about informers to journalists undertaken in 1982 by Joe Mounsey, an Assistant Chief Constable from Lancashire. According to an RUC Special Branch officer, this caused a souring of relations between the Special Branch and Hermon, who had instituted the inquiry. Special Branch officers regarded it as a 'witch-hunt' and it was seen as 'counter-productive'. According to one of the officers, 'Hermon was paranoid about leaks. [He] had an intense mistrust of the media and was concerned about the management of news-related material . . . He wanted to be in control of what the public was told.' Dillon, p. 393.
11 HOC *Hansard*, cols 1175–6, 5/7/90.
12 *New Statesman*, 14/12/84.
13 Adams/Morgan/Bambridge, p. 93. Prince, pp. 158–161.
14 Stalker, p. 66.
15 Ibid., pp. 82–3.
16 Ibid., p. 85. P. Taylor, pp. 107 and 109.
17 P. Taylor, p. 108.
18 Ibid., pp. 109–10.
19 Stalker, p. 86, P. Taylor, p. 196. It is beyond the scope of this book, but the author believes that there was a conspiracy to remove Stalker

from the inquiry, which had strayed into too many sensitive areas of the secret state. The purpose of the conspiracy was not to sabotage the whole inquiry but to blunt its edge. Whitehall had wanted the inquiry to succeed, if only as a public relations exercise, but dragging it out as long as possible would lessen its impact considerably. To this extent, the *Yes, Minister* tactics were successful. The true nature of the conspiracy is partially revealed in Stalker's own book: 'It seemed that for well over two years, in Northern Ireland, in MI5, and now in my own police force and the Home Office, decisions have been constantly delayed, discussed behind closed doors, altered, amended, shaped and then passed to someone else to endorse them. In the meantime the clock had ticked away.' This theme is repeated: 'Time had been bought . . . five years after the events themselves the reasons for bringing charges had become obscured . . . So far as I am concerned the time for prosecutions was in late 1985, when the evidence was fresh and strong – not in 1988.' Stalker, pp. 221–2 and 272. *Guardian*, 16/6/86.

20 P. Taylor, p. 196. Stalker, pp. 68 and 89. *Guardian*, 14/6/91. *Public Eye*, BBC TV, 14/6/91. Dillon, pp. 400–1.

21 *Guardian*, 30/1/88.

22 By the mid-eighties, there were reports of even more secretive units operating but which were outside of RUC control. These were known as 'ghost squads' and comprised civilians who were SAS trained, something akin to the older MRF units. *Sunday News*, 21/7/85.

7 Gibraltar

1 Geoffrey Morton, *Just the Job*, quoted in the *Guardian*, 5/2/92.

2 See *Magill* Murray, for details of the inquest evidence on the shooting and the autopsy reports.

3 *Independent*, 14/9/88. *Observer*, 18/9/88.

4 *New Statesman and Society*, 17/6/88.

5 *Scotland on Sunday*, 22/11/91. Campbell/Connor, p. 297.

6 *Observer*, 26/11/89.

7 Adams, *Secret Armies*, p. 199.

8 *Independent*, 6/9/88. *New Statesman and Society*, 17/6/88.

9 *Independent*, 20/9/90.

10 *Private Eye*, 'Rock Bottom: The Gibraltar Killings, Government and Press Cover-up', February 1990.

11 *New Statesman and Society*, 21/4/89, quoting the leading Spanish daily, *El Païs*, 7/9/88 and 15/3/89. *Guardian* 8/9/92.

12 *Independent*, 23/5/89. *New Statesman and Society*, 21/4/89. The 'lost' scenario may be connected to the fact that two other terrorists involved

in the IRA unit were lost – a woman reconnaissance expert, 'Mary Parkin', and 'John Oakes', who was responsible for transporting the explosives to the Costa del Sol.

13 *New Statesman and Society*, 21/4/89.

14 *Observer*, 20/11/88. At the inquest, Revagliatte insisted that he was on 'general patrol' and that the siren hoot was unconnected to the shootings.

15 Adams, *Secret Armies*, p. 402. After a spate of similar killings in Northern Ireland by the security forces, a Whitehall inter-departmental committee was asked to carry out a formal examination of the case for creating new legislation for offences of lethal force. At the moment, murder is the only charge that can be laid, and the Director of Public Prosecutions is naturally reluctant to proceed with cases which have little chance of success. Whatever the result of the committee's deliberations, we have not seen the last of what many people consider to be a policy of assassinations.

8 The Gulf War detainees

1 *Sunday Times*, 13/1/91. *Independent*, 8/9/91. *Guardian*, 8/9/91.

2 CAB (Cabinet Office) 65/7, WM (War Minister) (40) 141, 144 of 27 and 28 May; FO (Foreign Office Joint Intelligence Committee) 371 25246. JIC (40) 47 of 2 May. The following paragraphs on internment in 1940 are based on the excellent *Collar the Lot!* by Peter and Leni Gillman and on Hinsley/Simkins. It is interesting to note that the latter ignores Latham's cricisism of MI5, Hinsley/Simkins, p. 59.

3 FO 371 25247 and 371 25210.

4 FO 371 25192. Snell's report was later published in 1940 (HMSO Cmnd., 6238) with all mentions of criticism of MI5 deleted. FO 371 25210, folio 312. CAB 93/3, HD(S)E 48 of 21 January 1941. Hinsley/Simkins, p. 60.

5 *Sunday Times*, 13/1/91.

6 *Sunday Telegraph*, 20 and 27/1/91. *Independent*, 18/1/91.

7 *Sunday Times*, 13/1/91. *Daily Telegraph*, 8/1/91.

8 *Independent*, 24 and 27/1, 6/2 and 6/3/91.

9 Ibid. *Guardian*, 17 and 18/4/84.

10 Northern Ireland Council for Voluntary Work, *Political Vetting and Community Work*, summarised in *Scope*, October 1990, pp. 14–16.

11 *Independent*, 19/2/91.

12 *Sunday Telegraph*, 20 and 27/1/91. *Independent*, 6/3/91. *Sunday Times*, 20/1/91.

13 *Independent*, 24 and 27/1/91. *Sunday Times*, 27/1/91.

14 *Sunday Telegraph* and *Independent on Sunday*, 20/1/91. *Sunday Times*, 13/1/91. Channel 4, *Dispatches*, 30/1/91.
15 *Guardian*, 11/2/91. *Independent*, 27/1/91.
16 *Guardian*, 30/1/91 and 11/2/91. *Independent*, 5 and 7/2/91.
17 *Observer*, 27/1/91. *Independent*, 8/2/91.
18 *Observer* and *Independent on Sunday*, 27/1/91.
19 *Observer*, 27/1/91. *Guardian*, 18/3/91. BBC Radio 4, 5/2/91.
20 *Independent*, 6/2/91.
21 Ibid., 16/12/91. *Guardian*, 21/1/92.

9 Stella Rimington

1 *Sunday Telegraph*, 20/6/92.
2 *Guardian*, 17/12/91.
3 *Sunday Telegraph*, 11/8/91.
4 'Spies that Bind', *Harpers and Queen*, July 1992.
5 Ibid.
6 *Sunday Express*, 24/5/92 and 7/6/92.
7 *Daily Express*, 18/12/91. *Independent*, 17/12/91. *Scotland on Sunday*, 22/11/91. *Observer*, 10/3/85. Mrs Rimington can be contacted at Box 1604, London, SW1.
8 *Independent*, 17/12/91.
9 *Scotland on Sunday*, 22/11/91.
10 *Sunday Times*, 27/11/89.
11 *Sunday Telegraph*, 29/12/91.
12 *Tatler*. 'The Spy-fishing Season', June 1984. *Harpers and Queen*, July 1992.
13 *Independent*, 5/9/89.
14 Ibid. *Observer*, 25/11/90.
15 *Guardian*, 13/7/83. *Independent*, 5/9/89.
16 *Independent*, 5/9/89.
17 Ibid., 25/7/90.
18 *Sunday Telegraph*, 16/12/90. *Guardian*, 19/1/90.
19 *Guardian*, 19/1/90 and 24/7/91. *Independent*, 15/8/91.
20 Wright, *Encyclopedia*, p. 49. *Harpers and Queen*, July 1992.
21 Wright, *Encyclopedia*, pp. 48 and 260. *Independent*, 3/1/91.
22 *Observer*, 25/1/90.
23 *British Journal of Addiction*, quoted in *Guardian*, 25/1/92.
24 *Tatler*, June 1984. *Sunday Telegraph*, 29/12/91. *Guardian*, 18/4/84. *Harpers and Queen*, July 1992.
25 *Observer*, 10/3/85. *Guardian*, 5/2/92.

26 *Tatler*, June 1984. *Observer*, 12/5/85. *Sunday Telegraph*, 29/12/91. *Harpers and Queen*, July 1992.
27 *New Statesman*, 21/10/88.
28 HOC *Hansard*, 15/1/88. *New Statesman*, 5/12/86. *New Society*, 31/5/84.
29 Hollingsworth/Norton-Taylor, pp. 43 and 50. *Guardian*, 6/3/84.
30 *Sunday Times*, 27/11/89.
31 Bok; p. 266.
32 *New Society*, 31/5/85. Jung, *Modern Man in Search of a Soul*, p. 21, quoted in Bok, pp. 46 and 199.
33 *Harpers and Queen*, July 1992.
34 *Sunday Express*, 23/2/92. *Daily Telegraph*, 6/6/92.

10 MI5: The Branches

1 *Guardian*, 29/3/91. BBC2 *Late Show*, 4/2/92. Thames House was bought at the top of the market by the troubled property company Mountleigh. It is now estimated to be worth only £50 million.
2 Cockerill, p. 185.
3 *Sunday Telegraph*, 16/12/90. Kuzichkin, pp. 104, 106 and 116.
4 *Independent*, 10/12/91.
5 *Harpers and Queen*, July 1992.
6 *Guardian*, 21/5/92. *Security Service Act 1989, Report of the Commissioner for 1991*, London, HMSO.
7 *New Statesman*, 5/3/82.
8 Campbell/Connor, chapter 10, 'National Security Surveillance'. *Guardian*, 21/5/92.
9 *New Statesman*, 2/3/84. *New Scientist*, 11/3/84. Spackman: information from John Sweeny, see also Rusbridger, p. 16.
10 Allason, *The Branch*, p. 168. *New Statesman*, 5/3/82 and 24/4/87.
11 Channel 4, *20/20 Vision*, 8/3/85.
12 *Guardian*, 16/7/91.
13 Cathy Massiter affidavit quoted in House of Commons, *Independent*, 13/5/87.
14 HOC *Hansard*, col. 1125, 7/2/85. Fitzgerald/Leopold, pp. 57–8. Lee/Pratt, p. 206.
15 *New Statesman*, 11/4/80. *Guardian*, 18/4/84.
16 HOC *Hansard*, cols 210 and 241, 12/3/85. *Police Review*, 15/2/85.
17 *Sunday Times*, 27/2/83.
18 Hollingsworth/Norton-Taylor, pp. 84 and 90–1. *Observer*, 6/10/85.
19 Quoted on Channel 4, *20/20 Vision*, 8/3/85.

20 *Observer*, 30/10/88. *Guardian*, 20/4/91 and 14/6/91.
21 *Observer*, 5/8/84. Wright, *Encyclopedia*, pp. 47 and 105. *Intelligence Newsletter*, 23/7/92.
22 *Guardian*, 15/6/85.
23 *Time Out*, 12/2/82. Fitzgerald/Leopold, p. 184.
24 *New Statesman*, 1/2/80. *Observer*, 10/3/85.
25 Wright, *Encyclopedia*, pp. 49 and 255.
26 *Time Out*, 12/2/82.
27 Franks Committee on the Reform of the Official Secrets Act, 1972, vol. 3: *Oral Evidence*, p. 245. *The Times*, 7/5/85.
28 *Guardian*, 19/1/90 and 21/5/92. *New Statesman*, 3/12/82.
29 *Guardian*, 29/1/90 and 25/7/90. *Independent*, 25/7/90 and 29/1/91. *Daily Telegraph*, 25/7/90.
30 *Guardian*, 21/5/92.
31 *Security Procedures in the Public Service*, Lord Radcliffe Report, Cmnd. 1681, 1962. Hollingsworth/Norton-Taylor, pp. 66–7. *Daily Telegraph*, 14/11/92.
32 See Cornwall, *The Industrial Espionage Handbook*.
33 See *Guardian*, 21/10/88, and *Independent*, 23/3/89, for details of journalist Isabel Hilton's experience of MI5-controlled vetting at the BBC. She was blacklisted on the basis of MI5's assessment that the Scotland–China Association, of which she was secretary in the seventies, was 'subversive'. The association included prominent churchmen and academics. *Observer*, 20/10/85. *Guardian*, 24/10/85 and 25/6/90. *Sunday Correspondent*, 24/6/90.
34 *Observer*, 7/2/88.
35 *Independent*, 25/6/91. Ian Linn, *Application Refused: Employment Vetting by the State*, Civil Liberties Trust, 1990.

11 The Special Branch

1 Porter, *Vigilant State*, pp. 45–6 and 86. May, quoted in Porter, *Plots and Paranoia*, pp. 88–9.
2 *City Limits*, 2/9/83.
3 *The Christie File*, Cienfuegos Press, 1980.
4 *Leveller*, June 1978.
5 *Guardian*, 18/4/84.
6 *Guardian*, 17 & 19/4/84. *Monochrome*, April 1985.
7 House of Commons Home Affairs Committee, *Special Branch*, HMSO, May 1985. HOC *Hansard*, 2/3/78. Campbell/Connor, pp. 259–61. *Guardian*, 22/5/85.

8 *Monochrome*, April 1985.
9 *The Times*, 30/5/85. *Report of the Police Committee Support Unit, Greater London Council*, 23/11/84.
10 *The Times*, 30/5/85. Connor/Campbell, p. 268.
11 *Report of the Data Protection Committee*, Cmnd. 7341, 1978, p. 200.
12 Connor/Campbell, p. 268.
13 *Time Out*, 20/8/74. *County Council of West Midlands Police Committee, Report by the Chief Constable*, 16/11/83.
14 *Guardian*, 15/6/85. *Observer*, 10/1/82. Norton-Taylor, p. 22.
15 *The Times*, 22/5/85. *Guardian*, 22/5/85 and 31/1/85.

12 Oversight

1 Evidence to the House of Commons Treasury and Civil Service Select Committee, 12/2/86.
2 HOC *Hansard*, col. 781, 23/1/89. *Lord Denning's Report*, September 1963, Cmnd. 2152, London HMSO, 1963.
3 HOC *Hansard*, col. 225, 23/11/88.
4 *Guardian*, 21/4/89 and 11/12/89. *Observer*, 10/3/85. HOC *Hansard*, Security Service Bill, col. 52, 16/1/89. *Police and Constabulary Almanac*, R. Hazell & Co., Henley, 1986, p. 7.
5 HOC *Hansard*, col. 959, 5/12/86.
6 *Daily Express*, 19/11/79. *The Times*, 11/12/89.
7 *Guardian*, 32/1/90. *New Statesman*, 21/10/88.
8 Norton-Taylor, pp. 57 and 59. *The Times*, 8/5/87. *Guardian* and *Independent*, 20/5/92.
9 Denning Report, p. 80. *Guardian*, 17/4/84.
10 House of Lords Judicial Committee (Law Lords), 22/11/84.
11 Evidence to the House of Commons Treasury and Civil Service Select Committee, 12/2/86.
12 *Observer*, 21/7/91. *Independent*, 20/5/92. Tribunal's address: PO Box 18, London SE1 0TL.
13 *Independent*, 14/3/90.
14 *Independent* and *Guardian*, 20/5/92.
15 *Guardian*, 9/12/88. Wright, *Spycatcher*, p. 54. Court of Appeal, 22/1/88.
16 HOC *Hansard*, cols 1665–6, 31/7/52. *Observer*, 24/1/88.
17 *Independent*, 31/3/92. *Guardian*, 15/2/92.
18 Pincher, *Inside Story*, p. 167. Hennessy, *Whitehall*, p. 349. HOC *Hansard*, col. 60, 16/1/89.
19 *Guardian*, 12/2/91 and 8/1/92.

20 Duncan Campbell, *Phonetappers and the Security State*, 1981, p. 40. *New Statesman*, 5/3/82. *Independent on Sunday*, 25/2/90. HOC *Hansard*, col. 52, 5/12/88.
21 *Guardian*, 20/1/88.
22 Ibid., 24/6/92. *Independent*, 7/3/92 and 24/6/92.
23 *Guardian*, 25/11/87 and 24/6/92. Amery appears to have been referring to former Communist Party members.
24 *Sunday Telegraph*, 20/6/92.
25 *Guardian*, 15/5/92. *Interception of Communications Act 1985, Report of the Commissioner for 1991*, HMSO.

13 Ireland

1 See Verrier, chapter 10.
2 Ibid. P. Taylor, pp. 44–7.
3 DIS document published in Faligot.
4 Urban, pp. 24 and 97–8.
5 Ibid., p. 23.
6 *Guardian*, 16/2/91.
7 *Independent*, 5/8/89.
8 *Guardian*, 30/1/88.
9 Urban, pp. 98 and 159. HOC *Hansard*, Security Service Act, col. 287, 17/1/89.
10 *Sunday Telegraph*, 9/2/92. Urban, p. 95.
11 *Guardian*, 4/2/92.
12 Ibid., 16/2/91. Urban p. 101. Irish National Liberation Army (INLA) member Alexander Patterson had been a Special Branch informant for a betting shop robbery in the Falls Road in January 1990 which was subject to an SAS-style ambush by members of 14th Int. Ten months later, Patterson was himself the victim of a similar counter-action when he was shot dead by SAS troops while sitting in a car during an INLA operation. Patterson had not run away because, as an informer, he had no fear of the approaching soldiers. IRA bomb-maker Patrick Flood was an important informer for the RUC Special Branch. In May 1990, he was found in a ditch in South Armagh's 'bandit country' with a single bullet in his head, the victim of an IRA interrogation and execution squad. Flood had been betrayed when, after informing on a bombing operation and receiving guarantees from his handlers that to 'cover his back' there would be no arrests, an SAS patrol then arrested the three men involved in the attempted bombing. Attention immediately focused on Flood as the source of the RUC information. His days were numbered. *Guardian*, 19/9/91 and 16/2/91.
13 Holroyd, p. 47.

14 Urban, pp. 109 and 116–17.
15 On Michael Moore, see *The Middle East*, September 1981.
16 *Republican News*, 19/10/89, and *New Statesman*, 20/10/89.
17 It is understood that some of the agents named in the documents are living peacefully in Southern Ireland. Urban, p. 128. *NOW*, December 1989.
18 *Intelligence Newsletter*, 3/7/91.
19 *Independent*, 9/1/92.
20 Ibid. Urban, p. 109.
21 *Independent*, 9 and 26/1/92. Before accepting the deal which ensured his evidence would not be heard in open court, Nelson had claimed that an Army contact had a role in a UDA plot to plant a bomb in the Irish Republic. An FRU operation code-named 'Snowball' involved Nelson encouraging the paramilitaries to bomb commercial targets in the South. 'The military logic is said to have been that the bombing would lead to the Irish government seeking to extradite loyalists to the South – Dublin would then be under pressure to reciprocate by extraditing more republicans to the north.' Although Nelson had made a reconnaissance trip to the South and photographed selected targets, Snowball was never launched. Similar claims were made by Fred Holroyd concerning bombings and kidnappings in the Republic in the mid-seventies. Interestingly, the *Independent* attempted to rubbish Holroyd's character, while, five years later, publishing Nelson's claims in full.
22 *Intelligence Newsletter*, 1/3/89 and 25/6/92. *Independent*, 8/6/92.
23 Ibid., 9/1/92 and 4/2/92. *Intelligence Newsletter*, 25/6/92.
24 *Guardian*, 30/1/92. *Sunday Telegraph*, 9/2/92.
25 *Sunday Telegraph*, 9/2/92.
26 Urban, pp. 116–17
27 Enclosure, *Sunday Times*, 8/9/92.
28 *Daily Telegraph*, 11/7/92, *Intelligence Newsletter*, 23/7/92.

14 Europol

1 It has been argued that the collapse of the old Soviet bloc and the likely failure of economic reforms in the short term will lead to mass emigration, with up to two million or more economic refugees flooding into the EC. The Institute for European Defence and Strategic Studies used the argument in their January 1992 document. *After the Soviet Collapse: New Realities, Old Illusions*, to call for a strengthening of border controls, quotas, and the reversal of defence cuts. This seems like a redrafting of old illusions of the Cold War about the threat

coming from the East. Although the ethnic conflict in Yugoslavia has created mass emigration, most refugees have ended up in the buffer zone countries of Central Europe. Refugees remain a problem for Germany mainly because of its unique constitutional regard for their plight.

A secret file code-named 'Odos' was set up by American, British and French intelligence after the Second World War. Originally intended to monitor German prisoners of war returning to the West, it lists all refugees arriving from Eastern European countries. In 1958 responsibility for keeping the data up to date was transferred to the BND and recently the BfV. The computerised list contains details of education, employment, politics and plans in the West. *Intelligence Newsletter*, 8/11/92.

2 *Guardian*, 30/11/91. In June 1991, at the European summit in Luxembourg, Prime Minister John Major called for a clamp-down on illegal immigration into the EC. He warned that the rate of immigration could trigger a 'right-wing backlash' and told EC colleagues that action was needed urgently to tighten controls on the Community's external frontiers to curb the rising tide of immigrants and asylum seekers. It should be noted, however, that only 5 per cent of the world's refugees seek asylum in Western Europe. Britain has a small refugee population of about 140,000. In 1991, 50,000 applications were received by the British authorities, while there is expected to be a 60 per cent fall in 1992. However, despite this sharp rise in applications the number of those granted refugee status remains low – in 1987, only 536, 16 per cent of those who applied being accepted. Much of the rhetoric on this area has had a racial tone, and even John Major has used language which recalls Mrs Thatcher's fear of being 'swamped'. 'We must not', he told the summit, 'be wide open to all-comers just because Rome, Paris and London are more attractive than Bombay or Algiers.' Only 3 per cent of applicants come from Eastern Europe. *Independent*, 25/6/92.

3 *Independent*, 30/4/92.

4 Ibid., 4/6/92.

5 *The Times* and *Guardian*, 25/7/91.

6 *Guardian*, 26/7/90 and 2/7/92.

7 In the late sixties, as a member of Special Branch, Kendall was involved in the surveillance of Welsh extremists who threatened Prince Charles's investiture as Prince of Wales.

In 1986, Interpol's old HQ at St Cloud was bombed by the ultra-left Action Directe. Its two million typewritten files were slow and difficult to process and it took up to two months to respond to a request for information. At its new headquarters in Lyon, the massive

IBM computer, it has been claimed, now takes only two minutes to process and pass on intelligence. However, some sources suggest that an 'Automated Search Facility' as announced has not yet been installed. *Guardian*, 26/7/90. *The Times*, 27/2/85. *Daily Mail, Plus Magazine*, 28/2/90. *Intelligence Newsletter*, 10/10/90 and 10/6/92.

8 *Guardian*, 26/7/90. Friends of Trevi also attend, including Sweden, Austria, Norway, Switzerland, Canada and the USA. *Intelligence Newsletter*, 26/9/92 and 12/2/92. *Statewatch*, May–June, 1992.

9 *Daily Telegraph*, 23/2/77.

10 *Observer*, 7/7/91.

11 *Guardian*, 28/1/91. *Independent*, 29/6/91. The German end of the computer is known as the Staatsanwaltliches Informations System (SISY), while its French counterpart is JUDEX (JUdiciary Documentation and EXploitation system). *Intelligence Newsletter*, 24/5/89, 19/7/89 and 25/7/90.

12 *Guardian*, 28/1/91. *Independent*, 3/8/92. Channel Four *Dispatches*, 25/10/92. *New Statesman and Society*, 30/10/92.

13 Regulating the use of personal data in the police sector. Recommendations R (87) 15. Council of Europe, 1988.

14 *Advanced Imaging*, June 1991. *New Statesman*, 24/4/87.

15 *Fifth Report of the Data Protection Registrar*, Appendix AA3, London, HMSO, 1989.

16 *Independent*, 20/4/92. *New Statesman and Society*, 27/12/91.

17 *Guardian*, 2/7/89 and 19/7/91.

18 Ibid., 27/11/90 and 8/12/91.

19 *Guardian*, 26/7/90 and 18/12/91. *Independent*, 18/12/91 and 1/4/92. *Sunday Telegraph*, 5/4/92.

20 *Daily Telegraph*, 10/6/91.

21 Sir John Wheeler, chair of the Commons Home Affairs Committee, proposed a central national detective agency which would take over all Special Branch duties and investigations carried out by Regional Crime Squads. *Intelligence Newsletter*, 20/11/91.

15 Counter-Terrorism

1 *Scotland on Sunday*. 9/4/92, HOC *Hansard*, col. 198, Security Service Bill, 17/1/89. *Guardian*, 18/6/92. *Sunday Express*, June 1992 (day unknown).

2 *New Statesman*, 24/2/84.

3 *Sunday Times*, 5/8/90 and 9/4/92.

4 *Independent* and *Daily Telegraph*, 9/5/92. *Sunday Times*, 19/4/92.

5 *Daily Telegraph*, 9/5/92. *Guardian*, 23/7/84 and 21/9/92. *Sunday Express*, 20/9/92. *The Times* 21/9/92.
6 Leppard, pp. 58–9.
7 Ibid., pp. 63 and 131.
8 Ibid., pp. 63–4 and 130–1.
9 Ibid., pp. 93 and 146. *Observer*, 12/7/92.
10 Lockerbie Fatal Accident Inquiry report, p. 92, quoted in the *Guardian*, 15/2/92.
11 *The Times*, 22/7/91. *Guardian*, 2/8/91.
12 *Sunday Times*, 30/9/90. Khreesat, who was a double if not triple agent for German intelligence and others, was arrested for questioning about the bombing and was instead released.
13 Leppard, p. 212. *Sunday Times*, 24/11/91.
14 *Daily Telegraph*, 15/11/91. *Guardian*, 23/1/92. *Sunday Times*, 23/2/92 and 1/3/92.
15 Leppard, p. 218.

16 The Turf Battle

1 *Independent*, 29/9/90 and 6/7/91.
2 *Sunday Times*, 17/6/90 and 19/4/92. *Daily Telegraph*, 19/2/91.
3 *Sunday Times*, 19/4/92.
4 Ibid., 25/2/90. *Daily Telegraph*, 19/2/91. *Guardian*, April 1992.
5 *Guardian*, 19/6/90 and 5 and 6/3/91.
6 Urban, p. 100. Letter from Mark Urban, 10/6/92. *Guardian*, 25/7/90.
7 *Sunday Express*, 16/2/92. *Sunday Times*, 9/2/92. *Sunday Telegraph*, 9/2/92 and 22/3/92.
8 *Sunday Telegraph*, 26/1/92 and 9/2/92. *Sunday Times*, 1/3/92. *Independent*, 7/5/92.
9 Anthony Bevins later spotted this change of policy from a statement made by Home Secretary Kenneth Clarke in May 1992, though it had slipped through with other leaks a year before. *Independent*, 12/5/92.
10 *Independent*, 22/7/92.
11 *Guardian*, 7/3/91 and 10/6/92. *Sunday Express*, 7/6/92. *Independent*, 19/6/92. *Sunday Times*, 14/6/92.
12 Ibid., 19/4/92.
13 *Daily Telegraph*, 9/8/91. *Sunday Telegraph* and *Observer*, 11/8/91. *Guardian*, 11/12/91. *Intelligence Newsletter*, 4/12/91. Commander Tom Jones, on secondment from the Metropolitan Police, runs the unit, which relies on a well-established national surveillance system coupled to a computer database of prisoner intelligence.
14 *The Times*, 17/12/91 and 9/5/92. *Observer*, 26/4/92.

15 *Observer*, 26/5/92. *Daily Telegraph*, 9/5/92.
16 *Daily Telegraph*, 24/2/91. *Guardian*, 10/2/92. *Sunday Times*, 19/4/92.
17 *Sunday Telegraph*, 22/3/92.
18 Ibid.
19 *Daily Telegraph*, 22 and 23/4/92.
20 *Guardian*, 9/5/92. *Observer*, 10/5/92. *Daily Telegraph*, 9 and 14/5/92.
21 *Guardian*, 23/4/92.
22 *Statewatch*, May–June 1992. *Intelligence Newsletter*, 7/6/89.
23 *Guardian*, 15, 23 and 30/4/92, 23/7/92. Information from James Rusbridger.
24 *Independent*, 2/3/92 and 26/5/92. *Sunday Telegraph*, 17/5/92.
25 *Guardian*, 18/4/84. Urban, p. 105. *Statewatch*, May–June 1992.
26 *Guardian*, 15/5/92. *Interception of Communications Act 1985, report of the Commissioner for 1991*. *Sunday Times*, 3/2/80. *Intelligence Newsletter*, 8/5/91.
27 *Observer*, 26/4/92 and 10/5/92. *The Times*, 9/5/92. *Guardian*, 23/4/92.
28 *Daily Telegraph*, 10/5/92. *Guardian*, 26/6/92.
29 *Guardian*, 22/7/92. *Intelligence Newsletter*, 1/3/89.
30 *Guardian*, 13/4/92 and 26/6/92. *The Times*, 25/2/92. *Observer*, 9/12/91.
31 *Observer*, 21/6/92. *Guardian*, 30/10/92 and 11/11/92. ITV *This Week: The Enemy Within*, 15/10/92.
32 *The Times*, 23/4/92 and 9/5/92. *Observer*, 26/4/92.

17 Mysterious Deaths, Deniable Operations and Private Spooks

1 See Tony Collins, *Open Verdict*.
2 McRae: Scott/Macleay. *Carn*, no. 61, Spring 1988. *Independent Magazine*, 28/3/92.
3 Scott/Macleay, p. 123.
4 Ibid., pp. 155 and 160. *Carn*, quoting *Sunday Mail*, 16/6/85.
5 Scott/Macleay, p. 176.
6 BBC Radio 4 News, 6/7/92.
7 *Monochrome*, April 1985.
8 Ibid. *Guardian*, 4/2/89.
9 Murray: *Lobster*, 'Death in the Private Sector', no. 16. *New Statesman*, 4/1/85, 8/3/85 and 17/5/85. *Private Eye*, 25/1/85 and 22/2/85. *Guardian*, 21/3/85 and 27/6/85. *Sunday Telegraph*, 21/4/85. *The Times*, 27/6/85.
10 BBC Radio 4 News, 6/7/92.
11 Hamilton: Currer-Briggs, p. xi.
12 Norris: Dorril/Ramsay, p. 358.
13 This section is based on Cook and on Smith. The home of Cecil Woolf

was burgled the day after he agreed to publish a book by Graham Smith on the murder. Mail was also opened on a number of occasions. At the time of Dalyell's statement to the House of Commons, the flat of Rob Green's colleague in Naval Intelligence, Paul Hurst, was burgled and papers inspected.

14 Lynx publicity pack.
15 *Guardian*, 3 and 16/2/85.
16 *Observer*, 3/2/85. HOC *Hansard*, Official Secrets Bill, col. 1120, 25/1/89.
17 *Sunday Express*, 12/4/92. Biography of Ian Withers: *Phoenix*, 24/7/92.
18 *Observer*, 22/2/87 and 2/4/89. *Independent*, 17/2/87. *Guardian*, 20/2/87.
19 *New Statesman*, 20/2/81. Interview by Dorril: 23/1/82, see also Dorril/Ramsay. BBC *Panorama*, 23/2/81.
20 *New Statesman*, 22/2/80, and company records.
21 Research by Richard Taylor and Fred Holroyd.
22 Adams, *Financing of Terror*, pp. 240–8.
23 Taylor op. cit.; Holroyd, op. cit.
24 In the past, the clearing house for mercenary operations was organised by SAS Major Clarence 'Dare' Newell, who ran SAS Group Intelligence at the Duke of York Barracks in Chelsea.
25 *Time Out*, 21/7/78.
26 See Block on Airwork.
27 Research by Nick Davies and *This Week*. *KMS*: Special Forces magazine, 6/3/87 amd 14/7/87. *GQ* magazine. December 1992.
28 See Fiennes. Taylor op. cit.; Holroyd, op. cit. *Sunday Times*, 6/10/91. *Daily Telegraph*, 23/10/91.

18 Honourable Correspondents

1 *Guardian*, 2/11/91.
2 Philby, p. 156. Blake, p. 186.
3 Blake, pp. 185–7.
4 Ostrovsky, p. 86.
5 See Dorril/Ramsay.
6 *Sunday Times*, 8/12/91.
7 *Sunday Express*, 15/3/92.
8 *Independent*, 3/1/92. *Sunday Times*, 15/12/91. *Daily Telegraph*, 2/3/92.
9 *Sunday Times*, 15/12/91.
10 *Financial Times*, 15/6/92. *Daily Telegraph*, 17/6/92. There is no doubt

that Maxwell was extremely paranoid in the last years of his life. From 1988, he employed his bodyguard and driver, Les Williams, to organise the bugging of the *Mirror* offices. Head of security John Pole, a former CID detective who had served in Scotland Yard's Anti-Terrorist Squad, was helped by a former Army Intelligence officer with experience of undercover surveillance in Northern Ireland. Their services cost over £40,000. This, of course, may have offered the Security Service a unique opportunity to infiltrate their own spy into Maxwell's entourage. *Financial Times*, 15/6/92.

11 *Spectator*, 9/1/88. *Daily Telegraph*, 14/11/92.
12 Blake, p. 185. *Sunday Times*, 24/3/85.
13 Knightley, pp. 386–7.
14 *Guardian*, 16/11/89.
15 *The Times*, 5/9/84. *Guardian*, 11/9/84. *Daily Telegraph*, 23/9/84.
16 *Guardian*, 4/4/91.
17 *Sunday Telegraph* and *Independent on Sunday*, 7/4/91.
18 *Independent*, 18/6/91. *Private Eye*, 1/2/91. In March 1990, Customs officials investigating the export of arms to Iraq raided the offices of Global Technical and Management Services International, a Deeside company which specialised in the clearance of underwater mines and explosives which had long been involved in the survey and clearance of ordnance from Iraqi waters. The project involved the supply of personnel, many of whom were former members of British special forces. Darwish, p. 169.
19 *Independent*, 13 and 14/8/91.
20 *Guardian*, 4/4/91. *Sunday Times*, 24/11/91.
21 *Observer*, 24/11/91. *Guardian*, 19/12/91, quoting John Walcott and David Martin, *Best Laid Plans*. See also Hewitt.
22 *Observer*, 15/11/92 and 24/11/91. *Sunday Telegraph*, 8, 15 and 22/11/92.
23 *Independent*, 20/11/91, quoting Geoffrey Smith, *Reagan and Thatcher*.
24 *Sunday Times*, 24/11/91.
25 Ibid.
26 *Intelligence Newsletter*, 26/9/90. *Observer*, 24/11/91.
27 *Independent on Sunday*, 27/9/92.
28 *Independent*, 20/11/92.
29 *Sunday Times*, 24/11/91.

19 Abu Nidal, Black Networks and BCCI

1 *Wall Street Journal*, quoted *Guardian*, 12/3/92.
2 *Intelligence Newsletter*, 17/7/91.

3 *Financial Times*, 9–17/11/91.
4 Ibid., 13/11/91. *Independent*, 15/7/91. *Guardian*, 23/7/91, 1/8/91 and 1/8/92.
5 Norton-Taylor, p. 99. Kochan/Whittington, p. 22.
6 Kochan/Whittington, pp. 220–1.
7 *Guardian*, 26/7/91. *The Times*, 12 and 23/7/91.
8 Abu Nidal was born Sabri al-Banna and adopted the nom de guerre Abu Nidal, 'father of the struggle'.
9 *The Times*, 29/3/84 and 5/7/84. *Guardian*, 19/5/84, 21/6/84 and 12/7/84. *Observer*, 8/7/84.
10 *The Times*, 21/5/84 and 4/7/84. *Guardian*, 12/7/84. *Sunday Telegraph*, 30/6/85.
11 *Sunday Telegraph*, 30/6/85.
12 Seale, pp. 271 and 235–7. *Intelligence Newsletter*, 8/11/89.
13 *Independent*, 15/7/91. *Guardian*, 23/7/91.
14 *Sunday Telegraph*, 16/2/92. Kochan/Whittington, pp. 17 and 118–19. One source has suggested that there was a deal between the CIA and Najmeddin to finance the defection of a Polish general who was demanding $1 million to move to the West. The deal was to be financed by the CIA but given to the general by Najmeddin from the proceeds from the covert sale of CIA arms.
15 *Independent*, 15/7/91. *Guardian*, 23/7/91. Kochan/Whittington, pp. 113–14 and 221.
16 Adams, *Trading in Death*, pp. 130–2. Kochan/Whittington, pp. 117 and 121.
17 Kochan/Whittington, pp. 116 and 123. Najmeddin was expelled from Poland in 1988 after diplomatic pressure was applied by the United States.
18 *Guardian*, 25 and 30/7/91. *Independent*, 23/7/91. Kochan/Whittington, pp. 123–4.
19 *Financial Times*, 15/7/91. *Sunday Telegraph*, 16/2/92. *Guardian*, 25/7/91. *Independent*, 23/7/91. *Intelligence Newsletter*, 31/7/91.
20 *Guardian*, 22 and 26/7/91.
21 *Observer*, 23/8/92.
22 *Sunday Times*, 2/7/91. *Guardian*, 22 and 23/7/91.
23 Channel 4 News, 22/7/91. Lord Justice Bingham, who has for some reason a reputation as a giant-killer. He investigated oil company sanction-breaking against Rhodesia in 1977.
24 *Guardian*, 31/7/92 and 1/8/92. *Private Eye*, 21/5/92.
25 *Independent*, 13/8/92. *Guardian* 2 and 10/10/92. *Independent on Sunday* and *Observer* 4/10/92.
26 *Guardian*, 2/3/93.

20 Banks, High-tech and the man who never was

1 Hennessy, p. 76. See Tom Nairn, *The Enchanted Glass.*
2 Cavendish, pp. 38 and 47. Wright, *Spycatcher*, p. 72.
3 *Private Eye*, July 1992.
4 Cavendish, pp. 76, 134 and 138.
5 Ibid., pp. 53, 106, 117 and 119. See *Lobster*, no. 15, for a review of Cavendish's book by the present author.
6 *Independent on Sunday*, 19/1/92.
7 *Business*, November 1987.
8 *Observer*, 16/8/92.
9 *Guardian*, 4/10/83. *The Times*, 17/10/83.
10 *Observer*, 4/12/83. *Mail on Sunday*, 20/5/84.
11 *The Times*, 16/4/84 and 17/5/84. *Guardian*, 16/4/84. *Independent*, 27/8/92.
12 *Daily Express*, 1 and 18/10/83. *The Times*, 16/4/84. *Daily Express*, 26/3/84. *Guardian*, 16/4/84. *Observer*, 20/5/84. *Financial Times*, 15/7/91.
13 *The Times*, 20/10/83. *Daily Express*, 26/3/84.
14 *Observer*, 5/2/84. *The Times*, 17/5/84. *Private Eye*, 21/10/83. *Independent*, 27/8/92.
15 Tuck, pp. 3–4 and 14. Cahill, pp. 126 and 191.
16 Tuck, p. 50.
17 Cahill, pp. 16 and 121–2.
18 West, *Games of Intelligence*, pp. 162–4. Tuck, p. 200.
19 *Sunday Times*, 26/6/83 and 30/10/83. Tuck, p. 69. Cahill, pp. 85–6, 122, 158 and 184.
20 Cahill, p. 56.
21 Ibid., p. 4.
22 *Lobster* Special Issue. *GQ* magazine, April 1992.
23 Cahill, pp. 17 and 90.
24 Ibid., p. 184. *GQ* magazine, August 1992. In April 1990, the United States dropped many COCOM restrictions on the sale of high-technology exports to Eastern Europe, though stiffer ones were imposed on sales to Iraq, Iran and North Korea.
25 *Intelligence Newsletter*, 16/1/91.
26 *Spectator*, 22/2/92.
27 Tuck, pp. 180–1.
28 *Guardian*, 13 and 22/12/83. *International Herald Tribune*, 28/12/83. *Daily Telegraph*, 15/6/85.
29 *Intelligence Newsletter*, 5/12/90. Shears/Gidley, p. 173.
30 Shears/Gidley, pp. 55–6. West, *Games of Intelligence*, p. 168.
31 Shears/Gidley, pp. 104–5. *New Statesman*, 21/11/86.

32 *Sunday Times* Insight Team, *Rainbow Warrior*, pp. 194–5 and 268. De Marenches, p. 163. Shears/Gidley, pp. 174 and 192.
33 *Sunday Times* Insight Team, *Rainbow Warrior*, p. 272.
34 *Intelligence Newsletter*, 6/12/89.
35 West, *Games of Intelligence*, p. 167. *Intelligence Newsletter*, 22/11/89.

21 Economic Intelligence

1 Quoted in *The Socialist Register*, 1979, p. 279.
2 *Intelligence Newsletter*, 23/4/92. *Daily Telegraph*, 24/4/92.
3 *Spectator*, 22/2/92.
4 *Independent*, 20/8/90.
5 *Intelligence Newsletter*, 23/6/90. *Guardian*, 21/9/91. *Daily Telegraph*, 24/1/92.
6 *Daily Telegraph*, 24/1/92. *Intelligence Newsletter*, 23/5/90.
7 *Sunday Times*, 5/4/92.
8 *Daily Telegraph*, 24/1/92. *Sunday Times*, 16/6/91.
9 *Independent*, 14/11/90. *Daily Telegraph*, 24/1/92. *Guardian*, 29/12/90.
10 *The Times*, 2/4/84.
11 Ibid. *Guardian*, 19/7/91. *Observer*, 30/6/85. *Independent*, 16/6/92.
12 *New Statesman*, 19/11/82. *The Times*, 16/1/83.
13 *Financial Times*, 15/6/92. *Guardian*, 23/7/91.
14 Lanning/Norton-Taylor, pp. 67–8.
15 *Guardian*, 17/6/92. Lanning/Norton-Taylor, p. 68.
16 *Intelligence Newsletter*, 23/4/92. *New Scientist*, April 1992. *Scientific American*, January 1992.
17 *Guardian*, 3/2/92.
18 *Intelligence Newsletter*, 23/4/92.
19 *Guardian*, 29/7/89. *Independent*, 3/3/92.
20 Cornwall, *Data Theft*, p. 127.
21 *Observer*, 30/6/85. *Spectator*, 22/2/92. *Guardian*, 19/7/91. Wright, *Spycatcher*, pp. 110–12.
22 *Guardian*, 10/2/89. *Sunday Times*, 22/7/90. Ranelagh, pp. 83 and 255–6.
23 *Intelligence Newsletter*, 25/4/90 and 16/1/91.
24 *Guardian*, 12/9/90 and 16/8/91.
25 *Daily Telegraph*, 24/1/92. *Independent*, 4/1/92 and 22/3/92. *Guardian*, 13/11/92.

22 Arms, MI6 and the Death Merchants

1 *Guardian*, 14/5/91 and 23/7/92.
2 *Independent*, 14/3/92. *New Statesman*, 22/5/84. *Guardian*, 14/5/91 and 19/7/91.
3 *Financial Times*, 15/7/91.
4 Ibid. *Observer*, 8/3/92. *Independent*, 20/2/92. Timmerman, p. 349. *Observer*, 15/11/92, quoting from Cowley's book, *Supergun: a Political Scandal*.
5 *Financial Times*, 15/7/91. Adams, *Trading in Death*, p. 122.
6 According to Martin Short, author of *Inside the Brotherhood*, masonic lodges are strong within the MoD. 'The MoD lodges are very peculiar; procurement officials in the same lodge as people who supply military goods and services to the procurement department of the MoD.' *Independent*, 2/7/92. *Private Eye*, July 1992.
7 *Independent*, 16/7/91 and 28/2/92. *Guardian*, 26/2/92.
8 *Private Eye*, 16/9/92.
9 *Observer*, 28/6/92.
10 *Guardian*, 13/3/92. Bourn was once invited by Stefan Kock to visit the Astra factory at Grantham.
11 *New Statesman*, 25/1/85.
12 Ibid.
13 The Argentinian weekly *El Otro* claimed that in January 1989 'functionaries of the British Embassy in Uruguay, said to belong to the British intelligence service' had plotted an assault by guerrillas on an Argentinian army barracks. *Independent*, 13/1/89.
14 *Independent on Sunday*, 20/5/90. *Sunday Times*, 3/6/90. *Guardian*, 3/8/91.
15 Darwish, p. 161. Timmerman, pp. 168–9.
16 *Guardian*, 3/8/91.
17 *Independent*, 9/6/90. *Guardian*, 10/7/90 and 10/9/91.
18 *Guardian*, 10/7/90, 23/11/90, 3/8/91 and 10/9/91. Channel 4 News, 12/4/91.
19 *New Statesman*, 3/5/85. Channel 4 News, 12/4/91. *Guardian*, 14/5/91.
20 *Daily Telegraph*, 19/6/92. *Guardian*, 5/10/92 and 10/1/92. *Independent*, 13/11/92. Allivane International Group Ltd, a British company which folded in 1988, was involved in illegal arms deals to both sides in the Iran–Iraq War. Later it supplied ammunition parts to Dr Gerald Bull's Space Research Corporation (SRC). Allivane had been set up in the early eighties by a former employee of James Guerin, head of International Signal and Control (ISC), an arms dealer who supplied cluster bomb know-how to Cardeon. In co-operation with Chilean

secret police, blueprints and design technology were carried to Santiago in suitcases in 1985. Guerin had been operating since 1974 with the knowledge of the US National Security Agency, who used him as a cut-out for arms sales to South Africa, and 'the quiet approval of the CIA'. Cardeon was also shipping arms to South Africa, from where in turn the cluster bomb fuses were shipped to Iraq. Guerin was sentenced to fifteen years' imprisonment in July 1992 for his part in the massive defrauding of British arms/electronics company Ferranti, which had paid $700 million to buy ISC based on inflated and often non-existent sales to countries. *Guardian*, 4/5/92. Timmerman, p. 168.

Allivane had also been approached by SRC and Cardeon to set up a fuse manufacturing company in Iraq. Ultimately owned by Lagan Investments, a Panama company controlled by Cardeon, it was a paper company used to disguise arms shipments with, it appears. government knowledge – 'a buffer between illegal sales and the Government'. It negotiated credit arrangements with BCCI. The company was raided by British Customs officials in 1987 for exporting explosives to Iran. Mysteriously, twenty-four hours earlier 'someone had flown from London to [Glasgow to] remove documents from the company's files'. Further raids took place in 1988 following allegations of embezzlement and illegal shipments to Iran, but the case never reached the courts, following alleged 'interference from Whitehall'.

Following the collapse of the company in 1988, the Cardeon/SRC project was taken up by former Allivane executive John Grecian and Stuart Blackledge, a former MoD and SRC employee. They received suspended sentences in February 1992 for exporting arms to Iraq after threatening to subpoena government officials and documents on the illegal arms sales. *Guardian*, 4/5/92. *Private Eye*, 17/7/92.

23 Iraqgate

1 Darwish, p. 224.
2 Timmerman, p. 130. *Guardian*, 8/2/92.
3 Adams, *Trading in Death*, pp. 130–2. Timmerman, p. 340.
4. *Guardian*, 29/7/91.
5 *Independent*, 5/8/91.
6 *Sunday Times*, 14/4/91 and 26/5/91. *Guardian*, 14/5/91 and 10/11/92. *Daily Telegraph*, 11/11/92. *Independent*, 15/11/92.
7 *Guardian*, 23/11/92.
8 *Observer*, 8/3/92. *Daily Telegraph*, 22/1/92. *Independent*, 10/11/92.
9 *Guardian*, 10/11/92. *Financial Times*, 15/11/92.
10 *Guardian*, 19/10/92. *Independent*, 12/11/92.

11 *Guardian*, 10/11/92. *Financial Times*, 15/11/92. *Independent*, 14/11/92.
12 *Guardian*, 19/10/92 and 14/11/92
13 Ibid., 4/11/92. *Financial Times*, 10/11/92.
14 *Independent*, *Guardian* and *Financial Times*, 10/11/92.
15 *Sunday Times*, 2/12/90.
16 Another company approached by Iraqi go-betweens working indirectly for intelligence chief Barzan al-Tikriti was the Coventry-based machine-tool makers, Wickman Bennet, owned by the Berisford Group and chaired by Ephraim Margulies, rumoured to have been an MI6 paymaster. Timmerman, p. 272. *Sunday Times*, 2/12/90 and 14/4/91. *Guardian*, 27 and 28/10/92.
17 *Guardian*, 30/11/92. *Sunday Times*, 15/11/92.
18 Timmerman, pp. 48–9. *Independent*, 15/4/91, 5/8/91 and 28/10/92. *Sunday Times*, 15/11/92. Darwish, p. 96.
19 Ibid., p. 129.
20 *Daily Telegraph*, 23/4/91.
21 Ibid. *Sunday Times*, 28/4/91. Bazoft was given special glass containers which were later switched for plastic ones as given to him by British nurse, Daphne Parish.
22 *Private Eye*, April 1990. Timmerman, p. 376.
23 *Guardian*, 21/10/92 and 11/11/92.
24 Ibid., 10 and 14/11/92. *Sunday Times*, 15/11/92.
25 *Guardian*, 14/11/92. *The Times*, 13/11/92.
26 *Guardian* and *Independent*, 11/11/92.

24 Murder, Intrigue and the Supergun

1 *Guardian*, 31/5/90 and 7/3/92. Documents reached the Commons Committee inquiry into the supergun affair in the last days of its deliberations, which indicated that Sheffield Forgemasters had not been completely truthful in its account of the company's links with continental companies involved in the supergun project. The documents indicated much closer links than previously acknowledged and raised doubts about the reliability of statements made to the committee. They indicated that the two companies had good reason to suspect that they were involved in the manufacture of a weapon. *Guardian*, 13/3/92. *Observer*, 28/7/91 and 22/9/92. Lowther, p. 192.
2 Timmerman, p. 299. *Observer*, 8/3/92. *Intelligence Newsletter*, 29/1/92.
3 *Guardian*, 14/5/91, 6/2/91 and 7/3/92. Lowther, p. 209.
4 *Independent*, 5/8 /91, 14/3/92 and letter, 18/3/92. *Intelligence Newsletter*, 26/3/92. Lowther, pp. 124–5 and 145.
5 Darwish, p. 166. Lowther, pp. 236–7 and 239.

6 *Daily Telegraph*, 22/1/92. *Independent*, 5/8/91 and letter, 18/3/92. *Guardian*, 14/5/91.
7 *Guardian*, 16/1/92 and 6/2/92.
8 *Independent*, 11/10/91.
9 Ibid., 16/7/91. Lowther, pp. 248–9.
10 *Independent*, 16/7/91, 28/2/92 and 23/3/92. *Guardian*, 26/2/92. Aitken was Middle East consultant for Slater Walker in the seventies.
11 *Observer*, 8/3/92. *Independent*, 20/2/92. *Guardian*, 31/5/90. Darwish, p. 190.
12 *Guardian*, 6 and 20/2/92. *Observer*, 8/3/92. *Independent*, 28/2/92.
13 *Guardian*, 28/2/92. *Independent*, 28/2/92.
14 *Guardian*, 6/2/92. *Observer*, 8/3/92.
15 In March 1990, Astra's new chair accepted a deal on the return of PRB to the vendors of the company, Gechem, for £3.5 million. Shortly afterwards, PRB went into receivership. *Independent*, 11/10/91.
16 *Guardian*, 20/2/92 and 20/3/92.
17 *Financial Times*, 17/3/92. *Guardian*, 6/2/92. *Independent on Sunday*, 15/3/92. Lowther, p. 281.
18 Darwish, pp. 186–7.
19 *Independent*, 13/6/91. Timmerman, p. 261.
20 *Sunday Telegraph*, 3/5/92 and 23/2/92. Darwish, p. 169.
21 *Independent on Sunday*, 15/3/92.
22 *Guardian*, 16/1/92. *Independent*, 17/3/92.
23 *Independent*, 17/3/92.
24 *Independent*, 16/7/91, 5/8/91 and 20/3/92.
25 *Observer*, 22/3/92. *Independent*, 24/2/92.
26 *Daily Telegraph*, 31/1/92.
27 Ibid., 17/3/92. House of Commons Trade and Industry Committee, *Exports to Iraq: Project Babylon and Long-Range Guns*, London, HMSO. *Guardian*, 17/3/92.

25 MI6 and The Secret State

1 *Financial Times*, 22/5/92.
2 *Guardian*, 9/1/91. Verrier, p. 5.
3 Block/Fitzgerald, p. 53. Verrier, p. 9.
4 *Guardian*, 9/1/91.
5 *The Times*, 3/4/84. *Sunday Express*, 28/7/91. *Guardian*, 16/4/92. Norton-Taylor, p. 57. Verrier, p. 10.
6 Norton-Taylor, pp. 57–8.
7 *Independent*, 28/1/91 and 16/2/92. *The Times*, 3/4/84. Verrier, p. 9.
8 Read/Fisher, p. 199. *Labour CRISIS*, no. 4.

9 *Independent*, 3/7/91. *Sunday Express*, 22/3/92.
10 *Guardian*, 3/1/90. *Observer*, 9/9/84.
11 *Private Eye*, 7/10/83. *Sunday Times*, 7/11/82. *The Times*, 1/5/87. *Covert Action*, Winter 1983. *Newsday*, 13/11/83.
12 *Sunday Telegraph*, 21/6/92. *Guardian*, 9/1/91 and 2/10/91. Bok, p. 6.
13 *Guardian*, 2/3/92.
14 *The Times*, 2/4/92. *Independent*, 8/10/90.
15 Norton-Taylor, p. 49. Verrier, p. 341. *Guardian*, 2/3/92.
16 *The Times*, 2/4/92. Verrier, p. 362. *Guardian*, 2/3/92, reporting on BBC2's commemorative series on the invasion.
17 *The Times*, 2/4/91. *Independent*, 8/10/90.
18 *Guardian*, 4/4/91. *Sunday Times* and *Observer*, 27/3/88.
19 Owen, p. 391. 'Spies that Bind' *Harpers and Queen*, July 1992.
20 Woodward, pp. 78 and 212. *Sunday Times*, 29/3/92.
21 *Independent*, 30/5/89. Bodman: *Sunday Times*, 9 and 16/10/83. *Daily Mail*, 4/10/83. *Observer*, 9/10/83.
22 *Sunday Times*, 11/12/83.
23 *Time* magazine, 11/6/84.
24 *Independent*, 30/5/89.
25 *New Statesman*, 12/7/91. *Independent*, 8/10/90. *Intelligence Newsletter*, 7/11/90 and 16/1/91. *Guardian*, 16/10/90.
26 *Sunday Telegraph*, 3/5/92, quoting the *London Review of Books*. Pincher, *Inside Story*, p. 28.
27 Peter Hennessy and Caroline Anstey, 'Money Bags and Brains: The Anglo-American "Special Relationship" Since 1945', Department of Government, Strathclyde University. *Independent*, 28/1/91.

26 The Defence Intelligence Staff

1 *The Times*, 2/4/84.
2 Owen, p. 132.
3 *The Times*, 15/1/83. Block/Fitzgerald, pp.26–7. Bunyan, pp. 191–2.
4 Bailly, letter to *The Times*, 3/8/84.
5 *Independent*, 26/2/90. *RUSI Journal*, Summer 1988. Hennessy, p. 414.
6 *Independent*, 26/2/90.
7 *Guardian*, 22/8/90. *Lobster*, no. 19.
8 *Independent*, 20/8/90.
9 *The Times*, 20/12/91. *RUSI Journal*, Summer 1988.
10 *New Statesman*, 11/1/85.
11 Adams, *Trading in Death*, pp. 225–6 and 229.
12 Bailly, letter to *The Times*, 3/8/84.
13 *Guardian*, 14/3/85. *RUSI Journal*, Summer 1988.

14 Hennessy, p. 414.
15 *Guardian*, 30/3/84. Security Commission Report, Cmnd. 9212. *The Times*, 15/11/83.
16 *Independent*, 26/2/90. *Guardian*, 2/5/92. *Sunday Express*, 10/5/92.

27 Desert Storm

1 *Sunday Correspondent*, 12/8/90.
2 *Independent*, 10/8/90 and 17/1/92.
3 Ibid., 24/8/90, 10/1/92 and 9/5/92. *Guardian*, 10/1/92. IFF, p. 57.
4 *Guardian*, 22/8/90. Owen, p. 361.
5 *Sunday Times*, 19/8/90. *Independent*, 10/8/90. *Guardian*, 10/1/92.
6 *Sunday Times*, 17/1/91. *Independent*, 30/9/90 and 15/3/91.
7 *Independent*, 30/9/90. *Daily Telegraph*, 19/1/91.
8 *Guardian*, 8/3/91. *Independent*, 30/9/90 and 15/2/91.
9 *Daily Telegraph*, 21/1/91.
10 *Independent*, 17/2/91.
11 Ibid., 13/8/90 and 30/9/90.
12 *Sunday Times*, 19/8/90 and 27/1/91. *Independent*, 17/2/91.
13 During the Gulf War there was a fierce debate by the intelligence agencies about analysis of the damage done to the Iraqi war machine. Battlefield estimates made by the military were openly derided by the CIA. It appeared that the intelligence estimates were conservative, while the military's were often overly optimistic. *Guardian*, 20/2/91. *Independent*, 30/9/90.
14 *Sunday Times*, 16/12/90. *Daily Telegraph*, 8/1/91.
15 *Guardian*, 1/11/91. *Observer*, 20/3/91. *Independent*, 21/7/92. The UN had use of an American U2 spy plane whose film was developed and analysed by the US, while Britain was very closely involved in interpreting the aerial reconnaissance photographs. *The Times*, 30/7/92.
16 *Independent*, 5/10/91.
17 *Daily Telegraph*, 21/5/92. *Independent*, 5/10/91.
18 *Independent*, 5/10/91.
19 *Daily Telegraph*, 22/2/91. *Sunday Express*, 3/2/91. *Guardian*, 21/5/91.
20 *Private Eye*, 1/2/91. Information from Colin Wallace. *Guardian*, 7/1/91.
21 The spin-doctors and the disinformers went to work smearing Peter Arnett of the US television network CNN, who had reported accurately on the incident (see *Sunday Telegraph*, 24/2/91, for details). The BBC's chief overseas correspondent, John Simpson, was another victim of ugly rumours and of the assault by the media on those that failed to toe the MoD/government line (see the *Spectator*, 8/2/91). Cold War warriors such as Ray Whitney, Conservative MP and former head

of the Foreign Office's Information Research Department, which had dealt in all kinds of propaganda from white to black and had been responsible for setting up Information Policy, continued to spread the old anti-communist line with claims that hundreds of Soviet advisers were helping the Iraqi regime. Criticism of the war was allegedly led by communist-controlled front organisations. *Sunday Telegraph*, 24/2/91.

22 Ibid., 11/1/91. *Intelligence Newsletter*, 30/1/91.
23 *Independent*, 19/1/91. *The Times*, 17/1/91. *Daily Telegraph*, 21/1/91.
24 *The Times*, 17/1/91. *Observer*, 2/6/91. *Daily Telegraph*, 20/1/91 and 29/6/92. *Independent*, 19/1/91.
25 *Independent*, 19/1/91. *Daily Telegraph*, 23, 24 and 25/1/91.
26 Radio 4 News, 9/2/91.
27 *Independent on Sunday*, 12/1/92.
28 *Sunday Times*, 17/2/91. *Daily Express*, 15/2/91. *New Statesman and Society*, 22/2/91.
29 *Guardian*, 10/7/92. *The Times*, 11/3/91. *Independent*, 11/2/91.
30 *Independent*, 17/6/91.
31 *Guardian*, 16/1/91. *The Times*, 22/7/91. *Sunday Times*, 9/2/92.
32 BBC Radio 4, 23/1/92. *Sunday Telegraph*, 15/3/92.
33 *Guardian*, 8/1/92 and 26/10/92. *The Times*, 8/2/92. *Sunday Times*, 1/3/92. *Independent*, 22/10/92.
34 *Sunday Times*, 5/1/92. *Sunday Telegraph*, 18/12/88. *Intelligence Newsletter*, 18/1/89. Verrier, p. 349, note 3.

28 The Secret Intelligence Service

1 *Daily Telegraph*, 11/8/92.
2 *Observer*, 10/5/92. *Daily Mail*, 9/5/92. *Esquire*, Winter 1992.
3 Ibid., 8/5/92.
4 *Guardian*, 5/7/91, 2/5/92 and 19/6/92. *Independent*, 15/11/91 and 16/9/92. BBC2 *Late Show*, 4/2/92.
5 *The Times*, 2/4/84. *Observer*, 3/3/85. *Observer Magazine*, 25/11/90.
6 Norton-Taylor, p. 50. Block/Fitzgerald, p. 34. *Observer*, 10/5/92.
7 *Sunday Telegraph*, 2/2/92. *Observer Magazine*, 10/5/92. *New Statesman*, 17/12/84.
8 *Observer*, 25/11/90.
9 Sampson, p. 241. *Tatler*, June 1984. Block/ Fitzgerald, p. 38.
10 Blake, p. 168. Cavendish, pp. 12–13. *Independent Magazine*, 10/5/92. McDermott, p. 142.
11 Block/Fitzgerald, p. 39. BBC Radio 4, *The Profession of Intelligence*, 30/8/81. *Observer*, 15/7/84. McDermott, pp. 149–50.

12 *Observer*, 10/5/92.
13 Block/Fitzgerald, p. 38. McDermott, p. 142.
14 *Guardian*, 10/1/92. Block/Fitzgerald, p. 38. Copeland, p. 93.
15 *Independent*, 9/5/92. *Observer*, 16/2/92.
16 *Guardian*, 3/2/92. *Observer*, 16/2/92 and 10/5/92.
17 *Independent*, 9/5/92. *Guardian*, 19/7/91.
18 *Benn Diaries*, vol. 4, p. 40.
19 Owen, pp. 342 and 347. Block/Fitzgerald, p. 53. McDermott, p. 149.
20 *Sunday Express*, 10/5/92. Verrier, p. 10.
21 Verrier, p. 11.
22 *Guardian*, 15/10/92.
23 *Sunday Telegraph*, 14/6/92.
24 *Guardian*, 5/6/85. *Private Eye*, 21/9/84.
25 *Independent*, 18/9/92.
26 *Guardian*, 30/4/92. *Independent*, 20/4/92.
27 International Freedom Foundation (IFF), p. 116.
28 *Intelligence Newsletter*, 20/12/89. *Guardian*, 12/5/92.
29 *Guardian*, 26/3/92. *Independent*, 29/6/92.
30 *Sunday Telegraph*, 19/1/91.

29 'The Violent Peace'

1 *Sunday Times*, 3/5/92.
2 *Independent*, 9/5/92. *Guardian*, 10/1/92.
3 *Guardian*, 17/2/90 and 22/8/90. *Independent*, 27/10/92.
4 *Guardian*, 2/6/89. *Daily Telegraph*, 18/2/92. *Independent*, 6/3/92. *New Statesman and Society*, 14/8/92.
5 *Sunday Times*, 2/8/92.
6 *Guardian*, 19/10/92 – this profile was written by Michael Hartland, a former MI6 officer. *Independent*, 20/8/90. *Sunday Express*, 17/6/90.
7 *Sunday Express*, 30/6/91. *Intelligence Newsletter*, 3/7/91 and 6/11/91. IFF, p. 31.
8 *Guardian*, 14/8/92 and 30/10/92. *Daily Telegraph*, 13 and 14/8/92. *Sunday Times*, 16/8/92 and 6/9/92.
9 IFF, p. 41.
10 Ibid., p. 157.
11 Ibid., pp. 158, 166, 168.
12 Ibid., pp. 161 and 162. *Sunday Times*, 16/8/92.
13 *Intelligence Newsletter*, 22/5/91. *Sunday Times*, 27/9/92.
14 *Sunday Times*, 16/8/92 and 27/9/92. IFF, pp. 23–5 and 167.
15 *Guardian*, 16/12/91.
16 Ibid., 22/6/92. *Intelligence Newsletter*, 27/8/92.

17 *Sunday Telegraph*, 6/10/91.
18 Ibid., 2/2/92. Timmerman, 'Weapons of Mass Destruction; The Cases of Iran, Syria and Libya', Simon Wiesenthal Centre, *Mednews*, 1992, pp. 52–3. *European*, 30/4/92.
19 *Sunday Times*, 22/12/91 and 18/10/92. *Athens News*, 12/10/89. Associated Press report, 10/10/92.
20 *Independent*, 29/5/92. *Guardian*, 2 and 3/1/92. *Sunday Times*, 24/11/91. *Sunday Telegraph*, 12/1/92.
21 *Sunday Telegraph*, 6/10/91 and 12/1/92. *Guardian*, 19/10/91. *The Times*, 14/1/92 and 8/2/92. Timmerman, p. 49. *Independent*, 25/2/92.
22 *Independent*, 18/3/90.
23 *Guardian*, 2/7/92.
24 *The Times*, 15/1/92. *Observer Magazine*, 25/11/90. *Guardian*, 7/2/92.
25 *Sunday Times*, 5/1/92. *Independent*, 21/11/91.
26 *Independent*, 30/6/92. *Observer*, 23/2/92.
27 *Daily Telegraph*, 7/7/92. *Sunday Times*, 12/7/92.
28 *New Statesman*, 12/12/80 and 4/3/83. *Independent*, 26/1/92.
29 *South China Morning Post*, 6/8/78. *Guardian*, 10/6/92. *Independent*, 5/7/91.
30 *Independent*, 27/2/92. *Daily Telegraph*, 28/3/92.
31 *Sunday Times*, 18/8/91.
32 Ibid., 11/8/91.
33 Ibid. *New Statesman*, 4/3/83. *Guardian*, 29/6/92.
34 *Guardian*, 12/5/92.
35 *Observer*, 28/6/92.

Conclusion

1 *Independent*, 3/12/92.
2 *Intelligence and National Security*, Winter 1992.
3 Hollingsworth/Norton-Taylor, p. 8.
4 HOC *Hansard*, cols 1139, Security Service Bill, 15/12/88.
5 *Guardian*, 13/3/90.
6 *Private Eye*, 31/7/92. *Guardian*, 16/7/92, 5/9/92 and 20/11/92. *Sunday Times* and *Observer*, 2/8/92.
7 Lanning/Norton-Taylor, p. 71–2.
8 *Guardian*, 16/7/91. *Observer*, 28/6/92.
9 Lanning/Norton-Taylor, pp. 137–8. *Observer*, 28/6/92. *Guardian*, 4/2/91.
10 *Observer*, 10/5/92. *Sunday Times*, 10/5/92.
11 Ditchley Conference Report, no. 88/11.
12 Institute for European Defence and Strategic Studies, *The Secret*

Services: Is there a Case for Greater Openness?, Occasional Paper no. 41, 1989, pp. 43–45.

13 *The Listener*, 12/8/92. International Freedom Foundation, pp. 142–3. Although the IFF's policies are at total variance with the author's, its publication *Intelligence and the New World Order* is an interesting and recommended read.

14 A note by the director, Ditchley Conference, 11/88.

15 Kennedy, p. 482. Lanning/Norton-Taylor, p. 35.

16 Lanning/Norton-Taylor, pp. 35–7.

17 Kennedy, p. 482.

18 *Independent*, 7/9/92. Ranelagh, p. 307.

Bibliography

Adams, James, *The Financing of Terror*, London, New English Library, 1986.
—— *Secret Armies*, London, Pan, 1989.
—— *Trading in Death: Weapons, Warfare and the New Arms Race*, London, Pan, 1991.
Adams, James, Morgan, Robin and Bambridge, Anthony, *Ambush: The War Between the SAS and the IRA*, London, Pan, 1988.
Allason, Rupert, *The Branch: A History of the Metropolitan Special Branch 1883–1983*, London, Secker & Warburg, 1983.
Andrew, Christopher and Gordievsky, Oleg, *KGB: The Inside Story*, London, Hodder & Stoughton, 1990.
Asher, Michael, *Shoot to Kill: A Soldier's Journey Through Violence*, London, Penguin, 1991.
Bamford, James, *The Puzzle Palace: America's National Security Agency and Its Special Relationship With Britain's GCHQ*, London, Sidgwick & Jackson, 1982.
Ben Menashe, Ari, *Profits of War*, New York, Sheridan Square, 1992.
Benn, Tony, *Conflicts of Interest 1977–80*, London, Hutchinson, 1990; Benn Diaries, vol. 4.
Bethel, Nicholas, *The Struggle Between the British, the Jews, and the Arabs 1935–48*, London, André Deutsch, 1979.
Blake, George, *No Other Choice*, London, Jonathan Cape, 1990.
Block, Jonathan and Fitzgerald, Patrick, *British Intelligence and Covert Action*, London, Junction, 1983.
Bok, Sissela, *Secrets: On the Ethics of Concealment and Revelation*, Oxford University Press, 1984.
Bunyan, Tony, *The History and Practice of the Political Police in Britain*, London, Quartet, 1983.
Cahill, Kevin, *Trade Wars: The High-Technology of Scandal of the 1980s*, London, W. H. Allen, 1986.
Campbell, Duncan and Connor, Steve, *On the Record: Surveillance,*

Computers and Privacy – The Inside Story, London, Michael Joseph, 1986.
Carver, Michael, *Out of Step*, London, Hutchinson, 1989.
Cavendish, Anthony, *Inside Intelligence*, London, Collins, 1990.
Cloake, John, *Templer, Tiger of Malaya*, London, 1985.
Cockerill, A. W., *Sir Percy Sillitoe*, London, W. H. Allen, 1975.
Collins, Tony, *Open Verdict: An Account of 25 Mysterious Deaths in the Defence Industry*, London, Sphere, 1990.
Cook, Judith, *Who Killed Hilda Murrell?*, London, New English Library, 1985.
Copeland, Miles, *The Real Spy World*, London, 1978.
Cornwall, Hugo, *Data Theft: Computer Fraud, Industrial Espionage and Information Crime*, London, Mandarin, 1989.
—— *The Industrial Espionage Handbook*, London, Random House, 1990.
Coughlin, Con, *Hostages: The Complete Story of the Lebanon Captives*, London, Little, Brown, 1992.
Currer-Briggs, Noel (ed.), *'Security'*, London, Hutchinson, 1968.
Darwish, Adel and Alexander, Gregory, *Unholy Babylon: The Secret History of Saddam's War*, London, Victor Gollancz, 1991.
Deacon, Richard, *'C': A Biography of Sir Maurice Oldfield, Head of MI6*, London, Macdonald, 1985.
De Marenches, Alexandre, *The Evil Empire*, London, Sidgwick & Jackson, 1988.
Dillon, Martin, *The Dirty War*, Hutchinson, 1988.
Dorril, Stephen and Ramsay, Robin, *Smear!: Wilson and the Secret State*, London, Fourth Estate, 1991.
Elliott-Bateman, Michael (ed.), *The Fourth Dimension of Warfare*, vol. 1: *Intelligence, Subversion, Resistance*, Manchester University Press, 1970.
Faligot, Roger, *Britain's Military Strategy in Ireland: The Kitson Experiment*, London, Zed, 1983.
Farran, Roy, *Winged Dagger: Adventures on Special Service*, London, 1948.
Fiennes, Sir Ranulph, *The Feather Men*, London, Cygnet, 1992.
Fitzgerald, Patrick and Leopold, Mark, *Stranger on the Line: The Secret History of Phone Tapping*, London, The Bodley Head, 1987.
Geraghty, Tony, *Who Dares Wins*, London, Fontana, 1980.
Gillman, Peter and Leni, *Collar the Lot!: How Britain Interned and Expelled Its Wartime Refugees*, London, Quartet, 1980.
Greenslade, Roy, *Maxwell's Fall*, London, Simon & Schuster, 1992.
Hennessy, Peter, *Whitehall*, London, Fontana, 1990.

Hennessy, Peter and Jeffries, Keith, *States of Emergency*, London, Routledge & Kegan Paul, 1983.
Hewitt, Gavin, *Terry Waite: Why He Was Kidnapped*, London, Bloomsbury, 1991.
Hinsley, F. H. and Simkins, C. A. G., *British Intelligence in the Second World War*, vol. 4, London, HMSO, 1990.
Hollingsworth, Mark and Norton-Taylor, Richard, *Blacklist: The Inside Story of Political Vetting*, London, Hogarth Press, 1988.
Holroyd, Fred with Burbridge, Nick, *War Without Honour*, Hull, Medium, 1989.
International Freedom Foundation, *Intelligence and the New World Order: Former Cold War Adversaries Look Toward the 21st Century*, London, IFF, 1992.
Junor, John, *Memoirs: Listening for a Midnight Tram*, London, Chapman, 1990.
Kitson, Frank, *Low Intensity Operations: Subversion*, London, Faber & Faber,
—— *Insurgency, Peace-Keeping*, London, Faber 1971.
Knightley, Phillip, *The Second Oldest Profession: The Spy as Bureaucrat, Patriot, Fantasist and Whore*, London, André Deutsch, 1986.
Kochan, Nick and Whittington, Bob, *Bankrupt: The BCCI Fraud*, London, Victor Gollancz, 1991.
Kuzichkin, Vladimir, *Inside the KGB*, London, André Deutsch, 1990.
Lanning, Hugh and Norton-Taylor, Richard, *A Conflict of Loyalties: GCHQ 1984–91*, Gloucester, New Clarion, 1991.
Lee, Dick and Pratt, Colin, *Operation Julie*, London, W. H. Allen, 1979.
Leigh, David, *The Wilson Plot: The Intelligence Services and the Discrediting of a Prime Minister 1945–76*, London, Heinemann, 1988.
Leppard, David, *On the Trail of Terror: The Inside Story of the Lockerbie Investigation*, London, Jonathan Cape, 1991.
Lowther, William, *Iraq and the Supergun*, London, Pan, 1992.
McDermott, Geoffrey, *The New Diplomacy and its Apparatus*, London, Plume, 1973.
Murphy, David, *The Stalker Affair and the Press*, London, Unwin Hyman, 1991.
Murray, Raymond, *The SAS in Ireland*, Dublin, Mercier, 1990.
Nairn, Tom, *The Enchanted Glass: Britain and Its Monarchy*, London, Radius, 1988.
Norton-Taylor, Richard, *In Defence of the Realm?: The Case for Accountable Security Services*, London, Civil Liberties Trust, 1990.
Ostrovsky, Victor and Hoy, Claire, *By Way of Deception*, London, St Martin's Press, 1990.

Owen, David, *Time to Declare*, London, Penguin, 1992.
Philby, Kim, *My Silent War*, New York, Grove, 1968.
Pilger, John, *Distant Voices* , London, Vintage, 1992.
Pincher, Chapman, *Inside Story*, London, Sidgwick & Jackson, 1979.
—— *Too Secret, Too Long: The Great Betrayal of Britain's Crucial Secrets and the Cover-up*, London, Sidgwick & Jackson, 1984.
—— *Traitors: The Labyrinths of Treason*, London, Sidgwick & Jackson, 1987.
—— *The Truth About Dirty Tricks*, London, Sidgwick & Jackson, 1991.
Porter, Bernard, *The Origins of the Vigilant State*, London, Weidenfeld & Nicolson, 1987.
—— *Plots and Paranoia*, London, Unwin Hyman, 1989.
Prince, Michael, *God's Cop*, London, New English Library, 1989.
Ranelagh, John, *Thatcher's People*, London, Fontana, 1992.
Read, Anthony and Fisher, David, *Colonel Z: The Secret Life of a Master of Spies*, London, 1984.
Richelson, Jeffrey T. and Ball, Desmond, *The Ties that Bind*, London, Unwin Hyman, 1990.
Rogers, Paul and Dando, Malcolm, *A Violent Peace: Global Security After the Cold War*, London, Brassey's, 1992.
Rusbridger, James, *The Intelligence Game: The Illusions and Delusions of International Espionage*, London, I. B. Tauris, 1991.
Sampson, Anthony, *The Changing Anatomy of Britain*, London, Hodder & Stoughton, 1982.
Scott, Andrew Murray and Macleay, Iain, *Britain's Secret War: Tartan Terrorism and the Anglo-American State*, Edinburgh, Mainstream, 1990.
Seale, Patrick, *Abu Nidal: A Gun for Hire*, London, Random Century, 1992.
Seymour, William, *British Special Forces*, London, 1985.
Shears, Richard and Gidley, Isobelle, *The Rainbow Warrior Affair*, London, Counterpoint, 1986.
Smith, Graham, *Death of a Rose-Grower*, London, Cecil Woolf, 1985.
Spence, Martin, *1992 and All That*, London, Civil Liberties Trust, 1990.
Stalker, John, *Stalker*, London, Penguin, 1988.
Summers, Anthony and Dorril, Stephen, *Honeytrap: The Secret Worlds of Stephen Ward*, London, Weidenfeld & Nicolson, 1987.
Sunday Times Insight Team, *Siege*, London, Hamlyn, 1980.
—— *Rainbow Warrior*, London, Arrow, 1986.

Taylor, Kevin with Mumby, Keith, *The Poisoned Tree*, London, Pan, 1991.
Taylor, Peter, *Stalker: The Search for Truth*, London, Faber & Faber, 1987.
Timmerman, Kenneth R., *The Death Lobby: How the West Armed Iraq*, London, Fourth Estate, 1992.
Tuck, Jay, *High-Tech Espionage: How the KGB Smuggles NATO's Strategic Secrets to Moscow*, London, Futura, 1987.
Urban, Mark, *Big Boy's Rules: The Secret Struggle Against the IRA*, London, Faber & Faber, 1992.
Verrier, Anthony, *Through the Looking Glass: British Foreign Policy in the Age of Illusions*, London, Jonathan Cape, 1983.
West, Nigel, *GCHQ: The Secret Wireless War 1900–86*, London, Weidenfeld & Nicolson, 1986.
—— *Molehunt: The Full Story of the Spy in MI5*, London, Weidenfeld & Nicolson, 1987.
—— *Games of Intelligence*, London, Weidenfeld & Nicolson, 1989.
—— *Seven Spies Who Changed the World*, London, Secker & Warburg, 1991.
Whitehead, Philip, *The Writing on the Wall*, London, Michael Joseph, 1985.
Wilson, Harold, *The Governance of Britain*, London, Weidenfeld & Nicolson, 1976.
Woodward, Bob, *Veil: The Secret Wars of the CIA 1981–87*, London, Simon & Schuster, 1987.
Wright, Peter, *The Encyclopedia of Espionage*, Melbourne, Heinemann, 1990.
Wright, Peter with Greengrass, Paul, *Spycatcher*, Melbourne, Heinemann, 1987.

Index